Capitalism's Contradictions

Capitalism's Contradictions

Studies in Economic Theory before and after Marx

Henryk Grossman

Translated by Ian Birchall, Rick Kuhn and Einde O'Callaghan

Edited and Introduced by Rick Kuhn

Haymarket Books
Chicago, Illinois

Chapter Four, "The Evolutionist Revolt against Classical Economics" originally appeared in two parts as "The Evolutionist Revolt Against Classical Economics: I. In France—Condorcet, Saint-Simon, Simonde de Sismondi" and "The Evolutionist Revolt Against Classical Economics: II. In England—James Steuart, Richard Jones, Karl Marx," by Henryk Grossman in *Journal of American History* 51, no. 5 and 6, University of Chicago Press. © 1943, *Journal of Political Economy* The University of Chicago Press

Published in 2017 by
Haymarket Books
P.O. Box 180165
Chicago, IL 60618
773-583-7884
www.haymarketbooks.org
info@haymarketbooks.org

ISBN: 978-1-60846-779-2

Trade distribution:
In the US, Consortium Book Sales and Distribution, www.cbsd.com
In Canada, Publishers Group Canada, www.pgcbooks.ca
In the UK, Turnaround Publisher Services, www.turnaround-uk.com
All other countries, Ingram Publisher Services International,
IPS_Intlsales@ingramcontent.com

This book was published with the generous support of Lannan Foundation and Wallace Action Fund.

Cover design by Viktoria Ivanovna.

Printed in Canada by union labor.

Library of Congress Cataloging-in-Publication data is available.

10 9 8 7 6 5 4 3 2 1

Contents

Introduction

Rick Kuhn

The boundaries among Henryk Grossman's works on politics, economic history, economic theory and the history of economic thought are arbitrary.[1] From his first publications as a leader of Jewish workers in the Austrian province of Galicia, around 1905, he was concerned to make the case for revolutionary working-class action. His economic investigations were always linked to this end.

This collection contains five of his longer studies. All deal extensively with the history of economic thought; their pivot is the work of Karl Marx. The first part of this introduction outlines Grossman's life and the content of his writings. The second part, "Insights," focuses on several issues that recur in his work: aspects of Marx's theory that had been overlooked or misunderstood before Grossman and mostly still are neglected or distorted, weakening efforts to analyze contemporary capitalism in order to overthrow it.

Grossman and His Studies of Economic Theory

Born in Kraków to a bourgeois Jewish family in 1881, Grossman became active in the Polish Social Democratic Party (PPSD) of Galicia—the Polish province of the Austro-Hungarian Empire—and the Jewish workers' movement around the turn of the century. As the class struggle in the Austro-Hungarian Empire heated up, paralleling developments across the border in tsarist Russia that led to the revolution of 1905–6, Grossman was a founding leader, the secretary and the main theoretician of the Jewish Social Democratic Party (JSDP) of Galicia, established on May Day 1905. He was

---

1. Grossman's name in most of his German publications was rendered as "Henryk Grossmann." The source for the present account of Grossman's life and work, unless otherwise referenced, is Kuhn, *Henryk Grossman and the Recovery of Marxism.*

also involved in smuggling literature for Rosa Luxemburg's organization, the Social Democracy of the Kingdom of Poland and Lithuania, into Russian-occupied Poland. Despite the hostility of the PPSD and the federal Austrian Social Democratic Party, the JSDP grew rapidly, organized many Jewish workers into trade unions for the first time, mobilized them in struggles against their exploitation as workers and their oppression as (mainly Yiddish-speaking) Jews, undertook extensive educational and propaganda work and published a weekly newspaper. The JSDP led Jews in strikes and street protests alongside workers of other nationalities, particularly in the struggle for universal male suffrage. During this period Grossman was still a university student. After completing his first degree, he moved from Kraków to Vienna in late 1908 to continue his studies, particularly under the economic historian Carl Grünberg, the most prominent socialist academic at a university in the Austro-Hungarian Empire, with whom Grossman had already worked during the winter semester of 1906–7.

In his academic work before and during World War I, Grossman dealt with eighteenth-century economic policies and ideas in the Habsburg Empire. His main research project was a study of the empire's trade policy for Galicia.[2] After army training in 1915 and service on the eastern front, Grossman held military, administrative and research posts during the war. The extent of these duties apparently left time for other investigations. One result was a substantial article on the relationship between the early theory of public policy (*Polizeiwissenschaft*, literally "police science") and the origins of official statistics in Austria.[3]

Poland and Sismondi

Unable to take up the offer of a senior post in the Austrian Statistical Commission in Vienna after the war, as a result of the racist policies of the new, rump Austrian state, Grossman moved to Warsaw, where he joined the Communist Workers Party of Poland in 1920. He worked for over two years at the Polish Central Statistical Office, where he was in charge of the design of the first population census of the new republic and published several articles related to his work, before being appointed to a full professorship in economic policy at the Free University of Poland. Because of his political activity, particularly in the illegal Communist Party's front organizations, Grossman was arrested five times and did prison stretches of up to eight months.

Before moving to Warsaw, Grossman delivered a paper to the Polish Academy of Science in Kraków in June 1919. This was the first evidence of his work on Marxist crisis theory. Substantial manuscripts, written in Warsaw, elaborated on these ideas and a breakthrough he achieved by extending Otto Bauer's model of capitalist growth beyond just a few cycles. In Poland, apart from an abstract of the Kraków paper, he published statistical studies of the country in the past and present, a very brief defense of Marx's

---

2. Grossmann, *Österreichs Handelspolitik*. See also Grossman, "Polityka przemysłowa i handlowa."
3. Grossmann, "Die Anfänge und geschichtliche Entwicklung."

economic theory against critics, an introduction to his own translations of criticisms by Marx of the German socialists' draft Gotha Program, which included an account of the early Polish reception of Marx, and a monograph, **"Simonde de Sismondi and His Economic Theories: A New Interpretation of His Thought."**[4] The Sismondi study arose from a lecture to the Polish Society of Economists in December 1923, was published the following year in French by the Free University in Warsaw "with the co-operation" of the Institute for Social Research in Frankfurt, and remains an important reference point in the literature on Sismondi's economic works.[5]

Jean Charles Léonard Simonde de Sismondi was a Swiss political economist and a prolific and pioneering historian, notably of France (in twenty-nine volumes), the Italian republics of the Middle Ages (sixteen volumes), and southern European literature (four volumes). His first economic works accepted the framework established by Adam Smith. But he became critical of capitalism and classical political economy at its most sophisticated, in the work of David Ricardo. This was apparent in his two-volume *New Principles of Political Economy*, published in 1819 and in a revised second edition in 1827, as well as the two volumes of his *Studies on Political Economy* of 1837–38.[6] Following the publication of the *New Principles*, Sismondi engaged in controversies with Ricardo as well as Jean-Baptiste Say and John Ramsay McCulloch, whom Marx identified as proponents of the first phase of "vulgar" political economy, which abandoned the insights of their classical predecessors.

Sismondi's work on the nature of capitalism was a reference point for Karl Marx and in two major socialist controversies. The first was between Marxists, preeminently Vladimir Ilyich Lenin, and Narodniks (populists), who invoked Sismondi, over the scope for the development of capitalism in Russia. In the second, over the nature of imperialism before World War I, Rosa Luxemburg drew critically on Sismondi.[7] The issue, in both cases, was the underconsumptionist argument that crises arose because, under capitalism, there is insufficient consistent demand to ensure the sale of all that has been produced.[8]

Unlike most of his predecessors, including Marxists but not Marx himself, Grossman's primary focus was not on Sismondi's underconsumptionism but on its deeper causes.[9] Moreover, he wrote, "we do not propose to give a systematic exposition of Sismondi's

---

4 Grossman, "Ekonomiczny system Karola Marksa"; Grossman, "Przyczynek do historii socjalizmu"; Grossman, *Simonde de Sismondi et ses théories économiques*. Titles in bold are included in the present volume.

5. International Institute of Social Research, *International Institute of Social Research: A Short Description of Its History and Aims*, 14. For a more extensive account of the significance of Grossman's Sismondi monograph, see Kuhn, "Sismondi, Marx and Grossman."

6. Sismondi, *New Principles of Political Economy*; and Sismondi, *Études*.

7. Lenin, *A Characterization of Economic Romanticism*, 140–41, 142–45, 207–8, 247–48; Luxemburg, *The Accumulation of Capital*, 218, 217, 328–31.

8. For a more detailed account of the main Marxist attitudes to Sismondi, see Kuhn, "Sismondi, Marx and Grossman." Of underconsumptionist arguments, Marx wrote: "It is a pure tautology to say that crises are provoked by a lack of effective demand or effective consumption." *Capital*, vol. 2, 486–87.

9. Grossman, *Simonde de Sismondi et ses théories économiques*. See chapter 1 in the present volume, "Simonde de Sismondi and His Economic Theories," 71. Subsequent citations are to this translation.

ideas but just to draw out the essence of his thought."[10] Grossman gave greater coherence to Sismondi's rather fragmented and unsystematic presentation, in accord with the logic of his arguments, and stressed his originality.[11] This elucidation highlighted Sismondi's method and grasp of the contradiction between commodities' *use values*—the concrete, practical and unquantifiable ways in which commodities with specific material, technical properties serve human purposes—and their *exchange values*—social aspects arising, in Marx's more precise formulation, from the amount of socially necessary abstract labor embodied in them. Abstract labor is the common element of human labor—the expenditure of human energy, abstracting from its specific, concrete forms—that is the basis for determining the ratios at which commodities are exchanged for each other or money, under capitalism.[12] Like Grossman's 1919 lecture, his Sismondi monograph dealt not only with these issues, explored at greater length below, but also the way disequilibrium could be intensified as producers increased output to compensate for falling prices.

The monograph also identified the antecedents of Marx's concept of the fetishism of commodities in Sismondi's work. In 1923 and 1924, Karl Korsch, Georg Lukács and Grossman pointed out how Marx had accounted for both the material *realities* and the fetishized surface *appearances* of capitalism, for both the logic of capital accumulation and the mystifications of bourgeois economics.[13] "The real contradiction of the economic system," the then-Warsaw-based economist wrote, "appears in science in the form of incoherent notions and definitions and futile quarrels about words."[14] Sismondi had demonstrated how the fetishism of mainstream political economy, with its focus on exchange value to the exclusion of use value, fundamentally flawed its analysis.

According to Sismondi the exchange-value-based system necessarily gives rise to disproportion between production and needs and hence to crises, because production and consumption are separate.[15] Consequently, production is governed by individuals'

---

10. Grossman, "Simonde de Sismondi and His Economic Theories," 67.

11. Aftalion, "L'oeuvre économique de Simonde de Sismondi," 41.

12. Marx distinguished value (the amount of socially necessary labor time embodied in a commodity) from its "manifestation" as exchange value but observed that "Once we know this, our manner of speaking [referring to value as exchange value] does no harm; it serves, rather, as an abbreviation." *Capital*, vol. 1, 152. On abstract labor, see ibid., 142, 150, and 188, as well as Carchedi, *Frontiers of Political Economy*, 7–13.

13. Korsch, "Marxism and Philosophy," 64; Lukács, *History and Class Consciousness*, xlvi–xlvii, 11, 50, 164, 169; Grossman, "Simonde de Sismondi and His Economic Theories," 54, 67–8. Marx's early discussion of alienation gave rise to the observations about commodity fetishism in *Capital*. See Marx, "Economic and Philosophic Manuscripts of 1844," 290–91 and *Capital*, vol. 1, 163–77.

14. Grossman, "Simonde de Sismondi and His Economic Theories," 54

15. Cf. Marx: The "antithetical phases" of exchange involving money, that is, the "immanent contradiction" arising from the separation between the sale of one commodity and the purchase of another with the proceeds, intrinsic to the commodity form with its antitheses including that "between use value and value," "imply the possibility of crises, though no more than the possibility. For the development of this possibility into a reality a whole series of conditions is required, which do not yet even exist from the standpoint of the simple circulation of commodities." *Capital*, vol. 1, 209. Likewise: "Hence, the quality of money as mediator, the separation of exchange into two acts, already contains the germ of crises, at least their possibility, which cannot be realised except where there exist the basic conditions of classically and fully developed circulation corresponding to its concept." Marx, "Outlines of the Critique," 133.

pursuit of "their private aims, [and] loses sight of the general interest";[16] specifically capitalists adjust production to their pursuit of profit, not demand. So demand does not tend to match supply, as mainstream classical political economists believed. The problem is more profound than the concern about distribution and working-class poverty that previous commentators had identified in Sismondi's work.[17] Crises of underconsumption can lead to increased, rather than decreased output, intensifying the disequilibrium between production and demand. Technological change also continuously disrupts the proportion between production and demand, and gives rise to concentration of ownership, crises, pauperism, unemployment and unequal distribution of wealth.[18]

Grossman pointed out how Sismondi had contributed to the development of a series of Marx's concepts: socially necessary labor time as the foundation of commodities' values;[19] the commodity labor power (capacity to work), as distinct from the activity of labor, which solved the conundrum of the creation of surplus value under conditions of equal exchange;[20] capital as "permanent, self-multiplying value";[21] and crises as a necessary feature of capitalism, arising from its contradictions between forces and relations of production, use and exchange value, production and consumption, capital and wage labor. His "inkling . . . that the bourgeois forms are only transitory" was also distinctive.[22] But while Marx praised and built on Sismondi's theoretical insights, he was critical of the Swiss economist's policy proposals.

Sismondi, Grossman argued, had an ideal of a fundamentally different future economic system in which, thanks to the elimination of competition and exchange value, the necessary proportions for crisis-free growth could be maintained. This was Sismondi's *implicit* "maximum program." He *explicitly* advocated a range of palliative measures to ameliorate or slow down the destructive effects of capitalism: his "minimum program."[23] Sismondi was not an advocate of the abolition of private property, the only means by which exchange value could be dispensed with, and was therefore not a socialist. Nor, in the circumstances of the early nineteenth century, could he conceive of the working class as the agent of radical social change.

The description of Sismondi as "the first economist to scientifically discover capitalism" was overblown, particularly in light of Marx's respect for the earlier scientific achievements of Smith and Ricardo. But when, at the end of his monograph, Grossman qualified this depiction—Sismondi was the "first economist to scientifically demon

---

16. Grossman, "Simonde de Sismondi and His Economic Theories," 56 (citing Sismondi, *Études*, vol. 1, 69).

17. Grossman, "Simonde de Sismondi and His Economic Theories," 45, 48, 50, and following.

18. Ibid., 65, 67; see also Grossman, "The Theory of Economic Crises," 171–80.

19. Grossman, "Simonde de Sismondi and His Economic Theories," 59, 69, 73, 74; Marx, *The Poverty of Philosophy*, 135–36; Marx, *Contribution to the Critique*, 300.

20. Marx, "Economic Manuscript of 1861–63 [Notebooks I to VII]," 149, 157–58; Marx, "Economic Manuscript of 1861–63 [Notebooks XX to XXIII]," 271, 418, 423; Marx, *Capital*, vol. 1, 277.

21. Marx, "Economic Manuscript [Notebooks I to VII]," 12; see also "Economic Manuscript of 1861–63 [Notebooks XV to XX]," 341.

22. Marx, "Economic Manuscript of 1861–63 [Notebooks XII to XV]," 248, 274, 393.

23. Grossman, "Simonde de Sismondi and His Economic Theories," 81–82.

strate that an economic system based on abstract exchange value as the sole purpose of production and regulator of it necessarily leads to disruptions and to 'insoluble questions'"—his conclusion was and remains persuasive.[24]

Sismondi was a recurrent figure in Grossman's research program. After leaving Poland in 1925, he joined the Institute for Social Research in Frankfurt. In 1927 he was awarded his higher doctorate (*Habilitation*) for a major study of Austrian trade policy in Galicia, completed in Vienna under the supervision of Carl Grünberg (now the Institute's director), and for a trial lecture on Sismondi and classical political economy.[25] Grossman's principal and best-known work, on Marxist crisis theory—*The Law of Accumulation and Breakdown of the Capitalist System*, published in 1929—drew attention to Sismondi's innovative stress on capitalism's transitoriness, a point on which he elaborated in his 1943 study of the emergence of evolutionist thinking in economics.[26]

Unlike the 1924 monograph, *The Law of Accumulation* included criticisms of Sismondi's unsatisfactory underconsumptionist explanation of crises, which blamed capitalism's proneness to economic crises on its restricted internal market. So did two reviews and his entry on Sismondi in the *Encyclopedia of the Social Sciences* in 1934. That entry and his account of the development of Marxism, discussed in the next section, endorsed Lenin's critique of Sismondi's underconsumptionism, shared by Karl Kautsky and Luxemburg, and referred to Sismondi's hostility to democracy.[27] The arguments in the monograph were briefly recapitulated in the encyclopedia entry, which offered a broader overview of Sismondi's work, referring to his studies of French and medieval Italian history, as well as the way he and Madame de Staël "paved the way" for the modern sociology of literature.[28]

In his 1941 study of dynamics in economics, Grossman highlighted Sismondi's pioneering critique of mainstream economists' assumption of equilibrium. And he returned to Sismondi's insights into capitalism's transitoriness and developmental tendencies in his 1943 study of the emergence of evolutionist thinking in economics and his 1948 article on William Playfair.[29]

---

24. Ibid., 54–86.

25. Kuhn, *Henryk Grossman and the Recovery of Marxism*, 119.

26. Grossmann, *Law of Accumulation*, 35, and Grossman, "The Evolutionist Revolt against Classical Economics." Citations to "The Evolutionist Revolt" refer to pages in the present volume, where the text is included as chapter 4.

27. Grossmann, *Law of Accumulation*, 35; review of *Sismondi*, by Elie Halévy, 291; review of *La loi de Marx*, by Robert Bordaz, 314–15; "Sismondi, Jean Charles Leonard Simonde de (1773–1842)," 69–71; and *Fünfzig Jahre Kampf*, 121.

28. Grossmann, *Das Akkumulations- und Zusammenbruchsgesetz*, 32. See also Grossmann's review of *Sismondi*, by Elie Halévy, 291; his review of *La loi de Marx*, by Robert Bordaz, 314–15; and Grossman, "Sismondi, Jean Charles Leonard Simonde de (1773–1842)," 69.

29. Grossman, *Marx, Die klassische Nationalökonomie und das Problem der Dynamik*; chapter 3 in the present volume, "Marx, Classical Political Economy and the Problem of Dynamics"; "The Evolutionist Revolt against Classical Economics," chapter 4 in the present volume; and Grossman, "W. Playfair, the Earliest Theorist of Capitalist Development," chapter 5 in the present volume.

Frankfurt and Marxism after Marx

As a result of political repression, Grossman left Poland for a well-paid post at the Institute for Social Research, associated with the University of Frankfurt at which he also taught. Germany was less repressive than Poland. The Institute was funded by an endowment secured by Felix Weil, the radical son of a very wealthy businessman, to conduct Marxist research. It was an excellent place to work. His period in Frankfurt, between 1925 and 1933, was Grossman's most productive, although his publications while there built on arguments developed in manuscripts written in Warsaw. After Grünberg's retirement, his work was more publicly prominent than that of any other Institute member.

While *The Law of Accumulation* was very widely reviewed, there was a condemnatory consensus about it among most left-wing commentators, because it contradicted the explanation of capitalist crises that became the Stalinist dogma, while its emphasis on their inevitability was uncongenial to social democrats. Despite explicit statements to the contrary in the book, Stalinists, most council communists, as well as social democrats agreed that it expounded a mechanical theory of capitalist breakdown. This libel is discussed in this introduction's final section.[30]

Although politically restricted by his legal status in Germany, Grossman remained a revolutionary Marxist; he was a fellow traveler of the German Communist Party and the Communist International. His situation as an exiled Polish citizen and his job at the Institute for Social Research meant that he was free to conduct research and write unconstrained by a party line or the priorities of a normal academic post. He was insulated from the Stalinization of the German Communist Party and the International, completed by the end of the 1920s, which accompanied the defeat of the revolution in Russia and the rise of a new state-capitalist ruling class. Despite criticisms in Communist organs of his work on Marx's crisis theory, for its deviation from the Stalinist orthodoxy, Grossman continued to argue his position both in periods when he supported the principal political positions of the Communist International and when he did not.

After Grünberg was incapacitated by a stroke, Grossman took over his task of writing entries for Elster's *Dictionary of Economics*: a standard German reference work in three hefty volumes.[31] It was in this peculiar place that his distinctly Marxist biographical entries on prominent socialists, including Lenin, socialist and communist parties, Bolshevism, the Second and Third Internationals, anarchism, and Christian socialism, as well as his essay on Marxism after Marx, appeared. The editor, Ludwig Elster, allowed Grossman, as an expert, scope to express his own political and economic views in a forthright tone; the same was true of the item on "Socialist Ideas and Theories (National Socialism)" written by a Nazi economist.[32]

Carl Grünberg had written the initial sections of the item on "Socialist Ideas and Theories (Socialism and Communism)" for an earlier edition of the dictionary. In an additional

---

30. Kuhn, *Henryk Grossman and the Recovery of Marxism*, 138–46.
31. Elster, ed., *Wörterbuch der Volkswirtschaft*.
32. Jessen, "Sozialistische Ideen und Lehren."

part, "The Further Development of Marxism to the Present," also issued separately as **"Fifty Years of Struggle over Marxism, 1883–1932,"** Grossman provided a valuable survey of historical materialism's development after Marx's death. Published in 1932 and 1933, it examined major controversies over politics and economics, and the application of Marxist analysis, in the context of the history of capital accumulation and the labor movement. The final section summed up Grossman's own key contributions, discussed in the second part of this Introduction, and constituted an implicit reply to his critics.[33]

Only Karl Korsch's article "Marxism and Philosophy," which provided a shorter overview of the history of Marxism from Georg Wilhelm Friedrich Hegel to 1923, was an obvious immediate predecessor of Grossman's study. There were earlier discussions of the history of socialist ideas and Marxist organizations but none examined the development of Marxist thought, especially after Marx's death, more than superficially. Other works, the most outstanding of which was Lenin's *State and Revolution*, had dealt with particular controversies within Marxism.[34]

In his survey, Grossman condensed a huge literature by highlighting key works and arguments, focusing particularly on issues in Marxist economics and of socialist strategy. He started by noting that the appreciation of *Capital*'s full significance was very limited for decades.

After the Anti-Socialist Law lapsed in 1890 and the Social Democratic Party of Germany, the largest socialist organization in the world, could operate openly, the influence and sophistication of Marxist analysis grew rapidly. But the rise of revisionism in the party challenged the revolutionary core of Marxist politics and the validity of Marx's labor theory of value. Following Luxemburg, Grossman pointed out that Kautsky, then the foremost Marxist theorist in the world, who made some telling criticisms of Eduard Bernstein's revisionism, himself fundamentally revised Marxist politics. Marx's understanding of the state was only reconstructed by Lenin over twenty-five years later.[35]

Like Lenin, Grossman explained the rise of revisionism as the result of the emergence of a thin layer in the working classes of developed capitalist countries, an "aristocracy of labor", that gained material benefits from the imperialist exploitation of the colonial world.[36] This was a weak argument. To the extent that imperialism improved the living standards of well-paid workers, because of more buoyant labor markets and access to cheap raw materials and foodstuffs, it did so for the rest of the working class in the imperialist heartlands too. Better wages in developed capitalist countries have also frequently been associated with higher degrees of exploitation, because workers in them are better educated and use more efficient technologies, machinery and equipment. Workers with superior technology can produce more of the same commodity in a given time than those with inferior technology and therefore spend a smaller pro-

---

33. Grossmann, *Fünfzig Jahre Kampf* and Grossman, *Die Fortentwicklung des Marximsus*, published in the present volume as "Fifty Years of Struggle," 87–136. Subsequent citations are to this translation.
34. See Korsch, "Marxism and Philosophy"; Lenin, *The State and Revolution*.
35. Grossman, "Fifty Years of Struggle," 100.
36. Ibid., 90.

portion of their working days making the value equivalent of their wages and a larger proportion making profits. Furthermore, the successes of better paid and organized workers in fighting for their wages and conditions have often provided a model for the struggles of other workers.[37]

More compellingly, Grossman associated revisionism with a period of capitalist expansion, during which the working class was able to extract concessions from the ruling class, and the rise of a layer of full-time labor-movement officials, particularly in the trade unions.[38] While essential to the functioning of workers' key defense organizations and capable of leading important struggles, full-time union officials are not, by definition, workers themselves. They are employed by their unions, not a boss, and generally have better pay, superior conditions and greater autonomy than the unions' ordinary members. Their day-to-day activity does not involve creating profits for employers through their labor but rather organizing workers and making deals with employers. They are wary of militant action, let alone revolutionary struggles, that might risk the organizations on which they depend for their livelihoods.

Grossman did not devote much space to the application of historical materialist methods outside the areas of politics and economics. But he mentioned studies by Kautsky and "brilliant" writings by Franz Mehring and Georgi Plekhanov on philosophy, history and literary criticism. He also highlighted the work of Karl Korsch and, in particular, Georg Lukács's "fine and valuable book" *History and Class Consciousness*. The absence of Antonio Gramsci from Grossman's survey may seem surprising to contemporary Marxists. But very few of the Italian Communist leader's works appeared in languages other than Italian during his lifetime. Gramsci's prison notebooks were still being written in 1932. It was years after World War II before his major works appeared in translation.

In the period before World War I, international tensions and domestic class struggles intensified, as economic conditions changed and capital went onto the offensive. Against this background, Marxists started to devote more attention to the issue of imperialism. There was another gap in Grossman's survey here: the theory of permanent revolution, developed by Parvus and Leon Trotsky and tacitly embraced by Lenin and the Bolshevik Party in 1917.[39] It explained how socialist revolution was possible in a relatively backward country like Russia, because it was part of the international capitalist system and exhibited some particularly modern features, like a combative working class and advanced industry, even though the vast majority of the population was composed of peasants working with relatively primitive technologies. A socialist revolution in Russia could therefore occur but could only survive if it spread to more developed countries.[40] Grossman did refer to and reject this theory's basic content in

---

37. Cliff, "The Economic Roots of Reformism"; Post, "Exploring Working-Class Consciousness"; Bramble, "Is There a Labour Aristocracy in Australia?".
38. Grossman, "Fifty Years of Struggle," 90.
39. Lenin, *Letters from Afar*, 341.
40. See Trotsky, *Results and Prospects*.

his dictionary item on Bolshevism, where he acknowledged that it had been a component of "Leninism" but falsely suggested that, at the end of his life, Lenin had endorsed the notion of socialism in one country, which was advocated by Nikolai Bukharin and Stalin.[41] Contrary to the survey's assertion that the Russian Communists did not associate the possibility of revolution with a specific level of capitalist development, the theory of permanent revolution identified *the system of global capitalism's maturity* as a crucial precondition for socialist revolution.

The theory of permanent revolution was a much more profound argument than Bukharin's no doubt useful insight that in less advanced countries ruling class power was often more fragile. Grossman unnecessarily criticized Bukharin's contention, in the mistaken belief that it was incompatible with his own understanding of the Russian Revolution as a symptom and the start of capitalist breakdown, which made developed countries vulnerable to revolution. He also misleadingly denied that Bukharin's insight was also Lenin's and was silent about the vicious repressiveness of Stalin's regime. In this way, Grossman was able to avoid alienating the Stalinist leadership of the Communist movement more than necessary in defending his own position. He was aided by Stalin's own contortions on precisely the question of the implications of uneven capitalist development.[42] When he wrote this essay, Grossman was still a largely uncritical supporter of the Communist International, now thoroughly dominated by Stalin and his subordinates, and of the German Communist Party, which toed the line from Moscow.

Like very many other Communists of the time, who remained committed, in principle, to working-class self-emancipation, the essence of Marxism, Grossman did not recognize the defeat of the Russian Revolution, which was a massive setback for the international working class, in practice.[43] He was impressed by what he saw on a visit to the Soviet Union as the leader of an academic delegation in 1932. He did not, however, simply reproduce the Stalinist falsification of the history of the Russian revolutionary movement. His survey acknowledged contributions to the workers' movement by socialists and Communists whose positive role the Russian regime now simply denied, notably Parvus, Grigory Zinoviev, Bukharin, Herman Gorter and even its principal hate figure, Trotsky. Emphasizing the impact that the Russian Revolution had on Marxist theory, Grossman referred to Bukharin's specific version of the revolutionary argument that the development of capitalism in the womb of feudalism could not be the pattern for the transition to socialism. The survey also noted the contribution of David Riazanov, who had a close association with Carl Grünberg and the Institute for Social Research, to the history of Marxism and his leadership of the Marx-Engels Institute in Moscow, even though he had been arrested as an anti-Soviet conspirator and dismissed from that post in 1931.

---

41. Grossmann, "Bolschevismus," 437.
42. See Lenin, "The Chain Is No Stronger," and Stalin, "A Necessary Correction."
43. See Haynes, *Russia: Class and Power 1917–2000*, and Tony Cliff's classic, *State Capitalism in Russia*.

Exile and Fundamental Flaws of Bourgeois Economics

Soon after Hitler became the German chancellor in January 1933, most members of the Institute went into exile and most had settled in New York by October 1934. Grossman, however, moved to Paris. The Communist movement's blindness to the significance of the Nazis' rise and the German bourgeoisie's gift of power to them jolted Grossman into a much more critical attitude toward the leadership of the Communist International for several years. The Communists' equation of social democracy and Nazism prevented an effective response to Hitler that could have united workers who were social democrats, Communists, or just trade unionists. Grossman recommended Trotsky's discussion of the "German catastrophe" to Paul Mattick and in Paris associated with the former Communists Jacob Walcher and Paul Frölich who led the Socialist Workers' Party of Germany (SAP), originally a split from the Social Democratic Party.

In France, Grossman wrote a critique of Franz Borkenau's study of the emergence of the scientific worldview. This very substantial review article, along with the work of Boris Hessen and unlike Borkenau's fundamentally flawed position, was a pioneering Marxist account of the emergence of modern science.[44]

In early 1936, as international tensions mounted in Europe, Grossman moved to London. There, Russia's ambiguous backing for the Republican side in the Spanish Civil War seems to have prompted him to return to essentially uncritical support for Stalin's main domestic and foreign policies. This paralleled the SAP's endorsement of the Comintern's Popular Front tactic of alliances with "progressive" bourgeois parties and, eventually, "democratic imperialist" powers.

While Grossman was in London, Max Horkheimer, who had succeeded Grünberg as the Institute's director, suggested that he turn the discussion of methodology in *The Law of Accumulation* into an article for a 1937 issue of the Institute's journal. Grossman responded with a proposal for a more original piece to mark the seventieth anniversary of the publication of the first volume of Marx's *Capital*,[45] just as the JSDP's newspaper had celebrated the book's fortieth birthday.[46] The new essay would challenge the notion, shared by non-Marxists and most Marxists alike, that Marx had perfected classical political economy, arguing instead that he had revolutionized the work of his predecessors. It would identify elements that distinguished Marx's theory from those of the classical political economists and their bourgeois successors. In addition to new investigations, particularly of contemporary economics, Grossman could also draw on his previous publications, back to 1919 at the latest; research done by 1926; and courses he had taught: in 1928, "Exercises on the Question of the Relationship between Marx and Ricardo," and in 1930, "Marx as a Historian of Political

---

44. Grossmann, "The Social Foundations of the Mechanistic Philosophy and Manufacture."
45. Horkheimer to Henryk Grossman, September 9, 1936 (VI 9, Max-Horkheimer-Archiv), 349; Grossman to Max Horkheimer, October 1, 1936.
46. Anonymous, "Dos 40 yohriger yubileum."

Economy."[47] The essay included arguments previously intended for a sequel to *The Law of Accumulation and Breakdown*.[48]

Horkheimer liked the proposal. Hardly surprising, given that Grossman was building on and radicalizing themes in his own recently published article "On the Problem of Truth" and an earlier letter, which in turn drew on Grossman's exposition of Marx's method.[49] These two Institute members did not exercise a major influence on one another but did have friendly and fruitful exchanges until the late 1930s.

Grossman had completed a long draft of his examination of the relationship between Marx and his predecessors by May 1937. He considered issuing it as a book, rather than an article, and expanded its scope.[50] Work on the project continued after he rejoined Horkheimer and the Institute in New York, in October 1937. Eventually entitled *Marx, Classical Political Economy and the Problem of Dynamics* (henceforth referred to as *Marx and Dynamics*), its publication, to which the Institute had made a commitment, was delayed by the process of revision, including reductions of its length by a fifth and then a further quarter, and practical developments beyond the Institute's control. Even before the Nazi occupation of Paris, where it had previously been published, in 1940, the Institute's journal consistently failed to appear on time. The repeated postponements of the study's publication contributed to rising tensions between Grossman and the Institute, in the persons of Horkheimer and his administrative lieutenant and life-long friend, the economist Friedrich Pollock. In 1941 relations became poisonous.

The rift had theoretical, political and financial aspects. By 1939, Horkheimer and Theodor Adorno, adopted as his closest collaborator, had truncated Marx's "critique of political economy," validating only its negative aspect and rejecting its constructive side, the application of Marxist categories to the empirical analysis of capitalism, which they designated as "positivism," i.e., wrong.[51]

This was accompanied by rejection of the core of Marxist politics, recognition that the working class was capable of emancipating humanity, to which Grossman was still committed; a distaste for left-wing engagement; and an even more pronounced pursuit of the apolitical, academic respectability that Horkheimer had cultivated since arriving in the United States.[52] In contradiction with his views about the working class, Grossman was again favorably disposed not only to the Stalinist regime in Russia but also its foreign policies, while Horkheimer's circle recognized the reality of the vio-

---

47. Grossman, "The Theory of Economic Crises"; Universität Frankfurt am Main, *Verzeichnis*, 1928, 52; Universität Frankfurt am Main, *Verzeichnis*, 1930, 54.
48. Grossmann to Paul Mattick, February 19, 1935.
49. Horkheimer to Henryk Grossmann, October 12, 1936; Horkheimer, "On the Problem of Truth."
50. See Horkheimer to Grossmann, October 12, 1936, editorial note 2, 164, referring to a letter from Friedrich Pollock to Grossman of July 12, 1937, and "Marx und klassische Oekonomie oder die Lehre von Wertfetisch," unpublished manuscript, 1937, Folder 68, Henryk Grossman III-155 Collection.
51. Horkheimer and Adorno, "Diskussion über die Differenz," 438; also Adorno and Horkheimer, *Towards a New Manifesto*, 50. Compare Marx: "It is the ultimate aim of this work to reveal the economic law of motion of modern society." *Capital*, vol. 1, 92.
52. See, for example, Horkheimer to Friedrich Pollock, June 9, 1943.

lently oppressive police state there. And he resented pay cuts imposed by Horkheimer and Pollock on members of the Institute as a result of a crisis in its finances. Through brutal behavior, notably toward his fellow and more talented economist, Pollock also attempted to drive those regarded as peripheral to Horkheimer's higher theoretical ends off the payroll altogether.

Fed up with postponements in the study's publication as a monograph, Grossman eventually threatened to issue it as a book in English, prefaced by a statement about the Institute's two-year sabotage of its appearance, if it was not available by Christmas 1941.[53] Leo Löwenthal, who looked after the practicalities of the Institute's publications, complained that Grossman's inaccurate referencing held it up because stencils had to be retyped. As indicated in the translation below, several such errors were not picked up at that stage and it has still not been possible to identify a couple of Grossman's references to Marx.[54] Finally a mere eighty duplicated copies of the monograph were issued, dated 1941. Since then, it has been republished twice by the German new left and translated into Italian, French, Danish and English (three times).[55]

Earlier Marxist Critiques of Marginalist Economics

The fundamental assumptions and propositions of mainstream economics are, in the main, internally consistent and, where they are not, its usefulness as a class ideology and hence sponsorship by the capitalist class and states has ensured that theoretical doubts, conundrums and inconveniences have been concealed from broad public attention.[56] As part of the struggle against capitalism, Marx undertook a critique of its proponents' economic theories, which provided justifications for the existing order, and counterposed an alternative analysis. Henryk Grossman's study was conducted in this belligerent spirit of class warfare, not one of polite academic debate, identifying the flaws in bourgeois economics, notably the then- and still-dominant marginalist theory, and the superiority of Marxism.

---

53. There is an undated manuscript translation into English ("Marx Classical National Economy and Problem of Dynamics," Folder 74, Henryk Grossman III-155 Collection) of part of the draft essay in German, which includes material that did not appear in the published German version. See pp. 137–191 in the present volume.

54. Löwenthal to Henryk Grossman, July 30, 1939 (VI 9, Max-Horkheimer-Archiv), 286; Löwenthal to Max Horkheimer, November 26, 1941, 222.

55. Grossman, *Marx, die klassische Nationalökonomie und das Problem der Dynamik*, with appendix "Briefe Henryk Grossmanns an Paul Mattick über Akkumulation" (Frankfurt: Europäische Verlagsanstalt, 1969); Grossman, *Marx, die klassische Nationalökonomie und das Problem der Dynamik*, unauthorized edition, ca. 1970; *Marx, l'economia politica classica e il problema della dinamica*, trans. Giorgio Backhaus (Bari: Laterza, 1971); Grossman, *Marx, l'économie politique classique et le probleme de la dynamique*, with a preface by Paul Mattick (Paris: Champ Libre, 1975); Grossman, *Marx, den klassiske nationaløkonomi og dynamikken* (Copenhagen: Rhodos, 1975); Grossman, *Marx, Classical Political Economy and the Problem of Dynamics*, trans. Pete Burgess, *Capital and Class* 1, no. 2 (1977): 32–55 and 1, no. 3 (1977): 67–99; Grossman, *Marx, Classical Economics, and the Problem of Dynamics*, trans. Paul Mattick Jr., *International Journal of Political Economy* 36, no. 2 (2007): 6–83.

56. Dobb, *Political Economy and Capitalism*, 127; Varoufakis, *Foundations of Economics*, 352.

Earlier Marxists had undertaken critiques of marginalist economics.[57] Friedrich Engels began the job with a very brief comment on William Stanley Jevons's theory, accurately concluding, "Vulgar Economy everywhere!"[58] Conrad Schmidt devoted somewhat greater attention to the theory, in the Austrian variants of Carl Menger and Eugen Böhm-Bawerk. He condemned its subjectivist, psychological approach, its untenable assumption that individual judgments of utility could be aggregated, and its focus on consumption to the exclusion of production. Later Marxists have likewise rejected the methodological individualism of marginalist theory, which is particularly apparent in its foundation on subjective assessments of utility. While judging marginalist economics unsatisfactory for its understanding of values and prices, Schmidt thought the approach offered insights into the behavior of consumers faced with already established prices.[59] By referring to the choices individuals make about the amounts of different goods they purchase, marginalist economics has subsequently been able to dispense with the assumption that utility can be measured. Moreover, Schmidt's objection that the theory ignored production itself ignored the marginalist theory of the firm.

Henry Hyndman, the founder and leader of the Social Democratic Federation in England, while dogmatic and sometimes theoretically crude, did pay attention to the spread of marginalist theory. He made telling points against Jevons's individualist perspective, its continuity with earlier vulgar economics and incompatibility with Marx's labor theory of value. As Grossman did decades later, Hyndman also noted that demand no longer drove supply. Like Schmidt, however, he mistakenly regarded the theory as incapable of explaining supply in its own terms.[60]

In response to Bernstein's vague and eclectic suggestions that there was merit in both Marxist and marginalist theory and in the spirit of Engels's assessment, Kautsky insisted that it was impossible to construct a satisfactory economic theory on the basis of two quite different theories of value.[61] Furthermore, comparing Bernstein with the Fabians, he argued that

> the English, however, prefer not to break with settled forms but rather merely to change their content, remaining socialists even after becoming liberals and simply calling socialism what others call liberalism.
>
> Bernstein has undergone a similar development. But Marxism is not as vague a concept as "socialism." It is, rather, a quite definite concept that is incompatible with any bourgeois social outlook. If a declaration of incapacity to refute bourgeois criticism of Marxism, capitulating to bourgeois economics, is to be made, while nevertheless wanting to remain a Marxist or, as Bernstein expresses it, wanting to show that in the end Marx is right against Marx, then Marxism's bones must first be broken.[62]

57. For a valuable survey, see Chaloupek, "Marxistische Kritik an der Österreichischen Schule."
58. Engels to Nikolai Danielson, January 5, 1888, 137.
59. Schmidt, "Die psychologische Richtung."
60. Hyndman, *The Economics of Socialism*, 158–59, 261–66, 268–70.
61. Bernstein, "Sozialistische Oekonomie in England"; Bernstein, *Preconditions of Socialism*, 51–52.
62. Kautsky, "Bernstein über die Wertheorie," 80, 81; also see Kautsky, *Bernstein und das sozialdemokratische*

Rudolf Hilferding and Bukharin also judged marginalism and Marx's labor theory of value incompatible. Others regarded a coherent theory of value as dispensable. Otto Bauer followed Schmidt in thinking that marginalist economics shed light on demand and advocated Bernstein's eclectic approach; Kei Shibata argued that Marx's value theory could be an optional extra; and Oskar Lange rejected it while endorsing Marx's analysis of economic institutions.[63]

In his reply to Böhm-Bawerk's attempt to discredit Marx's economic ideas, Hilferding noted that marginalist theory's individualist approach made it ahistorical and that its characterization of labor as economically significant because it was a subjective "disutility" was inadequate, in addition to objections already raised by Schmidt.[64] In a later article, Hilferding drew attention to the marginalists' adherence to the quantity theory of money (that the total amount of money determines the value of each unit of money), which Marx had criticized.[65] Some other Marxists polemicized against marginalist economics without quite grasping its logic.[66]

The Bolshevik leader and theoretician Bukharin wrote the most systematic critique of contemporary bourgeois economics to appear between Marx's death and the post–World War II period. Following Marxist predecessors, he pointed out the weakness of the "subjectivist" approach of marginalist economics, that is, its methodological individualism: the assumption that social phenomena can be reduced to interactions of discrete individuals. He also criticized its ahistorical assumption that the fundamental features of modern capitalist society were eternal and its assessment of economic processes from the point of view of consumption (rather than production).[67] Less persuasively, Bukharin contrasted the Austrian variant, which he asserted was that of rentier capitalists, with John Bates Clark's American school, supposedly associated with the "progressive" bourgeoisie engaged in production. As these intellectual currents shared fundamental features, were hardly counterposed even when they emerged, and served the same broad interests of the capitalist class, such a distinction in terms of class affiliation was untenable.

Later, Maurice Dobb highlighted mainstream economists' unrealistic assumptions that individuals' preferences are independent of each other, the market and social relations, and are "fairly permanent and consistent."[68] Dobb, like Grossman, stressed conceptual continuity between the "revolutionary" marginalists, with their mathematical appurtenances, and their immediate vulgar economic predecessors.

Programm.

63. Bauer, *Einführung in die Volkswirtschaftslehre*, 288; Shibata, "Marx's Analysis of Capitalism" and "The Meaning of the Theory of Value"; Lange, "Die allgemeine Interdependenz."

64. Hilferding, *Böhm-Bawerk's Criticism of Marx*, 133, 184–85.

65. Hilferding, review of *Theorie des Geldes und des Umlaufsmittel*, by Ludwig Mises.

66. See Eckstein, "Die vierfache Wurzel des Satzes" and "Zur Methode der politischen Ökonomie." The latter repeatedly stressed Joseph Schumpeter's point (from *Das Wesen und der Hauptinhalt*) that marginalist economics is essentially static.

67. Bukharin, *Economic Theory of the Leisure Class*, 36–57.

68. Dobb, *Political Economy and Capitalism*, 136, 165, 161, 167.

Dynamics

Participation in one of Eugen Böhm-Bawerk's seminar courses at the University of Vienna before World War I underpinned Grossman's ability to deal not only with the earlier history of economics but also with marginalist theory. Böhm-Bawerk was the preeminent member of the second generation of the Austrian school of marginalist economics. Grossman did not recapitulate the arguments of earlier Marxist critics of mainstream economic theory at any length. Instead he grounded the contrast between its static approach—from the physiocrats[69] Smith and Ricardo through to the present—and Marx's ability to grasp capitalist dynamics in the contradiction between use value and value, and specifically the "dual character of labor." Marx had written to Engels that this was one of the two "best points" in *Capital*.[70]

Bourgeois economists' need to demonstrate that capitalism is rational and self-regulating resulted in the assumption that economies were characterized by a tendency to equilibrium. This approach was necessarily static and, as Grossman put it, "The concept of 'self-regulation' serves to divert attention away from the actually prevailing chaos of the destruction of capital, the bankruptcy of entrepreneurs and factories, mass unemployment, insufficient capital investment, currency disturbances and arbitrary redistributions of property."[71] Disturbances came from outside, according to mainstream economics back to Smith: war, crop failure, state intervention. Later attempts to attribute crises to monetary problems, by Knut Wicksell and subsequently Friedrich Hayek, Irving Fisher and Ralph George Hawtrey, were also static. Efforts to account for them in terms of technological change, disproportion among sectors, lengths of construction periods or the durability of production goods (the accelerator principle) were empirical observations divorced from theory.

Vulgar bourgeois economics had abandoned the labor theory of value and attempted to explain exchange value, understood as price, in terms of utility. Vilfredo Pareto solved the problem that it is impossible to measure the utility of commodities directly. He derived demand curves from the comparisons people make in their choices among different goods (commodities) in order to maximize their well-being. But for this "ordinal" approach to work, Grossman pointed out in one of the first Marxist critiques of the more sophisticated version of marginalist theory that emerged during the 1930s and 1940s, further unreal assumptions had to be made: the infinite divisibility of goods, unlimited substitutability between them (ignoring the material character of commodities as use values), and perfect knowledge. He also noted the importation, without

69. The physiocrats were an eighteenth-century school of French economists who stressed that productive work, which they identified with agriculture, was the source of wealth.

70. Marx to Friedrich Engels, August 27, 1867, 407. On the importance and previous neglect of use value in economic processes, see Rosdolsky, *The Making of Marx's* Capital, 71–95. The latter volume was originally published as an article in 1959.

71. Grossman, *Marx, die Klassische Nationaloekonomie und das Problem der Dynamik*. See the translation included in the present volume, as chapter 3, under the title "Marx, Classical Political Economy and the Problem of Dynamics," (henceforth referred to as "Marx and Dynamics"), 176.

justification, of theoretical physics's conceptual and mathematical apparatus, including the distinction between statics and dynamics, into marginalist economics.[72] Pareto's equilibrium equations were only possible because he, like his predecessors, excluded the dynamic factor of the production process and dealt only with exchange.

Equilibrium theory entails "the assumption of the simultaneous rhythm of all economic processes."[73] Economic processes, however, involve not just the circulation of commodities but also their production as use values. The duration of the periods of production and even the circulation of different commodities vary. Their coincidence, if it occurs at all, can only be accidental. Yet vulgar economics simply assumes such coincidence or the simultaneity of transactions. It cannot theoretically incorporate time and therefore history.

New York and Modes of Production

A long, early draft of what became *Marx and Dynamics* had included a discussion of whether Marx was the first to introduce a historical perspective into economics.[74] Material cut from that draft, extended and developed, was incorporated into **"The Evolutionist Revolt against Classical Political Economics,"** published in two parts by the Chicago-based *Journal of Political Economy* in 1943. Although he had already withdrawn from many of the Institute's activities, Grossman sent a draft of "The Evolutionist Revolt" to Horkheimer in early 1942. The director's comments were extremely hostile, reflecting his abandonment of Marxism. Grossman made only minor changes in response to them.[75]

The study demolished the misconception that Marx, under Hegel's influence, was the first to argue that the basic structure of economies had changed over the long term. Marx's originality lay elsewhere. Grossman examined the French works of Marie-Jean-Antoine-Nicolas de Condorcet (1743–94), Henri Saint-Simon (1760–1825) and Simonde de Sismondi (1773–1842); the English writings of James Stuart (1712–80) and Richard Jones (1790–1855); and Marx's treatment of modes of production. In this way, he showed "how dynamic or evolutionary thinking actually entered the field of economics."[76]

The most influential works of classical political economy, including those of Smith and Ricardo, the study explained, did not recognize that economic development took the form of successive modes of production. But from the late eighteenth century there were theorists outside the mainstream, in both France and England, whose views were

---

72. For a detailed account of marginalist economics' debt to physics, see Mirowski, *More Heat than Light*, 193–395.
73. Grossman, "Marx and Dynamics," 175.
74. Grossman, "Marx und klassische Oekonomie oder die Lehre von Wertfetisch," unpublished manuscript, 1937, Folder 68, Henryk Grossman III-155 Collection, 31–33, 53–62; see also Grossman, "Marx and Dynamics."
75. For a detailed discussion of the exchange, see Kuhn, "Henryk Grossman and Critical Theory."
76. Grossman, "The Evolutionist Revolt," 193.

shaped by the political revolutions in America and France and the industrial revolution in England. They made generalizations on the basis of contemporary and historical evidence. Jones went further, using these to criticize mainstream economic theories and formulate new positions. The concept of distinct stages of economic development, widely accepted by the middle of the nineteenth century, was most precisely formulated in Marx's analysis and then disappeared from economic orthodoxy.[77]

In contrast to the earlier evolutionists, Marx shared Hegel's dialectical concept of the development of the "cultural whole"—the totality of modern bourgeois society—as the object of his analysis. But Marx, like Sismondi and Jones, saw development as "a succession of objective economic stages of different economic structures." For Hegel the essence of development was "the progress within man's consciousness of an idea of freedom." Without using the expressions, Grossman therefore distinguished between the materialism of the evolutionist political economists and Hegel's idealism by distinguishing two meanings of "development": material evolution (in the work of the political economists he discussed) and development of the "notion" or "concept" (in Hegel's system). Unlike the evolutionist political economists, Hegel also believed that historical change had come to a halt with the "consolidation of middle-class society."[78]

Horkheimer's assessment that it was "a most rotten piece of work"[79] has not been endorsed by later appreciations of "The Evolutionist Revolt." The study was republished twice during the early 1990s, in a collection on Marx and in another on early political economists.[80]

A Missing Link in the History of Economic Thought and Return to Germany

"W. Playfair, the Earliest Theorist of Capitalist Development" was a supplement to the project embodied in *Marx and Dynamics* and then "The Evolutionist Revolt." The essay on pioneering economic evolutionists had only quoted a single empirical observation by Playfair in a footnote.[81] In a letter to his friends Christina Stead and Bill Blake, Grossman wrote:

> My "Playfair" is with Guterman for translation. I think that the paper itself is better than the "content." The point is: Sismondi went to England, to collect materials for his book on the basis of higher development of Engl. capitalism. So the English Capitalism influenced through Sismondi *French* economic literature. This must astonish, why this higher developed engl. capitalism *did not influence english* economic literature? Now, I found the

---

77. Ibid., 197–198, 214, 219.
78. Ibid., 195, 220, 223.
79. Horkheimer to Leo Löwenthal, January 21, 1943 (VI 16, Max-Horkheimer-Archiv), 105.
80. In *Karl Marx's Social and Political Thought: Critical Assessments*, vol. 1, edited by Bob Jessop (London: Routledge, 1990), 253–74, and *Thomas Tooke (1774–1858), Mountifort Longfield (1802–1884), Richard Jones (1790–1855)*, 1–16.
81. Grossman, "The Evolutionist Revolt," 196n19.

missing link, the *direct* trace in english literature. If [Harold] Laski could help publish in an English quarterly, would be better, than here in Journal of Polit. Economy. If you wish, I will send you a copy of MSS.[82]

The article was written during early 1947 and appeared in the English journal *Economic History Review* the following year.[83] Playfair had anticipated Sismondi's observations about the concentration of capital, polarization between a few in the wealthy upper class and more and more people who are poor, while the middle classes declined. He also linked the issues of growth and imperialism. Economic development transforms poor agricultural into rich industrial countries. But industrial nations have more capital than can be profitably invested at home. Moral and economic stagnation results, unless governments promote, most importantly, the "export of commodities and of capital" but also "decentralization of capital, further various forms of unproductive expenditure and waste." In Playfair's analysis of capitalism's underlying tendency to stagnate and its countertendencies, Grossman identified the first application of a methodology later employed by Ricardo, John Stuart Mill and Marx.[84] In the final two sentences of the last publication he saw into print, Grossman recapitulated an insight that underpinned many of his own contributions to the understanding of capitalism: that Marx had an original and accurate explanation, based on the long-term rise in the organic composition of capital (the ratio between living labor and means of production in the production process), of the system's proneness to crises and generation of poverty, which are discussed further in the second part, below.[85]

The translation of Grossman's article on Playfair into English was less polished than that on the early evolutionists and its material could have been better organized. The closest it came to discussion of the relationship between Playfair's insights and working-class strategy was to mention that socialization of production under capitalism presaged socialism. But, observing that when John Atkinson Hobson early in the twentieth century again raised the issue of the relationship between exports and stagnation, he stimulated a whole new literature, Grossman no doubt had Lenin's *Imperialism: The Highest Stage of Capitalism* particularly in mind.[86]

In addition to the Playfair article, after his estrangement from the Institute, Grossman also wrote a substantial study of René Descartes, only published in 2009. It was an extension of his review article on the rise of the scientific worldview.[87]

Although the Institute continued to pay his salary, its value severely eroded by wartime inflation, Grossman's work was now hardly of interest to Horkheimer, except as a

---

82. Grossman to Christina Stead and Bill Blake, May 4–5, 1947, Box 17, Folder 125, Stead Collection. [Editor's interpolation.]

83. Henryk Grossman to Bill Blake, March 3, 1947, Box 17, Folder 125, Stead Collection.

84. See Grossman, "W. Playfair," 246 (this and subsequent citations to the same essay refer to chapter 5 of the present volume). On the relationship between Mill's and Marx's use and application of this methodology, see Grossmann, *Law of Accumulation*, 73–74.

85. See Grossman, "W. Playfair," 250.

86. Ibid., 231, 241, 245, 247; Lenin, *Imperialism, the Highest Stage of Capitalism*.

87. Grossmann, "Descartes and the Social Origins of the Mechanistic Concept of the World."

possible source of embarrassment. They made a deal. Grossman accepted a lump-sum payment from the Institute to finance his return to Germany and in return agreed to terminate their relationship. He took up a professorial chair at the University of Leipzig, the oldest in the Soviet Occupation Zone, in early 1949. The university authorities recruited him and others exiled from Germany in the west to replace staff who had embraced national socialism and to raise the institution's prestige. The Stalinist authorities soon had second thoughts about this policy. But as he died on November 24, 1950, Grossman did not suffer from the wave of persecution of these unreliable elements.

Enthused by the task of contributing to "the construction of socialism," Grossman joined the Socialist Unity (that is, Communist) Party, participated in the intellectual and administrative life of the university and started to teach again. His health already weakened, particularly by Parkinson's disease, he did not undertake any new research projects but probably worked on ones already underway, including the Descartes study. He sought to have several of his essays of the late 1920s and early 1930s, now essentially inaccessible in Germany, republished together as a book. The contents would have contradicted the prevalent Stalinist orthodoxy in economics: none of Grossman's work was ever republished in East Germany. It only found a new audience when new left publishers in West Germany reissued *The Law of Accumulation* and other studies between 1967 and 1971, followed by translations into Italian, French and Spanish during the 1970s. English translations have taken longer.

Insights

In many of his works, including those in the present volume, Grossman contributed to interlocking controversies among Marxists over method, the contradiction between the use value and value sides of capitalist production, economic crisis and the revolutionary potential of the working class. His recovery and development of Marx's analyses in these areas paralleled and were influenced by Lukács's contributions to philosophy and Lenin's to political theory and practice. They are discussed in the following sections.

Method

The sorting of the myriad aspects of the reality that impinges on us according to their importance in influencing other aspects is intrinsic to scientific research. To understand falling bodies and develop the theory of gravity, for example, physicists "exclude the accidental and external influences of air"[88] as a first step in their explanations. Such thought experiments, involving initial abstraction away from less significant factors, are also a feature of economics as a science. But not all abstractions are accurate. Although Sismondi sometimes engaged in an antitheoretical, empiricist rhetoric, Grossman

---

88. Grossman, "The Theory of Economic Crises," 171.

pointed out that one of his most important criticisms of the classical political economy of Smith and Ricardo was that they abstracted from "*the essential elements* that characterize capitalist society." Contrary to the prevalent and superficial readings of his work, the Swiss economist's practice was far from empiricist. He developed François Quesnay's abstract model of reproduction, excluded survivals of previous modes of production and concentrated on crucial relations that the mainstream economists did not include, particularly the nature of the capital–wage labor relationship.[89]

The "process of successive approximation"—stripping away less important and relevant features, which clutter our perception, by making simplifying assumptions to identify fundamental relations, and then successively lifting those assumptions so that the abstract insights are embedded in an account closer to concrete reality—structured Marx's *Capital*. The model in the first volume abstracted, for example, from differences among the turnover times in the production of various commodities; competition among capitals; changes in the values of commodities; credit; changes in the value of money; systematic deviation of prices from values; differences in the organic compositions of capital among industries; and the concrete forms—industrial profit, commercial profit, interest, ground rent—taken by surplus value. In the course of the discussions in the second and third volumes, these and other aspects of empirical capitalism were introduced progressively to generate more complex models, incrementally closer to the reality we perceive.[90] A failure to grasp Marx's method and the reproduction schemas in the second volume of *Capital* invalidated Rosa Luxemburg's underconsumptionist explanation of economic crises.[91]

Use Value and Value

Ricardo and, before him, Adam Smith mentioned use value only to go on to ignore it and construct theories of abstract exchange value. Sismondi's critique of Smith and Ricardo highlighted the contradiction between the use value and exchange value aspects of commodities.[92] In mainstream economics, the neglect of use value became even more pronounced in the response to left Ricardians' employment of classical theory to justify socialist conclusions. Grossman quoted a very early text by Marx on the implications of an exclusive focus on exchange value: "By denying the importance of gross revenue, i.e., the volume of production and consumption [which Grossman identified as "the mass of use values necessary for the maintenance of the working nation"] apart from the value-surplus—and hence denying the importance of life itself, political economy's abstraction reaches the peak of infamy."[93] Marx's transformation

---

89. Grossman, "Simonde de Sismondi," 42.

90. Grossman, "The Change in the Original Plan," 30–31; Grossmann, "Eine neue Theorie über Imperialismus," 149.

91. For example, Grossmann, "Eine neue Theorie über Imperialismus," 183; "Fifty Years of Struggle," 133.

92. Grossman, "Simonde de Sismondi," 51, 67.

93. Marx, "Aus David Ricardo," 421 and following; Grossman, "Marx and Dynamics," 152.

of Ricardo's economic categories was like his transformation of Hegel's dialectic. An important feature of Marx's reconfiguration was the systematic exploration, drawing on Sismondi, of the dual character of economic processes, including their material aspects, as opposed to Ricardo's one-sided concentration on them as abstract value processes.[94] This provided a means of grasping the real relations behind the veil of appearances and the reasons for these misleading appearances: "The point is not to eliminate the mystifying factor and substitute another but rather to demonstrate the necessary connection between the two and to explain what is deceptive in the phenomena of value. Because capitalism has a dual reality—mystifying and nonmystifying sides—and binds them together in a concrete unity, any theory that reflects this reality must likewise be a unity of opposites."[95]

A fundamental aspect of capitalism, the dual character of commodities and labor, their use value and value sides, was not simply discussed in the first part of the first volume of *Capital* and then set aside, as many Marxist economists have assumed. The distinction between the use value (labor as an activity) and the value (labor power, a commodity) aspects of human labor was crucial in revealing the basis of surplus value, profits and exploitation. Capitalist processes of production are at once labor processes, in which specific kinds of concrete labor are applied, and value-creating (valorization) processes, in which quantities of socially necessary abstract labor are embodied into commodities.

Marx's method of successive approximation meant that, in *Capital*, the distinction between use value and value, gained at the highest level of abstraction, permeated the increasingly concrete analyses, progressively approaching the complex real world.[96] Capital and the organic composition of capital, for example, also have a dual character. The organic composition of capital is the ratio between the value of human labor power and other inputs into production processes "insofar as it is determined by" "the relation between the mass of the means of production employed on the one hand, and the mass of labour necessary for their employment on the other," that is, the relation between the means of production as use values and living labor, "and mirrors the changes in the latter."[97] The contradiction between the unlimited productive potential of the development of production forces and the constraints on output imposed by capitalist relations of production also expresses that between the use value and value aspects of economic processes under capitalism.[98]

The neglect of use value or its confusion with exchange value has remained a feature of mainstream economics. Much of Marx's critique of vulgar economics therefore

---

94. Grossman, "Marx and Dynamics," 147, 150, 156; Grossman, "Simonde de Sismondi," 58.

95. Grossman, "Marx and Dynamics," 144.

96. Ibid., 147, 158; Grossmann, *Law of Accumulation*, 147. In responses to criticisms of Marx by ecological economists, Paul Burkett has demonstrated that the reproduction schemas in volume 2 of *Capital* are concerned not only with flows of values but also flows of use values: "Marx's Reproduction Schemes and the Environment."

97. Marx, *Capital*, vol. 3, 762.

98. Grossmann, *Law of Accumulation*, 123.

also applies to its current, sophisticated and sophistical third, marginalist phase, preoccupied with psychology (the subjective theory of value) and mathematical technique, and popularly known as "economics."

There has been a long-running controversy over Marx's explanation of the way in which the values of commodities are transformed into "prices of production" as rates of profit equalize across industries with different organic compositions of capital. The neo-Ricardian Ladislaus Bortkiewicz identified a problem in Marx's failure to assume that economic processes occur simultaneously, as in equilibrium models, and "solved" it by means of systems of equations based on precisely this assumption.[99] Paul Sweezy's very influential *The Theory of Capitalist Development* popularized this "solution" among English-reading Marxists.[100] The acceptance of Bortkiewicz's solution to the "transformation problem" embedded the fundamentally static equilibrium approach of mainstream bourgeois economics into many Marxist economists' thinking. Subsequently, on the basis of a simultaneous equilibrium analysis, most cogently articulated by Nobuo Okishio,[101] not only non-Marxist economists but many Marxists also concluded that Marx's law of the tendency for the rate of profit to fall, the crux of his account of economic crises, was false. This refutation only holds if Marx's own "temporalist" approach, which eschews the implausible marginalist assumption of the simultaneous determination of the prices of inputs and outputs, is disregarded.[102]

In contrast with the static framework of both classical political economy and its vulgar descendents, both of which assume that capitalism has a tendency to equilibrium, the dual nature of commodities, especially as applied to the commodity labor power, allowed Marx to grasp capitalism as a dynamic system. The recovery of Marx's critique of the way classical political economists and their vulgar successors assumed "the simultaneous rhythm of all economic processes" allowed Grossman to expose many previous (and subsequent) Marxists' capitulation to bourgeois economics. They neglected the use value, therefore the time aspect of economic relations, and reverted to pre-Marxist equilibrium analysis. Between the 1980s and 2010s, the temporal single-system interpretation, in the process of resolving the "transformation problem," recapitulated the account Grossman provided of Marx's approach to capturing the dynamics of capitalism and his objections to the static methodology of vulgar Marxists.[103]

99. Bortkiewicz, "On the Correction of Marx's Fundamental Theoretical Construction" and *Value and Price in the Marxian System*, nb translated by Sweezy.
100. Sweezy, *Theory of Capitalist Development*, 109–28.
101. Okishio, "Technical Change and the Rate of Profit."
102. For a defense of Marx's approach, see Kliman, *Reclaiming Marx's "Capital,"* 113–38.
103. Grossmann, "Das Problem der Durchschnittsprofitrate in der modernen wirtschaftlichen Theorie," student's typed-up notes from Grossman's course, 1932, Folder 60, Henryk Grossman III–155 Collection; Grossman, "Zum Abschluss des Streites um die Wert- und Preisrechnung im Marxschen System," unpublished manuscript, n.d., Folder 61, Henryk Grossman III-155 Collection. See Kliman, *Reclaiming Marx's "Capital,"* for an impressive account of the controversy and the temporal single-system interpretation; and Moseley, *Money and Totality*, for a persuasive variant.

Crisis and Breakdown

Grossman subjected the crisis theories of mainstream economists and most of his Marxist predecessors to sustained criticism in the course of identifying two complementary theories of crisis in Marx's work. The first, which most commentators on Grossman's work have ignored, explained capitalism's dynamic instability. The second, based on Marx's law of the tendency for the rate of profit to fall, accounted for capitalism's breakdown logic and the cyclical nature of crises. Both were grounded in the contradictions between the capitalist production process as a labor process, creating use values, and as a process generating new values, in the form of surplus value. These theories were counterposed to explanations of crises and/or capitalism's tendency to break down in terms of underconsumption and value disproportion alone.

Heinrich Cunow, in 1898, offered an underconsumptionist explanation of capitalism's breakdown tendency: workers were not paid enough to buy all that they produced and export markets would only be able to absorb this excess for a limited period, until capitalism pervaded the whole world. At that point there would be no scope for exports to noncapitalist areas and the system would break down. Karl Kautsky, between 1901 and 1911, and Louis Boudin, in his widely read English-language work of 1907, also expounded this argument. Rosa Luxemburg, in 1913, provided a more systematic grounding for the underconsumptionist theory of capitalist breakdown than these earlier Marxist efforts. She drew explicitly on the work of Sismondi and argued that imperialism resulted from the pursuit of noncapitalist markets, which were essential for capitalism's survival. Luxemburg recognized that, contrary to Eduard Bernstein and his reformist successors, the theory of breakdown was a key element of Marx's analysis of capitalism and the case for socialism. As she was a consistent revolutionary, who sought like Cunow to justify a theory of breakdown with inadequate arguments, her position provided Grossman with a useful foil in making the case for Marx's explanation.[104]

The reproduction schemas in the second volume of *Capital* were inadequate, according to Luxemburg, because they did not show the necessary shortfall between the growth of output and its "realization," i.e. sale. Workers and capitalists could not buy the products embodying newly created surplus value. Those commodities had to be realized through sale to noncapitalist "third persons" at home or abroad. But the schemas, constructed at a high level of abstraction, were designed to illuminate the process of capitalist circulation, not the much more concrete issue of realization. The incorporation of foreign trade and investment would have undermined their provisional assumption that prices were the same as values, which was still crucial for the analysis the schemas embodied.[105] On the other hand, incorporating them into the analysis at a more concrete level presents no difficulties.

104. Grossman, "Fifty Years of Struggle," 103, 119, 121; Grossmann, "Eine neue Theorie über Imperialismus," 160.
105. Criticisms of Luxemburg are implicit in Grossman's "The Theory of Economic Crises" and "Simonde de Sismondi," 39. They are explicit in "Eine neue Theorie über Imperialismus," 183–84; "The Change in the Original Plan," 156–63; *Law of Accumulation*, 41–42, 47–48, 67–68; and "Fifty Years of Struggle," 133.

Luxemburg's approach could not account for cyclical crises and failed as a theory of breakdown because it did not accept that the logic of capital accumulation is "production for the sake of production," that is, profit making, rather than satisfying the final demand of individuals. In addition to their own personal consumption, *if it is profitable to invest*, capitalists in different sectors will expend newly created surplus value on expanding their capacity (by buying additional means of production and employing new workers who purchase additional means of consumption, produced in other sectors). In that way, all the commodities embodying surplus value can potentially find a market.[106]

Employing a model derived from Marx's reproduction schemas, Mikhail Tugan-Baranovsky, when a "legal Marxist" in tsarist Russia, claimed capitalist expansion could continue indefinitely, limited only by the rate of technological change. Crises, he argued, are the result of disproportional expansion in different industries. Tugan-Baranovsky reproduced the harmonious conclusions of Jean-Baptiste Say, the father of vulgar political economy, who contended that supply creates its own demand. "Neo-harmonist" Marxists, such as Hilferding, Bauer and Karl Renner, embraced this approach, including the focus, shared with mainstream economics, on the value proportions that are conditions for sustained growth and economic stability and the rejection of Marx's theory of breakdown. Their theories of disproportionality were unsatisfactory because they ignored the transformation of values into prices of production. From their analysis they drew the reformist conclusion that if proportional investment was imposed by the state, economic crises could be avoided. While Communists like Bukharin were committed revolutionaries, their theories of disproportionality drawn from Hilferding's shared its flaws.[107]

The contradiction between use value and value in the process of production pervaded the whole of Marx's economic theory, including his treatments of crises. In contrast to neo-harmonist, value-fixated accounts of the proportions required for stable capitalist growth, his inclusion of material use value conditions resulted in a radical theory of disproportionality with much more stringent and, in the real world, implausible conditions for capitalist equilibrium.[108]

Before September 1933, Grossman wrote that he had begun to work on a book on crisis under simple reproduction, which he described as his "life's work." He still referred to it as "my chief contribution to Marxist theory" in 1947.[109] While nothing like a book manuscript has survived, his published works contain elements of the argument, which built on his earlier, more general recovery of Marx's theory of radical disproportionality.

106. Grossman, "Fifty Years of Struggle," 119 and especially 121; *Law of Accumulation*, 41–42, 118–19; "Eine neue Theorie über Imperialismus," 183–85; "The Change in the Original Plan," 155–60.
107. Grossman, "Fifty Years of Struggle," 94; *Law of Accumulation*, 69; "Marx and Dynamics," 183.
108. Grossman, "The Theory of Economic Crises"; "Marx and Dynamics," 137–91, particularly 189.
109. Grossman to Paul Mattick, September 16, 1933, Paul Mattick Collection; Grossman to Christina Stead and Bill Blake, May 4–5, 1947. Also, for example, Grossman to Paul Mattick, July 18, 1937, Paul Mattick Collection.

In the second volume of *Capital*, Marx dropped the preliminary assumption of equal "production times" (the periods required for the production of commodities) of all capitals and also introduced the complication of "circulation time" (the period commodities spend in the sphere of circulation before they are sold). Together production and circulation time constitute "turnover time." Differences in turnover time are conditioned by the technical (that is, use value) characteristics of production processes and the commodities they create. Even in the model of simple reproduction (that is, without growth) in the second volume of *Capital*, which abstracts from the credit system among other aspects of the real world, crises are inevitable because of the use value distinction between fixed capital (embodied in commodities like machines, which function in multiple cycles of the labor process) and circulating capital (commodities like raw materials or wage goods, which are used up in one cycle). In some years, more fixed capital will have to be replaced than in others. But the model assumes a consistent level of output each year.[110] Unevenness in the accumulation of fixed capital will tend to become cyclical, clumped together during some periods, generating booms, and thinning out during others, resulting in slumps.

The analysis can be extended by considering different kinds of fixed capitals as use values with different average life spans to account for cycles of different periodicities. Hence there are cycles of investment in normal, productive fixed capital and longer cycles of investment in larger-scale fixed capital, infrastructure and buildings.[111] The existence of credit in the real world can even out fixed capital investments in different industries and enterprises, geographically, *at a given time*. It does not even out and may intensify fluctuations in fixed capital investment *over time*.

Furthermore, simple reproduction in value terms is not necessarily simple reproduction in terms of use values. Changed weather conditions in agriculture and large losses in output due to unforeseen circumstances in any industry can lead to a decline in the number of commodities produced, while the living labor and the value of the means of production used to produce them and therefore their total value, are unchanged. Such a development will disrupt simple reproduction in other industries to which it provides inputs.[112]

When the scale of reproduction expands and there is technological change, as Grossman argued much earlier, the situation becomes even more complicated. Even if new investment is proportional across sectors, in value terms the growth in the number of commodities produced by different sectors will vary according to the use value characteristics of their output.[113] So, for example, "No one who finds two trac-

110. Grossman to Paul Mattick, July 18, 1937; "Marx and Dynamics," 177–181 (see also 149); and Marx, *Capital*, vol. 2, 264 and 528–45 (particularly 543–45).
111. Roberts, *The Long Depression*, 219–21. The existence and basis in Marxist theory of still-lengthier "Kondratiev" cycles or "long waves" is more questionable (compare Trotsky, "The Curve of Capitalist Development" and Day, "The Theory of the Long Cycle.").
112. See Grossman, "Marx and Dynamics," 176–186; and Henryk Grossmann to Paul Mattick, 1937.
113. Grossman, "Marx and Dynamics," 177–81. For a more detailed explanation, see Marx, *Capital*, vol.

tors sufficient for the cultivation of their land will buy four simply because their price has fallen by half. Demand for tractors is, all other things being equal, not dependent on their price alone but is rather determined by the area to be cultivated, that is, quantitatively."[114] If technological change occurs, problems of disproportion will arise even when investment is not increased or increases in the same value proportions in different industries. Should technological progress leap ahead in the steel compared to the car industry, the quantity of steel will rise more rapidly than the number of cars. So even though the car industry may have the capacity, in *value* terms, to purchase the same proportion of the steel industry's output as previously, its *technical* requirements for steel will not have kept up with the expanded production of steel. The previous equilibrium, on the basis of the previous value proportionalities, will be disrupted.

The material characteristics of the technology used in production also mean that there is a minimum amount of accumulated value that has to be invested in specific sectors. This, too, is an obstacle to simultaneous proportional expansion of production.[115] For example, surplus value accumulated over a year or less may be sufficient to expand a clothing factory by an additional number of cutting and sewing machines. But a steel mill may have to accumulate over several years before it can invest in a new furnace and related equipment.

The contradiction between use value and value also underpinned Marx's theory of capitalist breakdown, another important aspect of his account of periodic crises. A tendency to breakdown was, according to Marx, inherent in the capitalist mode of *production*, but this has been denied by many Marxist economists for generations.

> It was a great historical contribution of Rosa Luxemburg that she, in a conscious opposition to the distortions of these "neo-harmonists," adhered to the basic lesson of *Capital* and sought to reinforce it with the proof that the continued development of capitalism encounters absolute economic limits.
>
> Frankly, Luxemburg's effort failed.[116]

Two circumstances facilitated Grossman's "reconstruction of Marx's theory of crisis and breakdown": recovering Marx's method of abstraction and successive approximation, which structured *Capital*, and the investigations associated with his theory of radical disproportionality.[117] Extrapolating Bauer's reproduction schema, designed to refute Luxemburg's defense of the idea that capitalism tended to break down, demonstrated the effects of the breakdown mechanism that Marx had identified but that had

---

2, 528–45.

114. Grossman, "Marx and Dynamics," 190. The same idea with a similar illustration was expressed in a manuscript response to a hostile review of *Law of Accumulation*. See Grossman, untitled manuscript beginning "Die Entwertung sollen die Zusammenbruchstendenz aufheben . . . ," n.d., Folder 45, "Stellungnahme zur Kritik am Hauptwerk," Henryk Grossman III-155 Collection.

115. Grossman, "Marx and Dynamics," 190.

116. Grossmann, *Law of Accumulation*, 41; Grossman, "Marx and Dynamics," 150–51, 181.

117. Grossman, "Fifty Years of Struggle," 133.

subsequently been neglected.[118] Bauer's model broke down in the thirty-fifth cycle because of this mechanism: the tendency for the rate of profit to fall.[119]

The dual character of economic processes is apparent in this tendency, which results from the long-term rise in the organic composition of capital.[120] For there is an "inverse movement of the mass of use values and values as a consequence of the increase in the labor's productive power. The richer a society, the greater the development of the labor's productive power, the larger the volume of useful things which can be made in a given labor time. At the same time, however, the value of these things becomes smaller."[121]

Capitalism spectacularly expands the number of use values produced while reducing the value of individual commodities, by channeling a progressively higher proportion of investment into new technologies embodied in constant capital as opposed to the purchase of living labor power. The ratio between the cost of constant capital used and the wages bill increases. Driven by competition among capitalists, this rising organic composition of capital expresses the progressive nature of capitalism, which increases the productivity of labor because workers using more sophisticated equipment produce more commodities in a given time. But it is only living labor that creates new, surplus value. The rate of profit, the ratio between the newly created value embodied in surplus value (profits) and capitalists' total outlays, falls. The requirements for the accumulation of constant capital encroach on the surplus value available for the consumption of the capitalists and/or workers. Eventually there is insufficient surplus value to maintain any given rate of accumulation: the model breaks down. The onset of the breakdown is accelerated as the absolute value of individual new items of constant capital grows.[122]

This analysis captures a long-term tendency of the capitalist system. To approach the real-world pattern of growth more closely, Marx continued his investigation by identifying countertendencies, also inherent in capitalism and shaped by the dual nature of capitalist production, that slow or temporarily reverse the tendency for the rate of profit to fall. These included the cheapening of both means of production and the items workers consume, a consequence of the increased productivity of labor; reduced turnover time; increases in the variety of use values, including through foreign trade; the transfer of surplus value from less to more developed territories through unequal exchange and profits from capital exports; and economic crises themselves, which devalue means of production, sold off cheap or left idle by bankrupt businesses. The effects of the countertendencies mean that capitalism's tendency to break down takes the form of recurrent economic crises. While exploitation, the rate of surplus value, rises and (up to a point) the mass of surplus value does increase, neither this nor

---

118. Bauer, "The Accumulation of Capital"; Grossman, "Zur Dynamik des kapitalistischen Wirtschaftsmechanismus," unpublished manuscript, 1924, Folder 37, Henryk Grossman III–155 Collection.
119. Grossman, "Zur Dynamik des kapitalistischen Wirtschaftsmechanismus" and "The Theory of Economic Crises"; Grossmann, "Eine neue Theorie über Imperialismus" and *Das Akkumulations- und Zusammenbruchsgesetz*.
120. Marx, *Capital*, vol. 1, 762; also vol. 3, 245; Grossman, "Marx and Dynamics," 149.
121. Grossman, "Marx and Dynamics," 150.
122. Ibid.; see also *Law of Accumulation*, 74–82.

the other countertendencies is sufficient to fully offset the effect of the rising organic composition of capital on the rate of profit in the long term. This is confirmed by empirical studies. Capitalism's tendency toward breakdown and inherent crises, grounded in the distinctively capitalist dual nature of the production process, are expressions of the contradiction between the forces and relations of production.[123]

Revolutionary Politics and Conclusion

A myth that Grossman had a mechanical theory of capitalism's collapse and the transition to socialism was fabricated by Stalinist and social-democratic reviewers of his *Law of Accumulation*. It was often associated with the implied or explicit accusation that Grossman was a proponent of political passivity. The myth was imported into the English literature by Paul Sweezy. His acolytes have continued to peddle it.[124] No act of esoteric divination was or is necessary to establish the nature of Grossman's commitment to political activity culminating in workers' revolution or that he did not mechanically apply his model of capital accumulation derived from Bauer's schema. His positions were apparent in his political affiliations and clearly expressed not only in unpublished responses to critics but also in his readily accessible publications, including *The Law of Accumulation*.

As a young revolutionary leader, Grossman emphasized the centrality of class struggle to both the formation of working-class consciousness and revolution. Decades later he expressed the relationship between capitalism's tendency to break down and the working class as an active revolutionary subject in Lukácsian/Hegelian terms. Marx "follows Hegel, for whom history has both an objective and a subjective meaning, the history of human activity (*historia rerum gestarum*) and human activity itself (*res gestas*)."[125] Consequently, "the point of breakdown theory is that the revolutionary action of the proletariat only receives its most powerful impetus from the objective convulsion of the established system and, at the same time, only this creates the circumstances necessary to successfully wrestle down the ruling class's resistance."[126] For

---

123. Grossman, *Law of Accumulation*, 83–85, 123, 130–200; Grossman, "Marx and Dynamics," 160. Grossman drew mainly on US statistics. For recent empirical confirmation of his exposition of Marx's theory see, for example, Kliman, *The Failure of Capitalist Production*; Maito, "The Historical Transience of Capital"; Basu and Manolakos, "Is There a Tendency"; Carchedi and Roberts, "The Long Roots of the Present Crisis." For refutations of the criticisms of Grossman's theory of breakdown and crisis, see Grossman, "Fifty Years of Struggle," 131–133, and Kuhn, *Henryk Grossman and the Recovery of Marxism*, 140–45, 151–52.

124. Sweezy, *Theory of Capitalist Development*, 211, 214; Foster and McChesney, "Listen Keynesians, It's the System!" 52–55.

125. Grossman, "Evolutionist Revolt," 228. Grossman's sensitivity to Marx's transformed Hegelian categories and his affinities with the returns to Marx of Korsch and Lukács in philosophy and Lenin in politics was even more evident in an early draft of "Marx and Dynamics." Grossman applied this understanding to economic analysis: "in the labor process, labor does not take the form of a tool, but rather 'labor itself appears as *the dominant activity*'; here the world of objects does not control labor; rather all of the means of production are subordinate to labor." "Marx und klassische Oekonomie oder die Lehre von Wertfetisch," unpublished manuscript, 1937, Folder 68, Henryk Grossman III-155 Collection, 111.

126. Grossman, "Fifty Years of Struggle," 133.

the working class's struggle over everyday demands is thus bound up with its struggle over the final goal. The final goal for which the working class fights is not, therefore, an ideal that is brought into the working class by speculative means, "from outside," whose realization, independent from the struggles of the present, is reserved for the distant future. Rather, as the law of breakdown presented here shows, it is a result that arises from everyday, immediate class struggles, whose realization is accelerated by these struggles.[127]

In *Capital*, Marx commented on the importance of knowledge about the laws of economic development: society "can neither clear by bold leaps, nor remove by legal enactments, the obstacles offered by the successive phases of its normal development. But it can shorten and lessen the birth-pangs."[128] It is clear from Grossman's survey of the history of Marxism that events other than a purely economic crisis may trigger an "objective convulsion." He stressed that, in the context of inter-imperialist rivalry leading to war, "the proletariat has the task of transforming war between peoples into civil war, with a view to the conquest of power and, for this reason, of preparing strategically and organizationally for revolution."[129]

The overthrow of capitalism by the working class is not possible at all times. In several publications, Grossman referred to Lenin's analysis of the circumstances in which revolution becomes a possibility. A revolutionary situation arises when the subordinate classes are suffering increased hardship, no longer want to tolerate the old order and are effectively organized to act, while the ruling classes are objectively unable to rule as before.[130] Luxemburg, also a proponent of capitalism's tendency to break down, had argued in the same spirit that the revolutionary position is not to passively wait for capitalism to collapse.[131] This position was counterposed to both faith in an act of revolutionary will by a minority, voluntaristic putschism, and reliance on subjectless history running its course. In suitable objective circumstances, Grossman was confident, the working class can become a historical subject capable of the revolutionary overthrow of capitalism.

No economic system, no matter how weakened, collapses by itself in automatic fashion. It must be overthrown. . . . "Historical necessity" does not operate automatically but requires the active participation of the working class in the historical process. . . .

The main result of Marx's doctrine is the clarification of the historical role of the proletariat as the carrier of the transformative principle and the creator of the socialist society. . . . In changing the historical *object*, the *subject* changes himself. Thus the education of the working class to its historical mission must be achieved not by theories brought from outside but by the everyday practice of the class struggle.[132]

127. Grossmann, *Das Akkumulations- und Zusammenbruchsgesetz*, 602–3.
128. Marx, *Capital*, vol. 1, 92, quoted in Grossman, "Evolutionist Revolt," 222.
129. Grossman, "Fifty Years of Struggle," 122; see also Grossman, "Eine neue Theorie über Imperialismus," 157.
130. Grossmann, "Eine neue Theorie über Imperialismus," 161–62, citing Lenin, "The Collapse of the Second International." See also Grossman, "Marx and Dynamics," 227.
131. Luxemburg, *Social Reform or Revolution*, 89.
132. Grossman, "Evolutionist Revolt," 227; see also *Das Akkumulations- und Zusammenbruchsgesetz*, 602–3, and "Eine neue Theorie über Imperialismus," 161–62.

Although hardly modest, Grossman's decision to conclude his 1932 survey with a third person summary of his own work on Marxist crisis theory and its relationship with Marxist politics, along with a refutation of arguments made against it, entailed a sober assessment of his contribution to Marxism.[133] Grossman vindicated Marx's sustained attention to the use value and value aspects of economic processes, which underpinned his reaffirmation of Marx's theories of economic crisis and capitalist breakdown and his powerful critique of bourgeois economics' equilibrium theories. His arguments are of immediate relevance. They provide a basis for decontaminating Marxism of a range of alien, bourgeois assumptions, which undermine its coherence, and they support important practical conclusions, particularly about responses to recurrent economic crises and the working class as a potentially self-conscious historical subject.

Structure and Conventions

The order of the studies below follows the dates of their publication. The original texts have been modified to comply with this book's citation and stylistic conventions, and to correct minor errors in Grossman's quotations and mistakes in his references. Where they exist, published English translations are used in quotations and references. Other things being equal, editions available free on websites such as http://archive.org have been preferred for references. References include the years of publications' original editions and/or during which they were written in square brackets, where relevant. Words in square brackets in quotations stem from Grossman, unless otherwise indicated; elsewhere they are the editor's. Emphasis in quotations is the original author's, unless otherwise indicated. The index includes micro-biographies of all people mentioned in the main text and explanations of abbreviations.

---

133. Grossman, "Fifty Years of Struggle," 128–133.

Simonde de Sismondi
and His Economic Theories

(A New Interpretation of His Thought)[1]

Translated from the French by Ian Birchall

This year we have the opportunity to commemorate several great economists, for it is the centenary of the death of [David] Ricardo, the fortieth anniversary of Karl Marx's death, the two hundredth anniversary of the birth of Adam Smith and the hundred and fiftieth of that of Simonde de Sismondi. Today I propose to draw your attention to the last of these. Compared with the numerous studies devoted to the physiocrats and the classical English economists,[2] those dealing with Sismondi are relatively few in number. And although a host of excellent authors in more or less recent times, such as Adolphe Blanqui, [Julius] Kautz, [Hugo] Eisenhart, Charles Périn, [John Kells] Ingram, Ludwig Elster, Luigi Cossa, [Alfred Victor] Espinas, [Heinrich] Herkner, [Albert] Aftalion, [Joseph] Rambaud, Hector Denis and Charles Rist, have attempted to expound Sismondi's ideas, those studies we do possess have not succeeded, in my view, in giving sufficient attention to his theoretical thinking.[3] In fact, while they pay ample homage to this hon-

1. Originally published in Warsaw as *Simonde de Sismondi et ses theories economiques*.
2. [The physiocrats were an eighteenth-century school of French economists who stressed that productive work, which they identified with agriculture, was the source of wealth. Grossman's references to English economists and England were inaccurate, as the British economists to whom he referred included people from Scotland and Wales.]
3. Adolphe Blanqui, *History of Political Economy*; Kautz, *Theorie und geschichte der national-oekonomik*; Eisenhart, *Geschichte der Nationalökonomik*; Périn, *Les doctrines économiques depuis un siècle*; Ingram, *A History of Political Economy*; Elster, "J. Ch. L. Simonde de Sismondi"; Cossa, *Histoire des doctrines économiques*; Espinas, *Histoire des doctrines économiques*; Herkner, *Die Arbeiterfrage*; Aftalion, "L'oeuvre économique de Simonde de

orary professor of the University of Wilno[4] and draw out his importance as the creator of new social policy, he is relegated to secondary status as a theoretician. It is precisely on this last point that I differ from generally accepted opinions. To set them right I will try to characterize in turn Sismondi's method, his theory and his social policy.

1. Sismondi's Method

As far as method was concerned, it previously seemed that Sismondi's viewpoint had been clearly established. It was generally claimed that Sismondi was an opponent of the abstract and deductive method and that his merit consisted solely in the fact that he had spoken out critically against the abstract and deductive method of the classical school and in particular of Ricardo, juxtaposing it to the method of historical and descriptive induction. According to Denis, "Sismondi's basic criticism of the [classical] school is for its abstract and deductive method."[5] Charles Rist in turn makes a very similar judgment. "Sismondi's disagreement was not upon the *theoretical principles* of political economy. So far as these were concerned, he declared himself a disciple of Adam Smith. He merely disagreed with *the method*, the *object* and hence the *practical conclusions* of the classical school." "Ricardo . . . is accused of having introduced the abstract method into the science . . . his spirit shrank from admitting those abstractions which Ricardo and his disciples demanded from him. Political economy, he thought, . . . was to be based on experience, upon history and observation. Human conditions were to be studied in detail." According to Rist, Sismondi's critique is directed against generalization. "It also prepared the way for that conception of political economy upon the discovery of which the German *historical school* so prided itself at a later date."[6]

Admittedly one can find in Sismondi many more passages similar to those noted by Rist. But we can see that the latter has stuck to a literal reading of Sismondi and has not grasped the spirit, that he has not seized the very essence of his method. Having asserted that Sismondi is an opponent of the abstract method, a few lines later he criticizes him for a certain inconsistency, because "Sismondi himself was forced to have recourse to it. It is true that he used it with considerable awkwardness and his failure to construct or to discuss abstract theories perhaps explains his preference for the other method."[7]

If there is an inconsistency, I venture to say that it is not in Sismondi but rather in Rist's standpoint and his rather scholastic logic. According to Rist, Sismondi's methodological merit entails the critique of the abstract method and the application of the

Sismondi"; Rambaud, *Histoire des doctrines économiques*; Denis, *Histoire des systèmes économiques*, vol. 2; Rist, "Sismondi and the Origins."

4. [Vilnius, now the capital of Lithuania; at the time Grossman wrote, under Polish rule.]

5. Denis, *Histoire des systèmes économiques*, 289.

6. Rist, "Sismondi and the Origins," 174–75.

7. Ibid., 176.

historical and descriptive method. But then Rist goes on to say that Sismondi "was forced to have recourse" to the abstract method.

Is it true that in Sismondi we are faced with contradictions and that these are a sign that he "creates . . . confusion" and has a "hesitating mind"—as Rist assures us?[8] To concede this would make our job a lot easier, all the more so since Sismondi is a powerful individual whose enormous influence on the development of economic thought, as well as on several great thinkers such as John Stuart Mill, [Pierre-Joseph] Proudhon, Karl Marx, Émile Laveley and so on, becomes more obvious with every passing day, as Hector Denis has quite rightly noted.[9]

If it were solely a matter of showing the need for an inductive, historical descriptive method, Sismondi's achievement in this respect would be quite dubious. In Germany [Johann Gottlieb] Fichte, it is true, applied an abstract constructive method to his "rational state," that is, the state as it ought to be. But where it was a question of economic relations, "real states existing at present," he demanded an explanation of "how everything that is came to be as it is," and it was for history to respond to this question, "since indeed all historical research of deep penetration neither can nor should be anything else than a genetic answer to the causal question: how has the present state of things arisen and what are the reasons that the world formed itself into what we find before us?"[10] In France it is Charles Ganilh who should take the credit, albeit problematic, for having opposed the abstract method. This economist, four years before the appearance of Sismondi's book, published a program for a statistical and descriptive method. In his work he criticizes Adam Smith and the physiocrats for using an "ambitious method" that, as a result of "their predilection for rational and speculative theories" and "by means of hypotheses, conjectures and analogies," aims to construct "general laws" by a means that "is independent of facts and experience." Political economy is "a practical science." Now "Adam Smith's system of unlimited freedom" is "a speculative theory." "When one looks carefully at Smith's admirable work, one finds there only assertions which do not fit the facts, conjectures with no basis in reality and unfounded hypotheses." To this method Ganilh contrasts the descriptive method and sees the solution in the progress of statistics.[11] It seems that he was inspired by the famous statistical treatise of Patrick Colquhoun (1814), which showed the distribution of wealth among the various classes in the population of England.[12] "Thus it seems to me that from the table of the present wealth of a people . . . one can progress not only to knowledge of the *causes* of this people's wealth but even to the establishment of the principles that create modern wealth and to the *true theory* of political economy."[13] He defines the relationship between statistics and economics as follows: "The former accumulates the materials

8. Ibid., 176, 190.
9. Denis, *Histoire des systèmes* économiques, 273.
10. Fichte, *The Closed Commercial State*, 38.
11. Ganilh, *La théorie de l'économie politique*, vol. 1, 1–2, 19, 37–8.
12. Colquhoun, *A Treatise on the Wealth*.
13. [Ganilh, *La théorie de l'économie politique*, 28–29. Grossman's emphasis.]

and the latter builds the edifice of the science." If the speculative theories that he criticizes "reasoned before having observed the facts . . . asserted instead of calculating," the method advocated by Ganilh leads *in short* to a rigorous theory, "to mathematical certainty." He briefly indicates the path to be followed. "We observe facts that can be subjected to observation and calculation and that, as a result, give economic science the right to lay claim to the same precision as the physical and mathematical sciences."

Thus it was not Sismondi who was the first to juxtapose a scientific ideal based on the statistical-descriptive method to the abstract and deductive method of the classical economists. However, I will not spend time discussing once more the banal question as to whether political economy should use induction or deduction. Half a century before Ricardo, James Steuart, to the great advantage of the science, applied *the two methods jointly* to economic research.[14] To employ induction and deduction simultaneously is in no way peculiar to economics but is practiced in all the sciences and indeed in every nonscientific operation of thought, for it is quite simply the very nature of our mind to move from the particular to the general and from the general to the particular. And that is why I consider that reducing the problem of method in political economy to the question of induction versus deduction is to deny any *specific method of study* in economics. And this is also why I think Wilhelm Hasbach has overstated Steuart's merit, as far as method is concerned, when he claims that "Steuart had no predecessor and until John Stuart Mill no successor who, with such clarity of thought, although it was in a less clear language, expounded *the methodological foundations* of our science."[15] And Hasbach concludes from this that Steuart "is the greatest economist of the eighteenth century."[16]

I have no intention whatsoever of belittling the value of Steuart. I should simply like to show that apart from the question of the involvement of induction and deduction in the field of knowledge and from ways of gaining knowledge as well as our mind's instruments of investigation—in short, all that we understand under the name of *Denkmethode* [method of thought]—the problem of method also has another aspect, not in relation to the properties of our minds but rather depending on the type of phenomena being studied; *Forschungsmethode* [method of research] While the former problem concerning knowledge itself is *common* to all sciences and is not specific to economics as such, the latter appears differently in each science, for in each science—and hence in political economy—it is necessary to create *specific methods appropriate to the character of the phenomena being studied*. "Every discipline," says Luigi Cossa, "has its own method, appropriate to its object, role and purpose, which distinguishes it from the others."[17] If, having set aside the question of induction and deduction, we ask what constitutes this specific research method of the classical English school, applied in particular to the character of economic phenomena, we will find it very difficult to give an answer.

14. Steuart, *Inquiry into the Principles*.
15. Hasbach, *Untersuchungen über Adam Smith*, 380. [Grossman's emphasis.]
16. Ibid., 381.
17. Cossa, *Histoire des doctrines économiques*, 77.

[François] Quesnay's *Formula for an Economic Table* (1758) was founded on the *constructive basis*, which was such a specifically economic method, effectively applied, although it was not justified theoretically. In respect of method, in relation to the problems of the totality of production and of social reproduction, the classical English school represents a retreat, a lowering of the level achieved by the brilliant creator of physiocracy.[18] This detrimental influence of the English school becomes visible in Jean-Baptiste Say, who in his *Treatise* of 1803 criticizes the physiocrats for founding "a principle upon some gratuitous assumption. . . . Political economy has only become a science since it has been confined to the results of inductive investigation."[19] This was a return to naïve empiricism and Sismondi takes up anew the methodological problem of the physiocrats, which entails the fact that the latter, in the study of economic phenomena, reject mere empiricism and use the *constructive method*. Sismondi develops this method in an original fashion and does so with all the expertise required of a theoretician. Sismondi's historical achievement in methodology is to have imagined and constructed this method and shown the necessity of applying it, not of having supposedly applied the descriptive-historical method of induction. For, as we will soon see, not only is Sismondi not hostile to abstract analysis but he uses it on a greater scale than the classical thinkers whom he criticizes, to such an extent that [Adolphe] Blanqui complains of his use of this abstraction, to which, it is claimed, Sismondi was opposed: "The principal defect in the method of M. de Sismondi lies in generalizing too much, like Ricardo himself, his most illustrious opponent."[20] The very fact that Sismondi's method has been evaluated in such diverse fashions should arouse our attention and encourage us to clarify the matter. So let us look at it more closely.

How does Sismondi proceed to analyze the phenomenon that interests him most and that, in his opinion, is "the fundamental question of political economy"—namely, the problem of the "balance between consumption and production"? Empirically there was the phenomenon of crises in the form of a glut on the market with goods that did not find buyers at a price that would make a profit possible. Ricardo saw the phenomenon itself as transitory and saw *the cause* as lying in an erroneous commercial or fiscal policy. In a discussion with Sismondi he "attributed this result . . . to constraints imposed on the circulation of goods, and to tariffs."[21]

At this time the effects of ruinous English competition were making themselves felt very powerfully in France. But instead of having recourse to the theoretical indication of the errors of free competition, first of all solutions were proposed in the form of *tariff protection*, as was done for example by [Jean-Antoine] Chaptal.[22]

What position does Sismondi take on this occasion? Does he follow the path traced out by Ricardo? Does he analyze "only what is"—empirical facts: the influence of taxes,

---

18. Quesnay, *Quesnay's Tableau Économique*.
19. Say, *A Treatise on Political Economy*, 36.
20. Blanqui, *History of Political Economy*, 473.
21. Sismondi, "On the Balance," 618–19. [Grossman's emphasis.]
22. Jean-Antoine Chaptal, *De l'industrie française*, vol. 2, 417 and following.

of duties and of import bans on the quantity of production and exports? Does he undertake descriptive and comparative studies of the quantity of production and consumption in the countries affected by the crisis, before and after the outbreak of the crisis? Does he perhaps study the decline in demand, imports and exports as a result of changes in fashion, warfare, or foreign competition? Does he try to examine the influence of the banks and of credit, or of paper money; the influence of the actual distribution of wealth, the total amount of wages, profits and so on? Not at all; instead of all that Sismondi *rejects the world of empirical phenomena* in the specific conditions of time and place and confines himself to a methodological fiction, taking his proof and his analysis into the world of *a constructed abstract example*. In fact he was perfectly well aware that the very object of his analysis was in no way empirical. We can study the level of wages, profits, prices, the quantity of production, or the number of workers employed empirically. But *the problem of the economic equilibrium* of production and consumption in a capitalist society cannot be studied under the microscope of descriptive analysis and, even if it were done by establishing as conscientiously as possible the effective state of overproduction, we would make no contribution whatsoever to demonstrating the extent to which this imbalance results *necessarily* from the very essence of the capitalist system. The object in contention in the analysis is therefore itself entirely abstract. "The question I had raised was so obscure, so *abstract* that I laid myself open to the most absurd interpretations. . . . However, I have never believed that I must forego the defense of what to me appeared to be the truth, because *that truth was abstract*, difficult to grasp."[23]

While he was in Geneva in 1823 Ricardo continued orally the polemic with Sismondi that the latter had begun in 1820 against [John Ramsay] McCulloch. Once again, empirical facts were put on one side. "But a spoken discourse cannot do justice to a question which calls for a difficult reconciliation of practical *arguments* with, *in some way, metaphysical considerations*."[24] We know what that means. In his 1824 treatise against Ricardo, where he reports the oral discussions he had with the latter, Sismondi, basing himself on certain arbitrary *a priori* principles (metaphysical considerations), constructs an abstract arithmetical example (calculations), and the polemic concerning the central problem of political economy was developed on this fictitious level.

While Ricardo, as a supporter of total freedom of exchange between nations, attributes crisis to "constraints imposed on the circulation of goods" and the empiricists, like Chaptal, seek salvation in the defense of the internal market through tariff protection, Sismondi *excludes in advance from his argument the factor of the commercial policy of governments*. The defense of the internal market and free export to foreign markets can undoubtedly get rid of excessive production but the problem is only provisionally resolved by this means and only for one particular country at the expense of another country. "In that system nations are rivals to each other; industrial prosperity in one causes the ruin of industry in the others." The export solution is likewise not viable for

---

23. Sismondi, "Clarification Relative to the Equilibrium," 596. [Grossman's emphasis.]
24. Sismondi, "On the Balance," 618. [Grossman's emphasis.]

all nations. "If all adopt this system at the same time, if all consign each year a greater amount of exports to foreign markets . . . their competition, that will embrace the world market, will be injurious to everyone."[25] "The immediate result of this universal battle can only be the impossibility of continuing it"—and all of them in turn would have to get rid of their excess.[26] Overproduction would then be revealed in its full extent. "What can be done if one will not be able to sell abroad anymore?" And then "the illusions of foreign trade" will disappear.[27] If therefore we take into consideration not a single state but "the world market," "for it there is no export." Starting from these thoughts, Sismondi continues the methodological construction of Quesnay's *Table*[28] and admits that the economic process of the world has already reached the stage where external markets no longer exist and that is why he takes as the starting point of his theoretical analysis *an isolated nation*, without external markets, "by either looking at the entire world market, or by postulating that every nation exists in isolation from every other." Elsewhere he expresses this thought even more clearly: "National *expenditure* must absorb . . . *total national production*. In order to follow this reasoning with greater certainty, and to simplify the problems, we have, till now, completely *abstracted from foreign trade*, and we assume an isolated nation; humanity is that isolated nation."[29]

It is only in such an isolated economic mechanism, without external markets, that Sismondi studies how the increase of production operates and in particular examines whether, as Ricardo and Say claim, an isolated nation, by increasing its production, *thereby* creates new consumers. If in fact there must be a balance, "it must be proven that it creates them itself when it increases its production." "To study this social mechanism," in order to analyze this equilibrium, Sismondi constructs the hypothetical arithmetical example that has already been mentioned, supposing, on the one hand, "a cultivator who, on a given area of land," employs a given number of agricultural workers and, on the other, an industrial capitalist employing a specific number of workers. "This is a hypothesis and an analysis presenting the least difficulty, and will force us to deal with the least detail."[30]

It is only in a system thus isolated and simplified that Sismondi, after having established a certain specific productivity of labor and a specific wage, studies the relations of supply and demand. Subsequently multiplying one of the elements, namely, the productivity of labor, and modifying the sum of wages by a fixed percentage, he studies afresh the influence of these changes on the relation of production to consumption.

Can there be anything more abstract than this method? How then has it been possible to claim that Sismondi is a representative innovator of the descriptive and inductive

---

25. Ibid., 619.

26. Sismondi, *New Principles of Political Economy*, 333.

27. Ibid.

28. Quesnay, *Quesnay's Tableau Économique*.

29. Sismondi, *Études*, vol. 2, 337; "On the Balance," 620; *New Principles of Political Economy*, 102. [Grossman's emphasis.]

30. Sismondi, "On the Balance," 620–21. [Grossman's emphasis.]

method? Here there is a misunderstanding resulting from the fact that people have not grasped the very basis of Sismondi's critique of the classical school. In his essay against McCulloch, Sismondi says, it is true, of the English school that it "loses itself in abstractions" and that it becomes, "to some degree, an occult science." He requires of science "that it finally deals with reality." We must "be watchful against all generalisations of our ideas that make us lose facts from sight."[31] Seven years later in the second edition of his work he denounces Adam Smith's disciples who "have thrown themselves even more into abstractions." "In their hands the science has become so speculative that it seems to separate itself from all practice. . . . Our mind is loath to accept the abstractions they require of us." However, Sismondi rejects this abstraction, not because it is abstract but because it is an abstraction that does not fit reality, because it *does not take account of the essential elements* that characterize capitalist society. The simplification of reality must have its limits. "The abstraction we are asked to make . . . is by far too strong: . . . this is not *simplification*, this is *misleading* us by hiding from our view all the successive operations by which we can distinguish truth from error." Sismondi criticizes Ricardo for having taken the state of equilibrium between independent producers as the basis of his proofs and of having, consequently, neglected such an important point as wage labor. "We will look at society in its actual organization, *with workers without property*, whose wages are fixed by competition, and whose master may dismiss them at the moment when he has no more need for their labor; for *it is precisely this social arrangement to which our objections apply*."[32]

Thus Sismondi is not opposed to abstraction in general but only to abstraction that sets aside essential elements of reality. Undoubtedly Sismondi too used the inductive, historical-descriptive method. But he applied it in order to establish *facts* that were to be the starting point of his argument. He observed, for example, with the help of an empirical analysis, the struggle of large workshops against small ones, the concentration of large assets under the same management and the increase of material wealth in contemporary society, parallel to the deep poverty and pauperism of the working classes.[33] But these "rebellious facts" merely enable him to *formulate the problem*.[34] He seeks the *explanation* of the phenomenon precisely by means of the abstract construction of a fictitious model with clearly established foundations, which enables him to draw from it conclusions that are rigorous even if, for the time being, hypothetical.

But Sismondi's methodological foundations are not limited to this. If science has the aim of reproducing realities in the mind and if, for this very reason, he indicts Say so vigorously for having said nothing about wage labor, he nonetheless recognizes, on the other hand, that not every empirical phenomenon belongs to the domain of the reality that he wants to explain scientifically. The task that he has taken on entails discovering the laws that govern the capitalist mechanism, that is, a mechanism based on free wage

31. Sismondi, "Analysis of a Refutation," 599.
32. Sismondi, *New Principles of Political Economy*, 55; "On the Balance," 621. [Grossman's emphasis.]
33. Sismondi, *Études*, introduction to vol. 1, 1–47.
34. Ibid., 47.

labor and the monopoly ownership by the capitalists of the necessary instruments of labor. Now, the empirical world showed that alongside these elements of the system there were independent artisans and land-owning peasants. Should these survivals of former economic formations, as elements of "*empirical reality*," be for Sismondi the object of the analysis of the capitalist system?

As a historian, Sismondi is well aware of the historical variety of successive forms of the organization of labor, as well as their *essential functional specificities*. As crises and the ills that they entail came into existence to the extent that wage labor—that is, economic organization based on the payment of wages—was constituted, he draws the far-reaching methodological conclusion that forms of independent labor (artisans, peasants) are absolutely irrelevant to him as a subject of his studies of the essence of capitalism.[35] But precisely these forms constituted the major part of the empirical reality of his time, while the system of wage labor he proposed to study was still only a new phenomenon, in its initial phase, although its pernicious influence had already made itself felt and had led to disastrous disturbances. The process of the expropriation of the artisan and the peasant, recently begun, was evolving rapidly. "We incline to separate completely any type of property from all types of labor. . . . This social organization is so new that it is not even halfway instituted."[36]

Now, if there exists "the universal tendency of wealth to separate the action of capitals from that of hands," it can be imagined that in its subsequent development this tendency will reach its final objective, that is, a complete separation of property from labor[37]; in other words it will lead to a social system composed exclusively of capitalists and workers. This will be a "purely" capitalist system, that is, the system that Sismondi wants to study. He therefore acknowledges that this process is in fact completed and *mentally he cleanses* the capitalist system of all infiltrations, of all survivals of earlier systems. In fact it is only in a system stripped of elements foreign to it that the laws and properties that characterize it can appear—for example, free competition, the antinomy of the interests of the entrepreneur and the worker as well as their struggle over the division of the social product and so on. "To examine this battle . . . it will be easier to abstract from all those workers who are at the same time capitalists, and [from] all capitalists who are at the same time workers."[38] Sismondi thus arrives at the methodological premise of an economic system based exclusively on wage labor, considered as a universally established system composed of capitalists and workers, excluding all third parties such as officials, soldiers, merchants and people practicing liberal professions, etc.

The result of our analysis is clear. In the central problem, which for Sismondi is the most important one—that of the equilibrium of the economic mechanism, meaning

---

35. It is true that Sismondi devotes long passages to the description of various forms of independent labor, but he does so where, as a historian, he is comparing the former economic organization to capitalist organization.

36. Sismondi, "On the Balance," 628.

37. Sismondi, *Études*, vol. 1, 241.

38. Sismondi, *New Principles of Political Economy*, 92. [Editor's interpolation.]

the equilibrium of production and consumption—he takes as the object of his theoretical analysis and as the basis of his proof *not empirical reality but a fictitious model of capitalist society based on arbitrarily assumed foundations.*[39]

In his arithmetical schema of annual production, Sismondi lists three branches of this production:

1. production of foodstuffs, represented by sacks of corn;
2. production of industrial articles absolutely essential for life; and
3. production of industrial luxury items.

He subsequently assumes *in all* branches of production a specific degree of productivity of labor, equal to the value of twelve sacks of corn a year per worker, and at the same time a specific standard of living for the workers, in other words the wage received, equal to ten sacks of corn, of which three sacks are consumed in kind by the workers and the seven others are consumed in the form of absolutely essential industrial articles. He then establishes that the whole surplus production of each worker beyond his wage—in other words, in this case, the value of two sacks of corn—accrues to the agricultural and industrial employers, and each of them shares his *indispensable* consumption in the same ratio: three sacks of corn in kind and seven in the form of indispensable industrial articles. It is only the remaining excess of their profit that they consume in the form of *luxury* industrial articles.

It is only after having simplified the problem by rigorously defining the data on which he is basing himself that Sismondi embarks on his subject properly speaking, namely, to study the influence of each element in particular: the number of workers and their productivity, the needs of society remaining immutable. Given the *productivity* of ten agricultural workers, the problem to be resolved will entail the quantitative determination of the number of workers in both branches of industry. If on the other hand, given the *number* of workers, the productivity of labor increases and overproduction appears, then the problem is reduced to the question either of limiting the number of workers or of reducing the increase in the productivity of labor.

As we can see, Sismondi's schema is only a refined form of Quesnay's *Table*; the refinement entails the fact that instead of Quesnay's three classes, corresponding to the situation in the middle of the eighteenth century—productive class, class of owners,

---

39. These are the same methodological foundations Karl Marx would adopt forty years later in his *Capital*, where, starting like Sismondi from the principle "of the universal and exclusive domination of capitalist production" (Marx, *Capital*, vol. 2, 422) he says, clearly making the connection with Sismondi's analysis of progressive reproduction: "Here we take no account of the export trade. . . . In order to examine the object of our investigation *in its integrity* free from all disturbing subsidiary circumstances, we must treat the whole world of trade as one nation, and assume that capitalist production is established everywhere and has taken possession of every branch of industry" (*Capital*, vol. 1, 727). Likewise: "In *theory*, we assume that the laws of the capitalist mode of production develop in their *pure form*. In *reality*, this is only an approximation; but the approximation is all the more exact, the more the capitalist mode of production is developed and *the less it is adulterated by survivals of earlier economic conditions* with which it is amalgamated." *Capital*, vol. 3, 275. [All emphasis, both in the main text and this note, is Grossman's.]

and sterile class—Sismondi introduces a division more appropriate to the capitalist system: capitalists and wage workers. *All* the branches of production are productive since they give the capitalists an income, here still envisaged in a general form and not in particular categories such as rent, profit, interest on capital, commercial profits, and so forth. This way of seeing things leads to the division between necessary consumption by workers and luxury consumption in which only capitalists participate. These are refinements that will later be adopted in full by Karl Marx in his reproduction schema at the end of the second volume of *Capital*.[40]

Are fictitious constructions of this sort, moving fundamentally away from Say's postulate, "study what is," admissible from the methodological point of view? We must respond that Sismondi's premises are not arbitrary fantasies of the mind, formed without any relation to concrete existence; they are a *construction* but a *necessary* construction, resulting from the character of the materials envisaged, from the fact of the mixture and simultaneous existence in empirical reality of phenomena that are aspects of organizations having completely different historical characters. The accepted bases therefore mark a *selection* of empirical materials, a limitation of the analysis to a specific group of phenomena, to the exclusion of all other alien elements; "they represent *positive facts, merely in the absence of disruptive causes.*" They are therefore in conformity with the conditions of methodological analysis, defined by [John Elliott] Cairnes for the circumstance in which one uses "*hypothetical cases framed* with a view to the purpose of economic inquiry. For, although precluded from actually producing the conditions suited to his purpose, there is nothing to prevent the economist from bringing such conditions before his mental vision, and from reasoning as if these only were present, while some agency comes into operation . . . the economic character of which he desires to examine."[41]

Sismondi's methodological construction, solidly ordered, is, therefore—to use Cairnes's expression—"a substitute for experiment,"[42] also known as a "hypothetical experiment" or a "thought experiment." Contrary to Hasbach's opinion, it accounts for Sismondi's incontestable superiority over the methodological procedures represented by James Steuart; by going far beyond the banal difference involved in the use of induction or deduction, Sismondi creates a method appropriate to the character and nature of economic phenomena, the objects of the analysis. This method is the expression of the stage of development reached by capitalism in Sismondi's day, a level it was far from having reached at the time of Quesnay and Steuart.

It is difficult to agree with Herbert Foxwell, professor at Cambridge University, who in his "History of Socialist Ideas in England" (1903) says that the time after Ricardo

---

40. Thus when Rosa Luxemburg states that in the history of political economy there are only *two* attempts at the *exact* exposition of the reproduction of the entire social capital—at the very beginning of this history with Quesnay, founder of the physiocratic school, and at the end in Marx—she is, as we have seen, mistaken. Between Quesnay and Marx, Sismondi's schema constitutes historically and logically a necessary intermediary link. (See Luxemburg, *The Accumulation of Capital*, 31).

41. John Elliott Cairnes, *The Character and Logical Method of Political Economy*, 62, 90. [Grossman's emphasis.]

42. Ibid., 93.

in England was "a period of indescribable confusion," of "sterile logomancy and academic hair-splitting," and that he saw the cause of this in the fact that "Ricardo had adopted what was intended to be a rigorously abstract and deductive manner, but without any of those formal aids to precision and clearness which scientific, and especially *mathematical, method* provides."[43] [Nicolas-François] Canard, who in his *Principles of Political Economy*[44] was the first to apply this method to economic problems, has shown that one could fill chapters with mathematical formulae without taking the science of economics a step further forward. That is why Sismondi, without mathematical formulae, is in my opinion more of a mathematician than those who apply such formulae in political economy. The value of the geometrical method of argument, as well as the accuracy and the effectiveness of its results, depend not on the construction of a formula but rather on the construction of a specific research method, based on clearly determined foundations that are appropriate to the character of the phenomena studied. Ricardo, despite all the subtlety of his *method of thought*, lacked this *method of research* into the problem of the totality of social reproduction. Hence it is Sismondi who has the merit of having continued on the methodological path indicated by Quesnay's *Table*, which later led to Karl Marx's brilliant methodological construction.[45]

2. Sismondi as a Theoretician

A. The Problem

The misunderstanding we have pointed out with regard to Sismondi's methodological approach is repeated in even more pronounced form when this economist is considered as a theoretician. Previously, the history of economic doctrines has told us that Sismondi's chief merit was being the creator of a new social policy and of a program of reforms where he "appeals for . . . the granting of the right of combination. Then follows a limitation of child labor, the abolition of Sunday toil, and a shortening of the hours of labor. He also demanded the establishment of what he called a 'professional guarantee,' whereby the employer . . . would be obliged to maintain the workman at his

---

43. [Foxwell, introduction to *The Right to the Whole Produce of Labour*, by Anton Menger, lxxii–lxxiii. Grossman's emphasis.]

44. Canard, *Principes d'économie politique*.

45. It was only in the *Études* published thirteen years after the essay against Ricardo that Sismondi, in his last years, revealed a certain apprehension against generalization and insisted on the study of details. [See vol. 1, iv]. At this time Sismondi, reproducing his memoir against Ricardo, gives us the arithmetical schema of social reproduction as a footnote. "Completely hypothetical calculations seem to me to have too uncertain a basis to deserve a place in the text." Ibid., 81. Here, as we can see, there is a restriction of the point of view adopted in 1824 and maintained in 1827 where, in the second edition of *New Principles of Political Economy*, these "calculations" still figure in the text.

own expense during a period of illness or of lock-out or old age."[46]

On the other hand, Sismondi the theoretician has been treated lightly. Rist assures us that "what really interested Sismondi was *not so much* what is called *political economy*, but what has since become known as *économie sociale* in France and *Sozialpolitik* [social policy] in Germany. His originality, so far as the history of doctrines is concerned, consisted in his having originated this study." "Sismondi thus becomes the first of the interventionists."[47] His role is quite different as far as theory is concerned: "Sismondi's disagreement *was not upon the theoretical principles* of political economy. So far as these were concerned he declared himself a disciple of Adam Smith."[48] "The principal interest of Sismondi's book *does not lie in his attempt to give a scientific explanation* of the facts. . . . His merit rather lies in having placed in strong relief certain *facts* that were consistently neglected by the dominant school of economists. . . . He deliberately shows us the reverse of the medal, of which others . . . wished only to see the brighter side."[49]

He was "the first to give *sentiment* a prominent place in his theory" and thought that "political economy . . . was best treated as a '*moral science*'" that must tend toward a just distribution of wealth. According to Rist, it is precisely *in this ethical conception that Sismondi distances himself from the English school*: "That is why he gave such prominence to a theory of *distribution* alongside of the theory of *production*, which had received the exclusive attention of the classical writers."[50]

Rist, as we can see, particularly insists on the importance of Sismondi as the creator of the ethical and socially reforming current and does not think much of him as a theoretician: "But to imagine anything more confused than the reasonings by which he attempts to demonstrate the possibility of a general crisis of over-production is difficult."[51] Elsewhere Rist says that "Sismondi . . . fell into the error of . . . Ricardo" (that is probably why he wrote the essay *against* Ricardo) and adds: "This shows what a hesitating mind we are dealing with." And having attributed such a modest place to Sismondi as a theoretician, Rist diminishes it even further by claiming that Sismondi's critique, far from being determined by theoretical principles, is only the result of "the violent reaction of humanitarianism against the stern implacability of economic orthodoxy. We can almost hear the eloquence of Ruskin and Carlyle, and the pleading of the Christian Socialists."[52]

I will not cite the opinions of other writers here. Almost all make a similar judgment and, whether it be Hector Denis or Eisenhart, [Werner] Sombart or [Gustav] Schmoller, they outdo each other in repeating that Sismondi inaugurated the "ethical current" in economics. "Sismondi's general approach," says Rosa Luxemburg, "is pre-

---

46. Rist, "Sismondi and the Origins," 195.
47. Ibid., 192. [Grossman's emphasis.]
48. Ibid., 174. [Grossman's emphasis.]
49. Ibid., 192. [Grossman's emphasis.]
50. Ibid., 173, 175, 177. [Grossman's emphasis.]
51. Ibid., 176.
52. Ibid., 189, 190, 196.

dominantly *ethical*, it is the approach of the social reformer." "He aspires . . . towards a thorough-going *reform of distribution* in favour of the proletariat."[53] And that means Sismondi's merit consists not in a theoretical explanation of the existing economic system but in a "normative" indication of what ought to be. He "never tire[s] of preaching," says Sombart, "not so much the Christian as the social spirit."[54] In Herkner's eyes, Sismondi is a classic of social reform.[55] On the theoretical level, Denis assures us, Sismondi "accepts the principles of Adam Smith," and he shows originality only in that "he came to draw quite different *conclusions*." "The most important feature of the revolution which he brings about in economic science" consists, according to Denis, in the fact that economics "appears to Sismondi as a science which is not merely theoretical but practical, that is, it proposes not only to illuminate the laws of what has been and of what is but of what ought to be." Sismondi prepared or pursued "the ethical moment of science, the subordination of political economy to morality."[56] Böhm-Bawerk agrees: according to him, Sismondi forms the link between the classical theory of value and the theoretical consequences the socialists were to draw from it later.[57] Even [Franz] Mehring saw in Sismondi nothing other than the "last representative of classical economics."[58]

Does this role attributed to Sismondi correspond to reality? This presentation is precisely intended to answer that question.

If Sismondi had only been an interventionist or a representative of the ethical current in political economy, he would have been in no way original. In England, some years before Sismondi, Robert Owen had published *A New View of Society, or Essay on the Principle of the Formation of the Human Character* in 1813.[59] It called for partial reforms in order to eliminate unemployment, on the basis of rigorous statistics about the labor market and of agencies that aimed to procure work and protect such work. At the same time, from 1815 onward, Owen put forward plans that included from the outset the principles of contemporary industrial legislation. Thanks to his persevering activity as well as the support of Robert Peel, the House of Commons in 1816 established the *first parliamentary enquiry* into the situation of children working in industry. That enquiry in 1819 led to a law protecting children working in cotton mills. Likewise, before Sismondi and under the influence of Fichte, Georg Sartorius in Germany published a critique of Adam Smith, of free competition and of the inequality in the distribution of wealth that it produced, while Julius Soden (1905) stated that economics was not the empirical science of what is but an ethical science laying down what ought to be.[60]

Contrary to current opinion, we do not see the historical merit of Sismondi in the

---

53. Luxemburg, *The Accumulation of Capital*, 220. [Grossman's emphasis.]
54. Sombart, *Socialism and the Social Movement*, 20–21. [Editor's interpolation.]
55. Herkner, *Die Arbeiterfrage*, 48 and following.
56. Denis, *Histoire des systèmes économiques*, 276, 283, 286. [Grossman's emphasis.]
57. Böhm-Bawerk, *Capital and Interest*, vol. 1, 244.
58. Mehring, *Geschichte der deutschen Sozialdemokratie*, vol. 1, 21.
59. [Owen, *A New View of Society*. Grossman's original text has the wrong year, 1816. Grossman's emphasis.]
60. Sartorius, *Abhandlungen die Elemente des Nationalreichtums betreffend*; Soden, *Die National-Oekonomie*, sections 20 and 138.

field of social reform but in the first instance in that of *theory*, and it is precisely to this too often neglected point of view that we should like to draw the reader's attention.

It must first of all be recalled that Sismondi himself claims a quite different role from the one historians have previously attributed to him: he considers himself above all a theoretician striving to *explain* facts that, in his view, the classical economists had not sufficiently elucidated, to explain them with the help of a new theory that he put in the place of the old one. "*I disturbed a science* which . . . appeared as one of the most noble creations of the human mind," in place of which "I had discovered new principles." Doubtless he does declare himself the disciple of Adam Smith. But he confines this agreement to the fact that "we declare, with Adam Smith, that labor is the sole source of wealth." However, Sismondi complements this principle with "the discovery of truths which he himself [Smith] had not known."[61] Sismondi insists on "the importance . . . of the modifications" he has made to Adam Smith's system. "When considered from *this new viewpoint* all that had heretofore remained obscure in this science, became clear." Sismondi differentiates himself from the classical school, it is true, in his conclusions and his practical proposals. But this difference in conclusions derives from the difference in the theoretical conception. That is why Sismondi rejects classical theory, which he believes to be false. "When the fate of millions of men *rests on a theory no experience has yet validated*, it is proper to regard it with some distrust." That is why, being dissatisfied with the theory of the classical economists, he takes "*a path quite different from theirs*." So here there is not only a difference in practical conclusions but in *the whole of the theory*. Classical theory, in the emerging world economy, sees harmony everywhere, while reality reveals discord. To combat the criticisms made of them, the defenders of classical theory deny the facts by asserting that it is contradictory to claim "that the increase in *wealth* can be a cause of *poverty*." Sismondi responds, "Since the *fact* is certain, it could not be contradictory, or rather if it presents a contradiction, it is in the *terms* used, in the definitions adopted."[62] And that is why he takes on the task of discovering the contradictions in the false theory. But it would be a mistake to confine ourselves to this critique of contradictory definitions. For beneath these contradictory definitions lies the contradiction of real phenomena. "Here we have set out only to . . . indicate that what seemed to be a contradiction in *terms*, growing poverty alongside abundance, could have *reality*." So it is necessary to "seek the fundamental principles of the science." In reality Sismondi succeeded in explaining, as he states, the facts in whose presence the classical economists found themselves mystified. "I have explained it *with a theory I believe to be new*."[63]

Moreover the very title of Sismondi's work, *New Principles of Political Economy*, shows that he had the ambition of creating a new theory. In fact he says so expressly. "This somewhat vague title might lead to the supposition that this book is merely a new man-

---

61. Sismondi, *New Principles of Political Economy*, 7, 53. [Grossman's emphasis; translator's interpretation.] See also p. 52.
62. Ibid., 2. See also "On the Balance," 630; *Études*, vol. 2, 210; *Études*, vol. 1, 114–15. [Grossman's emphasis.]
63. Sismondi, *Études*, vol. 2, 233; "Analysis of a Refutation," 600.

ual of the basic propositions of the science. I carry my pretensions much farther; *I believe that I have placed political economy on a new foundation*." This preponderance of theoretical considerations and purposes over practical information about economic policy is such that the writer deliberately omits any enumeration of practical means, in order not to divert attention away from the theoretical analysis of the central problem of economics. Foreseeing that he will be criticized because "it would have been better to show what remained to do," he says, "If I presented here what I consider to be a remedy for the actual ills of society, criticism would abandon the *examination* . . . of such ills, in order to judge my *remedy*, and to probably condemn it, and the question of the balance of consumption with production would never be decided."[64] That is why Sismondi always gives precedence to *knowledge*, to *theory* over practice. "Let us then conclude the *analysis* of the system we have taken up, before dreaming of what will have to replace it." "It is one of the greatest efforts to which we can force our mind to *visualize* the actual structure of society," for before indicating the remedy it is necessary to make the theoretical diagnosis.[65] If Sismondi begins by abandoning the old theory that should be "regarded with some *distrust*," because no experience has yet justified it, if for this reason he seeks a theory that seems to him to better explain the facts, he adopts a quite different tone a few years later, in the second edition of *New Principles*. Here he rejoices that the evolution of events has confirmed his theory and says forcefully, "Seven years have passed, and it seems to me that *the facts* have victoriously fought on my side." The supporters of the classical school "are forced to seek elsewhere new explanations for events which diverge so much from laws they have believed settled," and, Sismondi adds, not without pride, "Explanations . . . which I had given in advance have totally agreed with the results."[66]

So we can see that, contrary to what has been claimed previously, Sismondi disputes with his adversaries primarily *over a theoretical conception* of the economic system of his time and not over the implementation of practical policies!

ଔ

What does this "new theory" advocated by Sismondi entail? It is obvious that if we consider the social reformer and not the theoretician in Sismondi, we will not be able to elucidate this question adequately. The central point of Sismondi's ideas has been perceived as his views on the unequal distribution of wealth, on the insufficient participation of the working class in the social product of labor, in other words, as the fact of underconsumption, which Sismondi identifies as the source of social disruptions and poverty.

In fact no more clumsy misunderstanding could be imagined! If, in fact, the "new

---

64. Sismondi, *New Principles of Political Economy*, 12; "On the Balance," 634–35; *Études*, vol. 1, 105. [Grossman's emphasis.]

65. Sismondi, *New Principles of Political Economy*, 634.

66. Ibid., 7–8. [Grossman's emphasis.]

theory" of Sismondi were to consist in opposing the unequal distribution of wealth, it certainly would not have been new. Without mentioning older writers, a host of thinkers on the terrain of modern capitalism in England and in France had, from the middle of the eighteenth century, raised more energetically than Sismondi the redistribution of wealth to counter inequality and, above all, had put forward conclusions of much greater scope than his.[67] In reality Sismondi's "new theory" consists in something quite different!

The critical passages often found in Sismondi against the "chrematistic or abstract school" and against abstraction in general have been attributed to his methodological views.[68] However, since we have shown in the first part of our analysis not only that Sismondi did not oppose the abstract method but that he applied it with rare shrewdness, it is hard to explain against what, in this case, his criticism of abstraction was directed. Hence we are led to conclude *that the abstraction attacked by Sismondi must entail something quite other than a problem of method.* Certainly. We will try to show that Sismondi's critique strikes at the very heart of the contemporary economic organization of capitalist society. His criticism is not a matter of the *method* of research but of the *substance* and constitutive principles of the economic mechanism of his time, as well as of the economic *science* reflecting this mechanism.

Sismondi claims that the theory of the classical economists is incapable of explaining the mechanism around us. Every economic system has the aim of creating organizations, in order to meet the material needs of humanity. The periodically repeated crises of overproduction that provoke convulsions in this mechanism (bankruptcies of employers, enforced unemployment, and poverty of the working masses) are proof of some essential structural fault in the foundations of this economic system. Classical theory did not perceive this defect. Adam Smith, like Ricardo, acknowledged that the size of the productive apparatus had a spontaneous tendency to adapt to the size of the population and its needs. If the productive apparatus is too small, then—thanks to a rise in prices and profits—capitals and labor will move precisely to the branch where they are most needed. By means of the mechanism of prices and profits, given free competition—that is to say, the unfettered freedom of action of individuals seeking their own profit—the equilibrium of the productive apparatus with the extent of needs is therefore reestablished. Free competition is thus the regulator of the economic mechanism, a regulator that maintains it in a harmonious equilibrium. It is true that in Ricardo's time it was difficult not to see facts in contradiction with this theory; but for Ricardo these were only passing disruptions, "temporary reverses and contingencies" determined by war, by the whims of fashion, by commercial restrictions, by fiscal policy, and so on. Moreover "this . . . is an evil to which a rich nation must submit."[69] But

---

67. See Jaurès, *Histoire socialiste de la révolution*, vol. 7, 13 and following.
68. [Aristotle distinguished economics, gaining what is necessary for life, from chrematistics (gaining money). *Aristotle's Politics*, book 1, ch. 8 and 9, pp. 38–45.]
69. Ricardo, *Principles of Political Economy*, 175, 177. [English in Grossman's original text.]

they cannot permanently disrupt the equilibrium of the economic mechanism, since equilibrium is the normal condition—the "permanent state of things."[70]

It is precisely against this theory of harmony that Sismondi directs his criticism. He draws out the errors in the reasoning of the classical economists and shows *that the dynamic of the real capitalist mechanism is completely different* from the movement defined by classical theory. He therefore takes on the task of discovering the reasons why the actual course of phenomena diverges from the fictitious, harmonious course depicted in the theory of the classical economists.

Proceeding to the analysis of the capitalist system and the economic disruptions that are peculiar to it, Sismondi finds himself confronted by the fact that these disruptions appear and increase in time with the development of this new system, while they were unknown in earlier times. And he is led to historical comparisons. This analysis leads him to *distinguish two essentially different types* of economic system: systems without exchange and systems based on exchange. In the systems without exchange, human well-being depends directly on the *quantity* of goods obtained from production, that is, foodstuffs, clothes, housing; once these needs are satisfied, people rest. In such an organization "wealth may exist . . . *without any possibility of exchange*, or without trade. On the other hand it cannot exist without labor." Sismondi brings out the logic of his thought by describing to us a man on a desert island. *Ownership* of the land, woods, animals, fish, and metals does not ensure his well-being and amidst this abundance of natural goods the man can die of hunger and cold. It is only *by labor* that man acquires the goods that enable him to satisfy his needs, to become rich. "The measure of his wealth will not be the *price*, which he might obtain . . . in exchange, but the length of time during which no further labor will be requisite to satisfy his wants."[71] The totality of these goods acquired by labor and directly serving to satisfy his own needs will constitute true "territorial wealth." Sismondi does not mean thereby any agricultural product, as one might suppose, but what is called "natural economy," which the Germans describe more precisely by the expression *Bedarfsdeckungswirtschaft* in contrast to *Marktwirtschaft (Warenwirtschaft)*.[72]

To this organization without exchange, to this "territorial wealth" described in book III, Sismondi contrasts in book IV "commercial wealth." He keeps the same division in his *Studies*, where the first section (essays 3–12) covers territorial wealth, and the second (essays 13–17), commercial wealth. That the systems are identical in Sismondi's two major works is sufficient to show that here it is a question of essentially distinct economic types. If territorial wealth was not the agricultural economy, commercial wealth did not represent a separate category of commercial goods but *these same* goods, which inasmuch as they serve particular needs are territorial wealth, become commercial wealth when they are taken to market and intended to be sold. "From the moment

---

70. [English in Grossman's original text.]

71. Sismondi, *New Principles of Political Economy*, 61. [Grossman's emphasis.]

72. [Subsistence economy in contrast to market economy (commodity economy).]

that the products of the earth . . . had left the hands of the cultivator, to the moment they came into the hands of the consumer, they constituted commercial wealth."[73]

Now, "exchange had not in the least altered the nature of wealth: it was always *a thing* created by labor, saved for future need."[74] But now, in the course of exchange, alongside this character of real wealth, appears a new phenomenon: the *exchange value* of these goods, in its capacity as a special kind of wealth specific to the system of exchange. The use value of goods is an intrinsic wealth residing in goods and attached to them and, consequently, it is a real wealth, serving to satisfy needs, a wealth that is independent of exchange and hence always real in every economic system and it is the product of labor. "These goods are useful, are necessary to the very people who bring them into existence: they have an intrinsic value more legitimately than those that are commonly designated with this description; it is *independent of any exchange*, it is prior to any trade."[75]

In opposition to this real wealth, independent of the form of economic organization, exchange value is wealth deriving from exchange, hence exclusively linked to a certain economic organization based on exchange.

In the exchange system, the real value of goods, their intrinsic, use value—that is to say, what constitutes the essence of real wealth: the capacity to satisfy needs—is a matter of indifference to the producer of these goods, as soon as he creates them in order to sell them. "We come to goods which the manufacturer produces for the use *of others* . . . to the goods which only start to be useful to him at the moment when he exchanges them." The goods begin to exist for the producer of wealth if and when he sells them, for then they make real *their exchange value*. "We have included them under the name of commercial wealth, and we designate thus all goods which are evaluated only by their exchange value." The evolution of trade has transformed absolutely the character of the annual product of society: it has "suppressed its character of use value, in order to leave in existence only that of exchange value."[76] Since it is not the expression of the intrinsic value of goods, of true wealth, it is "false riches," an "illusion," a "shadow without reality."[77]

Since this exchange value plays a decisive role in Sismondi's theory, let us examine it more closely. We have seen that the exchange value of any object is distinct from and independent of the use value of this individual object: it is "appreciation of the thing evaluated in comparison not with one thing *in particular* but with *everything*." This fact confers on exchange value a *social character, generalizing and abstract*. "Value is therefore a social idea put in the place of an individual idea; *it is an abstract idea* put in the place of a positive idea."[78]

---

73. Sismondi, *New Principles of Political Economy*, 245.
74. Ibid., 68. [Grossman's emphasis.]
75. Ibid.; and *Études*, vol. 2, 227. [Grossman's emphasis.]
76. Sismondi, *Études*, vol. 2, 227, 230. [Grossman's emphasis.]
77. Sismondi, "Analysis of a Refutation," 613; *Études*, vol. 2, 230, 234.
78. Sismondi, *Études*, vol. 2, 375. [See also Marx:] "As *useful activity* . . . labor is . . . a condition of material

And we can already begin to understand what this "abstraction" is, against which Sismondi expresses his criticism. "The exchange price . . . *is one of the most abstract ideas* presented by economic science, which is so rich in abstractions."[79] If use value is a *thing* created by labor, exchange value is an *"abstract idea."*

This abstract value has found its most perfect expression in capital, which appears in the most abstract form. "We touch here on *the most abstract question* . . . in political economy." In fact for society, taken as a whole, real wealth continues to be merely the mass of actual goods and services that satisfy needs. Things are different for each individual producer. For the capitalist, the natural form of capital and the continual real transformations that it undergoes in the course of the labor process are a matter of total indifference. For him the only important thing is the abstract value that he has invested in production and the increase of this in the course of production itself and of circulation. Sismondi shows that the producer never lets this value escape from his hands—whatever may be the continual modifications of the external forms of his capital. In support of his thesis he gives the example of the agricultural producer: "The same object, passing from hand to hand, receives successively different names; while *its value, which separates itself from the consumed object* . . . appears to be a *metaphysical entity* which one spends, and another exchanges, which perishes . . . which renews itself and persists . . . as long as circulation lasts."[80]

For the cultivator, for example, the corn that he had harvested and used to feed productive workers "was a *permanent multiplying value which did not perish anymore*." This perpetual value has an independent life.

This value separated itself from that of the provisions that had created it: it remained like a *metaphysical* and *nonsubstantial quantity*, always in the possession of the same cultivator, for whom it merely took different *guises*. First it had been corn, then an equal value of labor (wage); then an equal value of the fruits of that labor; later a credit to the person to whom these fruits were sold for later payment; then money, then again corn or labor.[81]

"This movement of wealth is so abstract and it demands such great concentration to understand it well." This abstract character of capital in general likewise has repercussions on all its constituent parts and on all economic life. "Circulating capital is an *abstract* and elusive *quantity* and cannot be grasped."[82] "It is the *abstract image* of all the values which commerce has at its disposal."[83]

Following on from this analysis, Sismondi traces the properties of two different

---

interchange between man and nature, quite independent of the form of society. On the other hand, the labor which posits *exchange value* is a specific *social form* of labor." *Contribution to the Critique*, 278. [Grossman's emphasis. German in Grossman's original text.]

79. Ibid., 379. [Grossman's emphasis.]

80. Sismondi, *New Principles of Political Economy*, 79–80. [Grossman's emphasis.]

81. Ibid., 81–82. [Grossman's emphasis.]

82. Sismondi, *New Principles of Political Economy*, 84; *Études*, vol. 2, 395. [Grossman's emphasis.]

83. Sismondi, *Études*, vol. 2, 389. [Grossman's emphasis.])

economic systems. From the dynamic point of view, he observes that effective evolution means that the system without exchange—the substance of which is the production of wealth in the proper sense, in its natural, permanent, essential form, for it belongs to every economic system—disappears more and more, under the influence of trade in its capacity as regulator of the economic mechanism. To an ever-greater extent its place is taken by an accidental form of wealth, for it belongs only to a certain specific system, namely, exchange value. "Trade leads to the disappearance of *the essential character* of forms of wealth, utility, leaving behind only their *accidental character*, their exchange value."[84]

Now this abstract value puts its mark on the whole economic life of our epoch. If, from the point of view of essential wealth, the history of the well-being of society is nothing other than the *history of human labor*, then "it is most important that one thinks first of showing step by step all the *actions* by which [a human] can move from penury to opulence." Hence in the society of exchange the sole aim of every producer is not the labor process but "the hope of profit,"[85] in other words, the tendency to acquire a profit, that is to say a surplus of this exchangeable abstract value higher than the value laid out. *It is this abstract value*, in its capacity as the sole aim of production and as the regulator of it, that is the target *of Sismondi's sharpest criticisms, as he shows that it is the source of all the problems of our economic organization.*[86] If, therefore, Sismondi combats abstraction, abstract wealth, abstract ideas, he is thinking of wealth based on exchange value, in the same way that later Nassau Senior, Fryderyk Skarbek, or Karl Marx would call exchange value abstract wealth.[87] Hence Sismondi does not attack either wealth or the accumulation of wealth in general but attacks the accumulation of wealth *in the abstract form of exchange value* and describes as "chrematistic" economic organization based precisely on this exchange value. As the capitalist system races toward *the accumulation of abstract value*, which finds an adequate expression in the commercial export policy, Sismondi sees only a modernized form of the old mercantilism: "governments continue for the most part to behave according to the mercantile system, as though no argument had yet begun to undermine it."[88]

From this brief account it appears clear that Sismondi understood perfectly the very essence of the capitalist system, the aim of which is not the production of *real goods* serving to satisfy needs but the production and accumulation of an *abstract exchange val-*

84. Ibid., 378.

85. Sismondi, *New Principles of Political Economy*, 62; *Études*, vol. 1, 59. [Grossman's emphasis.]

86. "It contains the general possibility of commercial crises, essentially because the contradiction of commodity and money is the abstract and general form of all *contradictions inherent in the bourgeois mode of labour.*" Marx, *Contribution to the Critique*, 332. [German in Grossman's original text. Grossman's emphasis.]

87. "Money is *abstract wealth*. . . . The modes in which different individuals would employ it are infinitely diversified." Senior, *Outline of the Science*, 27. [Grossman's emphasis.] "Exchange value . . . can only be an abstract *idea*." Skarbek, *Théorie des richesses sociales*, vol. 1, 138. [Grossman's emphasis.] "Money as the end and object of circulation represents *exchange value* or *abstract wealth*." Marx, *Contribution to the Critique*, 389–90. [German in Grossman's original text; Grossman's emphasis.]

88. Sismondi, *Études*, vol. 2, 321.

ue. And that is why it is right to consider Sismondi as the first economist to scientifically discover capitalism; that is his immortal claim to fame in economic science.

CR

The characterization that we have just made of our *economic system* is only one of the aspects of the problem Sismondi was dealing with. This problem leads on to another: the relation of *economic science* to real phenomena. Now, according to Sismondi, the economic theory of his time was only the theoretical reflection of contemporary economic organization based on abstract exchange value. If this organization, as a result of its defective construction, is the source of lasting problems, this fact also has an impact on economic theory, which is likewise based on the same abstract foundation of exchange value. The real contradiction of the economic system appears in science in the form of incoherent notions and definitions and futile quarrels about words. Through a painstaking analysis of the contradictions of the economic system, Sismondi ends up with a search for the errors and contradictions in the theory. "This quest necessarily brings us back to the most abstract notions of the science, to the most disputed definitions, to a whole battle of words." In both organization and theory, the source of the problem and of the shortcomings is identical. "It is the opposition between *use value* and *exchange value* . . . which makes it impossible to give a satisfactory definition of these various terms: price, value, wealth." The abstract character of the science based on exchange value and the contradiction between this science and the phenomena of real wealth makes it difficult to define these notions—price of production, sentimental price, monopoly price, nominal price, real price, and so on—and this difficulty derives from the very nature of our system. In theory this again comes down to a battle of words, a dispute about meanings, and not to the very essence of the phenomena concealed by it. So it should not be forgotten that verbal disputes about a definition do not and cannot explain what these phenomena entail. Those who think they have dealt with the phenomena through the critique of a definition are greatly mistaken. The contradiction manifested in phenomena must be eliminated from these phenomena and this cannot be done by a critique that only examines words. The classical *theory* of the spontaneous harmony of interests is not in a position to resolve this *effective* contradiction: together with the continuous increase in wealth, capitalist production gives rise to "poverty growing together with abundance."[89] This phenomenon seems to be a contradiction; in fact it is a *real phenomenon* and hence the *idea* that expresses it is consistent with reality. So if theory has not succeeded in defining this concept adequately, that does not make it faulty; the error is in the definition, in the words. "If a more precise analysis makes us find a contradiction somewhere, it is not the *idea* which must give way but the *word*: it is in the *definition* and not in the *fact* that we find the defect of the argument."[90]

89. Ibid., 226, 229, 233. [Grossman's emphasis.]
90. Sismondi, *Études*, vol. 1, 116. [Grossman's emphasis.] In this profound characterization of the battle of

Sismondi was the first to present us with a deep analysis of the contradictions in theory, showing that it is not the accidental result of the incapacity of scholars but the necessary consequence of the contradictions presented by the economic system itself. That is why Sismondi uses the term "chrematistic" to describe both the economic theory based on the analysis of exchange value and the economic system itself that is built on this foundation. "The science which is commonly known as political economy, although its proper title is chrematistics, has taken on the task of studying wealth abstractly." He considers this economic science and the system itself to be "pursuing a shadow without reality." And he contrasts true science to this false theory. "We reserve the name of political economy for the study of the social organization of man in his relation with things, the man who *consumes* wealth and the man who *produces* it."[91] Sismondi wants to consider only real phenomena, the relation of man with the real usable goods that he produces and consumes, *independently of the question of the exchange value* of these goods. And this economy that is independent of exchange and of the calculation of value he calls the real economy, "the rule of the house and of the community."[92] As we will see, this problem has nothing in common with the question of the distribution of wealth that, according to the view held until now, constituted the very substance of Sismondi's doctrine.

The scientific problem that Sismondi was posing himself is hence double: critique of theory, critique of the system. Sismondi has to explain the functioning of the economic mechanism built on the basis of abstract exchange value, whose ideal aim—the aim of any economic system—is to satisfy all the needs of society, but in which the aim of each particular producer is to individually accumulate abstract exchange value. He proposes to "seek an *explanation* for so many facts which appear *contradictory*, to discover *what is the deception of the system of industrialism*, to show how it has abandoned the *substance* to run after the *shadow*, in order finally to replace chrematistics, or the abstract science of wealth, with *true political economy*."[93]

B. Positive Theory

So far we have tried to show what Sismondi considered to be the true problem in his research, and we have seen that this problem consisted in the dualistic character of capitalist production, which on the one hand is the production of real goods and on the other the production of abstract exchange value. It now remains for us to explain why he sees this fact as the *defect* of our economic organization and why in particular he criticizes one of these elements, abstract exchange value, as being the principal source of all the upheavals that trouble our economic system. The very location of the problem,

---

words, Sismondi anticipates the anonymous English author of *Observations on Certain Verbal Disputes*, as well as his belated epigone, the German Gottl (*Die Herrschaft des Wortes*).

91. Sismondi, *Études*, vol. 2, 234. [Grossman's emphasis.]

92. Ibid., 226.

93. Ibid. [Grossman's emphasis.]

no less than Sismondi's solution to it, are by their depth far removed from the horizon of classical economic thought and even of contemporary economic thought in general.

In the system producing for human needs and not for the market, for sale, an increase in production, that is, in the quantity of goods, is simultaneously an increase in wealth. "Before the introduction of trade and when everyone thought only of supplying themselves, the increase in the *quantity* of things produced was a direct increase in wealth." "That is doubtless the true understanding of wealth."[94] "As long as men work to satisfy their own needs, *utility* is for them the true measure of values, and the increase in quantity of a useful thing is a sure increase in wealth." It is nonetheless necessary *to produce these goods within strictly defined limits*. It is true that "the needs and desires of human beings are unlimited," but not the *concrete* needs: foodstuffs, housing, clothing, and so on.[95] "One can have too much, even of the best things." "Consumption cannot go beyond a certain limit, difficult to indicate precisely but nonetheless definite," and which no man could go beyond.[96] "All labor he performed *beyond that would be pointless*. Any product which he accumulated would be without value." Nonetheless, in the system without exchange "the glut of commodities was not possible."[97] Concrete needs gave an impulse to production, so that in practice the direction and scope of labor were adapted in advance to the extent of needs. Man, "after having supplied his stock for consumption and his reserve stock, will stop."[98] In these conditions one produces only as much as is necessary, and the goods produced are always wealth, for they fulfill the function appropriate to them—that is, they serve to satisfy needs.

It is quite different in the system with exchange. The whole, organized for a specific purpose, which was represented by the system without exchange, has now been fragmented into distinct functions that are independent of each other, if not diametrically opposed. The independent producers, left to themselves, produce for the market, that is, for other people, without knowing these people's needs, and remain in contact with them only by the mediation of exchange. Each cog in the clock has made itself free and functions independently of the others; the common movement, coordinated for a particular purpose, has been fragmented into private isolated fractions. "Trade or exchange has divided between the members of society the functions which tend toward a common purpose. Everyone, in pursuing their private aims, loses sight of the general interest. . . . They pursue their aims without really knowing how much of this thing society requires of them."[99]

This failure to adapt the behavior of individuals to the needs of the social whole has the necessary consequence of upsetting the whole. Society, in fact, although fragmented into specific and independent functions, nonetheless does not cease to constitute a *social*

---

94. Ibid., 378, 379. [Grossman's emphasis.]
95. Ibid., 229; and vol. 1, 139. [Grossman's emphasis.]
96. Sismondi, *Études*, vol. 1, 64, 151.
97. Ibid., 69; and vol. 2, 243. [Grossman's emphasis.]
98. Sismondi, *Études*, vol. 1, 68.
99. Ibid., 69.

whole. If in the economic system working for the producer's own needs it was necessary to adapt every act and every function to the needs of the individual producer, this same obligation exists for the system with exchange. "Production has limits which it is forbidden to exceed." "These rules . . . are equally true in *any state* of society, even if it is no longer directed by an intelligence which understands all the relations of its members with each other, by a will which makes them all cooperate for the common good." In a society based on the division of labor and functions, their coordination is a necessity; Sismondi compares it to a watch where all the cogs and all the motions, by the very nature of things, must be coordinated. "All movements in society are linked together; one follows from the other, as the various movements of the gears of a watch."[100]

However, from the time that society becomes divided into independent and even contradictory functions, this necessary adaptation can only be an objective *result* that is accomplished through the divergent interests and movements of individuals. "Civilized society seems to be subject . . . to those general laws . . . which propel the whole toward a common end, by disasters that pitilessly strike the different parts."[101] Thus it is these laws through which social union is achieved independently of the action of individuals.[102] In these conditions, economic disturbances are the natural and inevitable consequence of our economic organization. Since each individual acts independently, producing as much as possible, without taking account of *social need*, real goods exceeding this social need cease to be wealth. "All that is produced beyond this is useless and has no value."[103] The defect of the capitalist system consists precisely in the fact that, contrary to the law according to which all economic functions in society must be coordinated for a specific purpose, each producer tends to maximize production, thinking that by increasing the quantity of goods, he is also increasing the quantity of wealth. "The error on which the whole system of modern chrematistics is based . . . confuses the increase of *production* with that of *wealth*."[104]

And it is from this consideration, deriving directly as we will see from his new formulation of the law of value, that Sismondi starts in order to construct his theory. And over this issue Sismondi ceaselessly indicts the theory of the classical economists. "The error into which they have fallen stems entirely from the false principle that makes the annual output, in their eyes, the same thing as the income." This is the source of all the errors of the theory, of the confusion of concepts and of the inability to explain phenomena. "The confusion of the annual income with the annual product throws a dense

---

100. Ibid., 140; "On the Balance," 637. [Grossman's emphasis.]

101. Sismondi, *New Principles of Political Economy*, 503.

102. "The *exchange process* of commodities is the *real* relation that exists between them. This is a social process which is carried on by individuals independently of one another." Marx, *Contribution to the Critique*, 282. [German in Grossman's original text.]

103. Sismondi, *Études*, vol. 1, 69. "The commodity therefore has still to *become* a use value, in the first place a use value for others. . . . If this is not the case, then the labour expended on it was useless labour." Marx, *Contribution to the Critique*, 283. [German in Grossman's original text; Grossman's emphasis.]

104. Sismondi, *Études*, vol. 2, 312. [Grossman's emphasis.]

veil over the whole science."[105] "With this principle it becomes absolutely impossible to understand . . . the satiation of markets. . . . It is equally impossible to extricate oneself from the contradictions about the meaning that ought to be given to the words *value* and *wealth* with which Messrs Say and Ricardo mutually charge each other."[106]

Here Sismondi is referring to the well-known controversy between Ricardo on the one hand and Say and [Thomas] Malthus on the other. The latter two identify value with wealth. Malthus claims that revenue drawn out of the earth by a landowner is an increase in social wealth, "a new creation of riches."[107] Ricardo is in agreement with Sismondi, who regards revenue as a purely abstract value: "Rent . . . has a value purely nominal. . . . Consider it as no addition to the national wealth, but merely as a transfer of value."[108] Ricardo expresses a similar opinion in chapter 20 of the *Principles*, where under the obvious influence of Sismondi he shows that their theory has confused the ideas of value and riches. It is not value that determines wealth. "A man is rich or poor according to the *abundance* of necessaries and luxuries which he can command . . . whether the exchangeable *value* of these . . . be high or low."[109]

This way of seeing is undoubtedly in contradiction with the whole of Ricardo's system, which is based precisely and above all on exchange value. And that is why Ricardo draws no conclusion from this difference between exchange value and wealth. In Ricardo's system, chapter 20 constitutes a totally isolated point, unconnected with this system. Sismondi was the first to draw out all the implications for the economic mechanism that derive from the fact that it is precisely based on this abstract exchange value, "value purely nominal."[110] And in this fact he sees the cause of all the disturbances, all the disruptions, of this mechanism.

❧

It now remains for us to show in a detailed analysis why and how we must necessarily end up with these disturbances if we base the economic mechanism on abstract exchange value. Sismondi asserts that if we base the economic system on this principle it is *impossible to make a proportional fit between the amount of production and the extent of needs. Disproportion becomes then and as a rule a normal phenomenon.*

In the system without exchange, composed of producers independent of each other, it did not matter whether the number of producers increased, since each was producing only for his own needs, and the functions of production and consumption were dependent on each other and in close correlation; their equilibrium was thereby ensured in advance. But it is quite different in the system with exchange, where one

---

105. Sismondi, *New Principles of Political Economy*, 278.

106. Ibid. [Grossman's emphasis.]

107. Ricardo, *Principles of Political Economy*, 272. [English in Grossman's original text.]

108. Ibid., 273. [English in Grossman's original text.]

109. Ibid., 184. [English in Grossman's original text; Grossman's emphasis.]

110. [English in Grossman's original text.]

produces for other people. Here the separation of producer and consumer came into being: "Somebody had taken the place of the producer to consume." "But when trade was introduced, and each no longer labored for himself, but for someone unknown, the proportions . . . between the labor and the revenue . . . were independent of each other." And then it became necessary to regulate the mutual quantitative relations between total production and total needs. But as nobody carries out this regulation, these relations are entirely random; the number of producers and the extent of their production are different and arbitrary in each branch; *need* has ceased to be the regulator of the extent of production and has been replaced by the capitalist's *profit*, deriving from a product having a value "higher than the money advanced by means of which it has been obtained." This difference, this "surplus," is therefore itself exchange value and hence an abstract quantity. This profit, this abstract value, is henceforward the aim of the whole capitalist mechanism; it is its motor; it guides all actions, independently of real needs. "Profit making has become the first aim in life."[111] "The hope of profit makes capital circulate rapidly from one end of the known universe to the other."[112]

How does the exchange mechanism function under the influence of this regulator? And thus we find ourselves at the very heart of Sismondi's theory.

Although each social function has become independent, society has not ceased to be a whole in the economic sense, an organism controlled by the law of this whole and not by the elements that make it up, something that is manifested in the law of value. Sismondi corrects the individualist theory of value of Smith and Ricardo, which determines the value of a commodity by the labor expended on producing it, with this highly significant addition: that it must be the labor *necessary* for its production. "Mercantile value is always fixed, in the last analysis, by the quantity of labor necessary to obtain the valued thing."[113] To tell the truth, Ricardo also seemed to define value in this way: "I say that it is the comparative quantity of labour necessary to the production of commodities, which regulates their relative value."[114] But while Ricardo only speaks of the time technically necessary to produce a *unit* of a given commodity, Sismondi uses the word "necessary," as Marx will do later, in the sense of "time that is socially indispensible," that is, time necessary to produce *the whole mass* of a given commodity necessary for society.[115] "Value is the relation between the demand of all and the production of all." "Value results from the relation between the need of the whole society and the quantity of labor which has sufficed to satisfy this need." Only the labor required to satisfy the

111. Sismondi, *New Principles of Political Economy*, 68, 254; Sismondi, *Études*, vol. 1, 137; Sismondi, "On the Balance," 339.

112. Sismondi, *Études*, vol. 1, 59.

113. Sismondi, *Études*, vol. 2, 381.

114. Ricardo to Jean-Baptiste Say, January 11, 1820, 149.

115. Marx himself notes this: "Arguing directly with Ricardo, *Sismondi* not only emphasises the specifically *social* character of labour which creates exchange value, but states also that it is a 'characteristic feature of our economic progress' to reduce value to *necessary* labour time, to 'the relation between the needs of the *whole society* and the quantity of labour which is sufficient to satisfy those needs.'" Marx, *Contribution to the Critique*, 300–301. [German in Grossman's original text; Grossman's emphasis.]

whole need is necessary and the value of the products then corresponds exactly to the labor provided, measured by time. This condition would require the *quantitative fixing*, on the one hand, of the number of producers and the extent of their production, and on the other of the extent of total social needs. In the end it is only under these conditions that the process of production would be in proportion *to needs*, would be *normal*, without disturbances or losses for the producer. "To be sure of selling, he would have to know two things: the quantity of the thing he is producing that the public needs; the quantity of it that can be produced by all those who exercise the same profession as he does." "Whereas one or the other [wealth and population], considered by themselves, are only abstractions, and the real problem . . . is to find that combination and *proportion* of population and wealth."[116] Independently of the question of the unequal *distribution* of wealth between the various classes of the population, the key point is that reproduction is in proportion to the productive forces and the needs of society as a whole. "It is *on that proportion that my* New Principles *are founded*; it is in the importance that I attach to it that *I differ essentially* from philosophers who . . . have expounded the economic science of Messrs. Say, Ricardo, Malthus and McCulloch."[117] Assuming that total production corresponds to total need, if ten garments and twenty sacks of corn are produced by the same number of days of labor, they will exchange at equal values.

But in the real world nobody adapts production to needs; that is why the course of production and exchange does not follow this normal pattern. Given the fragmentation of the social whole into distinct functions independent of each other, the number of producers and the quantity of their production are arbitrary and random. To acquire a profit the producer would like to "produce indefinitely."[118] Now this excessive quantity of labor, accomplished in order to generate production exceeding total social need, does not count, because it has no purchasers *and hence does not create value.* "All that is produced beyond this is useless and has no value."[119] For "things become wealth only at the time when they find the consumer who agrees to buy them in order to use them."[120] Individual labor creates value only if this function is a *necessary organ of the whole*; otherwise it is a superfluous function, that is, time wasted.

If therefore the number of producers of clothing, for example, increases, although the need has not changed, the labor expended on this additional production of clothing does not create any value, the greater mass of clothes will have the same value as previously, and, as a result, the price of each garment must fall. A specific producer of

---

116. Sismondi, *Études*, vol. 2, 376, 379; vol. 1, 120; and *New Principles of Political Economy*, 2. [Grossman's emphasis; translator's interpolation.]

117. Sismondi, *New Principles of Political Economy*, 11. [Grossman's emphasis.] Rist commits a major mistake by understanding the problem of the proportionality of productive forces raised by Sismondi as a question of the *distribution of wealth* above all in the interest of the poor, that is, of waged workers. Rist writes that, according to Sismondi, "wealth only deserves the name when it is proportionately distributed." "Sismondi and the Origins," 178.

118. Sismondi, *Études*, vol. 1, 70.

119. Ibid., 69.

120. Ibid., 30.

clothing continues to manufacture, for example, ten garments, just like the previous year—that is to say, the same quantity as previously—but in view of the reduction in value of this production, he can no longer buy twenty sacks of corn, but only twelve, eight, or even none at all if he has not sold any of his ten garments. So despite the claims of Say and Ricardo, it appears that it was only in the system without exchange that the quantity of the product was identical to the income and in permanent conditions suffered from year to year to satisfy the same needs. In the system with exchange the quantity of products is not equivalent to income. This quantity of products must first of all be sold. Each producer now knows that "by making the same quantity of products, he might earn much or little, or he might even lose." The products of one year, identical in quantity and quality to those of the previous year, may and do represent a quite different income; *despite the identical nature of the products, the income is of a variable size.* In the exchange system, "products are not yet positive quantities, aliquot portions of wealth, as long as they are in the hands of the producer. Only sale . . . determines their value."[121] In these conditions the manufacturer of clothing produces, it is true, the same quantity as previously but his income will depend not on the quantity of goods created by him as an individual producer but on the quantity of goods created likewise by all the other producers and hence *will depend on productive processes taking place outside of each individual producer* and independently of him, in short, on competition. "Thus, in this new condition, the life of every man who works and produces depends not . . . on his labor but on what he sells. It matters little whether the work is done well. . . . It must be in *exact proportion* with production. The producer who cannot sell cannot live."[122]

From the point of view of society conceived as a whole, income is always a certain *given* mass of effective goods reproduced. "Income, of which we have seen all the different sources, is a material and consumable thing; it springs from labor."[123] But in the exchange system the producers act in isolation; for them income is always a *variable* amount: it is an abstract value subject to fluctuations. In this disproportion of production and income, of use value and exchange value, is found the original source of the disruptions that appear in our economic mechanism. The development of this thought constitutes the first part of Sismondi's theory. It was to this that Karl Marx's penetrating observation referred: "Sismondi founded on the *opposition* between use value and exchange value his principal doctrine, according to which diminution in *revenue* is proportional to the increase in production."[124] Despite these words written nearly eighty years ago, Sismondi's "principal theory" on the nature of income has not yet been understood.

---

121. Ibid., 65; and vol. 2, 231.
122. Sismondi, *Études*, vol. 1, 120. [Grossman's emphasis.] We have taken as the starting point of our argument the excessive number of producers of clothing, as a result of which some of these clothes could not be sold. But as the producers of clothing are in turn consumers of the products of other branches, the reduction of their incomes must also provoke a disproportion in other branches, namely, a "general obstruction." Sismondi, "Analysis of a Refutation," 600.
123. Sismondi, *New Principles of Political Economy*, 361.
124. Marx, *The Poverty of Philosophy*, 114. [Grossman's emphasis.] See also Sismondi, "Analysis of a Refutation," 600.

The classical school considered crises as accidental phenomena provoked by mistaken commercial policy and by restrictions. Even those who are called egalitarian socialists, like for example William Thompson, saw the real source of crises only in the luxury branches of industry, as the result of the whims and changes of fashion among the rich.[125] In contrast, for Sismondi crises are the *necessary* consequence of the construction, defective in principle, of our economic mechanism based on abstract exchange value.

Sismondi's analysis does not stop with this result. The classical school insisted that even when a crisis broke out, it could only be a transitory phenomenon, for our productive apparatus possesses a spontaneous tendency to reestablish the good order that has been disrupted. Sismondi had a quite different view. He showed that in an economic mechanism whose regulator is a variable exchange value there are causes that act permanently, that merely intensify the disequilibrium between production and needs and constantly create the tendency to enlarge production whether or not this is required by needs.

First of all on the commodity market. The mechanism described by the classical economists is well known: any excess production brings down prices and profits and has an automatic influence on the reduction in production. The tendency to equalize profits in the various branches of production brings about the withdrawal of capital from nonprofitable branches and prevents disequilibrium. On the other hand Sismondi argues that in a society where the producer's aim is not the production of a specific quantity of real goods but the highest profit possible, the lowering of the selling price and income caused by overproduction in no way leads to the *reduction* of production but, on the contrary, merely *extends* it, so that with a greater number of transactions the producer can recuperate his losses on prices. The producer "always seeks to produce more, to produce cheaper, to produce all the more . . . in order to regain by quantity what he loses on prices." "The result of the reduction of income is that he needs more capital to live, he needs more land to get the same amount of rent, he needs to lend more money to get the same amount of interest." Overproduction by lowering prices and incomes forces the individual producer to continue overproducing even more. "Because they had already too many goods, they have asked for more at a lower price." That seems like a paradox. However, there is a glut on the market and there is no means of selling all the increased production, since there was insufficient demand previously for less production. But the increase in production makes it possible to reduce expenses, thanks to which the large producer wins out over his competitors and disposes of his goods at his competitors' expense. "Each producer seeks to undercut his rival colleagues and by low prices to attract the buyer to himself in preference to someone else who cannot sell."[126] This producer prospers even at times of general stagnation; he increases his production even when there is no increased demand. It is an artificial

---

125. Thompson, *Inquiry into the Principles*, 195–210.
126. Sismondi, *Études*, vol. 1, 74; "On the Balance," 635; *Études*, vol. 2, 232.

buoyancy: "production is reviving," "but this sporadic activity is more often the result of risky speculation, of misplaced confidence, and of superabundant capital, than of new demand." "It is a deceptive activity," "a fallacious prosperity."[127]

"The necessary, inevitable consequence of undercutting by some is glut for all, or the arrival on the market of a quantity of goods in excess of needs, which can only be sold at a loss." Success in competition is conditioned by large-scale production, the purchase of cheap raw materials, the application of the division of labor, the use of machines, new inventions, and so on. But this success also depends on the abundance of capital and on a low rate of interest. "A decrease in the rate of interest begins a search for a productive use of superabundant capital." "The capitalists, in order to employ their funds, will set afoot industries which will not find an adequate market afterwards."[128] Finally we come to the key fact that it is not the increase in consumption that is the regulator of the extent of production but that increases in production are "determined, not by needs, but by the abundance of capital."[129] All the stimuli, directions, and dimensions of capitalist production today are in no way determined by the extent of concrete need; rather, "those who found themselves in possession of a certain quantity of accumulated wealth have in general undertaken the control of annual production."[130]

It is obvious that, in these conditions, the increase in production "without regard to the needs of the business world" intensifies competition "that enriched some individuals [and] caused a certain loss to others."[131] The increase in production is therefore parallel to the reduction of income and even to the ruin of the social whole. The increase in production, "always tied to a greater circulating capital, and to the use of a larger fixed capital, can give an advantage to the entrepreneur, and make his manufacture flourish, without having to again conclude that this leads to a social benefit."[132] Moreover, the source of disruptions is the same: the regulation of the extent of production by profit, that is, by an abstract exchange value. The shrinking of this abstract quantity leads to the enlargement of the real productive apparatus as well as the mass of real products, although demand is lacking—in short, the opposition between exchange value and use value. The result is that "the income of all is not the same thing as everyone's output . . . it would be possible that the product increases and the income decreases."[133]

CR

---

127. Sismondi, *New Principles of Political Economy*, 333; *Études*, vol. 2, 329.

128. Sismondi, *Études*, vol. 2, 233; *New Principles of Political Economy*, 299, 332.

129. Sismondi, *New Principles of Political Economy*, 278.

130. Sismondi, *Études*, vol. 1, 141. "As capitalist production develops, the scale of production is determined to an ever lesser degree by the immediate demand for the product, and to an ever greater degree by the scale of the capital which the individual capitalist has at his disposal, by his capital's drive for valorisation and the need of his production process for continuity and extension." [Marx, *Capital*, vol. 2, 221.]

131. Sismondi, *New Principles of Political Economy*, 303. [Editor's interpolation.]

132. Ibid., 299.

133. Sismondi, "Analysis of a Refutation," 600.

In the two instances we have just considered, since the available technology and the productivity of labor did not change, the reduction of exchange value was the result of an excessive increase either *in the number of producers* or in the extent of their production. This reduction of exchange value may occur as a result of *technical revolutions*, in other words, of progress in the productivity of labor. And here we come to the third part of Sismondi's theory. Ricardo had noticed the fact itself.[134] Sismondi develops it and shows the consequences. "Mercantile value is always fixed, in the last analysis, by the quantity of labor required to obtain the thing being valued; it is not what it costs at present but what it will cost in the future, perhaps with improved methods."[135] Whence *a constant devaluation of goods already produced* and put on the market, leading to a new source of disruptions. Moreover the old factories with their old equipment are reduced to struggling hopelessly against the competition of large factories that are better equipped. "The old machines, even the whole factory, replaced by new inventions, lose all their value. The immense capital which had been placed in their construction is destroyed."[136] "Every truly important discovery in engineering, each of those that produce . . . a considerable profit, immediately leads to the creation of a new factory in order to appropriate the profits exclusively." It is a never-ending race to monopolize profit through improvement but for a very short moment, for a newcomer in turn will soon reduce the value of this improvement. "It is in the nature of crafts that inventions succeed each other, that a new discovery comes to take away the fruits of the preceding one."[137]

This ceaseless competition produces a constant process of devaluation of the values already accumulated, a general dislocation of exchange value, and, as a result, a necessary disruption of the whole economic mechanism of which this value is the regulator. "It has been noted that *the violent shocks suffered nowadays by manufacturing industry derive from the speed with which scientific discoveries succeed one another*." And the effects of so many "revolutionary inventions" are deplorable for human society. "Not only is the value of all goods already produced diminished . . . but all the fixed capital, all the machines . . . are rendered useless."[138]

In these conditions, a fortune owned is always threatened with ruin, and the producer's income does not depend on labor effectively carried out. It is consequently not a positive amount, does not depend on the mass of effective goods produced but on the value he manages to obtain by selling them on the market and that he succeeds in preserving amid the continual upheavals to which this value is subject. "His operation takes on the character of a game . . . his profit depends on chance, or is based on the loss made by another."[139]

134. Ricardo, *Principles of Political Economy*, 182–91.
135. Sismondi, *Études*, vol. 2, 381.
136. Ibid., 302.
137. Ibid., 298, 305.
138. Ibid., 366, 367. [Grossman's emphasis.]
139. Ibid., 232.

The circumstances we have just noted, an unlimited quantity of producers and production and technical revolutions, must and did provoke disruptions even in a system composed only of independent producers possessing their own instruments of production. In both cases the reduction in profit and the subsequent depreciation of capital and of goods already produced causes the ruin of the small producers. "The prosperity of the producer who gets rich should not allow us to forget the poverty of the producer ruined by his competition." It is impossible to safeguard oneself from this competition by moving into another branch of production; "capitals leave an industry only *through the bankruptcy* of owners."[140] The spontaneous tendency to restore equilibrium between production and consumption does not exist. In the current system there is therefore overproduction: the impossibility of selling some of the products. "Hence, if production increases gradually, the exchange of *each year* ought to cause a small loss . . . if that loss is small and well distributed, everyone bears it." But, if the causes indicated act suddenly and violently, "there is a great disproportion between the new production and the previous production" and then one section of the producers gets rich but only because the other one gets poor; "capitals are reduced, there will be suffering." "New fortunes are built only by the overthrow of old fortunes."[141]

Hence the *natural tendency to concentration.* "Discoveries in the mechanical arts have always the remote result of concentrating industry within the hands of a smaller number of merchants."[142] Obviously this goes along with the bankruptcy and ruin of others, proletarianization, and pauperism. As we have seen, Sismondi does not merely observe this tendency empirically but shows that this concentration of industry and the consequent proletarianization are the necessary result of the current economic organization. "Pauperism is the state to which proletarians are *necessarily* reduced when they have no work. . . . This society, which gives all its support to the rich, does not allow the proletarian to work . . . and condemns him to idleness." In short, the causes that we have just set out are the historic basis of the tendency that has led to and continues to lead to the *separation of property* and labor. "We incline to separate completely any type of property from all types of labor." Hence, on the one hand, the concentration of capital, and at the opposite pole growth of the proletarian masses. "Already brought into the world, that population finds no longer any room to exist there."[143] But this excessive population "exists today, and . . . is the *necessary result of the existing order*." When a primitive hunter dies for want of finding any game, "he yields to a necessity which *nature* herself presents." Today it is a different matter for the artisan without work: "He is still surrounded by riches, . . . and if society refuses him the labor by which he offers, till his last moment, to purchase bread, it is *men*, not nature, that he blames."[144]

---

140. Ibid., 295; *New Principles of Political Economy*, 487. [Grossman's emphasis.]

141. Sismondi, *New Principles of Political Economy*, 104–5; Sismondi, *Études*, vol. 1, 31. [Grossman's emphasis.]

142. Sismondi, *New Principles of Political Economy*, 561.

143. Sismondi, *Études*, vol. 1, 44; "On the Balance," 628; *New Principles of Political Economy*, 548. [Grossman's emphasis.]

144. Sismondi, *New Principles of Political Economy*, 322, 556. [Grossman's emphasis.]

It is true that after the catastrophe of a crisis a new equilibrium is established at last. People have tried to see in this fact a proof that a crisis is only a passing ill and that equilibrium is restored automatically. Sismondi considers this theory of equilibrium restoring itself to be dangerous. "A certain equilibrium will reestablish itself in the long run,"[145] but the disaster nonetheless leaves a deep impression. Some of the producers go bankrupt and sink into the proletariat while others succeed in enlarging their businesses, and a concentration of industry results. *Equilibrium is restored, but on a new basis: the social structure has undergone a serious transformation*.

∞

This glance at Sismondi's conceptions enables us to conclude that economic science has previously considered the facts stressed by our writer—such as competition, the struggle between large and small industry, concentration, crises, pauperism, the reserve army, abuses committed in factories, and above all the question of the distribution of wealth—only as isolated, external facts, as *disjecta membra*.[146] Economists have not explained and have said nothing about the internal connection—the stimulus and the cause uniting all these phenomena into a set of parts of a common mechanism, in complete mutual dependence—hidden below these external manifestations. This connection is the fact *that abstract exchange value is the regulator of the extent of production*. The economic system serves to satisfy the concrete material needs of society by means of a given productive apparatus. These needs, just like the extent of the apparatus, are amounts and phenomena that can remain in mutual relations in natural conditions, without regard to value. On the other hand our economic system, in order to apply the dimensions of the aforesaid productive apparatus to the extent of the needs, takes as its regulator exchange value, a regulator that in a mechanism based on free competition *is necessarily a variable standard, whose movements are the opposite of those of the effective goods that it measures*, since the *value* of a given good diminishes if the general *mass* of goods increases. So these factors, like two worlds that are impenetrable to each other, do not have a common measure, and to try to harmonize them would be like measuring length in grams or weighing in meters. "The present suffering results from the increase of quantities, while values are being reduced."[147]

---

145. Ibid., 487.

146. ["Scattered fragments."]

147. Sismondi, *Études*, vol. 2, 478. See Marx: "It is a general law of commodity production that the *productivity* of labour and the *value it creates* stand in inverse proportion." *Capital*, vol. 2, 227. [Grossman's emphasis.] In a distorted form, we find this theory in Wilhelm Neurath, when he criticizes "the false calculation of value" and blames the fact "that the relation between the quantity of goods and the real need for them does not determine the estimated value of the goods." As a result of the application of this "false calculation of value," of this "phantom value," "the total value of the products can sink, even if the *quantity* . . . of the products increases, so that total use and total value come partially into contradiction with each other." In Neurath's eyes this is "something highly unusual" and "inappropriate." According to him, factories are free "of this calculation of value" (!) and possess "the capacity to produce wealth and to employ heads and hands"

Our system is like the mechanism of a factory in which every wheel, every machine set in motion by the transmission belt would have to experience disruptions in its movements if the belt contracted or stretched excessively. It is in this dual principle of organization of our economic mechanism—in the fact that to control the dimensions of the real apparatus we use a changing unit of measurement, an abstract and variable value; in this contradiction between use value and exchange value—that Sismondi sees the fundamental defect in the construction of our economic system, the real cause of crises, of overproduction, and of economic anarchy.[148] That is why the disruptions of this system are not temporary deviations from normal equilibrium but derive from a constitutive defect and are a phenomenon that recurs ceaselessly, periodically, and necessarily, to such an extent that it becomes possible to predict their regular repetition.

> The period of prosperity of any manufacture is promptly followed by a period of distress. It is enough for us to know that a manufacture is flourishing today for us to be able to foresee, almost with certainty, that in ten years or even much less time, according to all probability, it will have had to succumb to competition.[149]

CR

We do not propose to give a systematic exposition of Sismondi's ideas but just to draw out the essence of his thought. So far we have done this by analyzing phenomena on the market for commodities. We will complete our proof by *analyzing phenomena on the market for wage labor*. And there too we will encounter what we have already indicated. Critics have previously confined themselves to external aspects without reaching the very heart of the action, to apparent symptoms and not to essential and deep causes. Hence they have obstinately repeated that for Sismondi the source of all disturbances, of all crises, was to be found in the unequal distribution of wealth, in the underconsumption of the working masses. "The disproportion between capitalist production and the distribution of incomes determined by the former appears to him the source of all evil," writes Rosa Luxemburg.[150] According to [René] Gonnard, "in Sismondi's eyes, the questions of distribution take on a preponderant importance and there are almost socialist formulations on the right of the poor to a minimum consumption."[151] Nothing could be more wrong. Certainly nobody before Sismondi had exhaustively revealed the capitalist character of the creation and distribution of wealth and nobody before him had made such a penetrating critique of this system. In Sismondi we find in embryonic

---

even when they lose their value. *Die wahren Ursachen der Überproduktion*, 16–18. [Grossman's emphasis.]

148. "The *continual depreciation of labour* is only one side, *one consequence of the evaluation of commodities by labour time*. The excessive raising of prices, overproduction and many other features of industrial anarchy have their explanation in this mode of evaluation. . . . Instead of a 'proportional relation' we have a disproportional relation." Marx, *The Poverty of Philosophy*, 136. [Grossman's emphasis.]

149. Sismondi, *Études*, vol. 2, 306.

150. Luxemburg, *The Accumulation of Capital*, 178–79.

151. Gonnard, *Histoire des doctrines économiques*, vol. 3, 208.

form the doctrine later developed by Karl Marx and called by him *economic fetishism*, according to which in the capitalist system there exists an objective tendency to obscure the real nature of this system, of its institutions, and of the real source of its wealth. Monetary exchange is precisely the instrument whereby this process of artificial transformation is accomplished. In any economic system, "wealth . . . was always a thing created by labor."[152] "The history of wealth is, in all cases, comprised within the limits now specified—the labor which creates, the economy which accumulates, the consumption which destroys." But while nothing is so easy to grasp as this truth, exchanges "blur our vision and make a positive thing into an almost metaphysical one." Like wealth, income comes from this common origin—from labor. "It is however usual [and this is what this metaphysics entails] to recognize three types of income under the name of rent, profit and wages, as coming from the three different sources, the earth, accumulated capital and labor." We must lift the veil of monetary exchange to see what the phenomena really entail. "On closer inspection one realizes that these three divisions are three different ways in which to share in the fruits of the work of man." The worker produces by his daily labor more than his daily expenditure. But the landowner and the capitalist, thanks to the ownership of the instruments of production, have forced the worker to hand back to them the surplus "over and above his daily needs." The surplus constitutes the landowner's rent and the capitalist's profit. What remains forms the worker's wage. The worker has become the proletarian. "The latter is the man for whom what he needs to work and not die has been calculated exactly." "The master alone profited from the increase in productive power."[153]

Contrary to the trivial manner in which capital is identified with the material elements of the labor process, which in fact are common to all forms of production, Sismondi shows that *it is in the nature of capital that its function of exploiting the labor of others is determined*, that is, its power of taking possession of what the worker creates over and above what he has received from the capitalist in the form of wages. "Every time the rich man obtained a gain from using labor, he was situated, in all points, exactly as the husbandman who sows the ground. The wages paid to his workmen were a kind of seed which he entrusted to them, and expected in a given time to bring forth fruit." The capitalist knew "that this sowing would bring him a harvest,"[154] a "commodity, *of a greater value*," namely, what he would obtain in return, "first of all a value equal to . . . in total the capital he had employed" and subsequently a "*surplus* of goods he called his profit."[155] Here Sismondi opposes the idea, widespread then and later, that the capitalist's profit derives *from circulation* and, as a result, from what the capitalist sells for a higher price

152. Sismondi, *New Principles of Political Economy*, 68.
153. Sismondi, *Études*, vol. 1, 22; *New Principles of Political Economy*, 62, 80, 81, 83. So Marx's critique does not apply to Sismondi: "These bourgeois economists . . . instinctively and rightly saw that it was very dangerous to penetrate too deeply into the burning question of the origin of surplus-value." *Capital*, vol. 1, 651–52.
154. Sismondi, *New Principles of Political Economy*, 83.
155. Ibid., 81, 83. [Grossman's emphasis.]

than he paid for it; that, in a word, he sells above the value of the commodity (profit upon alienation).[156] Sismondi draws out the possibility of the capitalist making a profit even when he sells the commodity *according* to its value, that is to say, at the cost price measured by labor. "He does not profit because his enterprise produced much more than its costs, but because he does not pay all the costs." "The advantage of an employer of labor is often nothing else than the plunder of the worker he hired."[157] However, not only is the new capital *born* from the exploitation of the labor of others, but the already existing capital is likewise *preserved* by this exploitation.[158] "All wealth which one does not wish to destroy, must be exchanged against a future wealth that labor must produce. Wages were the price at which the rich man obtained the poor man's labor in exchange."[159] Thanks to that alone, capital "employed . . . to feed his productive workers . . . was a permanent, multiplying value which did not perish anymore." This value was detached from its material substratum; "it remained like a metaphysical and nonsubstantial quantity." Thus the real function of capital consists in the fact that, in the hands of the capitalist, it becomes a "fruit-bearing portion of accumulated wealth," an abstract value detached from its material base and constantly engendering a new value: it is a "multiplying value."[160]

Here we have the theory of "surplus value" set out with regard to both form and content, with a precision that nobody before Karl Marx had achieved. Sismondi explains here not only the particular forms of surplus value—rent, profit, interest and so on—but he considers it in its general and not yet differentiated form and seeks its origin not in the sphere of circulation but in that of *production*.

It is from this theoretical standpoint that Sismondi evaluates the ideology of unlimited labor and of endless production as propagated by the classical school. "Modern economists . . . do not cease to encourage nations to produce." They forget that "man does not tire himself, except to rest thereafter." Now, in the capitalist system things are quite different, because "today effort is separated from reward: it is not the same man who works and then rests; but it is because one man labors that the other can rest."[161]

So it is only in this system based on "the cooperation of the two classes of citizens with opposing interests . . . I mean the class of proprietors of accumulated labor . . . and the class of men who have only their natural strength" that superfluous production is possible.[162] If everyone had to devote their own labor to their luxury items, "there would not be one [manual worker] who would hesitate to choose less luxury and more

---

156. [English in Grossman's original text.]

157. Sismondi, *New Principles of Political Economy*, 83.

158. As we can see, Franz Oppenheimer is mistaken when he claims that Marx is the first "who recognized capital as a social relationship when *all his predecessors* had regarded it as a *thing*." *Kapitalismus, Kommunismus, Wissenschaftlicher Sozialismus*, 92. [German in Grossman's original text.]

159. Sismondi, *New Principles of Political Economy*, 82.

160. Ibid., 81.

161. Ibid., 74.

162. Ibid., 577. [See also Sismondi, *Nouveau principes d'économie politique*, vol. 2, 347. The published English translation has been modified to correct a serious inaccuracy.]

leisure." "Luxury is only possible if it is bought with the labor of others." So luxury is possible only because workers "produce wealth, and themselves obtain scarcely any share of it."[163]

Without any doubt, the theory of exploitation and of unequal distribution that is set out here is, by its purely objective economic argument, the product of a mature theoretical analysis, much better than the views of the contemporary English "egalitarian socialists" such as William Thompson, [John Francis] Bray, [John] Gray, and [Thomas] Hodgskin, who are not free from ethical judgment. But despite all the originality of the conceptions set out here, nothing would be more false than to claim that Sismondi saw the cause of crises in unequal distribution and in the underconsumption of the working masses and that he should be given credit for first propounding the theory that [Karl] Rodbertus took up in Germany a quarter of a century later.[164] Sismondi's analysis penetrates much more deeply into the very essence of the economic system based on exchange.

As in the capitalist system based on wage labor, labor itself (the vital force) has become a commodity that is bought and sold, and at the same time the valuation of labor operates as on the commodity market, in terms of money, that is, in abstract value; all the disruptions arising from the application of this *changing unit of measurement*, which we have observed on the commodity market, also appear on the labor market and thus merely accentuate the general anarchy of production. In the "pure" capitalist system analyzed by Sismondi, which is composed, as we know, solely of capitalists and workers, the former possess, at the end of the period of production A, all the product created by the latter during this period. Part of this product serves for the reproduction of fixed capital expended on this production, the remainder being given over to the consumption of capitalists and workers. Now, the part, destined for the maintenance of workers in the future period of production B, possesses—since it results from production during period A—an exchange value determined by the labor used in producing it and suffices to employ a specific number of workers in the given labor. But this workers' wage is a changing quantity taking into account their competition, that is to say, taking into account the fact that, just as on the commodity market nobody has fixed the number of producers required in a certain branch, so on the labor market nobody fixes the number of workers necessary for production. If in period B there are too many workers in relation to the capitalists' demand, their wage, that is, the value of labor (the vital force), is lowered. "If the value of his labor should be determined by competition, this value could diminish endlessly."[165] Therefore this same part of the annual product of period A, destined for the maintenance of workers, is now, in period B, sufficient to pay a greater number of workers and by this very fact to absorb a greater quantity of labor. "Wages do not represent an absolute quantity of labor, but only a quantity of goods which has sufficed to maintain the workers in the

---

163. Sismondi, *New Principles of Political Economy*, 75, 285. [Translator's interpolation.]
164. [Rodbertus, *Overproduction and Crises*.]
165. Sismondi, *New Principles of Political Economy*, 321.

previous year." Given the changed value of labor (of labor power), "the same quantity of provisions will set in motion, in the following year, a larger or smaller amount of labor."[166] The source of the disruption of economic equilibrium results precisely from the fact that in employing workers use has been made of an abstract measure of exchange values. The number of workers necessary to create the specific quantity of necessary products is in fact at the given moment a fixed amount, depending on the available technology and entirely independent of the level of the wage. But instead of this natural regulator, we use exchange value to establish the number of workers necessary.

> It is the income of the past year that must pay for the output of this year: it is a *predetermined* quantity that serves as a standard for the *undefined* quantity of labor *to come*. The error of those who urge an unlimited production comes from their mistaking this past income for future income.[167]

Therefore, although he does not need a greater number of workers, every capitalist who possesses a capital enlarges production in proportion to the cheapness of the labor force. "The masters are persuaded to produce an output, not because the consumer asks them for it, but because the workers offer to them to do it at a lower price."[168] The natural measure for fixing the number of workers necessary has been replaced by abstract value. *Wertrechnung* has been substituted for *Naturalrechnung*.[169] In total, an excessive number of workers are employed on a reduced wage; total annual production increases, although demand has not changed; the total income of the working class is reduced. Result: overproduction and crisis.

So we see that the mechanism which we have just described has nothing in common with the question of the unequal distribution of wealth, nor yet with underconsumption by the workers. Far from that being the case, intensified underconsumption is the *result* and not the *cause* of the crisis. On the other hand, the disproportion in production is the consequence of the application of a changing abstract measure to regulate the size of the productive apparatus in relation to needs—exchange value and not a natural measure: the quantity of necessary real goods, consequently the necessary quantity of labor power. "*It is the confusion between the estimation of a use value and that of an exchange value which is at the heart of the deception of modern systems of chrematistics*."[170]

CR

The results we have arrived at are entirely different from perspectives that have previously been accepted. Capitalism is an economic form in which all economic categories appear in the form of exchange value. But this form of exchange value is only

---

166. Ibid., 93.
167. Ibid., 104. [Grossman's emphasis.]
168. Sismondi, "On the Balance," 635.
169. ["Calculation of value"; "calculation in kind."]
170. Sismondi, *Études*, vol. 2, 229. [Grossman's emphasis.]

accidental, only belonging to a certain historical period and in no way constitutes the real substance of these categories. Thus, for example, the category of income appears in the exchange system in the form of a specific exchange value. But the category of income in no way depends on this form. It is an absolute category, belonging to every sort of organization of labor, hence also to the system without exchange. In this system, "there is no numerical price, since there is no exchange as yet; and nevertheless the idea of income is developed there much more clearly than in our complex societies." This income consists of "a specific *quantity* of food, clothing and furniture."[171] And it is only the introduction of an abstract exchange value, measured by labor, in the capacity of a regulator of production that has brought constant disruptions and upheavals into all economic relations. Constant technical upheavals, by the very nature of things, must in fact lead to a depreciation of labor and thereby to constant changes in the size of the standard by which we measure the value of all other goods and regulate the scale of their production. Thus, instead of a proportional relation between production and demand, a constant disproportion between them necessarily appears.

☙

It is a curious fact that these ideas of Sismondi have not been noticed; our mind is so accustomed to the routine categories in which we think about the capitalist economy that we have not been in a position to understand a system whose conceptions unfold along a quite different course. There is, however, an exception: Karl Marx alone got to the bottom of Sismondi's system and understood it clearly, although he only mentioned it in very brief notes almost in the form of aphorisms. It is true that in *The Poverty of Philosophy* (1847) he calls Sismondi reactionary and in the *Communist Manifesto* the head of the school of petty-bourgeois socialism.[172] But this negative attitude of Marx toward Sismondi's proposals for reform in no way detracts from his correct evaluation of the latter's theoretical ideas. For the English socialists contemporary with Sismondi and still today for many of Marx's epigones and hostile critics, the theory of value based on *labor* has an ethical character. They see something ennobling in it and at the same time a revolutionary postulate: a just basis for determining the reward for future labor, that is, for the distribution of the social product among the producers.[173] But Sismondi and later Marx see in it, on the contrary, a source of all the ills of current economic organi-

---

171. Sismondi, *Études*, vol. 1, 137, 138. [Grossman's emphasis.]

172. Marx, *The Poverty of Philosophy*, 137; Marx and Engels, *Manifesto of the Communist Party*, 509.

173. "Marx would like to reward every working citizen, if possible, with mathematical precision and believes this goal can be reached if a quantity of goods, as wages, equal to the particular quantity of values each has contributed to the national product, is allocated to every individual." "Marx demands that labor will form the measure for the distribution of goods." Kleinwächter, *Grundlagen der wissenschaftlichen Sozialismus*, 65, 68. [German in Grossman's original text.] "Marx's great merit is having uncovered *the world of daily work*. . . . We are bringing [!] in a new era, an era of detailed democratic work . . . social equality is founded on equality of work. . . . That, I would say, is the significance of Marx's theory of value." Masaryk, *Masaryk on Marx*, 237. [German in Grossman's original text; Grossman's emphasis.]

zation. They conceive labor as the source of exchange value not for ethical reasons but because an objective analysis of the phenomena of value and prices shows, in their view, a causal dependency between labor and value. But they never go so far as to idealize and "ennoble" labor as the source of exchange value. On the contrary, Sismondi finds in this fact the real source of all ills, of all economic crises; and Marx takes the same position in his polemic with Proudhon. "Labor time," Marx says, "serving as the measure of marketable value *becomes in this way the law of the continual depreciation of labor. . . .* Sismondi . . . sees in this 'value constituted' by labor time the source of all the contradictions of modern industry and commerce."[174] And in agreement with Sismondi, Marx develops the former's thought: "The continual depreciation of labor is only one side, *one consequence of the evaluation of commodities by labor time.* The excessive raising of prices, *overproduction and many other features of industrial anarchy have their explanation in the mode of evaluation.*" "Instead of a 'proportional relation,' we have a disproportional relation."[175]

In our view, not enough notice has been taken of this passage, whose connection with the whole of Marx's theory has not been sufficiently brought to light. Crises and overproduction, the relations of economic disproportion, are here, in conformity with Sismondi, deduced not from the unequal distribution of wealth nor from the fact of the underconsumption of the working class but rather *from the fundamental fact* on which the whole edifice of the capitalist system rests: that *labor time serves as a measure for exchange value* and that as a result all relations of exchange are based on a variable measure, constantly changing and constantly devaluing. In fact "every new invention," every perfected machine, depreciates labor and by that very fact the measure of exchange on which the capitalist system is based. That is why, when large industry has set out systematically to apply these new inventions, these new machines, disturbances have become a necessary and constant phenomenon—hence the criticism that Sismondi directs against machines. And after him Marx: "With the birth of large-scale industry this correct proportion [between supply and demand] had to come to an end, and production is inevitably compelled to pass in continuous succession through vicissitudes of prosperity, depression, crisis, stagnation, renewed prosperity, and so on."[176]

Some months later, in the *Communist Manifesto*, Marx declares that Sismondi's concrete proposals are reactionary and simultaneously utopian. But with a flattering deference that is very unusual in his writings, Marx stresses the "great acuteness" with which Sismondi analyzed the contradictions of the new relations of production. Sismondi's school

> laid bare the hypocritical apologies of economists. It proved, incontrovertibly, the disastrous effects of machinery and division of labor; the concentration of capital and land in a few hands; over-production and crises; it pointed out the inevitable ruin of the

---

174. Marx, *The Poverty of Philosophy*, 135. [Grossman's emphasis, apart from *depreciation*.]
175. Ibid., 136. [Grossman's emphasis.]
176. Ibid., 137.

petty bourgeois and peasant, the misery of the proletariat, the anarchy in production, the crying inequalities in the distribution of wealth, the industrial war of extermination between nations.[177]

Marx comes back to Sismondi again in his *Theories of Surplus Value*, written around 1865.[178] "Sismondi," he says,

is profoundly conscious of the contradictions in capitalist production; he is aware that . . . contradictions of use value and exchange value, commodity and money, purchase and sale, capital and wage labor, etc., assume ever greater dimensions as productive power develops. He is particularly aware of the fundamental contradiction: on the one hand, unrestricted development of the productive power and increase of wealth which, at the same time, consists of commodities and must be turned into cash; on the other hand, the system is based on the fact that the mass of producers is restricted to the necessaries. Hence, according to Sismondi, crises are not accidental, as Ricardo maintains, but essential outbreaks—occurring on a large scale and at definite periods—of the immanent contradictions.[179]

"*Sismondi was epoch-making in political economy* because he had an inkling of this contradiction."[180] Likewise, in *A Contribution to the Critique of Political Economy* (1859), Marx, clearly making the connection with Sismondi's analysis of the definition of "socially necessary" labor, stresses Sismondi's conception of "the antithesis of use value and exchange value."[181]

Even more important than these critical commentaries by Marx is the positive theory he formulated in *A Contribution to the Critique of Political Economy* and later in *Capital*, which for its part is only the deeper and more complete development of the conception that we already find briefly stated in Sismondi in his account of the contradiction between use value and exchange value.

In view of the preceding, [Charles] Andler's efforts to show the indirect influence on Marx of the epigones of Sismondi—[Eugène] Buret, [François] Vidal, and [Constantin] Pecqueur—seem superfluous, since it is possible to show the direct influence of Sismondi himself.[182]

But the problem entails defining the nature of this influence. Can we agree with Rist when he claims that of all the ideas Marx borrows from Sismondi, the most important is that of the *concentration* of fortunes among a small number of property owners and the growing proletarianization of the working masses? According to Rist, "this conception is the pivot of the *Manifesto* and forms a part of the very foundation of

177. Marx and Engels, *Manifesto of the Communist Party*, 509–10.

178. [Subsequent investigations have identified 1861–63 as the period during which Marx wrote the "Economic Manuscript of 1861–63" (*Marx and Engels Collected Works*, vols. 30–34), which was the basis for the posthumously published *Theories of Surplus Value*, edited by Karl Kautsky.]

179. Marx, "Economic Manuscript of 1861–63 [Notebooks XII to XV]," 247–48.

180. Ibid., 393. [Grossman's emphasis.]

181. Marx, *Contribution to the Critique*, 300.

182. Andler, *Introduction historique et commentaire*, 110, 175.

Marxian collectivism."[183] It belongs to Sismondi. Nothing could be more wrong. The concentration of fortunes and the proletarianization of the working masses are in no way theoretical *ideas* but empirical observations of the effects of economic evolution, frequently commented upon from the middle of the eighteenth century onward.[184] Marx had no need to borrow from Sismondi facts that were established by the industrial statistics of contemporary England. But what Rist does not see, what he does not understand, are the deep *causes* that necessarily conditioned this concentration of wealth at one pole and the poverty of the working classes at the other. What Sismondi proposes to do is precisely to *explain* these phenomena. Just as on this point Sismondi's fundamental idea has not been understood, has not even been noticed, likewise the genetic link between these conceptions of Sismondi and Marx's fundamental conception has not been noticed.

3. Sismondi's Social Policy: Conclusions

Attention has often been drawn to the inconsistency of Sismondi's conclusions and the contradictory nature of the means he proposed. He has sometimes been seen as the representative of the illusions of the petty bourgeoisie, sometimes as a timorous reformer who aims to get rid of "the abuses" of the present system without wishing to shake its foundations.

We have tried to show that Sismondi's strength and originality lie primarily in his theoretical analysis: he explains and understands the capitalist mechanism, while social policy has only a very modest place in his thought. Certainly, Sismondi never went so far as to make the practical conclusions drawn from his theory immediately concrete in a *clear program of action*. On the contrary, he proclaimed that "one can never rely with any certitude on even the best-established theories."[185] This conviction made him cautious as far as programs were concerned and forced him to restrict his proposals to the directly felt needs of the time. Moreover, clearly formulating programs of action for the future would have been difficult at a time when the capitalist system was only just emerging from the old organization.

But is it true, as Andler and Gonnard insist, that all Sismondi's reforming thought could be reduced to the proposal for "insurance legislation," for a "professional guarantee";[186] that Sismondi was *merely* concerned to restore to the worker a protection comparable to that which the guilds had provided; that his positive program of interventionism only asked the state to intervene in order to mitigate the effects of competition, to protect the weak against the strong, and in order "that the trade and agri-

---

183. Rist, "Sismondi and the Origins," 198.
184. "Wealth . . . accumulates gradually in a small number of hands; to favour a few skilful citizens, all the rest are reduced to indigence." Holbach, *Système social*, vol. 3, 74.
185. Sismondi, "On the Balance," 332.
186. [That is, provision of income by employers to employees who are no longer able to work.]

cultural employers should be formed into compulsory insurance societies, required to meet the needs of their workers in case of unemployment or distress"?[187] In the face of this opinion we nonetheless think that the position adopted by Sismondi in theory, the main feature of his diagnosis of the disease of the economic system, will facilitate our understanding of the means he proposes to cure it: perhaps then it will appear that the contradictions he is criticized for are sometimes only apparent and that in his proposals there is perhaps something more than what has been noticed thus far.

Sismondi's diagnosis has established that the disproportion of the productive apparatus in relation to demand is the inevitable consequence of the application of the abstract measure, always variable, of exchange value, as the regulator of this production. This measure is the necessary result of the present economic organization, based on the free competition of an arbitrary number of producers who are independent of each other and remain in a social union solely as a result of exchange. In these conditions, the disturbances and conflicts of the capitalist system cannot be avoided and necessarily occur in the system, just as in the economic doctrine which reflects it there are "*insoluble questions like all those in modern political economy*." Sometimes, for example, every effort has been made to force the worker to do excessive labor, and at the same time "there was no hesitation in condemning him to not working at all."[188]

The man who characterized the disease in this way, who saw in it the defect that constituted the very foundation of the current system, who, for this reason, criticized the economic science of his time for basing itself on abstract exchange value and thus finding itself in the dead end of "insoluble questions"—this man was bound to see a remedy in the reconstruction of the very foundation of the current system. If the root of the evil lies in organization based *on exchange* with its necessary consequence, an abstract measure of value, then a radical cure can be obtained only by basing the economic organization on quite different foundations: on movement toward a system *without exchange value*.

Is such a program to be found in Sismondi? Did he identify all the implications of the principles he laid down? We can only affirm one thing with certainty: that Sismondi possessed, if not the *postulation*, at least the *ideal* of a better system in the future. Although he has been accused of yearning for a past state of affairs, he says, "I do not desire any part of what has been, but I want something better of what is." He is interested in the past only as a historian and in order to draw lessons. "I cannot judge what that is, except by comparing it with the past, and I am far from wanting to restore ancient ruins." He is equally opposed to the present and his objections are directed against "the new organization of society which . . . gives [the working man] no guarantee against . . . competition." In defending the ideal that he pursues he cites various sociological arguments, denounces those who consider the defects of the present system to be inevitable and who declare that things must always be the same because this present system cannot be changed. "It

187. Andler, *Introduction historique et commentaire*, 177; Gonnard, *Histoire des doctrines économiques*, 213.
188. Sismondi, *Études*, vol. 1, 197. [Grossman's emphasis.]

is the belief in a sort of *fatality* which carries us along and a tendency to close our eyes to the precipice we are running toward, as soon as we think we cannot avoid it."[189] These people are so accustomed to the present system that they cannot even imagine a different one. "Our senses have become so accustomed to this new organization of society, to that universal competition which degenerates into hostility between the wealthy class and the working class, that we can no longer imagine any *other type of existence*."[190]

In opposition to this fatalism, resulting from the conviction that the existing system cannot be changed, Sismondi *describes the historical evolution of systems*. Society has the potential for modification, "for the organization of human society is our own work." Contemporary organization is, in fact, something very recent. "This organization is so new that it is not even halfway instituted." So it would be difficult to believe that it will last indefinitely: it has scarcely emerged from former systems that themselves had been modified in their turn. Each of these former systems had become a dominant organization because it had shown itself to be superior to the system that had immediately preceded it. "Each of these systems had seemed . . . to be an advance towards civilization. . . . *Slavery* itself followed a savage condition of universal war . . . [and,] following the slaying of prisoners, constituted progress in society."[191] And it was only in the long term that this system became an obstacle to further progress and contributed to the fall of the ancient world. Then came the feudal period, based on *bondage* and *serfdom*. This meant "an initial betterment in the status of the poor classes." "Feudalism had its shining and prosperous period," and it was only in the long term that the feudal system "became intolerable,"[192] for "social order, threatened so incessantly, cannot be maintained except by violent means." It then gave way to the system of *corporations* and finally to "the system *of liberty* we have now. . . . The revolution is not even half completed."[193] In the face of this historical evolution, can we claim that the "wage labor system" is the final stage of progress, since we cannot imagine that anything better will follow it? "When these three systems were dominant, likewise nobody conceived what might come next; *similarly the amendment of the existing order would have seemed either impossible or absurd*." If we base ourselves on the fact that the former systems proved themselves to be disastrous, in short "because, after having first done a little good, they later imposed terrible calamities onto the human race, can we then conclude that today we have moved into the true form of society?" From the preceding argument, the conclusion necessarily follows that "our actual social organization . . . the dependency of the worker"[194] is also historically temporary and will be replaced by a superior system in the future.[195] This will only happen when we "discover the fundamental evil of the

---

189. Sismondi, "On the Balance," 628; *Études*, vol. 2, 335. [Grossman's emphasis.]
190. Sismondi, "On the Balance," 628; *Études*, vol. 1, 92.
191. Sismondi, *Études*, vol. 2, 372; "On the Balance," 628, 629. [Grossman's emphasis; editor's interpolation.]
192. Sismondi, *New Principles of Political Economy*, 171; "On the Balance," 629.
193. Sismondi, *New Principles of Political Economy*, 170; "On the Balance," 629–30. [Grossman's emphasis.]
194. Sismondi, *Études*, vol. 1, 92; *New Principles of Political Economy*, 557–58. [Grossman's emphasis.]
195. Marx rightly points out that Sismondi had "the inkling that *new* forms of the appropriation of wealth

day labor system, as we have discovered the evils of slavery, of serfdom, of guilds." And it was only in thinking about this future system that Sismondi could say: "A time will doubtless come when our descendants will consider us no less barbarous for having left the working classes without protection than they and we ourselves consider as barbarous those nations which reduced those same classes to slavery."[196]

That is why Charles Rist tries in vain to interpret Sismondi's thought by arguing that the latter's criticisms are directed against the "abuses of competition,"[197] that he has shown the defects belonging to a period of transition between the old and new forms of social organization, and that the whole substance of his doctrine can be reduced to "the *protest he makes against the indifference* of the classical school in the face of the evils of these periods of transition." And Rist adds: "But Sismondi was a historian. His interest lay primarily in those *periods of transition which formed the exit from one regime and the entrance into another*, and which involved so much suffering for the innocent."[198]

To write in these terms is to obscure the very meaning of Sismondi's thought. No, he is not criticizing the periods of transition from one system to another but rather the very foundations of the present system—not the "abuses" of competition but the very principle of competition. Overproduction with all its consequences is not a temporary phenomenon but "the satiation of markets is on the contrary the inevitable result of a system to which everyone rushes;" it is the unavoidable effect of the "fundamental evil of the day labor system." Hence this is not a short-term phenomenon of the period of transition between the old and new organization but a phenomenon rooted in the defective structure of the new system, which is still establishing itself and will make itself felt more and more as this system develops and becomes the dominant economic form. This is what Sismondi expresses with the greatest possible clarity in his polemic with Jean-Baptiste Say in 1824: "For seven years I have pointed to that sickness of the body social, and for seven years it has not ceased to grow. I cannot see in such extended suffering *the frictions that always accompany change* and . . . I believe I have shown that the ills we experience are the *necessary consequences of the flaws of our system*, and that they are not yet at an end." And some years later, in his *Studies*, Sismondi can claim that the disease is making fresh progress and that although we are in a period of rare prosperity, "its only effect is to continually worsen the position of the poor classes."[199]

If, therefore, it seems certain that Sismondi foresees, for the future, the need for a system that is better than the present one based on competition, for the particular reasons we will set out below, he never draws a picture of this system. Anticipating the objection that he should "show what remained to do," he states, "We would want

---

must correspond to productive forces . . . that the bourgeois forms are only transitory and contradictory forms." "Economic Manuscript of 1861–63 [Notebooks XII to XV]," 248. [Grossman's emphasis.]

196. Sismondi, "On the Balance," 629; Sismondi, *Études*, vol. 1, 93.

197. Rist, "Sismondi and the Origins," 193.

198. Ibid., 181. [Grossman's emphasis.]

199. Sismondi, *New Principles of Political Economy*, 280; "Notes on an Article by M. Say," 647; *Études*, vol. 2, 334. [Grossman's emphasis, apart from *the frictions*.]

permission to convince the economists . . . that their science hereafter follows a *false* path. But we have not enough confidence in ourselves to show them what would be the *truth*." Yet in his eyes shines the ideal of a better system in the future, and he is not merely thinking of small corrections to the present social order: this omission results precisely from the fact that he insists on the *difficulty of conceiving* this future system. "It is one of the greatest efforts to which we can force our mind to visualize the actual structure of society. Who would then be the man enlightened enough to imagine *a structure that does not yet exist*, to see the future where we have already so much trouble to see the present?" Conceiving of a completely different system alone is difficult, while conceiving of detailed corrections would not be difficult at all. However, anticipating the tactics of socialism in the future, Sismondi merely shows the necessity of the advent of a superior system in the future but, at the same time, wants to confine himself to "the analysis of the system we have taken up"—"without being distracted by a comparison with an *entirely imaginary theory*" and "before dreaming of what will have to *replace*" the existing system.[200]

What could drive Sismondi to act in this way? We have already pointed out his scientific caution about formulating a program of action that, at most, could only have been "an entirely imaginary theory." But Sismondi mentions another reason, an even more serious one. For him, as a theoretician, the problem is above all to explain the existing mechanism and to discover its "fundamental evil," since, as we know, that is in his opinion the necessary condition for achieving the future system. That is why Sismondi does not want to indicate concrete means of change. "If I presented here what I consider to be a remedy for the actual ills of society, criticism would abandon the *examination* . . . of such ills, in order to judge my *remedy*, and to probably condemn it, and the question of the balance of consumption with production would never be decided."[201] This passage justifies us in concluding that Sismondi has what he considers a "remedy" for the ills of the social system, and if he does not set it out, it is solely in order not to distract attention from his theoretical aim: to establish the diagnosis of the sickness from which the system of his time is suffering. Moreover, the fact that concrete plans for remedying the situation had little success is demonstrated by those of the reformers of this time, Charles Fourier and Just Muiron, whose works had recently been published. So it is precisely because he does not go into detail that Sismondi is superior to these utopian socialists. While they draw up fanciful plans, Sismondi *through his critique undermines the very foundations of the system of his time* and indicates that "undoubtedly there is something wrong in the social order." For Sismondi this critique of the elements that make up this system is for the moment the essential thing, by reason of the passivity of the human mind, which is afraid of straying from principles once they have been accepted. "We have to fight against this laziness of the human mind, which, having reached the last results of a science, refuses to return to its first principles and

---

200. Sismondi, "On the Balance," 634. [Grossman's emphasis.]
201. Ibid., 634–35. [Grossman's emphasis.]

to shake the axioms on which it is based."[202]

Obviously the critique of these basic principles of the existing system, in itself, highlights in broad outline *the positive direction* of Sismondi's thought. He is thinking of an ideal organization in which *competition* among producers independent from each other will be replaced by a *rational regulation* of the scale of production according to the extent of need, independently of exchange and the oscillations of market prices. "It would not suit national security if its subsistence were to depend on the fluctuations of the market," he says with reference to agricultural production. We have seen above that it is on this *proportionality of the process of production to the needs* of society that Sismondi's *New Principles* is based and that this is the key point on which he differs fundamentally from Say, Ricardo, Malthus, and McCulloch. It is this ideal of a well-proportioned economic system that inspires Sismondi to this comparison: "All movements in society are linked together; one follows from the other, as the various movements of the gears of a watch."[203] In this well-regulated system, without free competition, human activity will find an outlet, not in the struggle of men against men but in the struggle to dominate nature. "It is not that there is no room for the progress of human effort in the creation of wealth every time that . . . man battles against nature, and not with another man."[204]

In an ideal system without competition, in which production is organized systematically in each of its branches, any change, such as for example the extension of production, cannot be brought about in one branch to the exclusion of another but must be achieved systematically for all branches, if the equilibrium of the system is not to be upset. "When [the progress of wealth] . . . is *well-proportioned*, when no one of its parts follows a precipitous course, it spreads universal well-being; but *if any one of its gears completes its actions earlier than all the others, there will be suffering*."[205]

---

202. Sismondi, *Études*, vol. 2, 334.

203. Sismondi, *New Principles of Political Economy*, 203; "On the Balance," 637.

204. Sismondi, *New Principles of Political Economy*, 306.

205. Ibid. [Grossman's emphasis.] The arithmetical diagram in the essay against Ricardo [Sismondi, "On the Balance," 621–27] is nothing but an attempt to establish, in a precise manner, *exactly determined quantitative proportions* for the extent of production in each of the branches of social activity. By accepting that, given a particular technology and a level of wages, agriculture employs ten people, Sismondi concludes that, to obtain equilibrium in the system, it is necessary to distribute the dimensions of production in such a way that the industrial capitalist employs 23 1/3 workers in industry producing indispensable articles and 1 2/3 workers in industry producing luxury articles, which—together with the ten agricultural workers and two entrepreneurs—makes a total of forty persons. It is only in these exactly determined proportions of the various branches of production and in the condition of constant value that equilibrium between consumption and production would be possible. But this constant value is not compatible with the exchange system where value, as a result of ceaseless technical revolutions, is subject to endless fluctuations, every time a technical improvement increasing the productivity of labor is introduced and by this very fact labor is depreciated in the given branch. As Sismondi shows, overproduction and disruption of equilibrium must and do in fact result, although, according to our author [Ricardo], this is not possible for the system based on exchange. Therefore, in opposition to the classical economists, Sismondi proves that in a system based on the abstract measure of exchange value a *constant disproportion* must result. That is why he attempts to fix the proportion of production in each branch according to a different principle, without having recourse to the measure of exchange value, and notably according to *the principle of the real proportions* of the extent of the productive apparatus in relation to the extent of needs.

Obviously this quantitative determination of the proportions of various branches of production cannot be the product of chance but must rather be the result of concerted action by the central authority. Sismondi therefore requires that the government should halt "a *disordered* expansion."[206] According to him, "the task of government should be to moderate these movements, *in order to equalize* them."[207] Envisaged from this point of view and under the influence of the Italian economic tradition of the eighteenth century,[208] political economy would become "a science of government" in the same sense as [Henri] Saint-Simon understands it when he speaks of the need to replace the present system "by an administrative system" or, again, what the German theoreticians understood by *Verwaltungswirtschaft*.[209] Chrematistics, that is, the free activity of individual producers, is replaced by a systematic *regulation* of the economy according to the principle of nonexchange, in other words by "household management" in the Aristotelian sense of *oikonomia*. "We consider political economy, the management of the house and the community, as being essentially the science of government. It amounts to . . . the *exposition of the plan of management* or influence that will be the most advantageous to society."[210]

This general principle, which Sismondi does not set out in detail, entails the ideal he aims at and, in the system of his thought, constitutes the *maximum program*, the fundamental "remedy" for the sickness he identifies in the economic system. If Sismondi does not indicate remedies, his caution is mainly related to this part of his ideas, to this maximum program. Should we see a contradiction if, in the face of the statement that he does not want to indicate remedies, he nonetheless indicates them repeatedly and in places only a few pages apart? For example, when he proposes to abolish all laws that interfere with the division of inheritances, or that protect employers' organizations against workers, or when he demands laws that could oblige the employer to guarantee the subsistence of the worker he employs, and so on. Or again when he proposes to guarantee every worker an assured ownership of his own labor in order to put limits on competition.[211] Let us examine the question more closely.

In Sismondi's theoretical thought, the real cure for the disease is possible only through a change in the structure of the present system. For him it is the only effective means of cleansing. Sismondi does not develop this question—we have already examined why—but he is convinced that this idea will be victorious in the future and prepares this victory by enlightening public opinion theoretically, while confining himself to posing practical conclusions for the present. "But *for as long as the present organization persists*, as long as the existence of the poor person is abandoned to the effects of free competition,"[212] it is necessary above all to *alleviate the effects* of this system by creating

---

206. Sismondi, *New Principles of Political Economy*, 312. [Grossman's emphasis.]

207. Ibid., 306. [Grossman's emphasis.]

208. Gonnard, *Histoire des doctrines économiques*, 206.

209. ["Administered economy."]

210. Sismondi, *Études*, vol. 2, 238. [Grossman's emphasis.]

211. Sismondi, "On the Balance," 636; *New Principles of Political Economy*, 324.

212. Sismondi, *Études*, vol. 1, 113. [Grossman's emphasis.]

obstacles to the natural tendencies originating in this system, for these obstacles "give time . . . allow to those who have been hurt the opportunity to *recover from their wounds*." Sismondi recommends to the economists "that they should leave the generations made superfluous time *to recover*." For *"first, one has to think of those who suffer, and then worry about the future."* And since, according to him, those who expand large-scale production with a view to personal profit are especially the big capitals, since above all "it is colossal fortunes which disturb the equilibrium of society," he finds here a reason for "legislation to put obstacles both to the accumulation and the amalgamation of capitals."[213]

So we see that Sismondi's struggle against big capital is in no way inspired by the desire for a more equal distribution of wealth or by any aspiration for the organization of medieval guilds. "No, I do not desire any part of what has been . . . I am far from wanting to restore ancient ruins." "It is not in any case the guilds that should be re-established." Moreover, these could not be a solution for workers employed in mechanized manufacturing industry, because "since the great perfection of machines, all those who worked almost like machines have had their influence diminished."[214] Repeatedly he protests that he has no intention of giving up all technical advances, machines, and inventions. If, nonetheless, as we have seen, he wants to create "constraints" on big capital, it is because of his deep pessimism, of the conviction that as long as the system of free competition, the system of wage labor, survives, economic disruptions are inevitable, that no cure could be found for them and that, we must, by means of constraints, slow down the course of this development, only in the interests of the victims of "a system that oppresses."[215]

It is only when one adopts this standpoint that Sismondi becomes comprehensible when he says, "We agree, in fact: to such extreme ills, we can offer only *palliatives* which must seem very much out of proportion." And a little later, he insists again: "To bring a remedy for such grave ills in the present . . . we know only of palliatives. The first and most important thing is *to enlighten opinion* . . ." and later he proposes means to delay development, that is, to attenuate disastrous effects. In this respect he says "that the remedies we are proposing are in no way illegal, in no way revolutionary, and in no way fanciful or requiring a new organization of society."[216] On the basis of these statements it has been denied that Sismondi had an ideal transcending the framework of the existing system. But the means he proposes can only be called palliatives by someone who assumes that no effective remedy exists or who, like Sismondi, recognizes in principle the historical necessity of evolution toward a higher form of organization and considers all other means as ineffective or as palliatives that are only partially effective. These palliatives are Sismondi's *minimum program* "for as long as the present organization survives," and that is why from this point of view "the first and most important remedy is to enlighten opinion." In the first place it is therefore a question of clearly

---

213. Ibid., 110, 113; *New Principles of Political Economy*, 332; Études, vol. 2, 459. [Grossman's emphasis.]
214. Sismondi, "On the Balance," 628; *New Principles of Political Economy*, 323.
215. Sismondi, *New Principles of Political Economy*, 285.
216. Sismondi, *Études*, vol. 2, 335, 363, 372. [Grossman's emphasis.]

realizing the causes of the sickness, of the structural defects of the present system, and that is the prior condition for any future fundamental reorganization.

It is precisely this pessimism that marks Sismondi's interventionism. Rist in fact is wrong to claim that Sismondi was the first interventionist. The mercantilists had also been interventionists. The essential difference consists in the quite distinct way of conceiving the *dynamic* of the economic mechanism. James Steuart, the most eminent representative of mercantilism in the eighteenth century, appeals at every moment for intervention by the authorities. And he does so because, he claims, government intervention can and must *maintain the equilibrium of the economic mechanism*. Sismondi's interventionism has an entirely different character. Half a century of capitalist development had dispelled these illusions, and Sismondi observes that the equilibrium of this mechanism is impossible. If "we invoke almost constantly that intervention of the government," it is merely to *protect the victims of the ills*. "We see the government above all as the protector of the weak against the strong, the defender of him who cannot defend himself."[217] And that is where Sismondi differs from the future party of social reform.

This party demanded the reform of the existing system while preserving the foundations of that system, whereas for Sismondi these were only half-measures, since for him it was the foundations themselves that were defective. The reforming school saw the state as an institution above classes, whose task was to safeguard the totality of social interests. On this point, too, Sismondi is pessimistic. For him *the state is the defender of the possessing class*. "The government, which most often protects the established order without even examining the rights of the parties, [gives] at all times powerful support to the haves against the have-nots."[218] The government gives its assistance to the capitalists against the workers. "While these unfortunates fight for a wage on which their lives and that of their children depend . . . soldiers and constables . . . watch them, who await eagerly the first disturbance to hand them over to the courts and their severe retribution." "The greater part of the charge arising from social establishments, is destined to defend the rich against the poor."[219]

These considerations of Sismondi on governmental power show that he was far from idealizing the current state as the school of social reform would later do.

If, however, he advocates state intervention in favor of the weak, he nonetheless sees in it only *a half-measure for a temporary period*. In principle these disadvantages could only be avoided in a system without competition.

◌੨

And now, to conclude, let us summarize our analysis of Sismondi's work. Can we consider him a socialist? Certainly, if we apply to him the normal criteria for social-

---

217. Sismondi, *New Principles of Political Economy*, 53.
218. Ibid., 446. [Translator's interpolation.]
219. Ibid., 285, 446.

ism—abolition of the private ownership of the means of production, abolition of the difference between rich and poor—Sismondi *was not a socialist*. It is not that he was a stubborn defender of private property. Far from it. While at this time (1818) Saint-Simon, for example, is proclaiming "It is on the preservation of the right of property that the existence of society depends," Sismondi in no way recognizes the perpetual and sacrosanct right to landed property.[220] "It must be judged as all the rest of social institutions, by the good or bad that has flowed from them for mankind." It is "*a gift of society, and in no way a natural right which pre-existed*." As a historian, he knows that many peoples did not have private ownership of land, that the institution of property is the child of historical evolution. The ownership of land is "not based on a principle of *justice*, but on a principle of *public utility*." Hence society can determine the conditions on which it entrusts property to individuals; it can regulate them. If the owners act against the interests of society, society "must submit property in land to legislation which will indeed bring about *the general good*."[221]

Yet despite these ideas about property, and although, as we have seen, his ideal is a system without competition, he never goes so far as to conceive the suppression of private property; he never imagines that the disruptions caused by exchange and exchange itself are phenomena indissolubly linked to an economic organization based on individual property.

Despite this attitude with regard to individual property, and setting the question of property to one side, Sismondi *constructs the ideal of the system without competition*, consciously and systematically regulating the scale of production in relation to the extent of needs. But we will be obliged to see Sismondi as a socialist if in order to analyze socialism as an aim, we adopt a different criterion "which characterizes economic socialism: the condemnation of competition and the appeal to a rational coordination of economic elements which is systematic rather than instinctive."[222] After having inquired on what basis a new organization can be established, Sismondi ends up with the truly original doctrine that such a rationally coordinated organization is not possible for a system based on the abstract measure of exchange value as a regulator of the extent of production. It is precisely on this point that the critique of the existing system and the positive economic views he opposes to it are much more profound and far-reaching than the theoretical statements of the utopian socialists of his time. These socialists, like John Gray, Robert Owen or later [John Francis] Bray and, during the 1848 revolution, Arthur Bonnard and Proudhon, attack only money and aim to abolish only the "privileges" of precious metals, *while preserving trade based on exchange and the exchange* of commodities. They formulate plans for exchange banks where the role of metal money is replaced by a currency based on labor—for example, the plans for certificates of value issued by the National Bank devised by John Gray in 1831 or Owen's Labour Exchange

---

220. Saint-Simon, *Vues sur la propriété*, 265.
221. Sismondi, *New Principles of Political Economy*, 132, 138, 139. [Grossman's emphasis.]
222. Gonnard, *Histoire des doctrines économiques*, 25.

in 1832, Bray's Central Bank in 1839,[223] and then, during the February Revolution in 1848, Proudhon's well-known scheme and Bonnard's Exchange Bank at Marseilles.[224] They thought that by basing exchange not on metal money but rather on labor, they were introducing a "fixed and invariable" measure of value and were thereby ensuring that the worker received the full fruits of his labor.[225] On this point, as we have seen, Sismondi clearly parts company with the utopian socialists and demonstrates—as Marx would later—that since labor is the source of value, this value cannot be fixed, that it must necessarily be subject to endless fluctuations and for this reason provoke upheavals in society. Likewise, Sismondi does not confine himself to merely suppressing monetary exchange but also wants to get rid of all exchange of values. He proposes to destroy not only money as a measure but all measurement of value and to replace this regulator of production with the regulation of the extent of production in the form of real proportions, in natural conditions. In this respect, then, Sismondi's idea is deeper and more consistent than that of the banks of the "exchange socialists."[226]

This is the result of views according to which the system he foresees and conceives would not entail the elaboration of concrete plans for remedies, of exchange banks or small communes dreamed of by certain rationalist socialists like Owen and Fourier, but would have to be the transformation of the present capitalist organization according to new principles of construction in the interests of the toiling classes. "I would seek," he said, "means to guarantee the fruits of labor to those who do the work, to make the machine benefit the one who sets the machine to work."[227] He considers the achievement of this proposition to be impossible within a system based on the measurement of exchange value and ends up with the conception of a system without exchange value. Sismondi strives to posit this new principle for constructing the future system not by way of an arbitrary creative fantasy but through the analysis both of the existing system and of former historical economic formations. In this regard we should see in Sismondi's analysis the first attempts at the method later applied by scientific socialism.

However, Sismondi evades the problem and does not examine how it is possible to abolish all measurement of exchange value as the regulator of the extent of production without abolishing private property. It is precisely on this point that we can apply to Sismondi the legitimate criticism of Marx against the attempts of the utopian socialists to abolish metal money, that "goods are to be *produced as commodities*, but *not exchanged* as

223. See Gray, *The Social System*; Bray, *Labour's Wrongs and Labour's Remedy*. [Cf. Marx, *The Poverty of Philosophy*, 138–44; *Contribution to the Critique*, 320–23.]

224. Gide and Rist, *History of Economic Doctrines*, 316; Knies, *Das Geld*, 240. [In 1849, Proudhon's scheme culminated in the People's Bank, which rapidly failed.]

225. Muckle, *Die grossen Sozialisten*, vol. 1, 53. All saw in labor taken as the basis of exchange the "revolutionary theory" of the emancipation of the proletariat from all exploitation. Marx replied to them: "Thus relative value, measured by labour time, is *inevitably the formula of the present enslavement of the worker*, instead of being, as M Proudhon would have it, the 'revolutionary theory' of the emancipation of the proletariat." [*The Poverty of Philosophy*, 125; Grossman's emphasis.]

226. Aucuy, *Les systèmes socialistes d'échange*.

227. Sismondi, *Études*, vol. 1, 105.

commodities."[228] Marx ridicules those utopian socialists who wish to retain commodities but not money,[229] and he asserts that between the commodity and money there is an "*inevitable correlation*."[230] "Beneath the invisible measure of value lurks hard money."[231] So in this respect Sismondi's idea goes further than the idea of the exchange socialists, but it too stops halfway. Thus Marx's criticism is quite justified when he states that Sismondi "forcefully *criticizes* the contradictions of bourgeois production but *does not understand them*."[232]

Sismondi does not tell us who will bring about or facilitate this evolution, this economic reconstruction of society. He does not address any social class; the proletariat in whose interests he was fighting was in his day a passive mass that was merely wretched. One can apply to Sismondi what Marx said of the theoreticians of the proletariat: "So long as they look for science and merely make systems . . . they see in poverty nothing but poverty, without seeing in it the revolutionary, subversive side."[233] In this respect Sismondi is better than Owen. Moreover, Sismondi's superiority to Saint-Simon is shown by the fact that while the latter foregrounds the struggle of "industry" against feudal reaction and this "industry" includes not only the most heterogenous spheres of agriculture and commerce but also factory owners and workers; in short, it conceals all the real contradictions existing at that time. Sismondi's opposition is completely modern. With a clarity shown by nobody before him, he draws out the antinomy of the class interests of the property owners and of the wage-earning proletariat, "so does Sismondi denounce large industrial capital," and with a penetrating critique he denounces *capitalism*, the scientific discovery of which should be attributed to him.[234]

Certainly Sismondi often deviates from the line we have attempted to characterize; it would be very easy to draw this out and to show contradictions in his fundamental conception. But these deviations merely prove that Sismondi's book is not an academic exercise but is based on living reality. From this heterogeneity of phenomena and in opposition to classical theory, Sismondi has created, in a flash of genius, a homogenous conception on which this heterogeneity of phenomena has here and there left its mark. Whether or not we call him a socialist, his immortal claim to fame in economic science is that he is the first economist to scientifically demonstrate that an economic system based on abstract exchange value as the sole purpose of production and regulator of it necessarily leads to disruptions and to "insoluble questions." It is on this point that Sismondi's doctrine constitutes one of the most important sources for the genesis of the scientific economic thinking of Karl Marx.

---

228. Marx, *Contribution to the Critique*, 322, [Grossman's emphasis.]
229. Ibid., 308.
230. Ibid., 323. [Grossman's emphasis.]
231. Ibid., 308.
232. Marx, "Economic Manuscript of 1861–63 [Notebooks XII to XV]," 248. [Grossman extended Marx's emphasis.]
233. Marx, *The Poverty of Philosophy*, 177–78.
234. Marx, *Contribution to the Critique*, 301.

Fifty Years of Struggle over Marxism

1883–1932[1]

Translated from the German by Rick Kuhn and Einde O'Callaghan

A. Marxists of the Early Period

Until the end of the seventies of the last century, the circumstances for understanding Marx's ideas were not very favorable, even within the socialist camp. A particular difficulty was that *Capital* was initially only available as a torso, the first of several volumes. Almost another three decades passed before the volumes completing the system appeared (the second volume in 1885, the third in 1895). A further fifteen years passed before Karl Kautsky brought out the last of the volumes of *Theories of Surplus Value* (1910). These, intended by Marx as the fourth part of *Capital*, are a magnificent history of political economy from the end of the seventeenth century, one that bourgeois historical writing has been unable to equal.

During the first decade after the founding of the German Empire it was hardly possible to speak of "Marxism" in Germany (and still less in other countries). There was only a very loose connection between the workers' movement and the theories of scientific socialism. Many years after [Ferdinand] Lassalle's death, the German workers' movement was still under the influence of Lassalle's theories and activities. Apart from that, it drew

---

1. Originally published in 1932 as *Fünfzig Jahre Kampf* and in 1933 as "Die Fortentwicklung des Marxismus."

its ideas and sentiments from memories of 1848, from [Pierre-Joseph] Proudhon, [Karl] Rodbertus, and Eugen Dühring.[2] Many socialists justified their demands by appealing to ethics and humanity or oriented themselves on the publications of the International Workingmen's Association.[3] When the two tendencies in the German workers' movement (the so-called "Lassalleans" and the Marxist "Eisenachers")[4] united at the Gotha Congress (1875), Lassalle's ideas and demands were in large part incorporated into the newly agreed Gotha Program (see Marx's criticisms in his *Critique of the Gotha Program*). Initially, workers in large-scale industry were not organized in either party. Rather, the bulk of the movement consisted of workers, such as shoemakers, tailors, book printers, tobacco workers, and so on, who still retained close ties with the petty bourgeoisie. Lassalle's pamphlets and demands, his woolly conception of the state, his complete lack of clarity about the party's goal evidently expressed much more the labor movement's lack of maturity at that time than the cohesive and magnificent edifice of Marx's theory. Even the leading figures in the labor movement were for a long time unable to grasp key aspects of Marx's theory. Characteristic of this is the request in 1868 (by Wilhelm Liebknecht, who, during his stay in London, had had a close relationship with Marx) that Engels make the actual differences between Marx and Lassalle clear in an article for the party organ.[5] From correspondence between Marx and Engels it is apparent how distressed Marx felt about the fact that German party circles were almost unbelievably indifferent to *Capital*.

Only gradually and in constant struggle against other views that were widespread in the labor movement (the struggle against Proudhonism and Bakuninism in the First International, Engels's polemic against Dühring in 1878, and so on) did Marxist ideas permeate the workers' movement. From 1883 Karl Kautsky (born 1854) sought to spread Marxist ideas as the editor of the party's theoretical organ, *Neue Zeit*. However, the period of the Anti-Socialist Laws (1878–90) was quite unfavorable for the theoretical consolidation of Marxism.[6]

The great popularity that Marx's lifework achieved was initially due to those sections of the first volume [of *Capital*] that describe the immediate process of production within the factory and thus make the situation of the working class, its exploitation by capital and everyday class struggles taking place before everyone's eyes intelligible. So the present volume became the "bible" of the working class for decades. The fate of the

2. [From February 1848 a wave of revolutions, starting in Paris, swept east across Europe. Marx wrote critiques of Proudhon, Rodbertus, and Dühring.]

3. [Marx played a vital role in the leadership of the International Workingmen's Association, later known as the First International, between 1864 and 1872, when it moved its seat to Philadelphia. It was shut down in 1876.]

4. [The Social Democratic Workers' Party, led by August Bebel and Wilhelm Liebknecht, who were influenced by Marx, was founded at a congress in Eisenach in 1869. After its fusion with the Lassallean General German Workers' Association in 1875, it became the Socialist Workers' Party of Germany, renamed the Social Democratic Party of Germany in 1890.]

5. [Liebknecht to Friedrich Engels, January 20, 1868, 88.]

6. [The Anti-socialist or Exceptional Law "against the public danger of social-democratic endeavors" banned social-democratic organizations, publications, and trade unions in Germany.]

parts of the work that present the historical tendencies of capitalist accumulation and the tendency toward the breakdown of capitalism that follows in their wake was quite different. Here Marx was so far in advance of his epoch intellectually that these parts of his work, at first, necessarily remained incomprehensible. Capitalism had not yet achieved the maturity that would have made its breakdown and the realization of socialism an immediate reality. So it is understandable that in a review of volume 2 of *Capital* (1886) Kautsky explained that in his opinion the present volume had less interest for the working class than the first, that for them only the production of surplus value in the factory was of importance.[7] The additional question of how this surplus value is realized was of more interest to the capitalists than to the working class! Kautsky's well-known book *The Economic Doctrines of Karl Marx* also exclusively confined itself to describing the contents of the first volume of *Capital*. Only an extremely deficient outline of the theories in the second and third volumes was added to later editions.

Two generations had to pass after the appearance of *Capital* before capitalism, as a result of capital accumulation, matured to its current heights, and conflicts developed in its womb that translated the problem of the realization of socialism from the domain of a programmatic demand, only appropriate for the remote future, to the sphere of daily political practice. The understanding of Marx's ideas has also grown in correspondence with the changed historical situation.

The situation was different after the end of the Anti-Socialist Laws (1890), when the socialist movement started to develop rapidly from a small, persecuted group into the largest party in Germany, and its appeal encompassed broad layers of intellectuals and the petty bourgeoisie, far beyond the working class. Outwardly, the strength of Marxism grew rapidly during this period. In the Erfurt Program (1891) it achieved a victorious expression. But precisely at the time when the appearance of the third volume of *Capital* (1895) publicly concluded Marx's theoretical system, the rapid blossoming of international capitalism and the strengthening of an opportunist labor aristocracy within the working class led to a change which was to be of the greatest significance for the further development of Marxist theory. Sooner or later social differentiation in the working class had to be expressed not only in politics but also in its theoretical conceptions of the goals and tasks of the labor movement.

B. The Advance of Reformism

a. Revisionism

The victory of opportunism, initially in England and then in France and Germany as well as a series of smaller European countries, is necessarily connected with the

---

7. [Kautsky, "*Das Elend der Philosophie*," 164.]

structural transformation of world capitalism, which exhibited extremely powerful development and increasingly showed its imperialist face during the last decade of the previous century. Its fundamental economic traits are the replacement of free competition with monopoly and colonial expansion combined with bellicose entanglements. Through capital exports, monopolistic domination, and exploitation of huge regions that supply raw materials and provide outlets for capital investment in Central and South America, Asia, and Africa, the bourgeoisie and the financial oligarchy of the capitalist great powers acquire billions in superprofits. These make it possible for them to win over an upper layer of the working class and the petty-bourgeois following of the socialist parties with higher wages and various other advantages, so that they take an interest in colonial exploitation, are politically bound to them, and enter a community of interests with them against the broad masses and other countries. These upper layers were the bourgeoisie's channels of influence into the proletariat. The emergence of the labor aristocracy, which found expression politically in the formation of "bourgeois workers' parties" on the model of the Labour Party in England, is typical of all the imperialist countries.

These layers, which found the revolutionary tenets of Marxist theory inconvenient and a hindrance to their practical efforts to cooperate with the bourgeoisie and the organs of the state, soon went onto the offensive against Marxist theory, with the argument that it was contradicted by capitalism's real tendencies. Their main difference with Marxism was that it denied the possibility of a lasting improvement in the conditions of the working class under the current economic order (apart from temporary improvements for shorter periods) and advocated the opposite point of view: that when capitalism reached its full development, its immanent powers would necessarily lead to a worsening of workers' conditions. In contrast, the representatives of reformism pointed out that even under the existing economic order, a lasting improvement in the situation of the workers—whether by means of state legislation (pensions, accident and unemployment insurance) or by means of self-help (by founding and expanding trade unions and consumer cooperatives)—was possible and already occurring. Here the rather slight improvement, confined to a narrow upper layer only, was overvalued and generalized, and its character was misjudged, to the extent that it was not considered temporary but the start of a transformation that was consistently expanding in breadth and depth.

The rising strength of the trade-union movement was, undoubtedly, the most effective lever for the enforcement of antiradical attitudes. For the leaders of the trade unions—the typical representatives of the labor aristocracy—reformism was tailor-made. For these men, conducting the small-scale war for entirely gradual improvements in the situation of the workers that were again and again threatened by setbacks, all radicalism represented a threat to the positions they had conquered, their organizations and trade-union funds. They therefore sought to nip every intensification of the methods of struggle in the bud. Under the Anti-Socialist Laws, there was no room for such efforts, as the trade unions then hardly suffered less than political social democracy. With the strengthening of the trade-union movement after the repeal of the Emergency Law—particularly from the foundation of the General Commission of the Free Trade Unions, which was connected with the tight centralization of the movement—the relationship of the trade unions to the party changed. The initial dependence on the political movement was soon transformed, and at both the Cologne Trade Union Congress in May 1905 and the Mannheim Party Congress in September 1906, the trade unions and their leaders knew how to impose their demands—often on decisive questions, too—against the will of the party authorities. Now their influence on the theoretical conceptions of the socialist workers' movement was also increasingly apparent. Gradually, certain essential elements of Marxist theory were eroded by the practical trade-union negotiators of wage agreements. In the hands of the trade union leaders the concept of "class struggle" experienced a gradual transformation, so that little of its original content remained. Under the same influences, the attitude of the trade-union leaders to the state also changed. They pointed out the benefits they saw for the working class in the state institutions of social insurance, a system they hoped to be able to expand further. Thus these circles felt compelled to revise the ideas previously inherited from Marx ("revisionism"). During the 1890s and after the turn of the century, a question was often raised as to whether a special trade-union theory that would justify reformism—the perspective of a gradual "socialization," "drop by drop" within the existing order—ought to be compiled for the socialist-inclined trade unions. But it never came to such a trade union theory. All the friendlier was the trade union welcome for efforts emerging within the political party that accommodated their desires.

Revisionism is inseparably linked with the name Eduard Bernstein (born 1850). He was the first to systematically demand a revision of Marx's theory, arguing that it did not correspond with the actual development of capitalism, even though the former radical Georg von Vollmar had earlier developed similar ideas—in his famous Eldorado speeches in Munich (1891) and in the pamphlet *State Socialism* (1892)—and advocated reformist tactics.[8] Bernstein, who seemed to be a true disciple of the theory while Engels was still alive, emerged as a critic only after the death of the master, in his *Neue Zeit* articles of 1896–97 on "Problems of Socialism" (published in book form as *The Preconditions of Socialism*). Other writings by Bernstein are relevant: *How Is Scientific Socialism Possible?*, *Guiding Principles for a Social Democratic Program*, *On the Theory and History of Socialism*.[9]

Bernstein never openly described Marxist theory as a whole as false. It is an essential feature of revisionism that it neither had the intention of nor succeeded in constructing a *complete theoretical edifice* to replace Marx's. Its historical significance lies pri-

---

8. [Vollmar advocated a program of reform and alliances with bourgeois parties in two speeches in Munich's Eldorado pub. See *Ueber die nächsten Aufgaben* and *Ueber Staatssozialismus.*]

9. [Bernstein, *Wie ist wissenschaftlicher Socialismus*; *Der Revisionismus in der Sozialdemocratie*; *Zur Geschichte und Theorie des Socialismus.*]

marily in the influence of *trade-union and political practice*. Theory was only of concern to the extent that it was an obstacle to this *practical reformism*. It was to be disposed of through the revisionist critique that adapted theory to practice, so that inconsistency between inherited revolutionary theory and reformist activity could be overcome. For this purpose, in his critique of Marx's theoretical edifice, Bernstein used the convenient procedure of sharply separating the enduring, generally valid elements of the theory—its fundamental theoretical propositions—from its variable elements, because they are propositions of applied science. Under the cover of this distinction, however, the fundamental propositions of the theory were also incorporated, albeit on the pretext that they were now reinterpreted as not fundamental. The goal of revisionism was never declared to be the defeat of Marxism; it was, instead, supposed to be a matter of rejecting certain remnants of "utopianism" that Marxism still allegedly carried in its baggage.

Bernstein's "act of purification" was an attempt to liberate socialism from Marx's *theory of value and surplus value*. Value is a construct in thought and not a phenomenon. Whether Marx's theory of value is correct or not, Bernstein argued, is superfluous for the demonstration of surplus labor, as surplus labor is an empirical fact that suffices alone as a rationale for socialism. Bernstein never offered such a rationale, a positive theory of capitalism, built on the fact of surplus labor, that led to socialism. He remained negative.

Bernstein concedes the accuracy of Marx's predictions about *increasing centralization and concentration of capital*, increasing concentration of enterprises, a rising rate of surplus value (exploitation) and the fall in the profit rate, but he maintains that the overall picture of capitalism in Marx's work is one-sidedly distorted. Marx supposedly neglects the countertendencies in the principal matter. Divisions among already concentrated capitals counteract the tendency to concentration. Income statistics show growth in the number of shareholders and the average magnitude of their shareholdings. Undeniably the number of property owners is growing both absolutely and relatively. And the employment statistics, for their part, prove that the middle classes are expanding. Finally, enterprise statistics irrefutably demonstrate that in a whole series of branches of industry, small- and medium-sized firms are quite viable alongside large concerns. This applies not only to industry but also to commerce. To the extent that large enterprises are concerned, developments in agriculture demonstrate either no change at all or a decline in the scale of operations. After Bernstein, Eduard David attempted to show that in agriculture, a development in the size of operations had begun that was diametrically opposed to Marx's prediction. His thesis contended that small-scale operations were not only viable but were even a superior form of production.[10]

Bernstein regards the Marxist *theory of crisis and breakdown* as an *a priori* construct in accordance with Hegel's scheme of development. In various ways, actual developments have taken a different course than they would have if breakdown was unavoidable for purely economic reasons. Bernstein concedes the possibility of local or particular cri-

---

10. [David, *Socialismus und Landwirtschaft*.]

ses, but the huge territorial expansion of the world market, the reduction of the time required for communications and the transport of goods, combined with the elasticity of the modern credit system and the emergence of cartels have created the possibility that local disturbances will cancel each other out. The occurrence of general crises should, therefore, be considered unlikely. Bernstein does not treat breakdown from the perspective of whether it was the necessary result of the immanent development of capitalism, whether with the existing level of economic development and the degree of maturity of the working class a sudden catastrophe might be to the advantage of social democracy. Bernstein answers these questions in the negative because there is a greater guarantee of enduring successes in a steady forward march than in the possibilities offered by a catastrophe. It is precisely in the theory of breakdown that Bernstein sees the quintessence of "utopianism" in Marxism, because this makes the victory of socialism dependent on its "immanent economic necessity."[11] Bernstein combats the "iron necessity of history" and the materialist conception of history as a theory of historical necessity and emphasizes the increasing effectiveness of ideological and ethical factors.[12] Against Marx he appeals to [Immanuel] Kant. The victory of socialism does not depend on economic necessity but on the moral maturity of the working class, that is, its realization that socialism is desirable.

Ultimately, Bernstein conjures away the final goal of socialism: "The final goal . . . whatever it may be, is nothing to me, the movement everything."[13] The final objective is subordinate; instead, the attention and energy of the working class should be concentrated on "immediate goals," on "daily, detailed work" that will lead to an advance in cultural development, higher morality and legal conceptions. It is apparent that such a formulation of the tasks of the workers' movement has nothing at all to do with socialism and coincides with the conceptions of bourgeois liberalism. The general perspective that in all individual goals there is always a pointer to a further goal, yet to be achieved, that has to be pursued later, only leads to "progression to infinity and that is diametrically counterposed to the essence of socialism, which at a particular stage of development wants to and should replace one definite system with another."[14]

It was only consistent that when Bernstein gave up the final goal he simultaneously abandoned the revolutionary tactics necessary to achieve it. In contrast to Marx's theory of class struggle and his conception that force is the midwife of every society that is coming into being, Bernstein emphasizes parliamentary activity as the means for emancipating the working class. The idea of conquering political power through revolutionary action is supposedly a foreign body in Marxism, a remnant of Blanquism from which Engels parted toward the end of his life.[15]

---

11. [Bernstein, *Preconditions of Socialism*, 199–200.]

12. [Ibid., 20.]

13. [Bernstein, "Der Kampf der Sozialdemokratie," 556; he makes a very similar statement in *Preconditions of Socialism*, 190.]

14. [Brauer, *Der moderne deutsche Sozialismus*, 142.]

15. [Blanquism is a political approach influenced by or similar to that of Louis Auguste Blanqui, who

From his critique, Bernstein drew the conclusion that it was false and disastrous to count on great social catastrophes and to focus the party's tactics on them. The utopia of a coming revolution had to be given up. Development blunts class antagonisms and democratizes society. It is appropriate to promote this development. In order to gain influence, social democracy has to find the courage "to make up its mind to appear what it is in reality today: a democratic socialist party of reform."[16]

From all this it is apparent, as Brauer correctly emphasizes, that Bernstein is no socialist in the Marxist sense, because he is caught up in political categories.[17] For Marx, the proletarian revolution is not just a "political act" that replaces the old power, based on parliament, with a new one, but is simultaneously a "social" revolution insofar as it abolishes the whole of the previous form of society to replace it with a new one. Class struggle—just like its highest form, civil war—is not, for Marx, the product of the good or bad will of the people and cannot be replaced at discretion by parliamentary activity. Instead, class struggle and revolution are inevitable concomitants of the immanent economic necessity with which development drives toward socialism.

The considerable influence Bernstein exercised on intellectuals can be explained by the fact that the boldness of his approach was initially captivating because, in contrast to the fear that Marxism was being petrified, it seemed to pave the way for the further development. At the same time he won over those who, for opportunist reasons, did not wish to "commit" themselves and found in Bernstein's limited determinations and qualifications the bolt holes they desired for their own indecision.

Among the critics of the Marxist theory of crisis and breakdown who, like Bernstein, proceed from an ethical perspective, the Russian professor Mikhail Tugan-Baranovsky particularly excelled, with arguments that were later used extensively by revisionists (*Studies on the Theory and History of Commercial Crises in England*, *Theoretical Foundations of Marxism*, *Modern Socialism in Its Historical Development*).[18] According to Tugan-Baranovsky, crises and the ultimate breakdown of capitalism cannot be due to a lack of markets, since in the course of the expansion of production, the individual spheres of production reciprocally create new market opportunities. Tugan-Baranovsky seeks to prove this, using a reproduction schema based on Marx's. Nor need the [relative] reduction of social consumption as a result of technological progress and the replacement of human labor by machines lead to overproduction. With the expansion of production, *human* consumption is replaced by *productive* consumption, that is, stronger demand for means of production. According to Tugan-Baranovsky, these results of abstract theoretical analysis are confirmed by the empirical facts. Recent capitalist de-

regarded revolution as the product of the efforts of a small group of dedicated conspirators, which would establish a temporary dictatorship in the interests of the masses.]

16. Bernstein, *Preconditions of Socialism*, 186.

17. [Brauer, *Der moderne deutsche Sozialismus*, 148.]

18. Tugan-Baranowsky, *Studien zur Theorie und Geschichte* [see also "Studies in the Theory and the History of Business Crises in England," a translation of chapters I and VII in *Studien zur Theorie und Geschichte*]; *Theoretische Grundlagen des Marxismus*.

velopment shows a strong expansion of the industries producing means of production, such sectors as coal and steel, mechanical engineering, chemicals, and so on, whose products do not flow into human consumption, while those sectors directly serving human consumption, such as textiles (cotton), have almost reached a standstill.

The absolute limit for the expansion of production is constituted by the productive forces that society possesses at any time. Capital can never reach this limit to the extent that this expansion of production occurs proportionately in all branches of production. Capitalist crises are thus exclusively the result of disproportional investment in individual spheres. With proportional investment, the productive forces of capitalism can develop without limit. "The capitalist economy cannot break down for economic reasons."[19] Marx's theory of value is superfluous for the demonstration of surplus labor. Surplus product is not the product of the wage laborer employed and exploited in production alone but is the produce of the whole of society as a unit. Capitalist society's defect is that the propertied class appropriates this surplus product. The end of this unjust system can thus only be the result of ethical causes. "There is, therefore, no occasion to suppose that capitalism will some day die a natural death; it will be destroyed by the conscious willing efforts of man, by that social class which has been the foremost object of capitalistic exploitation—the proletariat."[20] For this reason, Tugan-Baranovsky praises so-called utopian socialism, which was far more scientific than Marxism, to the extent that it did not attempt to provide untenable objective justifications for its ethical demands that the existing economic order be reorganized.

In addition to those mentioned, Conrad Schmidt, the author of a valuable book on *The Average Rate of Profit on the Basis of Marx's Law of Value* that was praised by Engels, ought to be mentioned. Yet he soon became one of the fiercest opponents of Marx's theory of value and surplus value. He was not, however, content to criticize and reject Marx's conception but himself undertook a systematic analysis of the capitalist economy and its laws (see his articles on the theory of value and crises in *Sozialistische Monatshefte* and, in particular "On the Method of Theoretical Political Economy").[21] Here Schmidt reached the same conclusion that Marx deduced for the capitalist economy: with the purchasing power in the form of wages to which he is entitled, the worker can only buy an amount of value for whose production only a fraction of the labor that he performed was necessary. In other words, if the commodities he produced are to be profitable for the employer, he must always perform surplus labor. But according to Schmidt, this basic result was achieved without having to use Marx's untenable law of value. In this way many contradictions associated with this law of value can be avoided.

---

19. [Tugan-Baranowsky, "Der Zusammenbruch der kapitalistischen Wirtschaftsordnung," 304 and following.]
20. [Tugan-Baranowsky, *Modern Socialism*, 96.]
21. Schmidt, *Die Durchschnittsprofitrate auf Grundlage*; "Nachträgliche Bemerkungen zur Bernstein-Diskussion"; "Zur Theorie der Handelskrisen"; "Positive Kritik des Marxschen Wertgesetzes"; "Zur Methode der theoretischen Nationalökonomie."

b. The Neo-Kantians

In addition to the revisionist movement, which sought to undermine the economic and political foundations of Marxism, a stronger revisionist current in the field of philosophy also arose within social democracy toward the end of the last century. The entry of broad intellectual layers into the workers' movement soon led to a discussion about the meaning and validity of the "materialist conception of history." Engels already made certain modifications, in letters to socialist university graduates who asked him for information (see, in particular, the letter of September 21, 1890, to Joseph Bloch). In these letters, Engels warned against exaggerations and observed that "some younger writers attribute more importance to the economic aspect than is due to it"[22] and that the economic situation was not the only but merely the determining moment of sociohistorical development in the last instance.[23] These intellectuals imported secondary idealistic currents into the workers' movement, which abandon the materialist conception of history or seek to combine it with idealism. This is particularly so in France, where Jean Jaurès in his Latin dissertation of 1891 develops an idealist conception of history, according to which it is the product of the human spirit—a conception that he also retained later as a socialist.[24] The idealist current is assisted by some supporters of the materialist conception of history, such as, for example, Paul Lafargue (1842–1911), whose crude interpretations helped discredit it.[25] In Germany, a current initially arising in university philosophy departments seeks to justify socialism idealistically and to link it with Kant. It originates with Hermann Cohen (1842–1918), the founder of Neo-Kantianism (the so-called Marburg School), who in his introduction to Friedrich Albert Lange's *History of Materialism* attempted to prove that socialism is "based on the socialism of ethics" and to this extent Kant was "the true and genuine initiator of German socialism."[26] In his book *Economics and Law according to the Materialist Conception of History,* Rudolf Stammler (of Halle) recognized this as, so far, the best and most consistent method for causal research into economic development but demanded that it be supplemented by goal-setting ("teleological") considerations. Only by means of the latter is it possible to achieve the highest social goal, which Stammler regards as the "community of people who want to be free," where "everybody makes the objectively justified purposes of the other his own."[27] Franz Staudinger (1849–1921) attempted even more in his writings (*Ethics and Politics; Economic Foundations of Morality*) to reconcile the Marxist standpoint with Kant's epistemological critique and ethics.[28] Each Kantian had to come to Marx by logically developing his own basic ideas. And vice versa: "As soon as Marxism no longer merely pursues social development scientifically in

---

22. Engels to Joseph Bloch, September 21, 1890, 36.

23. ["Moment" is a Hegelian term, here with the sense of "aspect."]

24. [Jaurès, *De primis socialismi germanici*. Grossman wrote an entry on Jaurès: see Grossmann, "Jaurès, Jean."]

25. Compare Lafargue, *Le déterminisme économique*

26. [Cohen, "Einleitung mit kritischem Nachtrag."]

27. [Stammler, *Wirtschaft und Recht*, 575–76.]

28. [Staudinger, *Ethik und Politik* and *Wirtschaftliche Grundlagen der Moral*.]

accordance with the causal viewpoint but makes conscious and planned transformation of the given into its goal, it arrives at Kant, as a result of consistent pursuit of its own principle."[29] Along similar lines to Staudinger, Karl Vorländer in his writings (*Kant and Socialism*, *Kant and Marx*, and *From Machiavelli to Lenin*) advocated a combination of "Marx" and "Kant," that is, a combination of an economic-historical with an epistemologically critical-ethical justification for socialism.[30]

This current, which initially arose outside the socialist movement, soon also created an echo within it, particularly in the ranks of the revisionists—Eduard Bernstein, Conrad Schmidt, and Ludwig Woltmann (*Historical Materialism*) —who also attempted to undermine Marxism through philosophy, but also in the ranks of the then-radical, younger Viennese Marxists such as Max Adler (*Causality and Theology in the Dispute about the Economy*, *Marx as Thinker*, *Kant and Marxism*, *Marxist Problems*) and Otto Bauer ("Marxism and Ethics," directed against Kautsky), who ultimately deviated into the camp of reformism.[31] They all demanded a stronger consideration of "ideological" moments, epistemological critique, and ethics in socialist theory. Similar attempts by Russian revisionism in the field of philosophy evoked the resolute resistance of [Georgi Valentinovich] Plekhanov and [Vladimir Ilyich] Lenin (*Materialism and Empiriocriticism*). On the whole, revisionism remains negative philosophically and proves itself to be just as infertile here as in the field of economics. With the victory of reformism in German social democracy during and after the [First World] War, however, these currents succeed in coming into their own. It is characteristic of the completely altered attitude of socialism in this period that the article on the philosophical foundations of socialism in *The Program of Social Democracy: Suggestion for its Renewal*, which appeared before the Görlitz Party Congress, was written by the above-mentioned Kantian Karl Vorländer, at the request of authoritative party circles.[32]

As far as revisionism as a whole is concerned, it is not only the circumstance that both Bernstein and Tugan-Baranovsky subscribe to the theory of marginal utility[33] that lends it an individualistic aspect but, as was shown, also its attempt to replace the Marxist materialist dialectic with Kantian ethics and epistemological critique. For in contrast to socialism insofar as it is a fundamental socialism, Kant's starting point, it must be insisted, is the autonomous personality. Here, however, there is a fundamental contradiction with socialism in general and Marxist socialism in particular, which only knows and explains individuals as conditioned by the social environment.

Revisionism as a whole has not been able to replace Marxist theory with one of its own that in any respect grasps the economic mechanism with its social interconnections.

---

29. [Staudinger, *Ethik und Politik*, 159.]

30. [Vorländer, *Kant und der Sozialismus*; *Kant und Marx*; and *Von Machiavelli bis Lenin*.]

31. [Woltmann, *Der historische Materialismus*. Adler, *Kausalität und Teleologie*; *Marx als Denker: Zum 25*; *Todesjahre von Karl Marx*; *Marxistische Probleme*; *Kant und der Marxismus*. Bauer, "Marxismus und Ethik." Kautsky, *Ethics and the Materialist Conception of History*.]

32. [Karl Vorländer, "Zu den philosophischen Grundlagen."]

33. [That is, mainstream neoclassical economics, as opposed to Marx's labor theory of value.]

It remained stuck in critique, and therefore the question of whether, in principle, revisionism should be pronounced to be socialism has to be answered in the negative. But also as pure critique the standpoint of revisionism has proved to be false. One only needs to compare its critique of the Marxist account of how artisanal production and the middle classes are prone to crises and concentration, and finally its conception of the superiority of small-scale operations in agriculture with the experience of the postwar period (see Friedrich Pollock, *Socialism and Agriculture*, and Julian Gumperz, *The Agrarian Crisis in the United States*) in order to see that history has proved that not revisionism but Marx is correct.[34] Anyone who delves into *Capital* today, after seven decades, has to concede with astonishment how correctly, indeed prophetically, Marx understood the large-scale tendencies of capitalist development.

Over the two decades before the World War, reformism became an international phenomenon. Much earlier than in Germany, it appeared in England. There, the first mass movement of the proletariat, the Chartist movement, was defeated in the 1830s and 1840s. But its struggle had shown the English bourgeoisie the danger that threatened it. Subsequently, it knew how to calm the dissatisfaction of the working class by means of concessions and the timely grant of real benefits to its upper layer, which its supremacy on the world market permitted. In this manner, over a long period, it successfully prevented the English proletariat from combining to create an independent political party. The whole energy of the working class turned to developing trade unions, mutual funds, and cooperatives. The great reorganization of local government gave workers the opportunity to represent their interests through autonomous local authorities in the field of municipal economic and welfare services. The trade unions developed a purely reformist practice. The revolutionary traditions of Chartism were forgotten. The reformist-socialist Fabian Society, founded in 1883–84 and consisting of a few hundred intellectuals, gained considerable influence in bourgeois circles and the trade-union bureaucracy under the leadership of Sidney Webb (born 1859) and George Bernard Shaw. The report they wrote for the International Socialist Congress in London (1896) provides a clear insight into the essence of the Fabians.[35]

The Fabians do not want to be a party; instead they want to permeate all existing organizations and movements with Fabian ideas. The "tactic of permeation" is one of the specific characteristics of the Fabians. "The Fabian Society endeavours to rouse social compunction by making the public conscious of the evil condition of society under the present system."[36] Apart from the Fabian Society's numerous pamphlets (tracts), English reformism found its theological expression above all in the works of the couple Sidney and Beatrice Webb (*History of British Trade Unionism*, with an afterword by Eduard Bernstein; *Industrial Democracy*; *The Prevention of Destitution*; *A Constitution for the Socialist Commonwealth of Great Britain*; *The Decay of Capitalist Civilisation*) and of James Ramsay MacDonald (*So-*

---

34. [Pollock, "Sozialismus und Landwirtschaft"; and Gumperz, *Die Agrarkrise in den Vereinigten Staaten.*]
35. [Shaw, *Report on Fabian Policy.*]
36. [Ibid., 7.]

cialism and Society).[37] The Labour Party, which was finally founded in 1900, immediately adopted the reformist principles and practice of the Fabians and the trade unions.

In France one already finds reformism in the pamphlets that Paul Brousse published in Paris in 1881–82.[38] Brousse was the founder of the party of the so-called Possibilists, which existed until 1899. Subsequently, reformist ideas were most strongly promoted by the activity of Jean Jaurès, who also advocated participation in a bourgeois government (ministerialism) in 1899. In the Socialist Party of Italy, too—despite the weak industrial development of the country—strong reformist currents appeared, essentially represented by petty-bourgeois intellectuals who participated in all the theoretical controversies about impoverishment and concentration that were fought out from time to time in the party's theoretical organ, *Critica sociale*, in the period 1895–1905, after the publication of volume 3 of *Capital*. The syndicalist Arturo Labriola, in his *Study of Marx*, was the foremost critic of the theory of impoverishment and breakdown.[39] In *Economic Speculation* and *The Dictatorship of the Bourgeoisie*, he dealt with the problem of imperialism.[40] With the stronger industrial development of the country after 1905, the related intensification of class struggles, and the advance of reaction within the bourgeoisie, numerous intellectuals abandoned socialism. Émile Vandervelde in Belgium worked with the same orientation as Jaurès in France (*Worker's Belgium*; *Collectivism and Industrial Evolution*; *Agrarian Socialism and Agricultural Collectivism*; *Essays on the Agrarian Question in Belgium*; *The Workers' Party of Belgium 1885–1925*).[41] Reformism took a specific form in Russia. Its most notable theoretical representatives were Tugan-Baranovsky and Peter Berngardovich Struve, who, however, soon swung over to liberalism. It achieved mass political influence in the workers' movement in Menshevism.

c. The Radicals on the Defensive

The efforts of revisionism were soon countered by the so-called "radicals" or "orthodox Marxists"—Karl Kautsky, Franz Mehring, Heinrich Cunow, Parvus, but above all Rosa Luxemburg, in *Neue Zeit* and in specific polemical writings—while the revisionists used the newly founded *Sozialistische Monatshefte*.[42]

---

37. [Webb and Webb, *Die Geschichte des Britischen Trade-Unionismus* (original edition: *History of Trade Unionism*); *Industrial Democracy*; *Prevention of Destitution*; *Constitution for the Socialist Commonwealth*; *Decay of Capitalist Civilisation*. MacDonald, *Sozialismus und Regierung* (original edition *Socialism and Society*).]

38. [Brousse, *Le Marxisme dans l'Internationale*.]

39. [Arturo Labriola, *Studio su Marx*.]

40. [Arturo Labriola, *La speculazione economica* and *La dittatura della borghesia*.]

41. [Vandervelde, *La Belgique ouvrière*; *Collectivism and Industrial Evolution*; *Le socialisme agraire*; *Essais sur la question agraire*; *Le Parti Ouvrier Belge*.]

42. [Kautsky, *Bernstein und das sozialdemokratische Programm*. When editor of the daily *Sächsiger Arbeiter-Zeitung*, Alexander Parvus wrote a series of articles, "Bernsteins Umwälzung des Sozialismus," which appeared in the paper from January to March of 1898. Franz Mehring's articles appeared in another daily party newspaper: "Sozialistische Selbstkritik," *Leipziger Volkszeitung*, February 9, 1898; "Das sozialistische Endziel," *Leipziger Volkszeitung*, February 10, 1898; "In Sachen Bernstein," *Leipziger Volkszeitung*, March 10, 1898. Cunow, "Zur Zusammenbruchstheorie." Luxemburg, *Social Reform or Revolution*. For writings by major contributors

Kautsky's *Agrarian Question* targets the revisionist critique of Marx's presentation of developmental trends in agriculture. This is Kautsky's most significant and independent economic work, although even here the historical-descriptive element crowds out the purely theoretical aspect. In his anticritique directed against Bernstein's critique (*Bernstein and the Social Democratic Program*), Kautsky deals with the questions of method, program, and tactics, particularly the tenets disputed by Bernstein: the theory of breakdown, developmental trends with regard to enterprise size (large and small enterprises), the increase in the number of property owners and the middle class, the theory of impoverishment and crisis.[43] Here Kautsky seeks to refute Bernstein's claims about the alleviation of capitalist contradictions by means of philological interpretation of Marx's texts and comprehensive company, tax, and other statistics, and to defend the thesis that class contradictions are intensifying. In the course of doing so, he relaxes or completely abandons important fundamentals of Marxist theory. Even the Erfurt Program (1891), which was drawn up by Kautsky and signified the high point in the Marxist development of German social democracy, portrays the decisive point of the political program very vaguely. The process of capitalist development seems to be the result of blind social forces. The conquest of power is wrapped in total darkness. The dictatorship of the proletariat is not even mentioned. As a result, the political aspect of Marxism was virtually decapitated until Lenin reconstructed it over twenty-five years later.[44] Engels's critique of the draft program of 1891 was disregarded and ineffective, just as Marx's critique of the draft Gotha Program had been in 1875.[45] In the dispute with Bernstein, Kautsky now intensified the reinterpretation of Marx's original theory even further. Compared with Bernstein's demand that the party should become a democratic socialist party of reform, he emphasized that social democracy "had to become a party of social revolution."[46] Here, however, Kautsky added that it was not a matter of the concept of revolution "in the sense of an armed uprising" but of "every large-scale political convulsion that sped up the political life of the nation and made it pulsate most energetically." Admittedly, "extralegal use of violence" could form an episode in such a convulsion, but it could never be the revolution itself. In this reinterpretation of the concept of political revolution, its real content—the transfer of power into the hands of a new class—was clearly lost. At the time, Engels's political testament, his famous introduction to *The Class Struggles in France*, written in 1895, played a not unimportant role in the debate over tactics. He allegedly revised the tactics of the workers' movement and supposedly counterposed barricade struggles—violent revolution—to

---

to the debate and an introductory overview, see Tudor and Tudor, eds., *Marxism and Social Democracy*. The contents of *Neue Zeit*, the official theoretical journal of the German Social Democratic Party, and *Sozialistische Monatshefte*, the organ of the right wing of the party, for that period are accessible online from http://library.fes.de.]

43. [Kautsky, *Bernstein und das sozialdemokratische Programm*.]
44. [This is a reference to Lenin's *Imperialism, the Highest Stage of Capitalism*.]
45. [Engels, "Critique of the Draft"; Marx, *Critique of the Gotha Programme*.]
46. [Kautsky, *Bernstein und das sozialdemokratische Programm*, 181–83.]

purely legal struggle—parliamentarism. It emerged thirty years later, thanks to David Riazanov who uncovered the correct text, that the introduction was published by the party executive in an abridged form that significantly distorted its meaning.[47]

Kautsky also reconstrued the economic side of Marxism on important points, by interpreting his own conceptions into Marx's text. Initially, this was not sufficiently recognized by the socialist public, since he appeared in the role of the defender of Marx's theory against Bernstein and adhered to Marx's traditional terminology. That was particularly the case for Marx's theory of breakdown and crisis. Instead of maintaining Marx's theory of breakdown, the theory of the objective necessity of the demise of capitalism, in its genuine form against the distortion in the revisionist critique—that the breakdown could happen "automatically," without the active intervention of the proletariat—Kautsky denied this decisive position of Marx's system altogether and portrayed the theory of breakdown as Bernstein's invention. At the same time and in contradiction to this, he maintained in relation to crises that, while production could expand practically without limit, external and internal markets had their limits. Consequently, "from a specific historic moment onwards the capitalist mode of production would become impossible." Not only a temporary crisis but "incurable chronic overproduction" would then set in, as the "final limit" on the maintenance of the capitalist regime. The significance of this "utmost limit of the viability" of today's society was that socialism [would emerge] from the sphere of nebulous ideas "to become a necessary goal of practical politics."[48]

That Kautsky's unclear and contradictory attitude to important elements of Marx's theory was unsatisfactory is clear and all the more so when Kautsky's theoretical confusion increased in his later writings. Three years later, in a series of articles on "crisis theory" directed against Tugan-Baranovsky's critique, he combats Tugan-Baranovsky's view that crises arise from lack of proportionality in production and argues against his assertion of the possibility that capitalism could expand without limit: "the capitalist mode of production has its limits, which it cannot transcend." Yet after a [further] quarter of a century, in his preface to the popular edition of the second volume of *Capital*, he embraced Tugan-Baranovsky's theory of disproportionality as the cause of crises, which he had earlier combated, without any reservations.[49] In his last large work (*The Materialist Conception of History*), in the autumn of his life, Kautsky finally abandoned the Marxist theory of the impassable limits of capitalist development and based himself on Tugan-Baranovsky's theory of the possibility of the unlimited expansion of capitalism, which he had criticized twenty-five years earlier, and with that disowned his lifework. The pattern in which every mode of production ultimately survives to become a fetter on production during its decline does not apply to capitalism. Industrial capitalism

---

47. [Engels, introduction to *The Class Struggles in France*. This edition indicates the abridgments made when the introduction was first published.]

48. [Kautsky, *Bernstein und das sozialdemokratische Programm*, 142, 145.]

49. [Kautsky, "Krisentheorien"; foreword to *Das Kapital*.]

does not lead to decline but "to an ever more rapid development of the productive forces." Kautsky claims that postwar capitalism has "demonstrated in practice in the most impressive fashion its ability to survive and to adapt to the most diverse, even the most desperate, situations. There are no arguments of economic theory that could call its vitality into question." Although Kautsky had anticipated a chronic crisis of capitalism three decades earlier, this proved to be false. "Capitalism . . . is today, considered from the purely economic standpoint, more solidly established than ever."[50]

If one bears in mind Kautsky's later development, already present in nascent form at the time of his disputes with Bernstein in his unclear and vacillating position on important points of theoretical principle, it is comprehensible that the controversy between these two theoreticians did not and could not result in the clarification of fundamental questions of Marxist theory. Both had abandoned Marxist theory on decisive points and conducted the struggle only over less important points, sometimes merely over words. At the time only a few (Rosa Luxemburg) noticed this. However great Kautsky's service was in popularizing Marxism, the real revolutionary character of Marxism remained alien to him. In Kautsky's struggle with Bernstein, ultimately Bernstein was the victor.

The arguments that Parvus (Alexander Israel Lazarevich Helphand), an enthusiastic social patriot during the [First World] War, advanced in a series of writings against revisionism were more effective (*Commercial Crisis and Trade Unions*, *The Trade Union Struggle*, *Socialism and Social Revolution*, *Colonial Policy and Breakdown*).[51]

Most impressive and enduring were Rosa Luxemburg's essays, the high point of which, on the theoretical side, is her *Social Reform or Revolution*, published against Bernstein's *Preconditions*.

If Bernstein was expecting the transition to socialism [to result] from the progressive development of the bourgeois legal system, from statutory social reform, Rosa Luxemburg explains, then he was committing a fundamental error with regard to the essence of capitalist class rule. This rests, in contrast to earlier class societies, not on legally anchored "acquired rights" but on real economic forces. "In our juridical system there is not a single legal formula for the class domination of today." "No law obliges the proletariat to submit itself to the yoke of capitalism. Poverty, the lack of means of production," which are taken from it not by law but by economic development, "obliges the proletariat to submit itself to the yoke of capitalism." The exploitation of the working class as an economic process cannot, therefore, be abolished or moderated by legal provisions within the framework of bourgeois society. "Social reform," factory laws, health and safety regulations do not indicate an element of "social control" in the interests of the working class; they do not constitute "a threat to capitalist exploitation but simply the regulation of exploitation" in the interests of capitalist society itself. In fact, development leads to

---

50. [Kautsky, *Bernstein und das sozialdemokratische Programm*, 421, 424–56.]
51. Parvus, *Die Handelskrisis und die Gewerkschaften*; *Der gewerkschaftliche Kampf*; *Der Sozialismus und die soziale Revolution*; *Die Kolonialpolitik und der Zusammenbruch*.

an accentuation and intensification of the contradictions of capitalism. From the stand-point of individual capitalists, credit, business associations and other means that allegedly serve to overcome these contradictions and to regulate production are only suited to adjust their insufficient means to the demands of the market: to raise falling profit rates in cartelized branches of industry at the expense of the others. Cartels cancel out their own effectiveness when they extend to all the more important branches of production. From the standpoint of the economy as a whole, credit helps increase production beyond the limits of the market and promotes the most reckless speculation. Far from being a means to moderate the contradictions of capitalism, business associations and credit, on the contrary, powerfully aggravate and promote crises and must accelerate its downfall. The breakdown of bourgeois society—says Rosa Luxemburg, not only against Bernstein but evidently against Kautsky too—is the cornerstone of scientific socialism. The histor-ical necessity of socialist upheaval is based, "first, on the growing anarchy of [the] cap-italist economy, leading inevitably to its ruin." If, however, the progressive moderation of contradictions is assumed, if it is assumed "that capitalist development does not move in the direction of its own ruin, then socialism ceases to be *objectively necessary*." Then its justification is only possible by means of "pure reason," that is, an "idealist explanation," while "the objective necessity of socialism, the explanation of socialism as the result of the material development of society, falls to the ground."[52]

With the same acuity, Rosa Luxemburg also develops her principal tactical ideas about the class struggle. Radical Marxism, too, desires everyday social reform work, a tactical orientation to current questions—the trade-union struggle over wages, the struggle for social reform and the democratization of political institutions—just as much as reformism. "The difference is not in the *what*, but in the *how*." Because it starts from the assumption that the political seizure of power is impossible, reformism wants, through "trade union and parliamentary activity[, to] gradually reduce capital-ist exploitation itself. They remove from capitalist society its capitalist character. They realize *objectively* the desired social change." By contrast, for Marxism trade-union and political struggle is significant only as necessary to prepare the *subjective factor* in social-ist upheaval—the working class—for the decisive revolutionary battle, first organizing the workers "as a class" and effecting the emergence of understanding, of united pro-letarian class consciousness. The socialist transition will not come of its own accord by fatalistically waiting for it to occur. It results, instead, from understanding, won in the everyday struggle of the working class, that the supersession of capitalism's objectively intensifying contradictions through social upheaval is indispensable. Thus for Rosa Lux-emburg, as later for Lenin, reforms are only by-products of class struggle oriented on revolution. Revisionism, by contrast, makes everyday work independent of the final socialist goal. It separates reform from revolution and, by raising the movement to an end in itself, changes its character. It is no longer a means to achieve that goal—social upheaval—but instead has itself become the goal. This undialectical attitude sees

---

52. [Luxemburg, *Social Reform or Revolution*, 45–7, 61, 90–2. Editor's interpolation.]

only mutually exclusive opposites—either/or, reform or revolution—but not the subsumption of these opposites in the totality of the social process.[53]

As we see, only with these explanations is the concept of the "final goal," neglected in the Erfurt Program, defined. Rosa Luxemburg does not understand the "final goal" as the ideal state of the future, to be erected after the socialist upheaval, but the conquest of political power, the *revolution* itself. If the future state is understood as the "final goal," then every democratic or economic achievement can be considered to be a step on the path to this goal. But if the conquest of political power through the revolution is regarded as the final goal, a sharp boundary is drawn with reformism, which replaces the strategic task of developing people's revolutionary capacity with current, opportunist work or the propagation of a more or less vague final goal to be awaited fatalistically. So Rosa Luxemburg's interpretation of Marxism assigns the decisive role to working-class political activism, through the orientation of current work on the final revolutionary goal, even though the seizure of state power is dependent on the objective course of material social development and "presupposes . . . a definite degree of maturity of economic and political relations."[54] Marxism is therefore sharply distinguished from both fatalism and pure voluntarism.

For the fate of the dispute between reformists and radicals, see the article "Internationals."[55] Reformism was defeated in all theoretical skirmishes, condemned by resolutions of party conferences and international congresses, refuted again and again by the prevailing intensification of class contradictions in the course of actual development. But, maturing on the basis of the aristocracy of labor, it nevertheless made a triumphal procession through the daily practice of the workers' movement. The growing power of Marxism was, however, demonstrated by the fact that of all the socialist tendencies in all European countries during the first half of the nineteenth century—Saint-Simonism, Proudhonism, later Blanquism and so on—it alone dominated the masses intellectually and that reformism, in order to be capable of winning over the masses, had to sail under the flag of Marxism.

d. Reformism in Marxist Disguise (The Neo-Harmonists)

Here we refer primarily to "Austro-Marxism," a group of Viennese intellectuals—Rudolf Hilferding, Otto Bauer, Max Adler, and Karl Renner—grouped around the newly established theoretical review *Kampf* (from 1908). They attempted to provide theoretical formulations for reformist practice. The most important book from this tendency, one that strongly influenced later theoretical development, is Rudolf Hilferding's *Finance Capital*. Its two components have to be distinguished. On the one hand, Hilferding

---

53. [Ibid., 66–69. Editor's interpolation.]
54. [Ibid., 95.]
55. [Grossmann, "Internationale: Die zweite Internationale" and "Internationale: Die dritte Internationale."]

strives to integrate the latest phenomena of economic life—trusts, cartels, export of capital, imperialist expansionism, in short, *monopoly capitalism*, which has replaced competitive capitalism—into the system of Marx's economics. On the other hand, following Tugan-Baranovsky's theory of crisis and renouncing the Marxist theory of breakdown, Hilferding endeavors to reinterpret the Marxist theory of breakdown in the harmonistic spirit of the limitless possibilities for capitalist expansion. Reviving Jean-Baptiste Say's old theory, which Marx always combated, that primarily general overproduction is impossible because individual spheres of production create markets for each other, Hilferding reaches the conclusion that crises are not necessarily associated with the essence of capitalism. They arise simply from disproportion in growth among individual spheres, that is, only from "unregulated production." If the distribution of capital among individual branches of industry is proportional, then there is no limit to production, "production can be expanded indefinitely without leading to the overproduction of commodities." In short, if production, even on a capitalist basis, can be regulated, crises can be avoided.[56]

The foundation of the work is Hilferding's theory of money and credit, which departs from Marx's theory of money and distorts it in the spirit of Knapp's "chartalism."[57] Certainly, for this purpose, Hilferding has to breach the general validity of Marx's law of value for the money commodity, which Karl Kautsky correctly asserted meant "the suicide of Marxism."[58] The theory of finance capital is built on the foundation of this theory of money. The characteristic feature of the most recent developments is the *dominant role of bank capital compared with industry*. With capitalist development, the total sum of money made available to the banks by the nonproductive classes and through the banks to the industrialists, that is, the role of bank capital in the form of money that is transformed into industrial capital, constantly grows. A particular role falls here to the type of enterprise known as a joint stock company. With shares, so-called fictitious capital, detached from productive capital functioning in factories, arises. It enables banks to rapidly concentrate ownership, independently of the concentration of factories, and is accelerated by speculation on the stock exchange and the accumulation of promoter's profit by the banks.[59] By means of this "mobilization of capital," an ever-growing portion of capital in industry becomes finance capital, that is, it no longer belongs to the industrialists working with it. The direction of capital invested in industry falls more and more to banks. "They become founders and eventually rulers of industry." The tendency toward concentration in banking, toward progressive elimination of competition among banks, "would finally result in a single bank or a group of banks establishing control over the entire money capital. Such a 'central bank' would then exercise control over social production as a whole."[60]

---

56. Hilferding, *Finance Capital*, 241.
57. ["Chartalism" is a theory of fiat money, issued and backed by law rather than precious metals, elaborated in Knapp, *The State Theory of Money*.]
58. [Kautsky, "Finance-Capital and Crises."]
59. [The profits made by floating shares in a new joint stock company.]
60. [Hilferding, *Finance Capital*, 105 and following; 226; 180.]

A parallel tendency toward combination is also at work in production. In a section on "The Historical Tendency of Finance Capital," probably intended to be a counterpart to Marx's famous chapter on "The Historical Tendencies of Capitalist Accumulation," Hilferding presents the course of historical development quite differently from Marx.[61] The latter depicted the limits of capitalist accumulation, which in a dialectical shift at a definite stage of development ultimately leads to the "expropriation of the expropriators."[62] Hilferding wants to demonstrate the peaceful and gradual growth of capitalism into a regulated economy. The cartelization of industry, in order to raise prices and profits, lowers the rate of profit in the noncartelized industries, intensifies competition in them and thus the tendency toward concentration. This leads to further cartelization in these industries too. So a tendency toward the continuous extension of cartelization emerges. The result of this concentration movement, its ideal, theoretical endpoint, will be the complete cartelization of all branches of industry, not only in the national but also in the world economy: a universal or "general cartel" that consciously regulates the entirety of capitalist production in all its spheres, sets prices, and also undertakes the distribution of products. With the advance of the concentration movement in industry, production is increasingly planned ("organized capitalism") and finally reaches its highest expression in the general cartel. The anarchy of production disappears; crises are eliminated and replaced by production "regulated" by the general cartel, even if still on the basis of wage labor. "The tendencies towards the establishment of a general cartel and towards the formation of a central bank are converging," hence a peaceful and painless transition from capitalism to socialism becomes possible.[63] "The socialising function of finance capital facilitates enormously the task of overcoming capitalism. Once finance capital has brought the most important branches of production under its control, it is enough for society, through its conscious executive organ—the state conquered by the working class—to seize finance capital in order to gain immediate control of these branches of production." "Even today, taking possession of six large Berlin banks would mean taking possession of the most important spheres of large-scale industry."[64]

After the war (1927), Hilferding declared that he had always "repudiated every theory of economic breakdown"; Marx had also considered them to be false. The overthrow of the capitalist system would "not happen because of internal laws of this system" but instead had "to be the conscious act of the will of the working class."[65]

During the postwar period, the other neo-harmonists, such as Otto Bauer ("The Accumulation of Capital") and Karl Kautsky, also derive crises simply from disproportion in the distribution of capital among individual branches of industry. They consider crises to be avoidable even under capitalism if the distribution of capital is regulated, and the

61. [Ibid., 227–35; Marx, *Capital*, vol. 1, 927–30.]
62. [Marx, *The Civil War in France*, 335.]
63. [Hilferding, *Finance Capital*, 234.]
64. [Ibid., 367, 368.]
65. [Hilferding, *Die Aufgaben der Sozialdemokratie*, 2.]

unlimited development of capitalism to be possible. Bauer's assertion that the capitalist mechanism automatically enforces this proportional distribution of capital—even if it is mediated by periodic crises—gives his harmonistic interpretation of Marx's theory of crisis a specific coloration. "The mechanism of capitalist production automatically [cancels out] overaccumulation and underaccumulation." While Marx had maintained that the progressive growth of the industrial reserve army of labor was necessary, Bauer tries to prove the opposite: "There exists in the capitalist mode of production a tendency for the adjustment of capital accumulation to the growth of population."[66]

C. The Resurgence of Revolutionary Marxism

a. The Decay of Revisionist Theory

As already shown, reformism was the result of the relatively peaceful period of capitalist development between 1872 and 1894. Revolutionary Marxist theory, itself the product of the revolutionary period of 1848, no longer seemed to suit this peaceful period. The reformist attempt to divest Marxism of its revolutionary character, in order to adapt it to the reformist practice of peaceful, constructive work, was ultimately doomed to theoretical failure. Economic development at the end of the previous century experienced a decisive shift, once more demonstrating that the "practice of the peaceful work of construction" was entirely questionable.

The policy of imperialist expansion, which in the most advanced countries was temporarily able to secure advantages for the upper layer of the working class, at the turn of the century led to a sharpening of all antagonisms in both domestic and foreign policy. The imperialist era of heightened colonial policy, feverish military and naval arms buildups, and finally bellicose collisions that led to the outbreak of the [First] World War began.

A sharpening of domestic class antagonisms in all capitalist countries ran parallel to growing tensions in foreign policy. The great advances of the socialist workers' movement accelerated the process of the combination of employers into powerful associations for struggle, which forced workers onto the defensive in all economic struggles. Kautsky demonstrated in 1908 "that the factors that had resulted in increased real wages over previous decades were all already going into reverse." The period of rising real wages was replaced by one of falling wages, and certainly not merely during periods of transient depression "but even in periods of prosperity."[67] The fact of the deteriorating conditions of working-class life over this period has been demonstrated by private and

---

66. Bauer, "The Accumulation of Capital," 106, 107. [This translation has been modified, as indicated by the square brackets. The previously published translation seriously distorted the meaning of Bauer's German text by rendering "aufhebt" as "generates." See Otto Bauer, "Die Akkumulation des Kapitals," 872.]
67. [Kautsky, "Verelendung und Zusammenbruch," 546, 549.]

public investigations in a series of advanced capitalist countries (America, Germany). [The advance of] state protection for workers also came to a halt under the pressure of employer associations. More and more, in this context, the trade unions' old methods of struggle proved to be insufficient. The period of isolated strikes in individual enterprises was past. Development drove on to large mass economic struggles in whole branches of a country's industry. On the other hand, the bourgeoisie became protectionist and reactionary. Political liberalism began to die out. There could no longer be talk of the further extension of democracy, which had been promoted earlier by a certain [degree of] cooperation between the liberal bourgeoisie and the working class. This entire development was strengthened and accelerated even more by the impact of the Russian Revolution of 1905. The development, predicted by the reformists, of progressive improvement in the condition of the working class and the weakening of class struggles did not occur. Instead, class struggles intensified. Since it was apparent that the old trade-union and parliamentary methods were no longer capable of achieving further gains, the working class was forced to look around for new methods of struggle that took into account rising economic and political pressure from the bourgeoisie. This was the significance of the discussion about the political mass strike.[68]

In such circumstances, during the era of bellicose imperialism and colonial expansion as well as reactionary domestic policies, reformism of the old kind was a typical product of epigones: repetition of dated lines of thought diametrically counterposed to reality. As an example of this oversimplified popularization of socialism that spread throughout the workers' movement at the beginning of the twentieth century and, despite its Marxist phraseology, retained nothing of the genuine content of Marx's socialism, mention should be made of a book by Morris Hillquit, the current leader of the American "Socialist Party," *Socialism in Theory and Practice*. In the chapter on "Socialism and the State," Hillquit settles accounts with two dozen definitions of the state, starting with Aristotle and Cicero, through [Anne-Robert-Jacques] Turgot and [Jeremy] Bentham, to [Pierre Paul] Leroy-Beaulieu and Anton Menger, according to whom the state is the organized humanity of a given territory. To this definition, designated as faulty, Hillquit counterposes the "entirely correct" "socialist definition of the state," according to Marx and Engels, and shows that the "state, as a product of class [divisions]," arose at the same time as the institution of private property and "has at all times been the instrument of the propertied classes" and, "as an organization of the ruling classes," necessarily "keeps the exploited classes in a condition of dependency." From this "entirely correct" definition, however, Hillquit draws no conclusions for working-class policy. In relation to the "present-day," "modern state," Hillquit nevertheless allows the validity of the bourgeois definition and asserts that it has experienced "deep inroads made in its substance and functions by the rising class of wage workers." "Under the pressure of the [socialist and] labor movement, the state has acquired new significance as an instrument of social and economic reforms." "The state which came into being solely as an instru-

---

68. [See Luxemburg, *The Mass Strike*.]

ment of class repression, has gradually, and especially within the last centuries assumed other important social functions, functions in which it largely represents society as a whole, and not any particular class in it." Its exploitative functions in the interests of the ruling classes are "curbed" more and more, while its "generally useful" functions claim its attention more and more, as it protects "workers from excessive exploitation," so it "is gradually coming to be recognized by the [workers] as a most potent instrument for the modification and ultimate abolition of the capitalist class rule." The ruling capitalist class will, indeed, never voluntarily give up its property and the supremacy that results. Hillquit draws the conclusion not that it has to be expropriated economically and politically but instead that the process of transformation will come to pass gradually, through "a series of economic and social reforms and legislative measures tending to divest the ruling classes of their monopolies, privileges and advantages, step by step." Violence does not, consequently, have to be employed. That would be "but an accident of the social revolution . . . [violence] has no place in the socialist program." Through these reforms, a "period of transition" will be entered, in which the state, although not yet socialist, is no longer an organ of the capitalist class but instead a "transitional state." "Definite lines of demarcation" where it begins and where it ends cannot be specified, but today "[a] number of municipalities and states are already wholly or partly under socialist control." Many of the political or social "transitional reforms" of socialism have, to a certain degree, been realized in countries in Europe, America, and Australia, and the "conceded tendency" of all modern lawmaking is directed toward the extension of such reforms. In this sense, it may well be said that we are in the midst or in any case at the start of the "transitional state." Hillquit, logically, recommends tactics that are confined to "electoral tactics" and the "positive work of parliament," "without violating the principle of the class struggle."[69]

If such theories were strongly utopian during the period before the war, they completely lost any connection with reality after its outbreak. In order to avoid shipwreck on this contrast with reality, reformist theory was forced to adapt to it. In pure logic, this correction was possible in two ways. From the proletarian standpoint: through a return to revolutionary Marxism. In a further, consistent development of its nature, reformism chose the other way and placed itself entirely on the ground of bourgeois society and the capitalist state. Karl Renner already drew this conclusion, contained in embryo in Hilferding's book, with great clarity in articles published in the Viennese *Kampf* and *Arbeiter-Zeitung* (which appeared in book form as *Marxism, War, and the International*).[70] Extending the conclusions of Hilferding's book, he seeks to portray the

---

69. [Hillquit, *Socialism in Theory and Practice*, 97–105, 174, 181, 189. Grossman wrote "class struggles" where the original had "class divisions" and left out "socialist and" from the quotation starting "Under the pressure . . ." Hillquit took the quotation "without violating the principle of the class struggle" from Kautsky, "Der sozialistischen Kongresse," 37. Kautsky in turn quoted his own letter to the *Petite Republique*, September 28, 1899.]

70. Renner, *Marxismus, Krieg und Internationale*. [The *Arbeiter-Zeitung* was the daily newspaper of Austrian social democracy.]

upheaval that has taken place in the fabric of the economy, the state, and society, the mutual relations of classes, the character of ownership and the external relations of economic territories, finally also in the tasks of today's proletariat, since Marx's death. Although Marx and he posit different developmental tendencies in all these areas and although he abandons all the fundamental components of Marx's theoretical edifice and finally identifies different goals and tasks for the workers' movement from those of Marx, he does not forgo a Marxist disguise for his theory. Instead, he claims to be a proponent of genuine Marxism who struggled against the "reactionary misconstrual" of Marx's thought against the "vulgar orientation . . . of Marxism," against the "ossification" and "oversimplification" "of the [Marxist] theory of class struggle." Not he but rather the supposed Marxists had distorted the theory of the master. In the short period since Marx was active, class relations have often, "almost every decade and a half," been transformed. Instead of lugging around the old "catechistic propositions" of Marx's system as "old goods," it is necessary to revise the theoretical baggage in all areas. So his book is a "Marxist examination" of the new material of social development, a draft of a "study program for Marxists."[71]

Marx's entire period of activity falls, according to Renner, into the liberal social epoch with its individualistic-anarchistic economic mode, for which the power of the state was a bogeyman. Marx researched this epoch and described it in *Capital*. In order to expose its laws in their pure, logical form, every state intervention had to be conceptually disregarded. This "capitalist society, which Marx experienced and described, does not exist any more," something that Marxists have so far overlooked. The essential feature of the fundamental changes in the structure of society, which were completed between 1878 and 1914, consists of the "statification" of the previously stateless economy, that is, precisely "what Karl Marx's system logically and practically excluded," what Marx did not experience or describe. There were important consequences of this statification, because "the economy more and more exclusively serves the capitalist class, the state more and more predominantly the proletariat." Consequently, the state is the tool with the help of which the historical overthrow of capitalism into socialism will be carried out. But it is a "crazy conception" to think that the conquest of political power by the proletariat can be carried out through a sudden overthrow of the system, through a political surprise attack. Those are conceptions that have been smuggled from the political history of the bourgeoisie into the world of socialist ideas. The state will, instead, be conquered step by step in daily struggles. Its transformation is carried out through the gradual socialization of all economic functions. Marx was far from condemning and negating the state—from "state nihilism," "with which contemporary Marxism coquettes." Through the state all economic categories are fundamentally transformed. The competitive price of the private economy is transformed into cartel price. Finally, during the period of high protection and under the influence of the state, regulated price develops into national price, whose form and extent differs from state

71. [Ibid., 61–62, 70, 90, 97.]

to state. "It is only one step further to state legislation directly prescribing the price": "tax price" or "political price." "The economy is not sufficient to explain such pricing"; overall "deviation from the natural laws of the economy" is determined by the process of statification. "An extra-economic law . . . imposed itself over the basic economic law. And that is now the new problem of Marxism," because the deliberate allocation of goods, that is, the exclusive mode of circulation of a socialist society, is today already merged into the system of automatic commodity circulation.[72]

What can be said of commodity prices can also be said of the category of wages. The wage system is being fundamentally reorganized by the state. Today the worker's wage is already comprised of an individual and a collective wage. The state socializes variable capital, that is, capital spent on wages, through compulsory contributions by workers and employers for health, accident, and old age insurance, after individuals are paid. Basically, the state has already long done this through certain public outlays, like public schools, that contribute to the maintenance and renewal of the working class. "The working class, consequently, already receives a part of its wages collectively." "Development is towards the collectivization of an ever-larger part of wages." To an increasing extent, the worker becomes the subject and object of "public institutions." "The process of socialization integrates him as an element into the state."[73]

This "process of socializing the worker's wage" has not yet been analyzed by Marxists. But large transformations of the individual components of the wage also take place. The individual wage is replaced by the trade-union wage and finally by the regulated wage. "These institutions . . . transform the worker from a serf into an economic citizen. The leap from the free wage contract to the regulated system is of the same significance as that from manorial subjection and patrimonial justice to the bourgeois court." "But the regulated wage is still not the highest point of development. Giant capitalist enterprises construct service programs for their white-collar employees and, to an extent, their workers," with "a wage scale that is calculated over their whole lives, including their deaths"—in short, forms of wage payment which Renner calls the "programmatic wage." "From this it is only a step to the direct setting of wages by the state, to a tax wage." Through statification, "today the working classes find themselves in a different social situation from Marx's period." Ownership becomes a "public institution," work a "public job." A "regrouping of classes" takes place. Industrialism is no longer the predominant form of enrichment in contemporary society. The factory owner of the old kind is no longer counterposed to the proletariat. Rather, the dominant powers within the capitalist class have become agrarianism and finance capital. An upheaval in the economic function of land ownership occurs. While the process of statification and socialization is very extensive in agriculture, landownership, encompassed economically as ground rent, has become more and more parasitic. The question of ground rent will become the principal

---

72. [Ibid., 7–12, 28, 41–43. According to Renner, the regulated price was a consequence of the interaction of cartels and protective tariffs.]
73. [Ibid., 46–47.]

social question over the next five years and decades.[74]

Loan capital has also experienced massive transformations. Loan capital of the old kind was usury, a merely parasitic economic function. The usurers were, however, defeated. "Credit capital" of the new kind is not parasitic and is "generally felt to be a blessing."[75]

The purpose of Renner's arbitrary construct, which cannot be fully itemized here, is the justifications that his conclusions provide: the working class has to affirm the contemporary state and, through the "policy of changing alliances" with individual bourgeois classes, painstakingly, step by step work its way up and "take power over bourgeois society intellectually," positioning itself everywhere on the basis of the state and bourgeois society. Such an alliance policy is "not a watering down of class principle but its fulfillment." As the proletariat affirms the state it must also affirm state policy. There is no "amorphous internationality"; internationality is, rather, only the result of the actions of groups of nation states, which is "specifically new" in our period. "Capital is not international but national." "National capital organized by the state has become the active agent on the tribune of the world." Marx's categories are universal; Marxists start with the category of the stateless world economy but for the time being this unit is still not a single state. For the time being development has achieved the level of na-tional-political, territorial states. Hence there is also no "world proletariat," which is only a "mystical unit"; in reality only national proletariats within state territories exist. The world economy is only coming into being, promoted by the tendency of individual states to extend their economic territories. "In terms of specific states, expansionist tendencies appear as colonial policy and colonial exploitation, domination and ser-vitude." But this "moralistic standpoint" lies "deep below Marx's mode of thought," as behind these "mundane complaints about colonial policy" the "secular greatness of the economization of the world" should not be overlooked.[76]

"In this way, to be an opponent of the colonial system means being an opponent of world history." So long as capitalism persists in the economy and the anarchistic antagonism of states in politics, wars are unavoidable, because competitive struggles among economic territories take place in two ways: peacefully, through states' trade agreements, and aggressively, through conquest. Imperialist war should not be judged ethically but should be accepted as a fact, just like trade policy. It is nothing other than the turning of "price competition" "into arms competition." At most, there should be efforts to "civilize war" and the extension of the organization of the world into a "peaceful association of nations," through international law. So long, however, as such a "future, supranational organization of the world" has not been achieved, "war" remains "possible and, in certain circumstances, necessary," because it concerns the existence of a state and its economy. Since the methods of struggle in trade-union work rest "on the basis of this capitalist order," trade unions must act positively in the struggle. No

---

74. [Ibid., 47–55, 61, 64–65, 67.]
75. [Ibid., 82–83.]
76. [Ibid., 63, 65–66, 101, 106, 112–13, 123.]

union desires the destruction of industry. "The existence, continuation and future of this capital" also affect the working class positively. "In bellicose periods the working class also struggles for that continuation." If there is war, the proletariat also has to take the path of war: this path is also "a path of history," and "as the proletariat cannot absent itself from history, it has to travel this path." From the moment of the outbreak of war, there is no other possible attitude than "alignment with its own state." The stand of the proletarian parties on August 4, 1914, was justified.[77]

Obviously Renner's theorems cannot be reconciled with proletarian socialism. They should be evaluated as an attempt to divert the proletariat from its tasks as a class and to bring it into the train of the imperialist bourgeoisie. In his works, reformism sank from the level of social criticism to apologetics for bourgeois society. It was therefore unavoidable that reformism, having come to power after the war and the outbreak of revolution in the defeated states, was incapable of fulfilling even one of the tasks posed by proletarian socialism.

Eclecticism and the tendency to turn away from Marxism are characteristic of reformist theory during the postwar period. Emil Lederer restricts the applicability of Marx's labor theory of value in two ways. In his *Outlines of Economic Theory*, he restricts it to the terrain of competitive capitalism.[78] He regards it as insufficient to explain monopoly prices and hence tries to construct a fusion of the labor theory of value with marginal utility theory. He regards Marx's labor theory of value, secondly, as suited only to the explanation of static economic processes but not of dynamic conjunctual cycles ("Economic Cycle and Crises").[79] Lederer's explanation of crises is in essence an underconsumptionist theory—on a detour through monetary theories of crisis (extension of the labor process "only through additional credit")—with all its attendant deficiencies.[80]

Alfred Braunthal's *The Contemporary Economy and Its Laws* is intended to be a textbook of socialist economics, "faithful to the idea of Marxism." In fact, Braunthal combats Marx's theory with arguments borrowed from bourgeois criticism of Marx: it provides "no information about the laws according to which the social product, in fact, is divided into wages and returns to capital." The (bourgeois) theory of productivity is, in this respect, "without doubt superior to Marxist theory." He refers further to the "secure results" of marginal utility theory. His account of the contemporary economy is essentially a simplified compilation of Hilferding's thoughts about the progressive organization of the economy and Renner's ideas about statification and the ever-stronger influence of the state that is being proletarianized. Through its growing regulation of the organization of the whole economy, finally through "cold socialization," that is, through the encroachment of the public economy, the free economy with its market mechanism is more and more superseded. For this reason, Braunthal thinks, we stand

---

77. [Ibid., 281–82, 331, 360–61, 328–29, 353.]
78. Lederer, *Grundzügen der ökonomischen Theorie*.
79. Lederer, "Konjunktur und Krisen."
80. [Ibid., 387.]

at the beginning of a social revolution, "a society which is changing from capitalism into socialism."[81]

With the transition in the leadership of the world economy from Europe to the United States of America and under the impression of Americian "prosperity" after World War [I], a flush of uncritical admiration of American methods of organization and work ("rationalization") arose in bourgeois Europe. The emulation of these methods by German capitalists found the fullest approval among the proponents of trade-union theory and practice. A typical product of this current is the work of the chairperson of the German Woodworkers' Association, Fritz Tarnow, *Why Be Poor?* "The old economic theories about the social question," Tarnow thinks, "originated primarily in England. . . . The new theories are being shaped in America." America has shown that poverty is no economic necessity but a social illness, "whose curability, even within the framework of the capitalist economy, is undoubted." Wages, as a cost factor, have declined in significance, but as a factor in purchasing power they have gained importance. Increasing consumption and, above all, mass consumption is the "key to the development of production." In view of the enormous development of the productive forces, from now on waste is a blessing and restraint a curse. Not only is labor dependent on capital but capital is also dependent on the purchasing power of worker consumers. High wages are in the well-understood interests of the employers themselves. Countries with high wages have accumulated most strongly and can compete most successfully. American employers are advancing along the track of this knowledge, which is the basis of the secret of the continuing boom in the United States of America. Henry Ford's book, *My Life and Work*, is "certainly the most revolutionary text of all economic literature to the present."[82]

In addition, the various subspecies and currents of reformism as they appear in individual countries or internationally should also be mentioned briefly. First, "municipal socialism," which is concerned with reformist activity in the area of local politics—among other things, also the effort to municipalize water, gas and electricity services for the urban population in the general economic interest, without reference to their private sector profitability (see Hugo C, that is, Hugo Lindemann, *City Administration and Municipal Socialism in England* and *Germany City Administration*).[83]

A current in the English workers' movement is known as "guild socialism." It aspires to the control of production and the supersession of the wage system through the organizational unification of all manual and intellectual workers, not according to profession or trade-union groups but in associations (guilds) of whole industries. It seeks to achieve this goal possibly through a general strike. Guild socialism differs from syndicalism in that it does not oppose the state but instead allocates it certain functions outside the sphere of production (see George Robert Stirling Taylor, *Guild Politics: A*

81. Braunthal, *Wirtschaft der Gegenwart und ihre Gesetze*, 62–63, 241, 63, 46, 220.

82. Tarnow, *Warum arm sein?*, 10, 19, 70, 71.

83. Lindemann, *Städteverwaltung und Munizipal-Sozialismus in England* and *Deutsche Städteverwaltung*.

Practical Programme for the Labour Party; George Douglas Howard Cole, *Self-Government in Industry* and *Guild Socialism*; and George Douglas Howard Cole and William Mellor, *The Meaning of Industrial Freedom*).[84]

So-called "liberal socialism" stands outside the workers' movement and has less to do with socialism than liberalism, that is, capitalism. Represented by the isolated efforts of Franz Oppenheimer (*Neither Capitalism nor Communism*), drawing on the theories of Eugen Dühring, it seeks to maintain the mechanism of exchange.[85]

b. The Development of the Materialist Conception of History

The materialist conception of history, drafted by Marx with Engels's collaboration in a series of youthful writings (1842–1859) in inspired outlines, was never systematically developed by them. It was only Marx's students who undertook to extend it philosophically and epistemologically, deepening it, above all, through fruitful, specialized research in various areas of social, economic, and cultural history. Karl Kautsky dealt with it philosophically, above all in *Ethics and the Materialist Conception of History*, *Class Antagonisms in the Era of the French Revolution*, *Thomas More and His Utopia*, and *Foundations of Christianity*.[86] In his last large work, *The Materialist Conception of History*, Kautsky revised his earlier conception of the driving force of historical development just as he had in relation to his economic and political conceptions (compare Karl Korsch, *The Materialist Conception of History: An Argument with Karl Kautsky*).[87] Franz Mehring (1846–1919), in his *The Lessing Legend*, chose the literature and the history of [Gotthold Ephraim] Lessing and Frederick II [Hohenzollern] as his field of application. In brilliant essays in *Neue Zeit*, he dealt with the most diverse areas of history and literary history. In his consummate, broadly conceived *History of German Social Democracy*, which admittedly only extended to the beginning of revisionism, he illuminated the economic and social context of the growth of the socialist workers' movement and combined this with a presentation of its theoretical developments.[88] Georgi Plekhanov, the creator of the materialist sociology of culture and art, entered the struggle against revisionism as one of the most brilliant proponents of dialectical materialism (above all in *Fundamental Problems of Marxism*, *Henrik Ibsen*, *Essays on the History of Materialism*). From the postwar period, the fine and valuable book *History and Class Consciousness: Studies in Marxist Dialectics*, by Georg Lukács, and Karl Korsch's *Central Points of Historical Materialism* and *Marxism and Philosophy* should be mentioned above

---

84. [The German edition of Cole's *Self-Government in Industry* referred to by Grossman, *Selbstverwaltung in der Industrie*, was introduced by Rudolf Hilferding. Cole and Mellor's *Meaning of Industrial Freedom* was published together with Cole's *Guild Socialism* in Cole and Mellor, *Gildensozialismus*.]

85. Oppenheimer, *Weder Kapitalismus noch Kommunismus*.

86. For the German edition of *Class Antagonisms*, see Kautsky, *Die Klassengegensätze im Zeitalter*.

87. Kautsky, *Materialist Conception of History*; Korsch, *Die materialistische Geschichtsauffassung*.

88. Mehring, *The Lessing Legend* and *Geschichte der deutschen Sozialdemokratie*. Mehring also published many hundreds of articles in *Neue Zeit*.

all.[89] Finally, in addition to the works by Max Adler, already mentioned, also Heinrich Cunow's *Marx's Theory of History, Society and the State*.[90]

Significant Writings on Historical Materialism in Particular Countries

France

Sorel, Georges. *La Ruine du monde antique: Conception materialiste de l'histoire* [*The Collapse of the Ancient World: The Materialist Conception of History*]. Paris: M. Rivière, 1925 [1901].

Rappoport, Charles. *La Philosophie de l'histoire comme science de l'évolution* [*The Philosophy of History as an Evolutionary Science*]. Paris: M. Rivière, 1925 [1901].

Italy

Croce, Benedetto. *Historical Materialism and the Economics of Karl Marx*. London: Allen & Unwin, 1915 [1901].

———. *Philosophy of the Practical: Economic and Ethic*. London: Macmillan, 1913 [1909].

Mondolfo, Rodolfo. *Il materialismo storico in Federico Engels* [*The Historical Materialism of Friedrich Engels*]. Genova: Formiggini, 1912.

———. "Il concetto marxistico della "umwälzende Praxis" e suoi germi in Bruno e Spinoza." ["The Marxist Concept of "Revolutionary Praxis" and Its Origins in Bruno and Spinoza."] In *Festschrift für Karl Grunberg: zum 70. Geburtstag*, 366–376. Leipzig: Hirschfeld, 1932.

Labriola, Antonio. *Essays on the Materialist Conception of History*. Chicago: Kerr, 1908 [1896].

———. *Socialism and Philosophy*. Chicago: Kerr, 1912 [1898].

Poland

Brzozowski, Stanisław. *Idee: Wstęp do filozofii dojrzałości dziejowej* [*Ideas: Introduction to the Philosophy of Historical Maturity*]. Kraków: Wydawnictwo Literackie, 1990 [1910].

Russia

Bukharin, Nikolai. *Historical Materialism*. New York: International Publishers, 1925 [1921].

Deborin, Abram. *Vvedenie v filosofiiu dialekticheskogo materializma* [*An Introduction to the Philosophy of Dialectical Materialism*]. Moscow: Librokom, 2012 [1916].

---

89. Korsch, *Kernpunkte der materialistischen Geschichtsauffassung*; "Marxism and Philosophy."
90. Cunow, *Die Marxsche Geschichts-, Gesellschafts- und Staatstheorie*.

Plekhanov, Georgi. Preface to *Vvedenie v filosofiiu dialekticheskogo materializma*, by Abram Deborin. In *Selected Philosophical Works*, vol. 3, 577–99. Moscow: Progress Publishers, 1976 [1916].

Holland

Gorter, Hermann. *Der historische Materialismus* [*Historical Materialism*]. With a foreword by Karl Kautsky. Stuttgart: Dietz, 1919.

WRITINGS ABOUT PARTICULAR AREAS OF APPLICATION OF HISTORICAL MATERIALISM

Law

Pashukanis, Evgeny. *Law and Marxism: A General Theory*. New Brunswick, NJ: Transaction, 2002 [1924].

Stutschka, Peteris. *Das Problem des Klassenrechts und der Klassenjustiz* [*The Problem of Class Law and Class Justice*]. In Eugen Paschukanis, *Allgemeine Rechtslehre und Marxismus*, edited by Hermann Klenne and Leonid Mamut, 233–68. Freiburg: Rudolf Haufe Verlag, 1991 [1922].

Compare with Kelsen, Hans. "Allgemeine Rechtslehre im Lichte" ["The General Theory of Law in the Light of the Materialist Conception of History"], *Archiv für Sozialwissenschaft und Sozialpolitik*, 66, no. 3 (1931): 449–521.

Szende, Paul. "Nationales Recht und Klassenrecht: Beiträge aus der ungarischen Rechts und Wirtschaftsgeschichte" ["National Law and Class Law: Contributions from Hungarian Legal and Economic History"]. In Max Adler et al., *Festschrift für Carl Grünberg–Zum 70. Geburtstag*, 445–78. Leipzig: Hirschfeld, 1932.

Economic History

Cunow, Heinrich. *Allgemeine Wirtschaftsgeschichte: Von der primitiven Sammelwirtschaft bis zum Hochkapitalismus* [*General Economic History: From the Primitive Gatherer Economy to Advanced Capitalism*]. 4 vols. Berlin: Dietz, 1926–31.

The process of transition from the feudal state of the eighteenth century to the modern capitalist state, using the examples of Austria and Poland in

Grossman, Henryk. "Struktura społeczna i gospodarcza Księstwa Warszawskiego na podstawie spisow ludnosci 1808–1810 roku" ["The Social and Economic Structure of the Duchy of Warsaw on the Basis of the Results of the Censuses of 1808 and 1810"]. *Kwartalnik Statystyczny* 2 (1925): 1–108.

Grossmann, Henryk. *Österreichs Handelspolitik mit Bezug auf Galizien in der Reformperiode 1772–1790* [*Austria's Trade Policy with Regard to Galicia in the Reform Period 1772–1790*]. Vienna: Konegen, 1914.

———. "Die Anfänge und die geschichtliche Entwicklung der amtlichen Statistik in Oesterreich" ["The Beginnings and Historical Development of Official Statistics in Austria"]. *Statistische Monatsschrift*, n.s., 21 (1916): 331–423.

Hartmann, Ludo Moritz. *Römische Geschichte* [*Roman History*]. Gotha: Perthes, 1919.

———. *Der Untergang der antiken Welt* [*The Fall of the Ancient World*]. Vienna: Heller, 1910 [1903].

Wittfogel, Karl August. *Wirtschaft und Gesellschaft Chinas* [*China's Economy and Society*]. Leipzig: Hirschfeld, 1931.

Sociology of Knowledge

Horkheimer, Max. "A New Concept of Ideology?" In *Between Philosophy and Social Science*, 129–50. Cambridge, MA: MIT Press, 1993 [1930].

Szende, Paul. "Verhüllung und Enthüllung: Der Kampf der Ideologien in der Geschichte" ["Masking and Unmasking: The Struggle of Ideologies in History."] *Archiv für die Geschichte des Sozialismus und der Arbeiterbewegung* 10, nos. 2–3 (1922): 185–270.

c. The Problems of Imperialism and War

We pointed out earlier that toward the end of the previous century, the development of capitalist states took on more and more imperialist features and was distinguished by arms buildups and colonial expansion. Socialists schooled in the Marxist approach to history very early recognized the significance of these processes. From the start of the new century, in a series of writings (*The Social Revolution*, *The Road to Power*, *Trade Policy and Social Democracy*), Karl Kautsky predicts the approach of a "*new epoch of revolution*" as a result of colonial policy and imperialism. Particularly in the East: an age of conspiracies, coups, and constant social upheavals, he explained, was beginning in East Asia and the entire Muslim world. Eventually the West would be caught up in these. "A world war is brought within threatening proximity." In all these writings, Kautsky describes the features of capitalism that had changed during its imperialist period, its inclination to aim for war, acts of violence and conquest in the struggle over the world market. At the time, these developments did not appear to him as consequences of the whims of individual power holders but as bound up with the inner nature of capitalism. "The iron necessity of economic requirements drives modern industrial nations towards ruin."[91]

This conception of capitalism's developmental tendencies, until then generally widespread in the workers' movement, could not be reconciled with Tugan-Baranovsky's and Hilferding's theories of the unlimited possibilities for the development of capitalism, already mentioned. The harmonist conception of capitalist development obviously contradicted the reality of steadily growing competition and the escalation of struggles among the advanced capitalist countries over markets and

---

91. Kautsky, *The Social Revolution*; *The Road to Power*, 107; *Handelspolitik und Sozialdemokratie*, 94.

spheres of investment; it also contradicted the fundamental notion of historical materialism that explains politics on the basis of the economy. In her book *The Accumulation of Capital: A Contribution to the Economic Explanation of Imperialism*, Rosa Luxemburg set herself the task of resolving this contradiction.[92] If the neo-harmonists' conception of capitalism's unlimited possibilities for development was right, then the imperialist features that were appearing with such intensity could not be explained in terms of the nature of capitalism. They were instead to be evaluated as merely accidental phenomena. On the other hand, as Rosa Luxemburg correctly emphasizes, "the theory of capitalist collapse . . . is the cornerstone of scientific socialism."[93] And this is the great historical significance of Rosa Luxemburg's book: that, in conscious opposition to the attempted distortions of the neo-harmonists, she adheres to the fundamental idea in *Capital* of an absolute economic limit to the development of the capitalist mode of production, even though the concrete justification that she provided for the theory of breakdown, today, has to be identified as mistaken. In her critique of Marx's analysis of the accumulation process, which assumes a society that consists solely of capitalists and workers and does not engage in foreign trade, she came to the conclusion "that Marx's schema of accumulation does not solve the question of who is to benefit in the end by enlarged reproduction." Purely abstractly, assuming the relations of dependence and proportions of Marx's schema, his analysis gives the appearance that capitalist production can by itself realize all surplus value and employ capitalized surplus value to satisfy its own requirements. That is, "capitalist production buys up its entire surplus product."[94] For example, coal mining is extended in order to make the expansion of the iron making and then machine building industries possible; the latter are expanded to make the extension of the production of means of consumption possible. This extension of industries producing means of consumption, however, creates markets for the extended production of the coal mining, iron making, and machine building industries. Individual branches of industry thus create markets for each other. Setting out Marx's analysis in this way, which Rosa Luxemburg regards as mistaken, production can be extended "*ad infinitum* . . . in circles," without it being apparent "who is to benefit . . . who are the new consumers for whose sake production is ever more enlarged."[95] Such accumulation does not serve consumption but is "production for the sake of production."[96] Actually, workers can really only consume a part of the enlarged product, the part that expresses the value of their wages. Part of the product serves to replace means of production that have been used up; the remainder that is

92. [Luxemburg, *The Accumulation of Capital*. This translation of Luxemburg is unsatisfactory in places. Where that is the case, new, more accurate translations from the German original are provided, and where Schwarzschild's translation has been used and her terminology diverges from the translations in the Penguin editions of *Capital*, her texts have been modified. The term "diagram," for example, has been replaced with "schema."]

93. [Ibid., 96.]

94. [Ibid., 330.]

95. [Ibid.]

96. [Marx, *Capital*, vol 1., 742.]

left, surplus value, consistently grows in the course of accumulation. Who realizes the consistently growing surplus value? The capitalists themselves only consume a part of it, while they employ an ever-growing part of it for further accumulation. But what do they do, then, with the even larger annual product, with their surplus value? Rosa Luxemburg comes to the conclusion that "the realisation of the surplus value for the purposes of accumulation is an impossible task for a society which consists solely of workers and capitalists," that is, such a capitalism cannot exist. The capitalist mode of production requires for its existence, "as its prime condition . . . that there should be strata of buyers outside capitalist society," that is, social layers "whose own mode of production is not capitalistic" and who realize the capitalist surplus value. But capitalism does not only require noncapitalist "milieus" to realize surplus value, even more in order to obtain a large part of the means of production, in particular raw materials (constant capital); and finally "only the existence of non-capitalist groups and countries can guarantee such a supply of additional labour power for capitalist production."[97] It is therefore apparent that "the process of capital accumulation is connected with noncapitalist forms of production in all its value and material relations: constant capital, variable capital, and surplus value."[98] Capitalist accumulation "as an historical process" is, in practice, dependent on "the given historical setting" of non-capitalist countries and layers: artisans, peasants. Without this milieu it is "in any case unthinkable." The result is capital's aggressive drive to bring noncapitalist territories under its sway. In this way, Rosa Luxemburg believes that she has explained not only accumulation and the conditions under which it takes place but also the driving force behind imperialism and the tendency to colonial expansion. Military occupation of colonies, the violent theft of their means of production and labor power, "planning for the systematic destruction and annihilation of all the non-capitalist social units," the struggle of capitalism against the natural economy, and the ruin of independent economies of artisans and peasants: all result from the drive to realize surplus value. In contrast to the "crude optimism" of [David] Ricardo, [Jean-Baptiste] Say, and Tugan-Baranovsky, for whom capitalism can develop without limit, "with the logical corollary of capitalism-in-perpetuity,"[99] her own solution seems to be in the spirit of Marx's theory of the final breakdown of the capitalist system of production, which is founded on "the dialectical contradiction that the movement of capital accumulation requires noncapitalist formations as its context . . . and can only exist as long as this milieu is present."[100] As natural economies are subordinated to capitalism, the situation Marx predicted in his analysis draws nearer, namely, capitalist production as "the exclusive and universal domination of capitalist production in all countries and for all branches of industry."[101] "But this is the start of a dead end. Once the final result

97. [Luxemburg, *The Accumulation of Capital*, 350–52, 361.]
98. [Luxemburg, *Die Akkumulation des Kapitals*, 314.]
99. [Luxemburg, *The Accumulation of Capital*, 365–66, 370.]
100. [Luxemburg, *Die Akkumulation des Kapitals*, 315.]
101. Luxemburg, *The Accumulation of Capital*, 417.

is achieved . . . accumulation becomes impossible.'[102] The historical limits of accumulation, the impossibility for the productive forces to develop further, is apparent here. The consequence is the end of capitalism. Its imperialist phase is thus the final period in its historical career. So the economic analysis of noncapitalist markets has the closest inner connection with the emergence of socialism. Socialism is not merely dependent on subjective-voluntarist factors but results from the economy's course of development, connected with the forces within capitalism that objectively work toward its necessary breakdown.

This theory, which places emphasis on the problem of markets, on the question of the realization of surplus value, is not capable of satisfactorily explaining the characteristic feature of capitalism's imperialist period: the export of capital (see Lenin's theory of imperialism, below). Furthermore, these ideas were not new; they have a history of more than a hundred years. In essence, they were already developed by Simonde de Sismondi in his *New Principles of Political Economy* of 1819 and Thomas Malthus in the chapter on accumulation in his *Principles of Political Economy* of 1820.[103] These ideas were later extended by socialist theorists to explain imperialism, by Heinrich Cunow ("On Crisis Theory"), Louis B. Boudin (*The Theoretical System of Karl Marx*, with a foreword by Karl Kautsky), and Kautsky himself (see above).[104] Luxemburg's achievement was new in that she used Marx's reproduction schemas to demonstrate the necessity of noncapitalist areas.

This is not the place to offer an extensive methodological and material critique of the theory. In this regard, refer to the works of Henryk Grossman, discussed further below. Directly opposed to Rosa Luxemburg's is the position of Vladimir Ilyich Lenin, who already argues against the Russian Narodniks in his *A Characterisation of Economic Romanticism (Sismondi and Our Native Sismondists)*.[105] The Narodniks adopted Sismondi's theory of external market as the condition for the existence of capitalism in full. Lenin repeatedly criticizes the theory that it was impossible to realize surplus value under "pure" capitalism in his principal work against the Narodniks, *The Development of Capitalism in Russia*. The contradiction between the limits of consumption and limitless expansion of "production for the sake of production" does exist.[106] But this is not a contradiction in a theory but a real contradiction in the capitalist system. Nothing would be more vulgar, however, than to conclude from the contradictions of capitalism, that is, from its irrationality, that it is impossible. This contradiction is not capitalism's only one. It can neither exist nor develop without contradictions. "Nothing could be more

---

102. Luxemburg, *Die Akkumulation des Kapitals*, 364.
103. [See Malthus, *Principles of Political Economy*, 308–438. Grossman wrote two studies of Sismondi's work, the 1924 essay included in the present volume and the 1934 entry in *Encyclopaedia of the Social Sciences*.]
104. Cunow, "Zur Zusammenbruchstheorie"; Boudin, *The Theoretical System of Karl Marx* [Kautsky's foreword was only published in the German edition, *Das theoretische System von Karl Marx*]; Kautsky, "Krisentheorien."
105. [The Narodniks were populists who opposed tsarism and identified with the peasantry in late nineteenth-century Russia.]
106. [Marx, *Capital*, vol. 1, 742; Lenin, *A Characterisation of Economic Romanticism*, 161, 182.]

senseless than to conclude . . . that Marx did not admit the possibility of surplus-value being realised in capitalist society, that he attributed crises to under-consumption, and so forth."[107] Instead, different branches of industry constitute markets for each other. Since, however, they develop unevenly and overtake each other, because there is no regulation to impose consistency on individual branches, "the more developed industry" necessarily "seeks a foreign market."[108] This uneven development of individual branches of industry is, therefore, the final cause of crises and capitalism's expansionist tendencies. After the outbreak of World War [I], as the problem of imperialism naturally attracted greater attention, Lenin undertook to lay bare the nature of imperialism, its economic and social roots in his book *Imperialism, the Highest Stage of Capitalism*. He identified these in the *structural transformation of world capitalism*, in the displacement of competition by monopoly, which opened the phase of capitalism's decline. Its characteristic feature is no longer the export of commodities but of capital. The monopolistic character of capitalism explains continuous colonial expansion and the division of the world among monopolist associations of capitalists, dominated by the financial oligarchy. Capital export, through the domination of enormous territories in Asia and Africa that supply raw materials, secures colossal superprofits for the bourgeoisies of the ruling capitalist countries. The essence of imperialist expansion does not lie in the sphere of circulation (the realization of surplus value) but in the sphere of production (raising profits).

The emergence of imperialism opened a period of constant war and threat of war. Wars are a product of imperialism, an unavoidable result of the antagonisms of the epoch of decline. In this respect, the character of wars has changed; the formal distinction between wars of defense and offense has lost any meaning. For in contrast with the wars of national liberation during the rising phase of capitalism, wars in the period of decline are predatory wars among imperialist countries and against less economically developed nations and states. As a consequence, the working class has special responsibilities in questions of war, civil peace, defense of the fatherland, and approving war credits. During the phase of capitalism's decline, the proletariat has the task of transforming war between peoples into civil war, with a view to the conquest of power and, for this reason, of preparing strategically and organizationally for revolution. Grigory Zinoviev (*The War and the Crisis of Socialism*), Vladimir Ilyich Lenin and Grigory Zinoviev (*Against the Current: Articles from the Years 1914–16*), Leon Trotsky (*The War and the International*), Nikolai Bukharin (*Imperialism and World Economy*, with an introduction by Vladimir Ilyich Lenin), and Hermann Gorter (*Imperialism, the World War and Social Democracy*) take similar stances on the problem of imperialism and war.[109]

---

107. [Lenin, *Development of Capitalism*, 58.]

108. [Ibid., 66.]

109. For the first Zinoviev piece, see Sinowjew, *Der Krieg und die Krise* [a section of the book is available in English translation as Zinoviev, "Two Eras of War"]; for Lenin and Zinoviev, see Lenin and Sinowjew, *Gegen den Strom* [a collection of seventy-four articles; the longest articles available in English are Lenin's "Collapse of the Second International" and "Discussion on Self-Determination"]. See also Gorter, *Der Imperialismus, der*

d. The Problem of the Proletarian Seizure of Power: Marxist Theory and the Soviet Union

The establishment of the Soviet Union is, in principle, not simply a turning point of great importance in the political and economic history of capitalism but also in the field of Marxist theory. The outbreak of the Russian Revolution confirmed the correctness of the prognosis of Marxists, who had predicted its advent and thus based their strategy and tactics on it for decades. Further, it proved the correctness of those who, like Lenin in 1905, had already predicted on the basis of Marxist theory that the coming revolution would be an upheaval of a new kind—proletarian revolution, which in its goal, organs, and tactics would move beyond the bourgeois world.[110] The international significance of the October revolution and its historical meaning from the point of view of Marxist theory is, moreover, that the sole rule of the capitalist system has reached its end. With the October revolution the bourgeois mode of production, before this turning point the dominant and the most progressive mode of production, lost its aura of permanence and indestructibility, proving to be a historical, that is transitory,category. Previously, only remnants of social formations that have gone under and are in comparison more backward (artisans, peasants, the primitive economies of colonial people in Africa and Asia) have survived alongside it. In contrast to capitalism, socialism was previously only a demand for the future arrangement of society. Now—as experience seems to confirm—a superior economic system in the Soviet Union confronts capitalism, which has been convulsed by the world economic crisis. Through the formulation of the first Five-Year Plan of 1928–32, it is on the best path to realizing, for the first time in history, the idea of a socialist, planned economy, after initial, transitional difficulties are overcome. In a sixth of the world, particularly in the previously most backward areas of Asiatic Russia, the Soviet Union knew how to construct a socialist economy on the basis of the most advanced technology at a gigantic tempo in the areas of economics and culture, for which there is no historical analogy and boldly leaping over whole historical stages of development. The great popularity of the planned economy's configuration in almost all the highly developed countries of Europe and in the United States of America expresses the shaken faith in the justification for and adequacy of the capitalist market economy. Capitalism's difficulties seem to have become more acute because of the fact of the very existence of the Soviet Union alone, as a consequence of its successful socialist construction. Social contradictions and class antagonisms are no longer, as earlier, contradictions between reality and a hoped-for socialist future but rather the ever more pronounced contradictions between two social and state systems

---

Weltkrieg und die Sozial-demokratie.

110. [In 1905 Lenin did argue that the working class would play a leading role in the revolution against the tsar in Russia and in the establishment of a "revolutionary-democratic dictatorship of the proletariat and the peasantry." This would clear the way for capitalist development. But he maintained that the coming revolution was definitely not a socialist revolution. *Two Tactics of Social-Democracy*, 28. Only in 1917 did Lenin conclude that socialist revolution was on the immediate agenda. *Letters from Afar*, 341.]

that exist side by side. The foundation of the Marx-Engels Institute in Moscow, under the leadership of the well-known Marx researcher David Riazanov, is of the greatest significance for the scientific deepening and development of Marxist theory. It took on the monumental task of [producing] the *Marx-Engels Collected Works* (in more than forty volumes), which will publish fundamentally important parts of Marx and Engels's world of ideas that were previously unknown.[111] *Marx-Engels-Archiv*, which also appears in German, is the organ of the Institute.

Research into the particular conditions of the existence and development of the peasant economy plays a specific role in the socialist literature of the Soviet Union. From the extensive literature only the following are mentioned: Alexander Vasilyevich Chayanov, *The Optimal Size of Agricultural Enterprises*, *The Theory of the Peasant Economy*, *The Theory of Peasant Co-operatives*; Nikolai Pavlovich Makarov, *The Peasant Economy and Its Evolution*. Further, the International Agrarian Institute in Moscow and its journal deal with these problems.[112]

Russian socialist literature, however, engages above all with the theory of socialist upheaval and the period of transition to socialism. In his speech on the program of the Third International in 1922, Bukharin criticized those who want to delay the socialist upheaval until socialism has ripened within capitalism. In contrast to the classical statement in Marx's *Capital* that "capitalism matured fully under feudal rule" until the new order was able to fully develop after the conquest of political power, the Russian Communists, especially Bukharin, insist that this theory does not apply to socialism. Under feudalism, the bourgeoisie could already possess a monopoly over industrial means of production, achieve leading roles in industrial production, and, drawing on its economic power, also overtake the feudal class culturally. In contrast, the working class cannot become the owner of the means of production and control production under capitalism. Nor can it rise to a higher cultural level than the bourgeoisie within the framework of capitalism. "Socialism can *never* ripen in this manner, even under the most favourable conditions. . . . It is impossible for the working class to take production in hand within the womb of capitalist society. . . . The proletariat . . . can learn all that only when it has already achieved the *dictatorship of the proletariat*."[113] "Socialism thus is not arise, it must be consciously constructed."[114]

---

111. [Marx and Engels, *Historisch-kritische Gesamtausgabe*. This project was terminated under Stalin, Riazanov was dismissed as the head of the Institute in February 1931.]

112. For *Optimal Size of Agricultural Enterprises* see Chayanov, *Die optimalen Betriebsgrössen*. [The Russian edition of *Theory of the Peasant Economy* published in 1925 was based on an edition published in 1923, to which Grossman refers]. Makarov, *Krestianskoe khozyaistvo i ego evolyutsiya*. [The International Agrarian Institute, *Mezhdunarodnii Agrarnii Institut*, published its journal *Agrarprobleme* in German from 1928 until 1934.]

113. Bukharin, "The Programme of the International," 491. [The first quotation is from Bukharin rather than Marx; but see *Capital*, vol. 1, 875.]

114. [This quotation does not appear in the English edition—Bukharin, *The Politics and Economics*—or the German edition to which Grossman referred, Bucharin, *Imperialismus und Weltwirtschaft*. Its sense, however, is apparent in the English edition, 99: the bourgeoisie did not build capitalism, but it was built. The proletariat, as an organized collective subject, is building socialism as an organized system. If the creation of capitalism was spontaneous, the building of communism is to a marked degree a conscious, that is, organized, process.]

Accordingly, for the Russian Communists, the possibility of a proletarian revolution is not tied to any definite developmental maturity of capitalist society. Only a sufficient concentration of production is required to make the planned organization of the economy possible and a correspondingly advanced union of proletarian atoms into a revolutionary class, to guarantee the overthrow of the bourgeoisie in the revolution and the construction of the apparatus of the proletarian dictatorship. In addition to these two objective moments, two subjective moments are required: the revolutionary enthusiasm of the proletariat and its desire to end the capitalist order, and the incapacity of the bourgeoisie to effectively resist the proletariat. All these moments, however, are compatible with the most diverse economic conditions. The breakdown of capitalism, according to this conception, can just as easily take place at a high or a relatively low level of capitalism's inner maturity. A country does not necessarily have to be among the leading capitalist countries in terms of its general level of economic development. On the contrary, since the capacity of the bourgeoisie is, all other things being equal, directly proportional to the economic maturity of capitalism, it is likely that "the collapse of the entire system ensues, beginning with the organisationally weakest links of that system."[115] Later we will see that this theory of breakdown, which constitutes nothing other than a formulation of the specific Russian situation during the [First World] War, neither corresponds with Lenin's conception of the overthrow of capitalism nor does it apply at all to the advanced capitalist countries of Western Europe.

The problems of socialist economic construction in industry and agriculture is of immediate, current significance, and at the same time present the greatest theoretical difficulties. No doubt the expropriation of the means of production has long been a fixed component of all socialist programs. But the question of the extent of the expropriation of industrial and commercial capital, the nature and extent of the connection between the socialist elements of the economy without markets and the remainder of the capitalist economy, that is, the question of the extent to which the market economy is to be retained and an economy without markets and money is to be introduced, now had to be answered. The problem of the socialist restructuring of the village had to be solved: whether a state monopoly over agricultural products should be introduced or private peasant production and private sales, only burdened with a tax in kind, should remain. Likewise, the question of whether collective agricultural production should be introduced and, finally, to what degree. Everywhere, the first tentative attempts at proletarian economic policy had to be made. They eventually achieved a preliminary resolution with the formulation of the first Five-Year Plan and of rules for a planned economy, which also laid the foundations for a new science.

Until the October revolution, it was almost only within the Russian workers' movement that the problems of the proletarian seizure of power were discussed concretely. With this event, most strongly inspired by Lenin's *The State and Revolution*,[116]

---

115. Bukharin, *The Politics and Economics*, 65.
116. [Lenin's *State and Revolution* was written in August-September of 1917 but not published until 1918.

they moved to the center of discussions within the workers' movement of the entire world, particularly Western Europe: the question of whether the conquest of power by the proletariat would take place by parliamentary or extraparliamentary means, that is, through the revolutionary action of the working class; the question of the choice between the dictatorship of the proletariat—the council system—as the realization of proletarian democracy and parliamentary democracy as the form of appearance of the dictatorship of the bourgeoisie; the question of the choice between spontaneous proletarian revolution and conscious organization through a party, and thus the fundamental relationship between party and class; the problem of the organization of a new proletarian international, whether it should be organized according to the principles of democratic centralism as a unitary world party, with the task of practically preparing for the world revolution; the task of conquering the middle strata in the towns and countryside as allies of the proletariat; the question of colonial peoples' struggle for freedom and the right of nations to self-determination, that is, the problem of mobilizing the oppressed masses of the entire world against imperialism.

The assessment of the tendencies of the economic development of world capitalism is, naturally, of decisive importance in answering these questions. At present, those like Kautsky and the speakers at the Brussels Congress of the Second International in 1928 are of the view that capitalism stands at the outset of a further era of upswing. Others, on the contrary, assume that it is in a period of decline, which is indeed punctuated by short periods of temporary stabilization, but that on the whole a continual sharpening of class antagonisms is apparent, which must finally lead to the decisive struggle for power.

The experiences and lessons of the Russian Revolution are a current problem for Western European capitalism if it is in the midst of decline, placing the question of the Western European revolution on the agenda for the next period. This is the significance of debates over the conquest of state power inside the left wing of the Second (Socialist) International, for example the debates at the Linz Congress of Austrian social democracy (October 30–November 3, 1926), at which the new party program was adopted.[117] The core problem was the question of whether civil war and the use of force should be avoided by the working class in its struggle for state power and socialism. The result of the discussion can be summarized thus: the working class should in principle make use of the legal means of democracy in its struggle. It should not, however, ignore the fact that it is probable that the bourgeoisie will have recourse to force against the working class and its state if the proletariat conquers political power by means of democracy, if therefore democracy is decisively deployed against the bourgeoisie itself, as no ruling class gives up its power without a struggle. Under such circumstances, the working class for its part cannot abstain from the use of force.

Its perspectives, however, underpinned Lenin's activity and published writings in the period leading up to the Bolshevik Revolution.]

117. [Sozialdemokratische Arbeiterpartei Österreichs. *Protokoll des sozialdemokratischen Parteitages 1926*.]

e. The End of Capitalism

While the sole rule of the capitalist system was convulsed by the victory of the Oc-tober revolution in Russia, it did not resolve the question of the end of capitalism in socialist theory, given the concrete circumstances in which this victory was possible. With the October revolution, the breakthrough from the capitalist system took place at its weakest point, namely, where the revolutionizing effects of capitalism had hardly begun at the moment of the social explosion. For the technological backwardness of old Russia was still more characteristic of feudalism than of capitalism. The Russian example is not, therefore, to be regarded as typical of the breakdown of capitalism in the industrially most developed countries. Their capacity to resist, as Bukharin says, is in direct proportion to their economic maturity, thus significantly greater than was the case in Russia, whose capitalist development was just beginning. If the October revo-lution was a symptom and also the beginning of the breakdown of the capitalist world system, the immediate, concrete causes of this event are still to be found in factors other than the likely causes of the breakdown of capitalism in fully capitalist countries like England, Germany, and the United States of America. After as before it, the break-down of capitalism therefore remains a problem from the standpoint of Marxist theory and the labor movement.

During the postwar period, Henryk Grossman undertook to reassert anew the va-lidity of this highly disputed but basic concept of Marx's system. Previously, there were two variants of the theory of breakdown. One (for example, Bukharin, *Imperialism and the Accumulation of Capital*) only speaks generally about the "limit . . . given to *a certain degree by the tension of capitalist contradictions*" that "will unavoidably lead to the collapse of capitalist rule," without proving this "unavoidability," that is, without providing the theoretical explanation of why these contradictions must culminate in the final impos-sibility of balance.[118] Just as little does this interpretation provide concrete indicators by which the "degree" of critical tension in the contradictions that make breakdown "unavoidable" can be identified in advance. This can only be determined after the fact, after the advent of the breakdown. Then, however, the theory of breakdown is super-fluous as an instrument of scientific knowledge. Such a "general" explanation of break-down must be considered to be unsatisfactory because of its scientific indeterminacy, as it really does not fulfill the "Marxist requirement of concreteness" (Lenin).[119]

The other variant of breakdown theory, represented by Cunow, Kautsky (in writ-ings of the period 1901–11, cited above), Boudin, and Rosa Luxemburg, sought to derive the necessity of the downfall of the capitalist system from the limitations of the market, thus from processes in the sphere of circulation ("the realization problem").

In his 1898 article, already mentioned, Cunow investigates the core problem of "whether our economic development drives towards a general catastrophe." Previous-

---

118. Bukharin, *Imperialism and the Accumulation of Capital*, 265.
119. [Lenin, "The Junius Pamphlet," 308–9, similarly, 316.]

ly, the steady expansion of colonial possessions functioned to weaken the tendency to break down, resulting from insufficient markets. As such an extension of markets has its limit, however, the "unavoidability of breakdown" is also a given. Without gaining external markets, "England would long ago have faced a conflict between the capacity of its domestic and foreign markets to consume and the gigantic escalation of its capitalist accumulation." For Cunow, breakdown is not in doubt; rather, [it is] simply [a matter of] "how long the capitalist mode of production can survive . . . and under what circumstances breakdown will take place."[120]

After Kautsky's endorsement in the preface, Boudin's book deals with "the decisive points of Marx's system." Boudin also sees in the sale of surplus value "the great problem" on which the existence of the economic constitution of capitalism depends. "It is the inability to dispose of that product that is the chief cause of the temporary disturbances within its bowels." Indeed, if crises have previously ended and further accumulation has been made possible again, it is only because "capitalistic countries . . . had an outside world into which they could dump the products which they could not themselves absorb." But this solution was only temporary. The thorough capitalization of the territories of agrarian markets signifies the "*the beginning of the end of capitalism*" and will lead to "the inevitable breakdown of the capitalistic mode of production."[121]

In contrast to all previous breakdown theorists, Henryk Grossman treads a new path in his principal work *The Law of Accumulation and Breakdown of the Capitalist System* and numerous methodological and critical essays ("A New Theory of Imperialism and Social Revolution," "The Change in the Original Plan for Marx's *Capital*," "Gold Production in the Reproduction Schema of Marx and Rosa Luxemburg," "The Value Price Transformation in Marx and the Problem of Crisis").[122] He explains the decisive cause of the inevitable demise of the capitalist system in terms of the *overaccumulation of capital in highly developed countries* and the resulting *insufficient valorization* of capital, thus in terms of the process of production itself ("the valorization problem"). With new proofs taken from modern economic relations, Grossman seeks to support the theory developed by Marx, today almost forgotten but already present in John Stuart Mill and Adam Smith in an embryonic form.[123] It holds that once a nation's capital exceeds a definite scale, its accumulation finds no further profitable opportunities for investment and consequently either lies idle or has to be exported. Since Tugan-Baranovsky's book on crisis, the problem of crisis and breakdown in the Marxist literature of the last thirty years has simply been dealt with from the point of view of disproportionality between individual spheres of production. Grossman demonstrates that, for Marx, the decisive

---

120. Cunow, "Zur Zusammenbruchstheorie," 425, 427, 430.

121. Boudin, *The Theoretical System of Karl Marx*, 150, 235, 244.

122. Grossman(n), *Das Akkumulations- und Zusammenbruchsgesetz*; "Eine neue Theorie"; "The Change in the Original Plan"; "Die Goldproduktion im Reproduktionsschema"; "Die Wert-Preis-Transformation bei Marx."

123. John Stuart Mill, *Principles of Political Economy*, book 4, chapter 4, 481–91; Adam Smith, *Wealth of Nations*, vol. 1, book 1, chapter 9, 78–89.

problem was not primarily partial crises arising from disproportionality but rather the primarily general crisis, "general glut," which is caused by "parallel production . . . which takes place simultaneously over the whole field."[124] "Precisely the possibility of such primarily general crises and not primarily partial crises arising from disproportionality is the object of Marx's dispute with the Say-Ricardo conception."[125]

That an ever-growing mass of means of production (MP: machines, buildings, raw materials, instruments of production) can be set in motion with a progressive decline in the expenditure of labor (L) is an empirical law characteristic of the capitalist mode of production as ever-expanding reproduction. On the basis of capitalism, the law is expressed in the constant growth in the amount of constant capital per worker in relation to variable (wage) capital (c:v, as the Marxists say, the organic composition of capital), which American census figures also confirm. As a result of the progressively higher organic composition of capital, because of the associated rising productivity of labor, wages do account for an ever-smaller portion of total production. To the extent that the surplus value generated by a given working population grows absolutely (the rate of surplus value increases), however, it falls in relation to the continuously expanding total capital (c + v). This is the fact that underlies the *law of the tendency for the rate of profit to fall*.

The classical economists (Ricardo) already correctly identified the tendency for the rate of profit to fall as a phenomenon but mistakenly attempted to explain it as a law of nature, resulting from the decline in the productivity of the soil. Ricardo drew pessimistic conclusions for the future of capitalism from this phenomenon, as without profit "there could be no accumulation." He consoled himself that "happily," from time to time, industrial and agricultural inventions (mechanical engineering and agronomy) can break through this pernicious tendency, so that it will only have an impact in the distant future.[126]

Many earlier theorists, like Boudin but above all Georg Charasoff (*The System of Marxism*),[127] felt that Marx also connected the breakdown of capitalism with the fall in the rate of profit. They could not, however, demonstrate the content of this connection, and "the great importance that this law has for capitalist production."[128] That is easy to explain, as they only ever pointed out the fall in the rate of profit alone. The rate of profit, however, only expresses a proportional relationship, nothing other than a numerical concept. It is apparent that this cannot lead to the breakdown of a real system. For that to happen, real causes are required.

Moreover, the tendency for the rate of profit to decline has been a constant, concomitant phenomenon of capitalism from its beginnings until today, that is, during the

---

124. [Marx, "Economic Manuscript of 1861–63 [Notebooks VII to XII]," 115, 136. "General glut" appears in English in Marx's and Grossman's original texts.]

125. Grossmann, *Das Akkumulations- und Zusammenbruchsgesetz*, 211.

126. [Ricardo, *Principles of Political Economy*, 71, 73.]

127. Charasoff, *Das System des Marxismus*.

128. [Marx, *Capital*, vol. 3, 319.]

whole process of its development. Where, then, does the sudden shift to breakdown come from? Why can't capitalism survive with a rate of profit of 4 percent just as well as with one of 13–15 percent, as the declining rate is offset by a rising mass of profit? Indeed, the growth in the mass of profit, as a consequence of the even faster growth in total capital, would indeed be expressed in ever-smaller percentages. The rate of profit would approach zero, that is, the boundary point in the mathematical sense, without reaching it, and yet the capitalist class could nevertheless feel comfortable as a consequence of the growth in the mass of profit.

Grossman was the first to point out that breakdown cannot be derived from or explained by the rate of profit, that is, by the index number of profits, but must be understood in terms of what is concealed behind it: the real mass of profit in relation to the social mass of capital. For according to Marx, "accumulation depends not only on the rate of profit but on the amount of profit."[129] If accumulation proceeds as a continuous process, the surplus value of the capitalists must be used for three purposes, be divided into three parts. First, one part must be used as additional constant capital (a_c); a second part as additional variable capital (a_v)—for the application of additional labor power; the remaining, third part can be used as funds [f] for the capitalists' consumption. Now, the mass of surplus value does grow absolutely with the development of the capitalist mode of production. If, however, the organic composition of capital grows—as is necessary for capitalist production and is also assumed in the theoretical analysis—then a relatively ever-larger part of the surplus value must be deducted for the purposes of additional accumulation (a_c). As long as the absolute mass of total social capital—with a low organic composition—is small, surplus value is relatively large, and this leads to a rapid increase in accumulation. For example, with a composition of 200c +100v +100s, constant capital c can be increased by 33 $1/3$ percent of its initial size (assuming the employment of all the surplus value for the purposes of accumulation). At a higher level of capital accumulation, with a significantly higher organic composition of capital, for example of 14,900c + 100v +150s, the expanded mass of surplus value is only 1 percent when it is employed as additional capital a_c. It is easy to calculate that with continuing accumulation on the basis of an ever-higher organic composition, a point must come when all accumulation ceases. This is all the more true because it is not any arbitrary fractional amount of capital that can be employed but rather a definite minimal amount is required, whose scale consistently grows with increasing accumulation of capital. With the progress of capital accumulation, therefore, an ever-larger part, not only absolutely but also relatively, must be deducted from surplus value for the purposes of accumulation. So at high levels of accumulation, when the extent of the total social capital is great, the part of surplus value required for additional accumulation a_c will be so large that it finally absorbs almost all of the surplus value. A point must be reached at which the part of surplus value destined for the consumption of the workers and the capitalists $(a_v + f)$ declines absolutely. That

---

129. [Marx, "Economic Manuscript of 1861–63 [Notebooks VII to XII]," 165.]

is the turning point at which the previously latent tendency to break down begins to take effect. Now it is apparent that the conditions required for the continuation of accumulation can no longer be entirely fulfilled, that the mass of surplus value, although it has grown absolutely, is not sufficient for the three functions. If, as previously assumed, the additional constant capital (a_c) is deducted from surplus value to the required extent, then the revenue part is not sufficient to cover the consumption of workers and employers to the previous extent. *An intense struggle between the working class and the employers over the division of revenue*, rising pressure from employers on the level of wages, becomes unavoidable. If, on the other hand, the capitalists are forced, under pressure from the working class, to maintain the previous level of wages, and consequently the part destined for additional accumulation a_c is reduced, the tempo of accumulation slows down. This would signify that the productive apparatus cannot be renewed and expanded to the extent required by technological progress. A relative technological backwardness in the productive apparatus would set in. Any further accumulation must in such circumstances increase the difficulties, because the mass of surplus value can only be increased to an insignificant extent with a given population. Surplus value flowing from previous capital outlays must therefore lie idle; an excess of inactive capital searching in vain for investment opportunities results. In this way, Grossman explains the technological backwardness of older capitalist countries, like England, with a higher level of capital accumulation, and the tendency apparent there for the level of wages to stagnate or decline.

In "pure," that is, isolated capitalism, these tendencies must soon prevail, that is, lead to the breakdown of the system under the pressure of intensifying class antagonisms. In capitalism that is interdependent with the world economy, numerous *countertendencies* operate to weaken the tendency to break down, which is then only expressed in temporary *crises*.

Valorization (the rate of profit) is repeatedly improved and increases the mass of profit by reducing the cost of producing constant capital and variable capital (the level of wages), shortening turnover time, improving the organization of transport, reducing stocks and commercial expenses and the periodic devaluation of available capital. The advantages derived from the domination of the world market operate in the same way. Unequal exchange takes place in foreign trade—the technologically advanced countries receive a higher value in exchange for the value of their commodities—which also increases profits. This also applies to the export of capital, Capital export occurs because an overaccumulation of capital predominates in the highly developed capitalist countries, and consequently there is a lack of opportunities for investment. As a consequence, the capital-exporting country receives an additional injection of surplus value, which improves the insufficient valorization of capital and weakens or temporarily suspends the tendency to break down. This explains the intensity of imperialist expansion during the late phase of capital accumulation. Imperialism is an attempt to improve currently insufficient valorization and hence to extend the life span of the capitalist system by weakening tendencies to break down, through the transfer of surplus profits from colonial territories to highly developed capitalist countries. In this way, Grossman combines the theory of breakdown with the theory of crisis. *Crisis is an expression of breakdown that has not fully developed, because it has been mitigated by countertendencies.* But soon it is apparent that, because of the nature of the above countertendencies, they are only temporary and only able to counteract the tendency to break down to a certain extent. Stocks can only be reduced to a definite lower limit, breaching which would disrupt the continuity of the production process. Wages can only be depressed to a definite limit, breaching which would mean that the labor power of the working class was not fully reproduced; instead, the intensity and quality of labor would decline. The reduction of commercial profits can only improve the profitability of industry to a limited extent. The more commerce is reduced, the smaller the mitigating effects of a further reduction will be. The countereffects of capital export can also only be temporary. To the extent that the number of countries with excess capital and consequently seeking to export increases in the course of accumulation, competition on the world market, the struggle over profitable spheres for investment, increases. For this reason, too, the tendency to break down must become more intense, at a definite point. The increase in fixed capital does not have a different effect. At higher levels of capital accumulation, at which fixed capital accounts for a larger component of constant capital, the contraction of production during the crisis has ever-smaller significance: a firm's burden of depreciation and interest payments for fixed capital does not decline when production is reduced.

So it is apparent that the immanent laws of capital accumulation themselves progressively weaken the countertendencies. Overcoming crises becomes ever more difficult; the tendency to break down more and more holds sway. The periods of upturn become ever shorter; the duration and intensity of crisis periods rises. In his formula for crises Grossman attempts to determine the phase length of the economic cycle theoretically, by means of mathematics, and to identify the factors on which the extension or contraction of the economic cycle depend. If crisis is, for him, the tendency to breakdown that has not fully developed, *the breakdown of capitalism is nothing other than a crisis that is not checked by countertendencies.*

So capitalism approaches its end as a result of its inner economic laws.

From the standpoint of a Marxist theory of crisis and breakdown, it is obvious to Grossman from the start that the question of perhaps fatalistically awaiting the "automatic" breakdown without actively intervening does not arise for the working class. Old regimes never "fall" of their own accord, even during a period of crisis, if they are not "toppled over" (Lenin).[130] According to Grossman, the point of a Marxist theory of breakdown is only to demarcate voluntarism and putschism, which regard revolution as possible at any time, without considering [whether there is] an *objectively revolutionary situation*, and as dependent only on the subjective will of the revolutionaries. The point

---

130. [Lenin, "Collapse of the Second International," 214.]

of breakdown theory is that the revolutionary action of the proletariat only receives its most powerful impetus from the objective convulsion of the established system, and at the same time only this creates the circumstances necessary to successfully wrestle down the ruling class's resistance.

Grossman could achieve these results, which he regards as a reconstruction of Marx's theory of crisis and breakdown, because he had previously researched and recovered Marx's method and the plan that underlies *Capital*.

Rosa Luxemburg assumed that there was a gap in *Capital*, that Marx had not considered foreign trade; the only explanation of this assumption is that the method that underlies the structure of *Capital* had not previously been recognized as a specific theoretical problem. For this reason, however, it was not possible for Luxemburg to fully understand Marx's solution.

If the process of isolation served the classical economists, Marx—according to Grossman—employs the so-called *procedure of successive approximation*. In order to research causes in the complicated world of appearances, Marx, like the classical economists, makes numerous simplifying assumptions by means of which he departs from the concrete totality of appearances, although this is precisely in order to explain it. The understanding achieved [in this way] can only have a preliminary character, can constitute only the first stage of acquiring knowledge in the procedure of successive approximation, which must be followed by a further, definitive stage. To each simplifying assumption there corresponds a subsequent correction, which in the final result takes into account the elements of actual reality that were initially neglected. All phenomena and problems are dealt with at least twice in this procedure: first under simplifying assumptions, then in their final form. This method underlies Marx's analysis in all three volumes of *Capital*. Those from whom this remains hidden must encounter continual "contradictions" between the individual components of Marx's theory.

Literature

Older literature is identified in the previous edition of this dictionary[131]; it is expressly referred to here. Of the more recent literature see:

Ashcroft, Thomas. *An Outline of Modern Imperialism*. London: Plebs League, 1922.

Bauer, Otto. *Kapitalismus und Sozialismus nach dem Weltkriege* [*Capitalism and Socialism after the World War*]. Vienna: Wiener Volksbuchhandlung, 1931.

Beer, Max. *The General History of Socialism and Social Struggles*. 2 vols. New York: Russell & Russell, 1957 [1922, 1929].

Bober, Mandell Morton. *Karl Marx's Interpretation of History*. Cambridge, MA: Harvard University Press, 1927.

Brauer, Theodor. *Der moderne deutsche Sozialismus* [*Modern German Socialism*]. Pader-

---

131. Grünberg, "Sozialistische Ideen und Lehren."

born: Salzwasser, 2012 [1929].

Graziadei, Antonio. *Capitale e colonie* [*Capital and Colonies*]. Milano: Casa editrice sociale, 1927.

Heider, Werner. *Die Geschichtslehre von Karl Marx* [*Karl Marx's Theory of History*]. Stuttgart: Cotta, 1931.

Heimann, Eduard. *Mehrwert und Gemeinwirtschaft: Kritische und positive Beiträge zur Theorie des Sozialismus* [*Surplus Value and Social Economy: Critical and Positive Contributions on the Theory of Socialism*]. Berlin: Engelmann, 1922.

—————. *Kapitalismus und Sozialismus: Reden und Aufsätze zur Wirtschafts- und Geisteslage* [*Capitalism and Socialism: Speeches and Essays on the Economic and Intellectual Situation*]. Potsdam: Protte, 1931.

Heimburger, Karl. *Die Theorie von der industriellen Reservearmee* [*The Theory of the Industrial Reserve Army*]. Halberstadt: Meyer, 1928.

Jenssen, Otto. *Der Kampf um die Staatsmacht: Was lehrt uns Linz?* [*The Struggle over State Power: What Does Linz Teach Us?*]. Proceedings of the Linz Congress of German-Austrian Social Democracy. Berlin: Laub, 1927.

Jostock, Paul. *Der Ausgang des Kapitalismus: Ideengeschichte seiner Überwindung* [*Capitalism's Exit: The History of Ideas of Overcoming It*]. München: Duncker & Humblot, 1928.

Laidler, Harry Wellington. *A History of Socialist Thought*. New York: Crowell, 1927.

Laurat, Lucien. *Un Système qui sombre* [*A System That Is Sinking*]. Paris: l'Églantine, 1932.

Lenin, Vladimir Ilyich. *Collected Works*. Moscow: Progress 1960–68 [from 1920].

Leubuscher, Charlotte. *Sozialismus und Sozialisierung in England: Ein Überblick über die neuere Entwicklung der sozialistischen Theorien und über die Probleme der Industrieverfassung in England* [*Socialism and Socialization in England: An Overview of Recent Developments in Socialist Theory and the Problem of the Industrial Constitution*]. Jena: Fischer, 1921.

Lewin, David. *Der Arbeitslohn und die soziale Entwicklung* [*The Wage and Social Development*]. Berlin: Springer, 1913.

Liebert, Arthur. "Materialistische Geschichtsphilosophie" ["The Materialist Philosophy of History"]. In *Handwörterbuch der Soziologie* [*Dictionary of Sociology*], edited by Alfred Vierkandt, 360–70. Stuttgart: Enke, 1931.

Louis, Paul. *Les Idées essentielles du socialisme* [*The Essential Ideas of Socialism*]. Paris: Rivière, 1931.

Luxemburg, Rosa. "The Accumulation of Capital: An Anti-critique, or What the Epigones Have Made of Marx's Theory." In *Rosa Luxemburg and Nikolai Bukharin, Imperialism and the Accumulation of Capital*, 44–153. London: Allen Lane, 1972 [1921].

—————. *The Crisis of Social Democracy*. New York: Socialist Publication Society, 1919 [1916].

Mallock, William Hurrell. *The Limits of Pure Democracy*. London: Chapman and Hall, 1918 [1917].

Spectator (Nakhimson), Myron Isaevich. *Mirovoe hozjajstvo do i posle vojny* [*The World Economy before and after the War*]. Vol. 3. Moscow: Izdatel'stvo Komakademii, 1929.

Pollock, Friedrich. *Sombarts "Widerlegung" des Marxismus* [*Sombart's "Refutation" of Marxism*]. Leipzig: Hirschfeld, 1926.

Ralea, Mihai. *Révolution et socialisme: Essai de bibliographie* [*Revolution and Socialism: Bibliographic Essay*]. Paris: Presses universitaires de France, 1923.

Rosenberg, Arthur. *A History of Bolshevism: From Marx to the First Five Years' Plan.* Oxford: Oxford University Press, 1934 [1932].

Séé, Henri. *Matérialisme historique et l'interprétation économique de l'histoire* [*Historical Materialism and the Economic Interpretation of History*]. Geneva: Slatkine, 1982 [1927].

Seligman, Edwin Robert Anderson. *The Economic Interpretation of History.* New York: Columbia University Press, 1967 [1902].

Seydewitz, Max, et al. *Die Krise des Kapitalismus und die Aufgabe der Arbeiterklasse* [*The Crisis of Capitalism and the Tasks of the Working Class*]. Berlin: Verlag der Marxistischen Büchergemeinde, 1931.

Sorel, Georges. "The Economic Interpretation of History." In *From Georges Sorel: Hermeneutics and the Sciences*, 191–208. New Brunswick, NJ: Transaction, 1990 [1911].

Sozialdemokratische Arbeiterpartei Österreichs. *Protokoll des sozialdemokratischen Parteitages 1926, abgehalten in Linz, vom 30. Oktober bis 3. November* [*Minutes of the Social Democratic Party Congress, held in Linz, from October 30 to November 3*]. Vienna: Verlag der Wiener Volksbuchhandlung, 1926.

Stalin, Joseph. *Problems of Leninism.* New York: International Publishers, 1934 [1924, 1926].

Trotsky, Leon. *Between Red and White: A Study of Some Fundamental Questions of Revolution, with Particular Reference to Georgia.* Westport, CT: Hyperion Press, 1975 [1922].

———. *The Third International after Lenin: The Draft Program of the Communist International, a Criticism of Fundamentals.* New York: Pathfinder Press, 1970 [1928].

———. *History of the Russian Revolution.* London: Pluto Press, 1977 [1930].

Turgeon, Charles. *Critique de la conception matérialiste de l'histoire* [*Critique of the Materialist Conception of History*]. Paris: Recueil Sirey, 1932.

Wilbrandt, Robert. *Sozialismus* [*Socialism*]. Jena: Diederichs, 1919.

Journals:

Die Gesellschaft: Internationale Revue für Sozialismus und Politik, since 1924.

Unter dem Banner des Marxismus, since 1925.

Archiv für die Geschichte des Sozialismus und der Arbeiterbewegung, 1911–30.

See, further, the literatures identified in the articles "Bolshevism," "Internationals," and "Social-Democratic and Communist Parties," and also the biographies of [individual] socialists.[132]

---

132. Grossmann, "Bolschevismus"; "Internationale: Die zweite Internationale"; "Internationale: Die dritte Internationale"; Grünberg and Grossmann, " Sozialdemokratische und kommunistische Parteien."

Marx, Classical Political Economy and the Problem of Dynamics[1]

Translated from the German by Rick Kuhn

1.

In the dominant view, Marx is merely a student of the classical political economists, someone who completed their work, or their successor.[2] A precisely delineated conception is thus erected: the labor theory of value developed by [Adam] Smith and

---

1. Originally published as Grossman, *Marx, die Klassische Nationaloekonomie und das Problem der Dynamik*.

2. Pareto, *Les systèmes socialistes*, 340; Croce, *Historical Materialism*, 138; Schumpeter, *Economic Doctrine and Method*, 15; Wilbrandt, *Karl Marx*, 101; Engländer, "Böhm-Bawerk und Marx," 380. "It was Karl Marx . . . who, as a value theorist, was indeed the last great figure in the classical school." Douglas, "Smith's Theory of Value," 65. The socialists Franz Mehring, Conrad Schmidt, and above all Rudolf Hilferding, however, are no different. See Mehring, *Geschichte der deutschen Sozialdemokratie*, vol. 2, 250; Mehring, *Aus dem literarischen Nachlass*, 557; Schmidt, *Die Durchschnittsprofitrate auf Grundlage*, 112. Hilferding not only regarded Marx as an opponent and conqueror of but also as perfecting "Classical Economy which begins with William Petty and finds its supreme expression in Marx." Hilferding, *Finance Capital*, 21. Maurice Dobb does not go beyond this traditional view in his new *book*. If Marx offered no adequate "proof" of his theory of value, this was because he was not dealing with a new or unknown theory. "Marx was adopting a principle." "The essential difference between Marx and classical political economy lay, therefore, in the theory of surplus value." Dobb, *Political Economy and Capitalism*, 67–8, 75. [Grossman indicated that the author of Croce's book was Antonio Labriola, who, however, fell into the category of Marxist proponents of the notion that Marx's economics were essentially Ricardian. Labriola, *Karl Marx, l'économiste, le socialiste*, 79.]

[David] Ricardo, in its innermost essence, leads to socialism. This consequence was not, however, articulated by its founders. Marx was the first to think Ricardo's theory through to its end, as it were, providing its previously unarticulated final word.[3] This conception must certainly already appear to be extremely questionable from the general position of the *critique* of political economy, if "the development of political economy and of the opposition to which it gives rise keeps pace with the *real* development of the social contradictions and class conflicts inherent in capitalist production."[4]

Marx distinguishes four phases in the development of political economy: the first embraces the period of "classical economics" and the remaining three the various stages of "vulgar economics." According to Marx, the identity of the historical situation combines the representatives of classical political economy into one consistent intellectual school, despite their sometimes great individual differences (for example between [William] Petty, [David] Hume, and the physiocrats, and between these and Smith or Ricardo).[5] This was the period during which modern capitalism and consequently the modern working class emerged, thus the "period in which the class struggle" between the proletariat and the bourgeoisie "was as yet undeveloped."[6] Classical economics is the expression of rising industrial capitalism, wrestling for power. Its theoretical and practical thrust is not directed against the proletariat, which is still weak, but against the representatives of the old society, the feudal landowners and old-fashioned usurers. The feudal forms of ground rent and "antediluvian" interest-bearing capital have "yet to be subordinated to industrial capital and to acquire the dependent position which [they] must assume."[7]

Ricardo's theory of ground rent, like Hume's critique before it,[8] is directed against feudal landownership. Ricardo's theory of value does, at the same time, articulate the struggle between the capitalist class and the waged proletariat, in theory. But the industrial bourgeoisie and its theory are still "naïve," that is, can afford to engage in the pursuit of truth without regard for possible dangers and implications, as yet unsuspected and in fact not yet present, that follow from their own principles. So the labor theory of value is developed without fear of emphasizing in theory the contradictions between the working class and the propertied class that can be derived from it, or of highlighting the distinction between productive and unproductive labor.[9] For it was

---

3. "Smith's formulation of the problems of exchange value and of the distribution of the national product . . . was such as almost inevitably gave rise to the doctrines of post-Ricardian socialists and to the labour theory of value and the exploitation theory of Karl Marx." Douglas, "Smith's Theory of Value," 53. Similarly, Frank H. Knight (Chicago): "[Marx] is certainly the thinker who above all others worked out the classical (Ricardian) theory to its logical conclusions." Review of *A History of Economic Thought*, by Erich Roll, 105.

4. Marx, "Economic Manuscript of 1861–63 [Notebooks XII to XV]," 500.

5. Ibid., 275.

6. Marx, *Capital*, vol. 1, 96.

7. Marx, "Economic Manuscript of 1861–63 [Notebooks XII to XV]," 463. [Editor's interpolation.]

8. Hume, *Essays, Moral, Political, and Literary*, chapter 4, 320–30; Marx, "Economic Manuscript of 1861–63 [Notebooks XX to XXIII]," 390–91.

9. For example, Adam Smith, *Wealth of Nations*, vol. 2, 63, where he states that ground rent and profit eat away the wage.

the representatives of the feudal occupations who were particularly ranked into the category of unproductive labor.

Those authors are "classical," according to Marx, to the extent that they express this front-line position; for example, John Locke, in his polemic against "unproductive" feudal landownership and ground rent, which according to him "is in no way different from usury."[10] This front-line position is particularly apparent in their theory of "productive" and "unproductive" labor, in which the relationship of the rising bourgeoisie to preceding classes and outlooks is entirely clear. This theory starkly contradicts both the perspective of the ancient world, "when material[ly] productive labor bore the stigma of slavery and was regarded merely as a pedestal for the idle citizen," and that of the social classes and occupations carried over from the feudal period, declared to be unproductive.[11]

The language of classical political economy is, Marx thinks,

> the language of the still revolutionary bourgeoisie which has not yet subjected to itself the whole of society, the state etc. All these illustrious and time-honored occupations—sovereign, judge, priest, officer etc.—with all the old ideological castes to which they give rise, their men of letters, their teachers and priests, are *from an economic standpoint* put on the same level as the swarm of their [i.e., the bourgeoisie's] own lackeys and jesters maintained by the bourgeoisie and by idle wealth—the landed nobility and idle capitalists. . . . They live on the produce of other people's industry, therefore they must be reduced to the smallest possible number.[12]

So long as the bourgeoisie has not yet confronted the "real productive laborers" in conscious, openly hostile antagonism—laborers who "moreover tell it that it [the bourgeoisie] lives on *other* people's industry"—it can still confront the "unproductive classes" of the feudal period as "the representative of productive labor."[13]

When the bourgeoisie has consolidated its position of social power in the course of economic development, in part taken possession of the state and in part concluded a compromise with the feudal classes and "ideological castes," and, in addition, once the proletariat and its theoretical representatives arrive on the scene and draw egalitarian and socialist conclusions from the classical economists' labor theory of value (the right of the working class to the full fruits of its labor), "things take a new turn." Political economy "tries to justify 'economically,' from its own standpoint, what at an earlier stage it had criticized and fought against."[14] At this point classical political economy disappears from the historical stage, and the hour of vulgar economics ([Thomas] Chalmers, John Ramsay McCulloch, Jean-Baptiste Say, and Germain Gar-

---

10. [Marx, "Economic Manuscript of 1861–63 [Notebooks XX to XXIII]," 89, summarizing Locke, *Some Considerations on the Lowering of Interest*, 36.

11. Marx, "Economic Manuscript of 1861–63 [Notebooks VII to XII]," 197. [Editor's interpolation.]

12. Ibid. [Marx also emphasized "industry" and "other."]

13. [Ibid., 32, 197.]

14. Ibid., 198.

nier) has struck (the second phase of political economy). The vulgar economics of the 1820s and 1830s, the "metaphysical period" of political economy,[15] is the expression of the existence of the victorious and now conservative bourgeoisie, which therefore apologetically obfuscated the prevailing order, and whose theoretical representative in England was [Thomas] Malthus. He combated any tendency in Ricardo's work that was "revolutionary in relation to the old society."[16] Like Ricardo, Malthus did indeed wish to have "bourgeois production," but only so long as "it is not revolutionary . . . but merely creates a broader and more comfortable material basis for the 'old society,'" a society with which the bourgeoisie had just struck a compromise.[17]

Now the classical theory of the distinction between productive and unproductive labor was abandoned (as in Say and Malthus)—out of fear of the proletarian critique that had already registered its demands—and replaced by the conception that all labor is equally productive. Malthus likewise turned the real meaning of Ricardo's theory of ground rent, aimed against the landowners, into its direct opposite, by introducing capitalism's problem of sales. Malthus does emphasize the inevitability of generalized overproduction, affecting all branches of production. He only does so, however, in order to prove the necessity of unproductive consumers and classes, that is, "buyers who are not sellers," so that the sellers can find a market in which they can dispose of what they supply. Hence the necessity of waste (including war).[18] Finally, Ricardo's labor theory of value is now also abandoned. By regarding the wage as a proportion of the total social product (relative wage), Ricardo articulated the class relation that is inherent in the capitalist economy.[19] With the development of the real antagonisms of capitalist production, the embryonic theoretical class antagonism contained in Ricardo's labor theory of value began to polarize. The (theoretical) opposition "to political economy has [already] come into being in more or less economic, utopian, critical and revolutionary forms."[20]

[William] Thompson (1824), Percy Ravenstone (1824), and [Thomas] Hodgskin (1825, 1827),[21] the theoretical representatives of the working class in England, draw egalitarian conclusions and demands from Ricardo's labor theory of value.[22] In the face of such demands, as an 1832 text by Malthus openly admits, the classical labor theory of value was abandoned through successive small changes and transformed into a meaningless theory of costs of production: the specific value-creating role of labor was

---

15. Ibid., 217. Compare also the postface to the second edition of *Capital*, in which Marx states that 1830 "sounded the knell of scientific bourgeois economics." *Capital*, vol. 1, 97.

16. Marx, "Economic Manuscript of 1861–63 [Notebooks XII to XV]," 245.

17. Ibid., 244.

18. Ibid., 216–43.

19 Ibid., 226–27.

20. Ibid., 500.

21. [See Thompson, *Inquiry into the Principles*; Ravenstone, *Thoughts on the Funding System*; Hodgskin, *Popular Political Economy*, and Hodgskin, *Labour Defended*.]

22. See "Opposition to the Economists (Based on the Ricardian Theory)" in Marx, "Economic Manuscript of 1861–63 [Notebooks XII to XV]," 373–449.

obliterated.[23] A particular productivity—a creation of value!—was now attributed to land and capital in and of themselves, and labor was now only acknowledged as another factor of production, alongside capital and land. In this way Ricardo's conception of the wage as a relation of the working class's share in total production that it has itself created was likewise overturned, justifying capitalists' profits as the result of the "productivity" of their capital (not of labor). In similar fashion, ground rent was justified as the fruit of the productivity of the land, which meant that antagonism toward landownership that characterized classical theory now lapsed and became meaningless.

The third phase of political economy, the period in the 1830s and 1840s following the July revolution, was a period of sharpening class antagonisms and cumulative proletarian critique of the prevailing social order in England (John Gray and [John Francis] Bray) and France ([Constantin] Pecqueur).[24] It also saw the first attempts to organize the workers' movement politically: the Saint-Simonians, [Philippe] Buchez, Louis Blanc, and [Pierre-Joseph] Proudhon's struggle against interest-bearing capital.[25] The result is an intensified phase of vulgarization and transformation of classical economics.[26] The last remnants of the original content of the theory were eradicated: those real contradictions of capital that were still admitted and highlighted by Malthus and Say (Say's disproportionality theory of crisis; Malthus's theory of generalized crisis) were now denied and disappear from economic theory. In Frédéric Bastiat's work (1848) capitalism is transformed into a harmonious system.[27]

The fourth phase of political economy, after 1848, falls into the period during which fully developed class antagonisms became unmistakably visible during the June days in Paris, as the working class first struggled for its own goals.[28] The result was the complete dissolution of the Ricardian school and a departure from all genuine theory. Economic theory was abandoned and replaced by the historical description of phenomena (the older historical school, with Wilhelm Roscher at its head).[29] Or economic theory was degraded to a pseudotheory, as it departed entirely from the terrain of economic reality and took flight to the higher regions of psychology (first attempts at a subjective theory of value by Nassau Senior and Hermann Heinrich Gossen, 1854). This likewise achieved the desired end: the turn away from real class antagonisms and granting equal rank to capital and labor in the creation of value. The theory of costs of

---

23. Marx, "Economic Manuscript of 1861–63 [Notebooks XII to XV]," 253–46.

24. [The French Revolution of July 1830 overturned the monarchy of the House of Bourbon, which represented the power of landowners, and replaced it with the reign of Louis Philippe of the House of Orléans, who served broader, bourgeois interests, though not those of industrial capital.]

25. [See Gray, *The Social System*; Bray, *Labour's Wrongs and Labour's Remedy*; Blanc, *The Organization of Labour*. The Saint-Simonians followed the teachings of the pioneering French utopian socialist Henri Saint-Simon.]

26. See Marx, "Economic Manuscript of 1861–63 [Notebooks XII to XV]," 499–503.

27. [See Bastiat, *Economic Sophisms*. But perhaps of greater relevance here is Bastiat, *Harmonies of Political Economy*.]

28. [In June 1848 the French government, brought to power by the revolution in February, brutally suppressed a workers' uprising provoked by its attack on state support for the unemployed.]

29. Marx, "Economic Manuscript of 1861–63 [Notebooks XII to XV]," 502.

production—the equation of labor, land, and capital as factors in the creation of value—was unsatisfactory, as it represented a trivial, circular argument. In attempting to explain the process of the creation of value, the value of products was reduced to the value of the factors jointly acting to produce the product, such that value is explained by value. (There is no such circle in Marx's labor theory of value, as labor creates value, but is not itself a value: it is the use value of the commodity labor power). Under the pressure of the left Ricardians' critique, the theory of costs of production had to be abandoned. But since a return to the labor theory of value was undesirable, a way out was found by transforming economics into psychology. In principle, Senior had already accomplished this change.[30] Basing himself on one of the two interpretations of labor provided by Smith, according to which labor is not seen as an objective expenditure of energy (measured by time) but rather as the subjective effort employed in producing an article, Senior treats labor as a psychological sacrifice. In order for capital to be granted equal status with labor as a parallel factor in the creation of value, it must also be turned into a psychological variable. If the wage is the reward for the effort of labor, then the interest on capital is the reward for the subjective sacrifice of saving, renunciation of immediate consumption of capital.

The "development" of the individual phases of political economy, as sketched above, imposes the formulation of the following question: can Marx, the theoretician of the proletariat at an advanced stage of capitalist development, take over and "complete" the theories and categories of classical economics— in particular those of Ricardo—as the dominant conception maintains, if Ricardo, like classical economists in general, expressed bourgeois interests at a much lower stage of capitalist development, a stage of undeveloped class antagonisms? And the thesis that Marx's original achievement in his "socialist critique" of capitalism is that he drew socialist conclusions inherent in Ricardo's labor theory of value—in short, that he was a "Ricardo turned socialist"—is just as much to be rejected. As pre-Marxist socialists also offered a socialist critique of capitalism, such a critique cannot be regarded as the specific essence of Marx's theory. But Marx reproaches the egalitarian left Ricardians for the "superficiality" of their critique, namely, that they base their critique on Ricardo's theory and only attack "particular results of the capitalist mode of production" instead of its "manifold presuppositions." An effective socialist critique could only be based on a specific, new theory, with the assistance of new economic categories.

In his critique, Marx proceeds from the mystifying character of the reified forms of value, that is, the fact that relations which people enter into in the process of production appear as relations between objects, things, and that these reified forms conceal true relations between people. Marx therefore speaks of the deceptive appearance of all forms of value. In contrast to transparent, precapitalist forms, the relation between exploiter and exploited in the modern capitalist form of value is opaque, because in the wage relation, which is a form of value that regulates the "exchange" between the wage

---

30. Senior, *Outline of the Science*.

laborer and the entrepreneur, it appears that the worker's wage fully compensates all his labor and no unpaid labor is performed.[31]

According to classical theory, all exchange transactions correspond strictly to the law of value, that is, equal labor times always exchange for equal labor times. This principle also applies to the exchange relation between the workers and the entrepreneur. Now, according to Marx, it is quite evident that there is no exchange of equivalents between worker and entrepreneur. If workers were to receive as much in wages (measured in labor) from entrepreneurs as they give in labor, then profit—surplus accruing to entrepreneurs and hence also the capitalist economy, which is based on this profit—would be impossible.[32] Since both profit and capitalism do, however, exist, no exchange of equivalents can take place. Marx's entire effort is directed at showing that the transaction between capitalist and worker is as much an exchange of nonequivalents as of equivalents, depending on whether this transaction is regarded within the sphere of circulation (on the market) or during the process of production. The exchange of equivalents between worker and capitalist on the market is merely an appearance arising from the form of exchange. Despite the alleged exchange of equivalents,

> the laws based on the production . . . of commodities become changed into their direct opposite. . . . The relation of exchange between capitalist and worker becomes a mere semblance belonging only to the process of circulation, it becomes a mere form, which is alien to the content of the transaction itself, and merely mystifies it. The constant sale and purchase of labour power is the form; the content is the constant appropriation by the capitalist, without equivalent, of a portion of the labour of others, which has already been objectified, and his repeated exchange of this labour for a greater quantity of the living labour of others.[33]

Marx regards it as one of Smith's great merits that he at least sensed that the exchange between capital and wage labor is a flaw in the law of value. Although Smith could not clarify it, he could see "that in the actual result the law is suspended."[34] According to Marx, it is precisely the form of exchange value that mystifies the real content. "The wage form thus extinguishes every trace of the division of the working day into necessary labour and surplus labour, into paid labour and unpaid labour."[35] Just as the wage form does, so too all the other forms of value that emerge in the process of exchange mystify.[36] The reified forms of value (exchange value, ground rent, profit, interest, wages, prices, and so on) conceal and invert the real relations between people, by making them appear as the "fantastic form of a relation between things," "a social

---

31. "On the surface of bourgeois society the worker's wage appears as the price of labour." Marx, *Capital*, vol. 1, 675.
32. Ibid., 676.
33. Ibid., 729–30.
34. Marx, "Economic Manuscript of 1861–63 [Notebooks I to VII]," 393.
35. Marx, *Capital*, vol. 1, 680.
36. Ibid., 169, 173–4; and Marx, *Contribution to the Critique*, 289.

hieroglyphic," "something dark and mysterious."[37]

Classical economics did seek to dissolve the mystifying categories of value into "labor," and thought that in doing so it grasped the essence behind the deceptive appearance of phenomena. Marx wants to demonstrate that this attempted solution leads to contradictions that could not be overcome on the basis of classical political economy. Any glance back at earlier economic epochs shows that mystifying forms of value first arose in the period of commodity production and exchange.[38] Resolving these forms of value into "labor" turns their mystifying character into an eternal feature of all social processes, as labor itself is definitely a "nature-imposed necessity" of human existence.[39] Experience contradicts this view, however, and this contradiction is insoluble from the standpoint of the classical economists.

For Marx, who wants to grasp the "concrete" in thought, the mystifying categories of value cannot simply be eliminated or ignored, to be replaced by other, "true" categories. Even though the phenomena of exchange value are mystifying, they are still an important component of reality. The point is not to eliminate one mystifying factor and substitute another but rather to demonstrate the necessary connection between the two and to explain what is deceptive in the phenomena of value. Because capitalism has a dual reality, mystifying and nonmystifying sides, and binds them together in a concrete unity, any theory that reflects this reality must likewise be a unity of opposites.

It has become almost banal to assert that Marx taught that monetary processes should not be regarded as the primary elements in economic events but only as their characteristic reflexive determinations, and that real processes should be sought behind the veil of money, on the side of commodities, within the process of production. The acknowledged polar opposition between commodity and money is repeated within the world of commodities itself as the opposition between the commodity's value and its use value. For it is not the metallic existence of money that is deceptive but rather its character as value.[40] Marx sarcastically criticizes the "crude . . . vision" of political economy, which only perceives what is misleading in exchange value, in its "developed shape" *as money*, but not in its preexisting form of the *values of commodities*, to the extent that they occur as mutual equivalents for each other.[41] It is precisely this equivalent form that Marx sees as a puzzle: the "internal opposition between use value and value" within the individual commodity becomes visible in the "external opposition" of two commodities, in which one counts "only as a use value" and the other commodity—money—"only as exchange value."[42]

---

37. Marx, *Capital*, vol. 1, 165, 167; vol. 2, 430–31; "Economic Manuscript of 1861–63 [Notebooks XII to XV]," 451.

38. Marx, *Capital*, vol. 1, 153–54.

39. Ibid., 175.

40. Marx, "Comments on James Mill," 213–14.

41. Marx, *Capital*, vol. 1, 147–49.

42. Ibid., 153.

The illusion is not due merely to the money form but to the value form in general. Consequently, real economic processes have to be sought not only behind the veil of money but behind the veil of value in general.

2.

In the section of the first volume of *Capital* dealing with "The Fetishism of the Commodity and Its Secret," Marx attempts to penetrate the mystification involved in the exchange value form.[43] Two different, [though] in their basic notion analogous methods serve this end. The first is the method of historical comparison between the period of commodity production and earlier periods when there was no production or exchange of commodities and consequently no exchange value. In these periods there was, therefore, no mystification: personal relations of dependence appeared in unconcealed form, and were not veiled by the process of exchange.[44] In order to illustrate this, Marx presents three different types of economy that do not produce commodities: Robinson Crusoe, medieval feudal lords with their serfs who perform compulsory labor, and finally the patriarchal peasant family. In all these cases producers create useful objects for the satisfaction of their own needs. As there are no exchange values, "all the relations between Robinson and these objects that form his self-created wealth are . . . simple and transparent."[45] What is mysterious and mystifying about the production of commodities evidently does not derive from the use value side of commodities but is instead connected only with the process of exchange and exchange value.[46]

Marx arrives at the same result by the method of comparing various sides of commodity production itself, value side with use value side, the process of valorization with the labor process. In short, the means of seeing through the mystifying character of the categories of exchange value is, in fact, use value! The use values of earlier historical periods are just as much the result of human labor as the products of the epoch of commodity production. But only in this contemporary period do products assume a mystifying character. The same source—labor—cannot yield such totally different results. It is not sufficient to say that commodities are the products of "labor," as such, just as those of earlier economic epochs were. Instead, it is necessary to distinguish two different moments[47] of labor, its "dual character." First, labor that is "concrete," "useful," creating not value but rather objects of use: the labor of the joiner, tailor, weaver, which functions in the technical labor process and as "productive activity appropriate to its

---

43. Ibid., 163–77.
44. Ibid., 169.
45. Ibid., 170.
46. "The whole mystery of commodities, all the magic and necromancy that surrounds the products of labour on the basis of commodity production, vanishes therefore as soon as we come to other forms of production." Ibid., 169.
47. ["Moment" is used here in the Hegelian sense of "aspect."]

purpose" of the appropriation of the natural world, is a nature-imposed necessity for all social formations.[48] Secondly, general human labor "that creates exchange value," functioning in the process of valorization, the moment of labor that only appears in one particular social formation (of commercial interaction).[49] Only with the arrival of exchange value does the object of use become a commodity.[50] It is evident that only this second side of labor, the characteristic that it "creates exchange value," is the origin of all that is mystifying and fetishistic. The reduction of the forms of value to labor pure and simple, as carried out in classical economics, is false because labor as such is an unreal abstraction, a "mere spectre."[51]

In this way Marx arrived at the differentiation of the "double character" of the labor represented in commodities, which in his own eyes constituted what was "fundamentally new" in his theory.[52] With a pride he seldom expressed, Marx emphasizes the importance of his discovery: the examination of the twofold character of labor was the "point . . . crucial to an understanding of political economy."[53] He saw in this element a decisive break between his conception and that of all his predecessors. And in fact, from the new standpoint of a two-dimensional conception of economic processes, he repeatedly criticizes the classical political economists in principle, reproaching them for their one-dimensional theory exclusively concerned with value. Time and again he raises the objection that classical political economists and their successors did not distinguish the dual character of labor. "Classical political economy in fact nowhere distinguishes explicitly and with a clear awareness between labour as it appears in the value of a product, and the same labour as it appears in the product's use value."[54] And then Marx makes this general objection more precise in specific criticisms of William Petty, Adam Smith, Ricardo, and Hodgskin.[55] This alone is sufficient to show that we find

---

48. Ibid., 133, 174–5, 176, 179.

49. [Marx uses the phrase "labor that creates exchange value" in *Contribution to the Critique*, 271.]

50. Marx, *Capital*, vol. 1, 153.

51. Marx, *Capital*, vol. 3, 954.

52. Marx to Friedrich Engels, January 8, 1868, 314.

53. Marx, *Capital*, vol. 1, 132. Marx himself, in other places in his work and letters, also repeatedly identified precisely this theory as his original contribution to the understanding of economic events, the "fundamentally new" element of his achievement. For example, in 1859 in *Contribution to the Critique* and in 1867 in *Capital*, vol. 1.

54. Marx, *Capital*, vol. 1, 173. Similarly, p. 313, and frequently elsewhere.

55. Against Petty: "Labor as the source of exchange value is confused with labor as the source of use value." Marx, "Economic Manuscript of 1861–63 [Notebooks XX to XXIII]," 248.

Against Adam Smith: "He does not distinguish the twofold character of labour itself: labour that creates value, by the expenditure of labour power, and labour that creates objects of use (use values), as concrete useful labour." Marx, *Capital*, vol. 2, 453 and similarly 460.

Against Ricardo: "What Ricardo does not investigate is the specific form in which labor manifests itself as the common element of commodities. . . . Ricardo does not sufficiently differentiate between labor in so far as it is represented in use values or in exchange value." Marx, "Economic Manuscript of 1861–63 [Notebooks XII to XV]," 325. [Marx emphasized "specific."] Similarly *Capital*, vol. 1, 174 and 313.

Against Hodgskin: "In his investigations into the productivity of capital, Hodgskin is remiss in that he does not distinguish between how far it is a question of producing use values or exchange values." Marx, "Economic Manuscript of 1861–63 [Notebooks XII to XV]," 401. Also see Koepp, *Das Verhältnis der Mehr-*

ourselves here at the real center of Marx's innovation in comparison with the classical political economists. The great significance of the new conception is that Marx found in it a means of eliminating what was deceptive in the pure categories of exchange value and thus created a foundation for his further research into capitalist production, which gave him the possibility of grasping the true interconnections of this production, behind the veil of value.

3.

The results of our analysis are particularly confirmed by those statements by Marx in which he deals with his relationship with the classical political economists and indicates the place he claims for himself in the development of political economy.

Such statements in *Capital* as well as *A Contribution to a Critique of Political Economy* reveal that Marx regarded classical political economy as fundamentally concluded, completed by Ricardo, because in Ricardo "political economy ruthlessly draws its final conclusion and therewith ends."[56] Marx judged John Stuart Mill's attempts to develop classical political economy beyond this limit and to accommodate the principles of classical theory to the demands of the working class as a "shallow syncretism" and "a declaration of bankruptcy by 'bourgeois' economics."[57] So did Marx himself yet again complete what already had been completed and "further develop" what had already been concluded? According to Marx's own conception, he stands in starkest opposition to classical theory and not only as regards its specific theories (such as theories of wages, ground rent, crises, and so on) but also to the very theoretical foundation of economics. He does not aim, therefore, "to develop classical theory further" but rather to undertake a "scientific attempt to revolutionize a science."[58]

He expressed himself quite clearly about the nature of this "revolutionizing." After first developing the dual character of the commodity in the first chapter of the *Contribution*, in the section "Historical Notes on the Analysis of Commodities," he provides a characterization of his theoretical position and its relation to those of his predecessors: "The decisive outcome of the research carried on for over a century and a half by classical political economy, beginning with William Petty in Britain and Boisguillebert in France, and ending with Ricardo in Britain and Sismondi in France, is an analysis of the aspects of the commodity into two forms of labor—use value is reduced to concrete labor or purposive productive activity, exchange value to labor time or homogeneous social labor."[59]

---

werttheorien, 32, 34, 39.

56. Marx, *Contribution to the Critique*, 301. He expresses himself similarly in the postface to the second edition of *Capital*, vol. 1, 96.

57. Marx, *Capital*, vol. 1, 98.

58. Marx to Ludwig Kugelmann, December 28, 1862, 436. [Marx emphasized "scientific."]

59. Marx, *Contribution to the Critique*, 292.

The issue is therefore one of a contrast between two conceptions, one of which (the English) took exchange value as its main object, the other (the French) use value. That is, each only grasped one side of reality. Marx's actual theoretical position only emerges in sharp profile when it is seen from the perspective of this historical background. Only then is it understandable why Marx identified the discovery of the dual form of labor as the "decisive discovery of the research carried on for over a century and a half by classical political economy." Marx's theory of the dual character of labor is the critical synthesis, and only as such a further development, of both conceptions.

The following analysis is intended to show that Marx fundamentally transformed the most important categories inherited from classical economics, based on the new viewpoint that he had elaborated. In Marx's work they all obtain a value and a material side.

The *commodity* is a dual entity, a unity of exchange value and use value. This is because its source, *labor*, has a twofold character, which of necessity reveals itself not only in the commodity but in all the products of labor. The commodity is the unity of exchange value and use value.[60] The *capitalist production process* is the unity of the technical labor process and the valorization process.[61] While the means of production, raw and auxiliary materials, are transformed by human activity into material products, use values, during the labor process, the valorization process is the site of the creation of new values, whose excess over the values used in production results in surplus value and its derivatives (industrial profit, ground rent, gains made through trade, interest, and so on). This dual character is also apparent in the *management of the capitalist production process*, the necessity of which results from the division of labor, the increasing scope of the means of production employed, and the necessity of controlling their proper use.[62] On the one hand the management function is necessary in any economic system, insofar as it arises from a social labor process with a division of labor, like the function of an orchestra conductor. On the other hand, under the capitalist mode of production the capitalist exercises the management function by virtue of ownership of capital; it is "made necessary by the capitalist and therefore antagonistic nature of that process."[63] The process of reproduction of total social capital is also "not only a replacement of values, but a replacement of materials, and is therefore conditioned not just by the mutual relations of the value components of the social product but equally by their use values, their material shape."[64] The category of wages has the same dual character. On the labor market, the worker does not sell "labor," that is, the activity, since labor does not take place on the market, but rather the commodity "labor power": the capacity to labor. For this the worker receives as countervalue, as the wage, an exchange value (as in the sale of any other commodity). Only later in the labor process, thus outside the market, does this labor power become an activity, that is,

60. Marx, *Capital*, vol. 1, 125–27.
61. Ibid., 283, 304, 425.
62. Ibid., 449.
63. Ibid., 450.
64. Marx, *Capital*, vol. 2, 470.

when it is used by the entrepreneur.[65] Surplus value is obtained precisely from this use value of labor. By splitting the classical category of (wage) labor in this way into its use and exchange value sides, the contradictions in which the classical economists entangled themselves could be avoided.

The category of *capital* also has a dual character. The classical political economists already made the distinction between fixed and circulating capital. Marx took this distinction over but gave it an entirely different meaning, in which, yet again, the difference between the value and use value sides of fixed capital became decisive. The difference between fixed and circulating capital in the sphere of circulation employed by the classical economists is meaningless. It is only valid for productive capital, that is, in the sphere of production, in the labor process.[66] As money or as a commodity, capital is neither fixed nor circulating.[67] The material bases of fixed and circulating components give rise to the distinct characteristics of the useful forms, in which they function as factors in the labor process.[68] Circulating capital is used up in a single working period, while fixed capital functions in a series of "repeated labour processes" due to the durability of its natural form. The result of this difference in the duration of the lives of different capitals, that is, the time aspect, is the completely different manner in which fixed capital is replaced, on the one hand as value and on the other as use value, in its natural form. Marx derived the necessity of periodic crises already under simple reproduction from this difference in the mode of replacement.[69]

The category of the *organic composition of capital* changes in a similar way. Ricardo already made the distinction between capital-intensive and labor-intensive spheres of production, which was important for his theory of profit. But he conceived of it purely in terms of value. Marx split Ricardo's category into its use value and exchange value sides in order to reunite them in a synthesis.[70] The category of organic composition, transformed in this way, takes on a completely different function, not only for the explanation of profit, as in Ricardo's work, but also as the "most important factor" in the accumulation of capital.[71]

---

65. Marx, *Capital*, vol. 1, 292.

66. Marx, *Capital*, vol. 2, 246–47, 269–70, 282, 288–89.

67. Ibid., 270, 278.

68. Ibid., 237, 241, 246.

69. Ibid., 237, 298, 246, 302; compare "Replacement of the fixed capital" (a) in the money form, (b) in kind, in Ibid., 528–45.

70. "The composition of capital is to be understood in a twofold sense. As value . . . [and a]s material, as it functions in the process of production, , , , I call the former the *value* composition, the latter the *technical* composition of capital." The mutual relation between the two is called the *organic* composition, which is apparent in the *value* composition, "in so far as it is determined by its technical composition and mirrors the changes in the latter." Ibid., 762. Similarly *Capital*, vol. 3, 244–45, 254, 264; and "Economic Manuscript of 1861–63 [Notebooks VII to XII]," 493.

71. Marx, *Capital*, vol. 1, 762. The importance of the distinction between the technical and value composition of capital is already apparent in Marx's creation of entirely different terminological designations for them: the technical composition in its material form is expressed symbolically as $MP:L$ (the relation of the means of production to labor) and the value composition as $c:v$ (the relation of constant to variable capital).

Finally, the same dual aspect is apparent in the category that occupies the central place in Marx's system: the *falling average rate of profit*, the "driving force in capitalist production."[72] Repeatedly in *Capital*, "the internal opposition between use value and value, hidden within the commodity" is emphasized, and the development and growth of this contradiction as capitalist production develops is explained.[73] The nature of the opposition between use value and value in the commodity and why it constantly assumes ever greater dimensions was never previously treated as a problem. Now, when seen in connection with the presentation of the development of the productive power of labor in the first volume,[74] the presentation of the tendency of the rate of profit to fall in the third volume of *Capital* shows that Marx also derives this category from the dual character of labor, namely, the inverse movement of the mass of use values and values as a consequence of the increase in labor's productive power.[75] The richer a society, the greater the development of labor's productive power, the larger the volume of useful things that can be made in a given labor time. At the same time, however, the value of these things becomes smaller. As with the development of labor's productive power, an ever-growing mass of means of production (MP) is set in motion by a relatively ever-falling mass of labor (L), the unpaid part of the labor (surplus value or profit) must also progressively fall [relatively]. In capitalist terms, growing social wealth is expressed in the tendency for the [rate of] profit of a given capital to decline. The decline in [rate of] profit, the factor that regulates and drives the capitalist mechanism, also calls the continued existence of this mechanism into question.[76] The greater the mass of use values, the more pronounced the tendency for the rate of profit to fall (in value terms).

In its interpretation of Marxist economics the dominant theory has, however, expunged the entire theory of the dual character of labor indicated above, that is, precisely

---

72. Marx, *Capital*, vol. 3, 368.

73. Marx, *Capital*, vol. 1, 153, 181, 198, 209; "Economic Manuscript of 1861–63 [Notebooks XII to XV]," 247–48.

74. Marx, *Capital*, vol. 1, 136–37.

75. Marx, *Capital*, vol. 3, 318–19.

76. For a more precise justification for this deduction it is noted that, with the development of the productive power of labor, by which "we always mean the productivity of concrete useful labour," the same labor produces a growing mass of useful goods, of material wealth. The rising mass of useful things can, however, correspond to a fall in the value of each thing and even of their total value. "This contradictory movement arises out of the twofold character of labour." Marx, *Capital*, vol. 1, 137. Now, it is an empirical law of the capitalist mode of production that its development is accompanied by a relative decline in variable in relation to constant capital. "This simply means that the same number of workers . . . sets in motion, works up, and productively consumes, within the same period, an ever-growing mass of means of labour, machinery and fixed capital of all kinds, and raw and ancillary materials." "It is just another expression for the progressive development of the social productivity of labour." Marx, *Capital*, vol. 3, 318. Looked at in terms of use value, constantly growing masses of useful things arise, which, however, represent ever-smaller amounts of value. "Since the mass of living labour applied continuously declines in relation to the mass of objectified labour . . . the part of this living labour that is unpaid . . . must also stand in an ever-decreasing ratio to the value of the total capital applied." In short, "The progressive tendency for the general rate of profit to fall is thus simply the expression, peculiar to the capitalist mode of production, of the progressive development of the social productivity of labour." Marx, *Capital*, vol. 3, 319. [Marx emphasized "the expression, peculiar to the capitalist mode of production."]

what is specific to Marxism and what distinguishes it from classical political economy, in order, subsequently, to incorporate it into classical theory's lines of thought. That this "incorporation" was no mere accident is apparent when Benedetto Croce virtually credits it as one of the merits of the dominant theory.[77] In showing the untenability of classical theory, the intention is to demonstrate thereby the invalidity of Marx's theory.[78]

4.

From its origins, theoretical political economy was a theory of abstract exchange value: where it did concern itself with production it dealt solely with the value side, passing over the labor process.[79] Since the rise of marginal utility theory and the mathematical school, the analysis of the concrete production process was increasingly excluded as a component of theory, only considered in establishing its preconditions and overall framework. Analysis was concentrated almost exclusively on relations between given market variables. It therefore had a static character and was unable to explain dynamic structural changes in the economy. Marx's economic theory deviates in principle from both of these tendencies.

The capitalist mode of production is governed by the relation: exchange value–increase in exchange value, (M–M').[80] As a faithful expression of the bourgeois economic system, classical theory was always only a theory of abstract exchange value.[81] Adam Smith does begin his work *The Wealth of Nations* by emphasizing the division of labor as the source of wealth. A people's wealth consists of an abundant supply of the results of labor: useful things. In the subsequent course of his work, however, he forgets use values; they are not used any further in the economic analysis.[82] Certainly, there are also presentations of material and structural relations. They have, however, an exclusively descriptive character. His theory is one of abstract exchange value. The social

---

77. "It has even been possible to unite with the body of admitted economic doctrines those of Marx, which seemed revolutionary, for these are only definitions of a particular casuistry." Croce, *Philosophy of the Practical*, 379.

78. In a book commemorating the 150th anniversary of the publication of *Wealth of Nations*, Paul H. Douglas endeavors to show that "the contribution of Adam Smith to the theory of value . . . [was] not great," which necessarily led to the failure not only of classical but also of Marx's theory. But "the failure was not the failure of one man, but of a philosophy of value, and the roots of the ultimate contradiction made manifest to the world in the third volume of *Das Kapital* lie embedded in the first volume of the *Wealth of Nations*." Douglas, "Smith's Theory of Value," 69

79. "The pivots of any theory of the economic process are their teachings about value and interest . . . and four fifths of theoretical economic literature consists of research into or controversies about these subjects." Schumpeter, "Eugen von Böhm-Bawerk," 67.

80. [M is the value represented by money capital laid out at the start of the circuit of capital; M' is the expanded value of represented by money generated at the end of the circuit.]

81. Marx consequently speaks of the "accentuation of quantity and exchange value" by the classical economists, in the "most striking contrast" to "the writers of classical antiquity" (Plato, Xenophon), "who are exclusively concerned with quality and use value." *Capital*, vol. 1, 486.

82. Compare Elster, "Smiths Lehre," vol. 3, 213. Further, Bousquet, *Essai sur l'évolution*, 199; and Myrdal, *The Political Element*, 61.

equilibrium between supply and demand, which yields the "natural price," is exclusively a value equilibrium.[83] The same applies to Ricardo. Chapter 20 of his *Principles*, where he elaborates the distinction between use value and value, and the importance of "wealth," of use values, remains an alien body in the book.[84] Ricardo's entire ingenuity is concentrated on value terms (profit), and the use value side of commodities plays no role in his analysis. The life of the working class depends on the mass of use values that can be bought with a capital. The entrepreneur, meanwhile, is only interested in exchange value, the expansion of exchange value, that is, profit. Ricardo expressed this in the now-famous dictum that for the employer who annually makes £2,000 profit on a capital of £20,000—10 percent—"it would be a matter quite indifferent whether his capital would employ a hundred or a thousand men . . . provided, in all cases, his profits were not diminished below £2,000."[85] Whether a given capital employs a hundred or a thousand workers depends on the specific economic structure. Ricardo is indifferent to this. Marx emphasizes that Ricardo is only concerned with net revenue (pure profit), with the excess, in value terms, of price over costs, not with gross revenue, that is, the mass of use values necessary for the maintenance of the working nation. For Ricardo these are considered only as costs, to be pushed down as low as possible. Marx says: "By denying the importance of gross revenue, i.e. the volume of production and consumption apart from the value-surplus—and hence denying the importance of life itself—political economy's abstraction reaches the peak of infamy."[86]

Ricardo's central interest is the theory of distribution: "To determine the laws which regulate . . . distribution is the principal problem in Political Economy."[87] In a letter to Malthus he calls political economy a theory of laws that govern the proportional division of a given wealth among the various social classes. He regarded the determination of the mathematical relation between the parts of this given totality as "the only true object of the sciences."[88] This point of departure renders Ricardo's method aprioristic and deductive: his theories can be derived from a very small number of premises. Classical theory is more a system of logical deductions than research into and presentation of the objective economic relations of the capitalist mode of production.

In postclassical economics this tendency to avoid the real labor process becomes even more pronounced. In itself the principle of labor [as the source of] value contains a revolutionary element. It indicates, as the classical political economists themselves stated, that workers do not receive the full product of their labor under the prevailing social order, and that rent and profits on capital represent deductions [from it]. The egalitarian

---

83. Elster, "Smiths Lehre," vol. 3.
84. [Ricardo, *Principles of Political Economy*, 182–91.]
85. Ibid., 234–35.
86. Marx, "Aus David Ricardo," 421 and following.
87. Ricardo, *Principles of Political Economy*, 1.
88. "Political economy you think is an inquiry into the nature and causes of wealth; I think it should rather be called an inquiry into the laws which determine the division of the produce of industry amongst the classes who concur in its formation. No law can be laid down respecting quantity, but a tolerably correct one can be laid down respecting proportions." Ricardo to Thomas Malthus, October 10, 1820, 175.

Ricardians in England merely drew the conclusion implicit in the classical labor theory of value when they explained that a social situation in which workers received the full product of their labor is, fundamentally, the only proper and "natural" one.[89]

The reaction of right-wing students of Ricardo to this theoretical turn of the left Ricardians was to become ever more conservative. They scented a threat to class peace in Ricardo's theory of value.[90] Any analysis of the production and labor processes was avoided, in order to avoid the awkward question of the labor theory of value and its dangerous implications for distribution and the prevailing social order. Analysis was restricted to market phenomena, exchange: "Exchange," says Bastiat, "is political economy."[91] According to Léon Walras, the founder of the Lausanne school, political economy is "the theory of exchange of value and of exchange; on the contrary, he [Walras] forbade us to study production and distribution entirely."[92]

For fear of ending up in opposition to prevailing propertied interests, every effort was made to give economic theory the most abstract and formal shape possible, abandoning any qualitative, concrete content.[93] In short, efforts were made to erect a theory of distribution based on a theory of markets in order to furnish proof, by means of a theory of allocation, that all factors of production are rewarded in proportion to their contribution to the product and that, consequently, workers receive in wages full compensation for their labor.[94]

A second line of development also begins to become apparent just as early. Out of the same need to flee from reality, it pushes economic theory onto another terrain,

---

89. See, in particular, the sharp formulation of workers' rights to the full product of labor in Hodgskin, *Labour Defended*.

90. See, for example, Charles Knight's book, which scathingly attacks all opponents of the prevailing rights of property, including Hodgskin, and characterizes them as "ignorant of mankind," "destroyers" and "ministers of desolation." *The Rights of Industry*, 210, 212. Somewhat later, [Henry Charles] Carey formulated this view most clearly: "Ricardo's system is one of discords . . . its whole tends to the production of hostility among classes. . . . His book is the true manual of the demagogue, who seeks power by means of agrarianism, war and plunder." *The Past, the Present and the Future*, 74–75.

91. [Bastiat, *Harmonies of Political Economy*, 97.] Compare Bousquet, *Essai sur l'évolution*, 226.

92. Bousquet, *Essai sur l'évolution*, 208. Walras's analysis is in fact confined to exchange relations. He disposes of the entire "production process" with one word. The production process is replaced by a symbol, the concept of "coefficients of production," which means those quantities of productive goods used in the manufacture of one unit of output. In this purely formal manner, each unit of production is then allotted a corresponding "production coefficient."

93. August Walras makes this quite clear in a letter to his son Léon on February 6, 1859: "Une chose qui me plaît parfaitement dans le plan de ton travail, c'est le projet que tu as et que j'approuve de tous points, de te maintenir dans les limites les plus inoffensives á l'égard de M.M. les propriétaires. Cela est très sage et très facile á observer. Il faut faire de l'économie politique comme on ferait de l'accoustique ou de la mécanique." ["One thing that I find especially pleasing in the plan for your work is the project you have, of which I totally approve, to stay within the least offensive limits as regards property owners. This is very wise and very easy to observe. It is necessary to do political economy as one would do acoustics or mechanics."] See Leroy, *Auguste Walras, sa vie, son oeuvre*, 289.

94. John Bates Clark constantly tried to prove the proposition that the formation of prices under free competition allocates to each individual exactly in accordance with his productive efforts. "Natural law, so far as it has its way, excludes all spoliation." In a polemic against von Thünen he affirms that "the natural law of wages gives a result . . . [that is] morally justifiable." *The Distribution of Wealth*, 324.

that of psychology. This begins with Jean-Baptiste Say, who starts with the use values of commodities, understanding them not as physical phenomena but rather as psychological variables, the subjective utilities of the objects, and who constructed a subjective theory of value on [the basis of] this "service." From Say through Senior (1836) in England, [Jules] Dupuit (1844) in France, and Hermann Heinrich Gossen (1854) in Germany, the subjective theory of value led on to the theory of marginal utility as a theory of general hedonism.[95] In the process, political economy's object of inquiry shifted from the realm of things and social relations onto the terrain of subjective feelings. "Böhm-Bawerk's analysis of subjective value is the purest and most rationalistic hedonism," as Böhm-Bawerk's tenth supplementary discussion "On the 'Measurability' of Sensations" particularly shows.[96] The process of production is passed over.[97] Analysis is confined to market phenomena, the explanation of which is sought in human nature.

An even higher level of abstraction is represented by those attempts to make economics into a mathematically "exact" science that consequently disregard any qualitative content in economic phenomena. Market phenomena are one-sidedly regarded as mere "economic quantities" and, where possible, are expressed in mathematical equations. This tendency in modern theory is, perhaps, formulated most clearly by Joseph Schumpeter.[98] The process of production, like all objective economic relations, lies outside the analysis. According to Schumpeter, the essence of economic relations rests on a relation "between economic quantities," which is indeed reduced to the relation of exchange; all other relations among economic quantities are neglected as inessential.

Summarizing, it can be said that although theoretical schools and tendencies have changed a great deal over the entire century since classical economics, they possess the common trait that the real labor process and the social relations entered into during its course are excluded from their theoretical analyses.[99]

---

95. [See Senior, *Outline of the Science*; Dupuit, "On the Measurement of the Utility"; Gossen, *Laws of Human Relations*.]

96. Compare Myrdal, *The Political Element*, 98; and Böhm-Bawerk, "On the 'Measurability' of Sensations."

97. One could easily respond that, on the contrary, there are the well-known sections on "The Capitalist Production Process" and "Roundabout Methods of Production" in Böhm-Bawerk, *Capital and Interest*, vol. 2, 79–88, 89–94. It would be self-deception, however, to anticipate that Böhm-Bawerk really does describe the capitalist production process. All that is learned are general concepts that do not seek to grasp the specific features of the period of capitalist production but are instead intended to apply, in their abstract universality, to all periods. Thus, for example, the statement that objects of use can be made in two ways: directly, such as picking wild fruit from a high tree; or indirectly, by first cutting a stick from another tree and then knocking the fruit down. Böhm-Bawerk, *Capital and Interest*, vol. 2, 82. The creation of such an "intermediary product," a tool, is the creation of "capital" and hence the conduct of "capitalist production," which for Böhm-Bawerk is identical with any form of indirect production. This confusion rests on a trivial confusion of the technical labor process with the valorization process, so that for Böhm-Bawerk, every tool is already "capital." Hence the wild [American] Indian or Zulu who uses a boat to catch fish is a capitalist and carries on "capitalist production." Böhm-Bawerk, "On the 'Measurability' of Sensations," 81. According to Böhm-Bawerk's terminology, capitalist production was already present at the most primitive level of culture.

98. Schumpeter, *Das Wesen und der Hauptinhalt*, 50 and following.

99. With the possible exception of the [younger] historical school in Germany dominated by [Gustav]

Marx's critique is directed against political economy's abstract value approach, as was the contrasting critique made by the older historical school. The latter sought, however, to overcome the abstract "absolute" character of classical theoretical deduction by means of superficially and indiscriminately drawing on concrete historical or statistical material about production, consumption, trade, tax, the conditions of workers or peasants, and so on. It remained purely descriptive, denying, in effect, the possibility of knowing theoretical laws. But Marx set himself the task of "revealing the economic law of motion of modern society."[100] This cannot be done, however, by abstracting from the "real world" and merely clinging to its aspect as "economic quantities." Such a procedure is not political economy but the "metaphysics of political economy," which, the more it detaches itself from real objects by way of abstraction, "the more [it] imagine[s] [itself] to be getting all the nearer to the point of penetrating to their core."[101] As reality does not merely consist of values but is rather the unity of values and use values, Marx's critique begins from the twofold character of economic phenomena, according to which the essential character of the bourgeois economic system is given by the specific connection of the valorization process to the technical labor process. Of course, subjectively, the entrepreneur is only interested in the value side, in the valorization process of his capital, in profit. But he can only realize his desire for profit through the technical labor process, by making products, use values. And the capitalist period impresses its specific stamp on precisely the specific character of this labor process: from being a means of satisfying needs it becomes an instrument of the valorization process.[102] Marx accuses previous economic theory of only looking at individual, isolated sectors instead of grasping the concrete totality of economic relations.

The monetary system of the mercantilists merely analyzed the circuit of capital in its money form within the sphere of circulation. The physiocrats (Quesnay) grasped the problem at a deeper level yet regarded the economic process as an eternal circuit of commodities, because the production of commodities was not actually the work of human beings but of nature. Finally, the classical economists (Adam Smith, Ricardo) did take the production process as the object of their analysis, but only to the extent that it is a valorization process. In this way, by detouring through production, they eventually arrive at the same formula that constituted the basis of mercantilism.[103] In contrast to

---

Schmoller, which, however, because of its descriptive and eclectic character and rejection of theory, can be passed over here. [Editor's interpolation.]

100. Marx, *Capital*, vol. 1, 92.

101. Ibid., 163, 165. [Editor's interpolation.]

102. "In the capitalist mode of production the labour process appears only as a means towards the process of valorisation." Ibid., 711; compare Marx, *Capital*, vol. 2, 461.

103. According to Marx, the deep similarity between capitalist production and the mercantilist system becomes particularly evident in crises. When all values and prices are subject to enormous disturbances, there is suddenly a hunt for stable metallic currency, hoarding of gold, as the one secure thing in the midst of general insecurity, as the "*summum bonum*" [highest good] "just as it is regarded by the hoarder." This hoarding of gold expresses how "the actual devaluation and worthlessness of all physical wealth" is the natural consequence of a mode of production based on abstract exchange value, because alongside abstract exchange value, "all other commodities—just because they are use values—appear to be useless, mere baubles and

his predecessors, Marx emphasizes the decisive importance of the production process, regarded not merely as a process of valorization but, at the same time, as a labor process. This does not mean, however, that the two other forms of the circuit of capital, as money and commodities, may be ignored. Capitalist reality is a unity of circuits: the process of circulation (of both money and commodities) and the process of production (as the unity of the valorization and labor processes). Only to the extent that it is the unity of the labor and valorization processes does the production process, according to Marx, constitute "The basis, the starting-point for the physiology of the bourgeois system—for the understanding of its internal organic coherence and life process."[104] When the production process is regarded as a mere valorization process—as in classical theory—it has all the characteristics of "hoarding," becomes lost in abstraction, and is no longer capable of grasping the real economic process.[105]

Because Ricardo's categories of value are the expression, if only one-sided, of concrete reality, namely, the valorization process, they are taken over by Marx in principle and developed further. At the same time, however, he modifies them, by rounding their exclusively abstract value character out with the material side, and elaborates their dual character. The meaning of Marx's critique of Ricardo's categories of value and the changes he made to them moves in the same direction as his critique and transformation of [Georg Wilhelm Friedrich] Hegel's dialectic.[106] Both exhibit the same basic feature, being directed against the abstract and final character which Ricardo's categories of value and Hegel's dialectic share, because both abstract from "real determinateness." In his critique of Hegel's dialectic, Marx compares, in characteristic fashion, the logic with which Hegel begins the *Encyclopaedia*[107] with money and value: it is "mind's coin of the realm" and the "mental value of man and nature," because it is "totally indifferent to all real determinateness" and has become "thinking which abstracts from nature and from real man: abstract thinking."[108] Similarly, money represents the "most irrational" form of capitalism, and in interest-bearing money capital, capital has achieved the

---

toys." Marx, *Contribution to the Critique*, 378. Although political economy imagines itself to be superior to the mercantile system and assails it as "utterly wrong," as illusion, it shares the same "basic presuppositions" as the mercantile system. As a consequence, the monetary system at present "remains not only historically valid but retain[s its] full validity within certain spheres of the modern economy." Marx, *Contribution to the Critique*, 390. [Editor's interpolation]. Compare *Capital*, vol. 3, 670, 706–7, 727.

104. Marx, "Economic Manuscript of 1861–63 [Notebooks VII to XIII]," 391.

105. Accordingly, for Marx, only concrete labor functioning in the technical labor process, creating use values, is "real," "genuine" labor. *Contribution to the Critique*, 293, 296–97. [This translation has been modified because it rendered "real" and "*wirklich*" as "concrete," which did not capture the full nuance of Marx's expression, especially as earlier in the German text he also used the phrase "*konkrete Arbeit*." Marx, *Zur Kritik der politischen Ökonomie*, 115, 130–31.] Abstract labor creating exchange values is merely the "bourgeois form" of labor; "labor which creates exchange value is a specifically bourgeois feature." Marx, *Contribution to the Critique*, 298. It is precisely this labor that sets exchange value, which is responsible for all market catastrophes, devaluations, overproduction, stagnation. Marx, *The Poverty of Philosophy*, 135–38.

106. Marx, *Capital*, vol. 1, 103.

107. [Hegel, *The Encyclopaedia Logic*.]

108. Marx, "Economic and Philosophic Manuscripts of 1844," 330. [Marx italicizes "mental value" and "abstract."]

"pure fetish form" "in which all its determining features are obliterated and its real elements [are] invisible; in this form it represents merely independent exchange value."[109]

Marx also puts this decisive philosophical position into practice in economics: the abstract study of value obscures "real determinateness," the qualitative content of the concrete labor process, which impresses its specific, differentiating features on the capitalist economy. These can only be grasped by demonstrating the specific connection of the valorization process to the technical labor process in each particular epoch.[110] The "value-form, whose fully developed shape is the money-form, is very simple and slight in content."[111] The category of exchange value leads an "antediluvian existence."[112] Exchange value can be found in ancient Rome, in the Middle Ages, and under capitalism. Different contents are hidden behind each of these forms of exchange value. Marx emphasizes that "exchange value," detached from the concrete relations under which it has arisen, is an unreal abstraction, as exchange value "cannot exist except as an abstract, one-sided relation of an already existing concrete living whole." Whoever says "exchange value" presupposes "population which produces under definite conditions."[113] Of course, "political economy . . . is not technology."[114] The point is not, however, to study the valorization process in separation from the particular labor process, on whose basis it arose and with which it constitutes a unitary whole. "The concrete is concrete because it is a synthesis of many determinations, thus a unity of the diverse." The task of science consists of the "reproduction of the concrete" "by way of thinking."[115]

Just as the paleontologist reconstructs the entire skeleton and even the presumed muscles and movements of an animal from a few excavated bones, Marx reads the necessary tendencies of capital that are peculiar to an epoch from the structure of the labor process in the particular epoch and the type of tools used in it. For "technology reveals the active relation of man to nature, the direct process of the production of his life, and thereby . . . the social relations of his life."[116] "The hand-mill gives you society with the feudal lord; the steam-mill, society with the industrial capitalist."[117] Since social rela-

---

109. Marx, "Economic Manuscript of 1861–63 [Notebooks XII to XV]," 462. [Editor's interpolation.]

110. Hegel already criticized this tendency to mathematicization, which only grasps one side, the relations between quantities, in the concrete totality of reality and neglects all the remaining qualitative moments. "Its purpose or principle is quantity. This is precisely the relationship that is non-essential, alien to the character of the notion. The process of knowledge goes on, therefore, on the surface, does not affect the concrete fact itself, does not touch its inner nature or notion, and is hence not a conceptual way of comprehending." Hegel, *Phenomenology of Mind*, 41. He consequently emphasized that the task of economics consists not merely in representing quantitative but also, at the same time, qualitative relations and movements of their elements in their "complexity." Hegel, *Outlines of the Philosophy of Right*, 187. [Grossman's original text has *Verwirklichung*, "realization," but given the passage he refers to and the structure of his own sentence, what seems to be meant is *Verwickelung* ("complexity").]

111. Marx, *Capital*, vol. 1, 90.

112. Marx, "Introduction," 38.

113. Ibid., 38.

114. Ibid., 24.

115. Ibid., 38.

116. Marx, *Capital*, vol. 1, 493.

117. Marx, *The Poverty of Philosophy*, 166. In a letter to Kautsky, Engels criticizes him for having paid in-

tions are closely bound up with the forces of production, changes in the tendencies of capital can be read from changes in these forces.

The best illustration of Marx's theoretical thought is provided by chapters 14 and 15 of the first volume of *Capital*, the chapters on "Manufacture" and "Machinery and Large-Scale Industry."[118] They are by no means historical-descriptive depictions, in which Marx seeks to present genetically how large-scale industry arose out of manufacture. Both chapters have an eminently theoretical character, which is proven by the fact that they are merely subsections of the part of *Capital* dealing with "The Production of Relative Surplus Value." What characterizes manufacture and large-scale industry by means of machines as two distinct phases of capitalist production? Both have a capitalist character; both are based on wage labor and are governed by the pursuit of profit. The technical labor process in each is, however, completely different. Manufacture represents a "productive mechanism whose organs are human beings."[119] In contrast, modern large-scale industry is based on machines. So precisely it [the technical labor process] marks the distinctness of capitalism's different phases. The example of the derivation of these objective tendencies of capital from the analysis of the concrete labor process and its instruments, machinery, illustrates the difference in principle between Marx and other theoretical tendencies in the study of economic events. Further consequences arising from this for the problem of crises and dynamics will be dealt with later.

While transformations in the mode of production during manufacture begin with labor, in large-scale industry they proceed from the instruments of labor: machinery.[120] The process is as follows: machinery makes muscle power dispensable and thus facilitates the incorporation of women and children into the production process on a massive scale. It lowers the price of labor power and increases surplus value, because the wages of the entire "parcelized family," doing labor that is many times greater, are now no higher than that previously received by the individual head of the family alone.[121] The degree of exploitation of labor increases in an avalanche.[122] Further, the tendencies to employ minors and immature people and simultaneously to strengthen the despotism of capital through the extensive employment of women and children break down the resistance put up by the male workers.[123] The material consumption of the ma-

---

sufficient attention to the role of the labor process. "You should not separate . . . technology from political economy as you do. . . . The tools of the savage condition his society just as much as do more modern ones capitalist society." Engels to Karl Kautsky, June 26, 1884, 156. [Engels emphasized "technology" and "his."]

118. Marx, *Capital*, vol. 1, 455–91 and 492–639. It is no accident that so large a part of the presentation in all the volumes of *Capital* is devoted to the technical labor process. The chapter on the shaping of the labor process by machinery, in the first volume alone, encompasses nearly 150 pages. But much space is also devoted to the presentation of the technical labor process in its connection with the valorization process.

119. Ibid., 457, 468.

120. Ibid., 517.

121. [This phrase is used by Marx in German but does not appear in the English translation of *Capital* referenced here. See Ibid., 518, and Marx, *Das Kapital*, 355.]

122. Marx, *Capital*, vol. 1, 517.

123. Ibid., 526. See pp. 489–90 on the insubordination of workers characteristic of the period of manu-

chinery, which represents a large capital value and which must have interest paid on it and be depreciated, does not only occur when it is in use but also when it is not in use, as a result of the destructive effects of the elements. Hence the capitalists' tendency to make labor continue day and night. It is further strengthened by the circumstance that every new invention threatens to devalue machinery. Hence the capitalists' efforts to minimize the danger of the "moral" depreciation of the machinery by reducing the period in which its total value is reproduced.[124] "Hence too the economic paradox that the most powerful instrument for reducing labour-time suffers a dialectical inversion and becomes the most unfailing means for turning the whole lifetime of the worker and his family into labour-time at capital's disposal for its own valorisation."[125]

A further impulse to the prolongation of labor time therefore comes from savings on outlays for additional machinery and buildings, otherwise normally required for the expansion of the scale of production. The expansion in the scale of production without these additional outlays signifies an increase in the mass of surplus value, with a simultaneous reduction in capital expenditure per unit of the commodity produced, which further increases the mass of profit.[126]

Machinery leads to the tendency for labor to become more intense and particularly in all areas where workers' resistance has made the extensive prolongation of the working day impossible because of legal prohibitions. In the factory, "the dependence of the worker on the continuous and uniform motion of the machinery had already created the strictest discipline."[127] The increased speed of machinery forces the worker to become more attentive and active.[128]

Here the tendency for the rate of valorization to fall and to create an industrial reserve army also comes into play. At higher levels of capitalist development and with its general application, machinery, whose purpose is to enlarge relative surplus value and hence the mass of surplus value, brings about a countertendency, that is, toward a fall in the rate of valorization. For the mass of surplus value that can be obtained depends on two factors: the rate of surplus value and "the number of workers simultaneously employed."[129] In the hunt for increased relative surplus value, the capitalist is driven to constantly develop labor's productivity by expanding the application of machinery in relation to living labor, and he "attains this result only by diminishing the number of workers employed by a given amount of capital."[130] A part of the capital that was previously variable and yielded surplus value progressively becomes constant capital, which produces no surplus value. The result is apparent in the tendency to create an excess

---

facture.
124. Ibid., 528.
125. Ibid., 532.
126. Ibid., 529.
127. Ibid., 535.
128. Ibid., 536–37.
129. Ibid., 530.
130. Ibid., 531.

working population; on the other hand, in the tendency for the mass of surplus value attainable, in relation to the size of the capital employed, to fall. "Hence there is an immanent contradiction in the application of machinery to the production of surplus value, since, of the two factors of the surplus value created by a given amount of capital, one, the rate of surplus value, cannot be increased except by diminishing the other, the number of workers."[131] Finally, Marx underlines the dynamic impulses that emanate from machinery. While manufacture traditionally "strives to hold fast to that [appropriate] form [of the division of labour] when once it has been found"[132] and was consequently unable to seize hold of society in its full extent and transform it in depth,[133] large-scale industry based on machinery is forced by the fall in the rate of profit to continually revolutionize the technology of the labor process and therefore the structure of society.

5.

The second characteristic feature of the dominant theories since classical economics (the first was their one-sided view of the valorization process) is their static character. No one disputes the static character of the theory of the physiocrats, who discovered the "economic circuit" (the "*tableau économique*").[134] The theories of Smith and Ricardo are both similarly static. All of their categories are based on the concept of an equilibrium in which "natural price" (value) asserts itself as an ideal point in economic activity, around which market prices oscillate. As a result, there is no room for crises in Ricardo's mechanism. For him, they are merely accidents, introduced from the outside (wars, bad harvests, state intervention, and so on).[135] Left to itself, the economic circuit always moves in equilibrium and always follows the same path. The deceleration and cessation of capital accumulation in the distant future that Ricardo forecast must be described as mere pseudodynamics, because the "dynamic" factor is not inherent in the economic process itself but is rather a natural force that influences the economic process from the outside (falling rate of profit as a consequence of growing population and hence increased ground rents).

This is how it remained with Ricardo's students, too. In France, Say's theory of markets, that is, the theory that every supply is simultaneously a demand, that consequently any production, through the very fact of its supply, creates its own demand, leads to the conclusion that an equilibrium between supply and demand is possible at any time and on any scale of production. But this implies the possibility of the unlimited accumulation of capital and expansion of production, because there are no obstacles

---

131. Ibid.
132. Ibid., 485. [Editor's interpolation.]
133. Ibid., 489.
134. [Quesnay, *Quesnay's Tableau Économique*.]
135. Compare Weiller, *La conception classique*, 11, and John Maurice Clark, "The Relation between Statics and Dynamics," 51.

to the full employment of all factors of production.[136]

John Stuart Mill does make the first attempt to consider the dynamic character of the economy, by distinguishing between statics and dynamics. But this division of the scientific object into two, taken over from the mechanics of physics, proved disastrous for the further development of political economy. Mill's analysis has an entirely static character. After having first analyzed the economic mechanism in a static state (with constant population, production, capital, and, likewise, unchanged technology) and investigated its laws, he subsequently sought to add "a theory of motion to our theory of equilibrium—the dynamics of political economy to the statics."[137]

A certain number of corrections are introduced into the static picture: population growth, growth of capital, and so on, as if such subsequent retouching removes the statically conceived character of the economic system's essence; as if there were two capitalisms, a static one and a dynamic one. But if capitalism is dynamic, what is the point of investigating the laws of an imaginary static economy without, at the same time, demonstrating how the transition from statics to dynamics is to take place?[138]

As equilibrium theories, the dominant theories cannot, in principle, derive generalized crisis from the system, because for them prices are an automatic mechanism for the restoration of equilibrium, for overcoming disturbances. Any attempt to incorporate into their system one of the empirically confirmed moments of disturbance, that is, the tendency to break through equilibrium that is actually observed, necessarily suffers from a fundamental contradiction. Consistent application of the lines of thought employed in equilibrium theory can only demonstrate that such disruptions of equilibrium are only generated precisely "from outside," that is, by changes in economic data. From the standpoint of equilibrium theories, the economy can always only react in one direction following changes in these data, by adjusting: by tending to create a new equilibrium. It is not apparent how a crisis can arise in such a system.[139]

Alfred Marshall (1890), who tries to combine classical theory with marginal utility theory, has a decidedly static construct. He does investigate shifts in a developing society. These merely constitute, however, an external framework for his analysis. It is only a matter of the adjustment of the economy to changing, external data, such as population, capital, and so on, but not of economic developments that arise from the economy itself. Marshall's economy does not develop. At the center of his system lies the concept of a general equilibrium enforcing itself in all parts of the economic mechanism.[140] Once it is achieved, no further changes take place. This basic idea is then

---

136. ["Full employment" is in English in the original text.]

137. John Stuart Mill, *Principles of Political Economy*, 461.

138. "The main problem now is to proceed from static to dynamic economics." John Maurice Clark, "The Relation between Statics and Dynamics," 46.

139. Compare Grossmann, *Das Akkumulations- und Zusammenbruchsgesetz*, 284.

140. "The general theory of equilibrium of demand and supply is a fundamental idea running through the frames of all the various parts of the central problem of distribution and exchange." Marshall, *Principles of Economics*, ix.

applied to individual problems. Equilibrium is not a heuristic device in theory but a tendency asserting itself in reality.[141]

The whole system is governed by the idea of a general state of equilibrium (maximum satisfaction), toward which the economy, under free competition, tends. Marshall only arrived at this static picture thanks to his inadequate method, because, despite his "general theory of equilibrium," he does not provide any theory of the system as a whole that deals with all the submarkets and the production process at the same time that is one which grasps the overall interdependence of the system. What he offers, in reality, is a theory of partial equilibria in submarkets, which is always concerned with relations between already existing economic variables, with the determination of the price level (if supply and demand curves are given), or with the determination of the demand curve, if quantities and prices are known. So Henry Ludwell Moore, quite correctly, characterizes Marshall's approach as "static and limited to functions of one variable."[142]

John Bates Clark, in Schumpeter's view the most influential American theorist of the previous generation, did "take a significant step beyond Mill's standpoint, already mentioned, and carefully defined the static state. . . . He also energetically advanced the proposal for a specific theory of 'dynamics.'"[143] But this remained a "proposal." In resignation, Clark says of dynamics: "But the task of developing this branch of science is so large that the execution of it will occupy generations of workers."[144] What he really gives is a picture of a fictional, static economy: year after year the mass of workers employed and the number of capitals remain unchanged, along with the tools and technologies in production. In this society, there are no transfers of capital or labor from one branch of production to another, and consumer demand also remains constant. Under these assumptions he investigates the principle of distribution and demonstrates the way that prices, wages, and interest on capital are formed in a static situation. Commodities are sold at their "natural," that is, cost prices, so that entrepreneurs gain no profit.[145] Clark admits that "this picture is completely imaginary. A static society is an impossible one."[146]

---

141. "When demand and supply are in stable equilibrium, if any accident should move the scale of production from its equilibrium position, there will be instantly brought into play forces tending to bring it back to that position." Ibid., 404 f.

142. Marshall was conscious of the weaknesses of his construct, of its unrealistic character. "He recognized the impossibility of solving real problems by his method unless his hypothetical, static constructions could be replaced by concrete, dynamic functions," which he hoped would follow the improvement of mathematical "scientific machinery." Moore, *Synthetic Economics*, 93. Hicks also emphasizes the static character of Marshall's construct, stating "how reluctant he is to abandon static conceptions even in his dynamic analysis . . . his dynamics are not made easier by running in terms of a very static equilibrium and by the fact that their central passage leads up to the introduction of the 'famous fiction,' the stationary state." In addition, Marshall's distinction between "short" and "long periods," with the further assumption that "a 'full adaptation' of supply to demand" will occur in the latter, "is not a concept that fits very well into a general dynamic theory." Hicks, *Value and Capital*, 120–21.

143. Schumpeter, *Theorie der wirtschaftlichen Entwicklung*, 100. [The English translation of this work is a revised version of the German edition and does not include the text quoted by Grossman.]

144. John Bates Clark, *The Distribution of Wealth*, 442.

145. Ibid., 400 and vi–vii.

146. Ibid., 400 and 29.

"Actual society is always dynamic. . . . Industrial society is constantly assuming new forms and discharging new functions."[147] But no conclusions are drawn from this observation. Clark thinks that static forces, isolated in this way, do nevertheless possess real meaning: they also always operate as a fundamental component force in the dynamic world; they indicate real tendencies.[148] But there is more. Despite all the emphasis on the "hypothetical" character of the "static state" and despite all his references to the dynamic essence of reality, Clark almost totally abandoned dynamics in his later, principal work, *Essentials of Economic Theory*. His picture of the economy and society is static. The static model asserts itself in a competitive economy—although not in an ideally pure form. As long as there is free competition, "the most active societies conform most closely to their static model."[149] The situation is not much different in contemporary society (with imperfect competition).[150] Precisely the mobility of the prevailing economy's elements enables a static state to be attained more quickly than if these elements were less mobile. The "normal" (static) form asserts itself better in the highly industrialized society of [the United States of America] than in immobile Asian societies.[151] "The static shape itself, though it is never completely copied in the actual shape of society, is for scientific purposes a reality."[152] In short, "static influences that draw society forever toward its natural form are always fundamental and progress has no tendency to suppress them."[153] What the economy's "dynamic" character consists of, and how disturbances can arise, Clark has not said. He presents dynamic development, with its rapid changes in the economic organism, as a succession in time of different static states.[154]

This static character becomes even more pronounced in the pure theory of marginal utility. Dynamic changes in the structure can hardly be reconciled with such a construct, because it assumes that production is governed by consumers (demand), and that the economy can be reduced to subjective choices between various subjective uses. They are merely external data, which this theory assumes. But it does not investigate or explain their emergence. Schumpeter (1912) could therefore state that "the static character of its theoretical edifice was unaffected by the great reform of theory, through the subjective theory of value. . . . In fact, the static character of the theory gained substantially in rigor and clarity as a result of the new analysis."[155]

---

147. Ibid., vi and 30.

148. "The static state which has here been pictured is the one towards which society is at every instant tending." Ibid., 402.

149. John Bates Clark, *Essentials of Economic Theory*, 195.

150. "The actual form of a highly dynamic society hovers relatively near to its static model though it never conforms to it." Ibid.

151. Ibid., 195.

152. Ibid., 197.

153. Ibid., 198.

154. Ibid., 196. A more recent critic of Clark says, quite correctly, that as a result of all his abstract assumptions, the picture he sketched is totally alien to reality. "Such an isolation of static forces, it is admitted, gives to the study an unlifelike appearance and makes it 'heroically theoretical.'" Homan, *Contemporary Economic Thought*, 38.

155. Schumpeter, *Theorie der wirtschaftlichen Entwicklung*, 100.

As [Maurice] Roche-Agussol states, the main object of marginal utility theory's analyses is an "essentially static problem," namely, the valuation and distribution of goods "at a *given* level of needs and the means for satisfying needs."[156] With the introduction of movement through time, this theory has to fail, even from its own standpoint, because no statements about future needs and means for satisfying them can be made. Conscious of this fact, Menger declares that "the conception of theoretical economics . . . as a science of the . . . 'laws of development in economy,' and other such things, is a one-sided monstrosity. . . . It is a living proof of the aberrations," et cetera.[157] The theory of William Stanley Jevons, the other founder of the marginal utility school, is also decidedly static. He operates with concepts borrowed from the science of mechanics (such as "infinitely small quantities"), on which he erects his theory of exchange. "The laws of exchange resemble the laws governing the equilibrium of a lever, as they are both determined by the principle of virtual velocities."[158] Jevons does know that all economic phenomena are in motion and must, therefore, be dealt with in units of time. But in chapter 3 of his book, he manages to exclude the time factor from his analysis by recourse to a methodological trick. From the outset, he dispenses with the idea "of a complete solution to the problem in its entire natural complexity" (that would be "a problem of motion—a problem of dynamics") and confines his analysis to "the purely static problem" of establishing the conditions under which exchange ceases and equilibrium is achieved.[159]

The marginal utility school has consistently retained this character to the present; for reasons of space, we have to restrict ourselves to a few typical examples from various currents. Frank Hyneman Knight does emphasize that history does not stop and that "evolution to other forms of organization as the dominant type" is inherent in capitalism,[160] but thinks that "such a social development falls outside the scope of the economic theorist," because the notion of equilibrium is entirely applicable to such changes.[161] He refers the study of these changes to the science of history and comes to the conclusion that "economic dynamics, in the sense which this expression should have in order to be applicable [in economic theory], does not exist. What is specified as being dynamic in it should be named evolutionary or historical economic theory."[162] Ewald Schams's position is no different. According to him, economics is a theory of "economic variables," and understanding the relations among variables and dependent variables necessarily requires the construction of functional concepts and the specifi-

---

156. Roche-Agussol, "Die Werttheorie," 36.

157. Menger, *Investigations into the Method*, 121. [This quotation is misleading. Menger's comments were not directed *against* subjective preference/marginal utility theory but rather *from* that position against the German historical school.]

158. Jevons, *Theory of Political Economy*, vii, 3.

159. Ibid., iv, 93–94.

160. Frank Hyneman Knight, "Statik und Dynamik," 25.

161. Ibid., 26.

162. Ibid., 7.

cation of equations.[163] Since, however, the theory of functional relations, as is generally conceded today,[164] is necessarily static, because it merely investigates relations between given value variables, Schams arrives at the conclusion (despite his acknowledgment of the dynamic character of the capitalist economy) that we must work with static conceptual tools. This is because we do not possess a specifically dynamic conceptual form that could grasp dynamic changes. The theory of economic variables [mathematical economics], as a theory of relations, has no more possibility of development than geometry. Quite independently of whether "there is a stationary reality or simply an economy in full motion," "logically defined statics will always be an assumption."[165] Schams therefore directs his criticism against the twofold division of theory into statics and dynamics. "Every theory of economic variables is entirely static." Economic movement can only be understood as the succession and comparison of various static states of equilibrium, as "comparative statics," as "the comparison of the two states of dependent variables over a certain interval of time."[166] There can be no specifically dynamic problems that are not theories of variables within the theory of economic variables but at most theoretical problems that are no longer questions of the theory of variables, and are thus theories of the development of economic data. But these lie outside the scope of economic theory.[167]

The realization that several interdependent movements and nonequivalent relations cannot be grasped mathematically has apparently led one part of the dominant theory into an intensified struggle against attempts to "dynamize" the theory and to a renais-

---

163. Schams, "Komparative Statik," 46–48.

164. Compare Mayer, "Der Erkenntniswert der funktionellen Preis-theorien."

165. Schams, "Komparative Statik," 49.

166. Ibid., 49–50.

167. Yet another of the grounds advanced by Schams for the passionate struggle being waged against attempts to "dynamize theory" and introduce the time factor directly into the analysis, despite acknowledgment of the dynamic nature of reality, is interesting. If economics is regarded as "a theory of economic variables," then the mathematical method will prove indispensable in the "exact" treatment of complex relations among variables, which cannot be mastered by means of "conventional logic." The most important methodological principle in the construction of systems of variables is the "equivalence of relations, that is, the construction of equations in which the relationships among the variables can be expressed." Schams, "Komparative Statik," 48. This method, however, is located right in the center of statics, as the functional method can only grasp relations between given values, quantities, and so on, but not their formation. If movement, that is, change through time, is now introduced, it is apparent that "the regularity of disproportional movement will destroy the equivalence of the relations," as Schams freely admits. "The simultaneity of more than two independent movements cannot be dealt with mathematically." Schams, "Komparative Statik," 49. "The use of differential and integral equations is scarcely possible with nonequivalent relations." Not beginning with given prices and quantities, however, and introducing change through time means confronting the task of dealing with future changes and, instead of establishing exact relations between given variables, "being content with the calculation of correlations and mathematical price expectations." Doing this, however, means turning away from "exact theory" and "entering the company of the dice-throwing probability theorists." Schams, "Komparative Statik," 55. The "mathematically exact" method, originally designated as indispensable on the grounds that it was supposed to be the best means for the exact investigation of reality, is here raised to the level of an end in itself. Reality is dynamic. As it is impossible to grasp dynamic movement by mathematical means, however, one is restricted to statics, in order to avoid having to dispense with the "exact" method of mathematics.

sance of static theories of equilibrium.[168] According to Conrad, an exchange economy without centralized management is a "self-regulating mechanism, which tends toward a steady state, that is, seeks to assume uniform movement." The essence of self-regulation is that the "mechanism is steered toward a stationary state"—"a tendency that never actually reaches its goal but which is alone to be thanked if an exchange economy, lacking centralized management, does not fall into chaos."[169] Conrad does know that there are crises and disturbances that cannot be regarded as movement toward a stationary state. The presupposition of the tendency toward equilibrium is therefore "that the regulative apparatus functions correctly" (sic!). If this were not the case, "then it is possible that the approach toward the stationary state will be constantly impeded."[170]

According to Conrad, movement should be understood as a succession of stationary states without making the intervening, nonstationary states intelligible.[171] Alexander Bilimovic concedes that previous theory merely succeeded in determining equilibrium equations for a stationary economy but not for a dynamic economy. This explains why "the schemas which have predominated until now do not express economic equilibrium in the real world." These schemas are, nevertheless, held to be capable of improvement, and Bilimovic hopes that it may also be possible to construct a mathematical model of a nonstationary economy, for previous attempts' lack of success in dynamizing the schemas of a stationary economy cannot be attributed to any fundamental defect in these schemas.[172]

Doesn't this twofold division of theory recall John Stuart Mill's similar proposition? And won't it remain as futile as Mill's, in view of the basic fact that no bridge can lead from statics to dynamics, even if this dynamics is thought of as a succession of static states? For these are various static states that follow one another. The static line of thought is unable to explain how successive new states arise, precisely for the reason "that the equilibrium of static analysis does not allow for growth, that this analysis can only describe an expanding system in terms of successive states of equilibrium, with the intervening stages of transition left, and left with danger to the validity of the argument, unanalyzed."[173]

These difficulties only really begin to accrue when statics are no longer regarded as a real tendency but as a heuristic device, because there is then even less of a bridge leading from this hypothetical state to reality, which moves in disequilibrium. "If the economic cycle's entire course is movement in disequilibrium—neither cumulative downward nor upward—what is the point of regarding particular states of equilibri-

168. On this, compare Conrad, "Die Grundannahme der Gleichgewichtstheorie," 243.

169. Ibid., 236 [citing Conrad, *Der Mechanismus der Verkehrswirtschaft*, 286].

170. Conrad, "Die Grundannahme der Gleichgewichtstheorie," 239.

171. [Ludwig] Lachmann (London) similarly understands "a dynamic theory of equilibrium" as one "which is concerned with changes in equilibrium through time and describes the complete process of transition from one equilibrium to the next." The difficulties with which the theory of dynamics wrestles are difficulties in neither its principles nor its content and are rather to be attributed to "the deficiencies of our analytical tools." Lachmann, "Preiserwartungen und intertemporales Gleichgewicht," 33–34.

172. Bilimovic, "Zur Verteidigung der Gleichgewichtsidee," 220–24.

173. Compare Harrod, "Studies in the Theory of Economic Expansion," 496.

um as the point of departure or a transition point in this movement? If equilibrium is nowhere departed from, tended toward, or passed through, why behave 'as if' this was the case?"[174] Proceeding from the assumption of static equilibrium, the entire problem of dynamics is reduced to the question of which factors "disturb" this supposed state. Thus, for [Gottfried] Haberler, there is an inherent tendency toward equilibrium in the economic system. Consequently, for him, only the downturn in the course of the economic cycle, the "long swing" "in the negative direction" but not the upswing, requires explanation, "since the upward movement, the approach to full employment, might be explained as a natural consequence of the inherent tendency of the economic system towards equilibrium."[175]

More recently still, criticisms of the concept of "the stationary state"[176] as a superfluous, because economically unreal, presupposition have multiplied in another area of the dominant theory. As Hicks says, this group is forced to concede "that the actual state of any real economy is never in fact stationary; nevertheless, stationary-state theorists naturally regarded reality as 'tending' towards stationariness; though the existence of such a tendency is more than questionable." "The stationary theory itself gives no indication that reality does tend to move in any such direction."[177] Still more, Hicks holds the concept of a stationary economy directly responsible for retarding the development of science, because it neglected problems of dynamics.[178]

We can deal with the mathematical tendency's lines of thought briefly, because our concern is not to offer an exhaustive critique of this school but rather to bring out its static character.[179] "No presentation is more static than that of Léon Walras."[180] As can be read on a memorial tablet in the Lausanne Academy, Walras was exalted as the theorist "who first established the general conditions of economic equilibrium." According to Walras, the economy can be compared with a lake, whose waves may well be temporarily whipped up by a storm, but which subsequently subside to form a new, mirror-flat equilibrium. Similarly, economic disturbances to general equilibrium spread out through the entire economic system. But Walras simply regards them as oscillations, whose amplitude falls over time until equilibrium is restored.[181] The question of whether, perhaps, such a static state cannot be realized at all is not posed. On the contrary, Walras is convinced of the possibility of the realization of an enduring equilibrium. "The more we know of the ideal conditions of equilibrium, the better we

---

174. Bode, "Prosperität und Depression," 599.
175. Haberler, *Prosperity and Depression*, 265. [Quotations in English in the original.]
176. [In English in the original.]
177. Hicks, *Value and Capital*, 119.
178. Ibid.
179. Hicks also includes Knut Wicksell in the Lausanne school, alongside Walras and Pareto, because he thinks just as statically as the other two. Wicksell's "capital theory is limited to considering the artificial abstraction of a stationary state." Ibid., 3.
180. Schumpeter, *Theorie der wirtschaftlichen Entwicklung*, 100.
181. Walras, *Elements of Pure Economics*, 380–81.

shall be able to control or prevent these crises."[182]

The same can be said of [Vilfredo] Pareto's work. Hicks calls Pareto's *Manual* "the most complete static theory of value which economic science has hitherto been able to produce."[183] Pareto distinguishes three areas of research: the theory of statics, the area of economic theory that is the most complete; the theory of successive equilibria, "we have only a very few notions about the theory of successive equilibria"; finally the theory of dynamics, which deals with the investigation of the movement of economic phenomena, "except for a special theory, that of economic crises, nothing is known about dynamic theory."[184] Pareto himself contributed nothing to the investigation of dynamics and, rather, impeded it by assuming that the above threefold division of research actually corresponded to reality.[185] His attention is only directed toward statics; his central, indeed only, problem is that of equilibrium,[186] to which he devotes chapters 3 to 6 of his book. He never indicates the bridge that leads from statics to dynamics.[187] Pareto underscores the significance of Walras's equations for economic equilibrium and attributes to them an analogous role to Lagrangian equations in mechanics, in that he conceptualized reality as a system of "continual oscillations around a central point of equilibrium" and thought that this center of equilibrium moved.[188] The question of whether the concept of economic movement is compatible with that of equilibrium is never raised and is almost completely excluded by the untenable assumption that all economic phenomena share a simultaneous, uniform rhythm.[189]

This static trait of Pareto's theory is understandable if it is considered that he deals exclusively with relations between already existing values on the market or, in Pareto's later formulation, with choices between indifference combinations that already exist. According to his conception, equilibrium is achieved if two people possessing a certain number of goods exchange them with each other on the market up to the point at which both parties agree that no further exchange is possible. The state of equilibrium attained can therefore be defined as "a state which would maintain itself indefinitely" if there is no change in its conditions or if this change is so slight that the system "tends

---

182. Ibid., 381.

183. Hicks, "A Reconsideration of Value," 52.

184. Pareto, *Manual of Political Economy*, 105.

185. "This division corresponds to reality." Ibid., 104. As if we had experienced two different objects, a static alongside a dynamic economy!

186. "The principal subject of our study is economic equilibrium." Ibid., 106.

187. Ibid., 103–290.

188. Consequently, Rosenstein-Rodan correctly says: "No doubt mathematical, like any static theory, only seeks to explain tendencies to equilibrium and understand the real course of the economy as deviations from the state of equilibrium." "In this it is supposed that, after numerous oscillations, a state of equilibrium, which continues to exist unchanged, will emerge." Rosenstein-Rodan, "Das Zeitmoment in der mathematischen Theorie," 136.

189. The assumption that economic phenomena share a simultaneous rhythm was explicitly emphasized in Pareto, *Manual of Political Economy*, 105. The same is true of a successor of Pareto, [Alfonso] de Pietri-Tonelli. [See, for example, Pietri-Tonelli, *Traité d'économie rationnelle*.]

to re-establish itself, to return to its original position."[190]

Pareto employs the concepts of statics and tendency to equilibrium, borrowed from mechanics, without investigating whether they make sense in economics. The essence of his method of the general interdependence of all economic variables, long regarded as a modern miracle, like the essence of any functional approach that abstains from genetic explanation, is their static character. It only shows the relations between already given economic variables (be they utilities or indifference combinations), but not the capacity of the system for movement, the evolution of these variables, and hence the direction in which the system is moving. To do this, it is necessary to look at the process of production as the source of all changes in "economic variables." But this is excluded from the analysis at the outset.[191] Although Hicks thinks that Pareto's exchange equations could be extended to production processes, given certain corrections, he makes the reservation that they would only be valid for a stationary economy in which no capital accumulation (Hicks says no net saving) and no other changes in given economic data take place. But this makes Pareto's equations, as Hicks concedes, "far from being a description of reality." "They are not a description of reality."[192]

As early as 1846, Marx wrote against Proudhon that "the relations of production of every society form a whole."[193] The same authors who emphasize the "general interdependence" of all economic variables and reject methods that seek to single out and explain only individual groups of phenomena from the process of economic life themselves break this totality down into sectors. They separate market phenomena from the sphere of the labor process and make this artificially separated sphere of exchange the main object of their analysis. Pareto could arrive at "equilibrium equations" by dealing with the functional connection between given market variables[194] and excluding the dynamic factor of the production process or, that is, by "completely dedynamizing the system."[195]

---

190. Pareto, *Manual of Political Economy*, 108, 109.

191. As Amoroso emphasizes, "a base della statica economica paretiana sono due concetti fondamentali: di richezza, di ofelimià. Non esistono differenze sostanziali fra produzione." ["Two concepts underlie Pareto's economic statics: wealth and ophelimity (economic satisfaction). No substantial distinctions exist in production."] Amoroso asks: What about the former division of economics into production, exchange, consumption, and distribution? And he answers the question, saying that according to Pareto, "non esiste nella realtà una distinzione di cose corrispondente a questa distinzione di parole . . . ma tutti i problemi economici sono compressi nelle condizioni generali dell'equilibrio, limitamente alla sola condizione che restano invariate le forze e gli vincoli quali esistono nella posizione iniziale." ["There is no distinction in reality that corresponds to this linguistic distinction . . . rather, all the problems of economics are contained in the general conditions for equilibrium, amounting to the sole condition that forces and constraints do not change from their initial state."] Amoroso, "La meccanica economica," 46–47.

192. Hicks, "Equilibrium and the Trade Cycle," 525, 526.

193. [Marx, *The Poverty of Philosophy*, 166.]

194. "The circulation of commodities has of course only to do with already existing, given values." Marx, *Capital*, vol. 2, 297.

195. Mayer, "Der Erkenntniswert der funktionellen Preis-theorien," 239. Of course, Mayer is not consistent enough. As a marginalist he regards consumer demand as the "driving force of the entire system" (ibid.). Demand, however, as the most recent works of the Keynesian school admit, is not a driving factor

At the same time, the above example shows how the accuracy of the mathematical process is invoked in the construction of the system of equilibrium equations. This accuracy is not related to the content of economic knowledge but rather to the technique of mathematical calculation. Despite the accuracy of these operations, mathematical treatment can be a source of the greatest errors, precisely because of the postulates that underlie the equations and determine the value of the knowledge they yield.[196]

In its youthful enthusiasm, the mathematical school (Walras, Marshall, [Ysidro] Edgeworth, Pareto in his *Cours*, but also Böhm-Bawerk)[197] believed it could measure everything and constructed an edifice of equilibrium equations, whose basis was the assumption that utility is, in principle, a measurable variable, or would be a measurable variable if we had knowledge of enough facts at our disposal. After one generation, a more sober assessment was made. The objection initially raised by a few was generally acknowledged: utility, as an intensely psychological variable, cannot be measured and subjected to mathematical operations.[198] But if marginal utility is not measurable, then nor is aggregate social utility, and hence all the equilibrium equations constructed on this unreal basis are invalid.

The critique of the marginal utility theory, which was initially made only by opponents of the mathematical school, is now pursued by its supporters and has led to the dissolution of marginal utility theory.[199] The breakdown of marginal utility theory did not, however, lead to the abandonment of equilibrium equations but rather to efforts to construct them on another basis. In his *Manual* Pareto took refuge in the concept of "ordinal" indifference curves, in order to use this as the basis, supposedly taken from experience, on which to construct his theory of preference and its equilibrium equations.[200] Criticism proved the untenability of this theory by highlighting the arbitrary nature of the assumptions behind the equations. The mathematicians' procedure presupposes the infinite divisibility of goods and the unlimited substitutability of various goods (for example, of nuts for apples) in the satisfaction of wants. Hence a gulf arose between the

---

but is instead only a result, a variable that depends on the extent of investment. Investments themselves are conditioned by the profitability that can be achieved in the process of production.

196. Ibid., 205.

197. [Pareto, *Cours d economie politique*.]

198. "Utility is, and will remain, only a comparable but not a measurable magnitude. . . . Attempts to treat utility like an ordinary extensive magnitude, in our opinion . . . are bound to fail. . . . One cannot subject utility to the ordinary arithmetic and algebraic operations." Compare Fisher, *Mathematical Investigations*, 88. [Bernadelli, "The End of the Marginal Utility Theory?" 192. Bernadelli emphasized "comparable" and "measurable." Grossman provided no reference for this quotation from Bernadelli. As the source of the quotation, Bernadelli cites Bilimovic, "Irving Fishers statistische Methode." It is not there but is in Bilimovic, "Ein neuer Versuch der Bemessung," 178. The page in Fisher's work that Grossman refers to does not seem directly relevant, although the entire monograph is devoted to the subjection of utility to algebraic operations.]

199. "It is a curious process of a self-decomposition of a theory—a supreme example of Hegelian dialectics . . . —which not so long ago had been hailed as the essential step in putting economics on a scientific basis." Bernadelli, "The End of the Marginal Utility Theory?" 192.

200. For example, someone who possesses 100 apples and 100 nuts can be asked how many nuts would compensate for giving up 10 or 20 apples. A combination of 80 apples and 140 nuts, for example, could result.

assumptions on which the indifference curves were based and reality.[201] Elevated to the status of a general rule, the assumption of the unlimited substitutability of goods "leads to the most absurd conclusions." For example, in the everyday consumption combination of bread and wine, a very little or even a minimum amount of bread can be "replaced" by a lot of wine, or increasingly small amounts of meat by more and more salt![202] These absurd results and the indifference curves, demand curves, price relations, and equilibrium positions derived from them are not an approximate reflection but "in truth a distorted picture of reality."[203]

Considering that even in the circumstances of a solitary individual with few commodities at his disposal there are an infinite number of possible indifference combinations, it is apparent that with forty million people and several thousand different types of commodities, "the time and energy of a whole generation would not suffice" to collect the incalculable amount of information needed to construct the hundreds of millions of indifference combinations. And the time and energy of a further generation would not suffice to solve the equations that were constructed on this basis.[204]

The static character of the monetary theories of crisis, which spread during the postwar period—Wicksellian and neo-Wicksellian efforts to overcome economic cycles and stabilize the economy, the value of money, and world prices in a purely monetary way, by means of the appropriate regulation of interest rates by central banks—is also apparent.[205] According to Wicksell, "in principle" the real causes of crisis do lie on the commodity side. But this plays no role in his thinking because, according to him, the connection between the economy and credit has shifted the economic system's center of gravity toward the monetary side. With an appropriate regulation of interest rates "the real element of the crisis" would fall away and be reduced to "an even fluc-

---

201. Mayer, "Der Erkenntniswert der funktionellen Preis-theorien," 214.

202. Ibid., 211–12.

203. Ibid., 212; compare 216. Compare also Ricci, "Pareto e l'economia pura," 43, Schultz, "The Italian School of Mathematical Economics," 77, and Mayer, "Der Erkenntniswert der funktionellen Preis-theorien," 207–8. Mayer stresses that the indifference combination only takes the form of a curve with two goods; with a combination of three goods, the diagram becomes three-dimensional; under real conditions, that is, with thousands of goods, indifference diagrams would be "inconceivable," thought of in a space of thousands of dimensions (!)—["diversities in hyperspace"—that would be purely imaginary and have nothing more to do with reality.

204. In addition, the Lausanne School's method—the method of the general interdependence of all economic variables—so admired in its time, is today held responsible for the school never going beyond worthless generalities. It led to the school's "theoretically idle state." Lange, "Die allgemeine Interdependenz," 56. Hicks underlines the "apparent sterility of the Walrasian system," because of its great distance from reality, in *Value and Capital*, 60. As Husserl correctly says, the danger of such failures is inherent in the essence of mathematics itself. It is a technique that can be and often is applied to the most various and also irrelevant areas. "The same thinkers who sustain marvellous mathematical methods with such incomparable mastery, and who add new methods to them, often show themselves incapable of accounting satisfactorily . . . for the limits of their right use." Husserl, *Logical Investigations*, 16. Hence, in the field of economic theory, the dazzling application of mathematical methods and their miserable results.

205. Wicksell, *Lectures on Political Economy*, 216, 223.

tuation."[206] This holds not merely for individual countries but primarily for the world economy. "It would then simply be the task of the [central] credit institutions to regulate their interest . . . rates against and with each other . . . so that the international balance of payments remains in equilibrium and the general level of world prices is unchanged."[207] And it is precisely this static conception of the economy that is identified by [Friedrich] Hayek as "the most important basis for all future monetary theory of the trade cycle."[208] In fact, this conception underlies all monetary theories of crisis (Irving Fisher and Ralph George Hawtrey).[209] For the latter, economic fluctuations are not of necessity bound up with the essence of the capitalist mechanism but instead "arise out of a world-wide contraction of credit."[210]

The crisis cycle is consequently "a purely monetary phenomenon," and changes in economic activity, "the alternation of prosperity and depression," have as their sole cause "changes in 'the flow of money.'" "If the flow of money could be stabilised, the fluctuations in economic activity would disappear," and prosperity could continue indefinitely without limit.[211]

Doubts within the dominant theory about the correctness of the static conception first arose under the pressure of the great crisis of 1900–1901 and then the economic disturbances of the postwar period. More attention was paid to the problem of crises and to collecting empirical material on the course of past crises. Using this material, economic research institutes founded to investigate these problems attempted to establish the laws of the economic cycle's course and its phases. Only now was attention paid to the material elements of the production process, in addition to the value side, and the distinction between the production of means of production and the production of means of consumption was introduced into the analysis, emphasizing their different roles in the course of the economic cycle. The specific role of so-called durable ("fixed") capital[212] was emphasized as a cause of crisis, for example by [Arthur] Spiethoff and [Gustav] Cassel.[213] The role of progressive technological improvements, the disproportion between the structure of the various branches of production,[214] and

---

206. Ibid., 212.

207. [Grossman does not reference this quotation, which is neither in Wicksell's *Lectures on Political Economy* nor in Hayek's *Monetary Theory and the Trade Cycle*.]

208. Hayek, *Monetary Theory and the Trade Cycle*, 116. Wicksell's neo-Malthusianism is also rooted in an undynamic conception of the productive forces, according to which a country can only support a particular optimum population, exceeding which must lead to the country's impoverishment. This conception represents an unambiguous relapse to the level of the outlook of the first half of the eighteenth century. Compare Süßmilch, *Die Göttliche Ordnung*, 142.

209. Compare Fisher, *Stabilizing the Dollar*.

210. Hawtrey, *Currency and Credit*, 141.

211. Compare Haberler, *Prosperity and Depression*, 15, 17, and Hawtrey, *Trade and Credit*, 98.

212. Haberler, *Prosperity and Depression*, 73.

213. [See Spiethoff, "Business Cycles," and Cassel, *Theory of Social Economy*.]

214. Haberler, *Prosperity and Depression*, 39 and 73. Haberler correctly says of nonmonetary theories of over-investment, whose representatives he names as Arthur Spiethoff and Gustav Cassel: "In the writings of these two authors . . . we find the culmination of a very important line of thought which can be traced

the influence of the length of the period of construction on the course of the cycle ([Albert] Aftalion) were emphasized.[215]

These attempts turned out to be unsatisfactory, as each of the authors simply made one individual, isolated material moment of the entire process the basis of his crisis theory, which gave these theories an accidental, eclectic character, resting on partial observations. The same can be said of the most recent attempts, by John Maurice Clark,[216] Simon Kuznets,[217] and Leonard Ayres,[218] to use the durability of the means of production as a possible basis for explaining periodicity itself and the more intense fluctuations in the industries producing "capital goods" (the so-called accelerator principle). An attempt is made to explain the special problem of crises by means of individual observable correlations. This means abandoning any connection with the theoretical foundations of political economy, because of the feeling that the old static theories are of little use in explaining a dynamic process. Since, on the other hand, no conclusive dynamic theory in which these material elements have been treated theoretically has been constructed, these more recent investigations of crisis have remained special theories of a subfield in economics, lacking a broader theoretical foundation.[219]

Only a very small circle within the dominant theory itself has perceived the lack of a general theory of dynamics. As Hans Mayer stated, "the unsatisfactoriness and deficiency of previous theories" was felt "more and more intensely," as was their fundamental error: that the apparatus of their system "could not assimilate and deal with certain problems thrown up by the actual course of economic events." "The evidently dynamic problem of the economic cycle and crises" cannot be grasped by the "previous, essentially static

---

back to Marx." *Prosperity and Depression*, 72. On the now-usual distinction between the production of means of production and the production of means of consumption, see Marx, "The Two Departments of Social Production," *Capital*, vol. 2, 471–74; on the specific role of durable (fixed) capital, "Replacement of the Fixed Capital," *Capital*, vol. 2, 524–45; on the influence of the length of the construction period on the course of the cycle, *Capital*, vol. 2, 387, 445, 552–53. [These pages do not seem relevant as compared with 306–68. Marx does not refer to "construction period" but distinguishes between "working period" and "production period."] This distinction among material elements was first introduced into the recent literature by Tugan-Baranovsky's book on crises in England (Tugan-Baranovsky, *Studien zur Theorie und Geschichte*) and subsequently by Spiethoff and others. They were influenced by Marx, as can immediately be seen from Tugan-Baranovsky's schemes of reproduction, which were copied from Marx. Tugan-Baranovsky, however, was celebrated by Sombart as the "father of modern crisis theory" in "Die Störungen im deutschen Wirtschaftsleben," 130, and his book was praised by Spiethoff as the "first scientific monograph on crises" in "Die Krisentheorien von M. Tugan-Baranovsky," 700.

215. [See Aftalion, *Les crises périodiques de surproduction* and "Les crises économiques et financières."]

216. John Maurice Clark, "Business Acceleration."

217. Kuznets, "Relations between Capital Goods." [Grossman mistakenly attributed this essay to Roy Forbes Harrod, in both the main text and a footnote.]

218. Ayres, *Turning Points in Business Cycles*. [Grossman reviewed this book for *Zeitschrift für Sozialforschung* in 1939.]

219. Thus Paul Thomas Homan writes, in an essay entitled "The Present Impasse": "It is probably no exaggeration to say that recent investigations into the causes of cycles have done as much to destroy adherence to older types of theory as any other single cause. And it has led to the casting of their problems by many economists into terms of a changing process, rather than into terms of a static situation." *Contemporary Economic Thought*, 453.

systems of price theory," as a consequence of its "purely static approach" to relations of exchange between given economic variables, which merely describes "existing price relations in a state of equilibrium that has already been reached." For the "analysis of the processes of movement in economic reality" requires "insight into the process of price formation."[220] As shown above, all these systems abstained from grasping the economic system's overall trend in a definite direction, that is, its developmental tendencies, and were also incapable of doing this, because they confined themselves solely to grasping exchange relations between given variables. But from the exchange equations it is apparent that all the quantities of goods or prices that an economic subject disposes of are received as increments by others. Hence all these (positive or negative) increments in the number of goods or prices result in a total sum of zero. There is no incalculable [sic] remainder that could be regarded as an index of a definite trend in the course of the system as a whole.[221] The relations of exchange of the "economic variables" on markets are, likewise, not real processes of movement, a sequence over time. They are transfers, a timeless "movement," a circular motion. If, however, the economic system's overall trend in a definite direction is to be grasped, not only the relations of exchange of given variables must be investigated but also their evolution, growth or passing away or (as Mayer says) the process of "price formation." It is insufficient to investigate exchange relations; the production process as well as the process of circulation, that is, the process as a whole, must also be investigated. It is then apparent that positive and negative changes no longer balance out in the full account to yield zero but that they assume definite values (for example, a falling rate of profit). That is, they reveal the direction of movement of the system as a whole, its developmental tendency. So the main task of theory for Marx in *Capital*, the investigation of "economic laws of motion," which was banished from the realm of economic theory by the marginal utility school, finally steps into the foreground of the dominant theory too. Now, for the first time, a small group of theoreticians within the dominant theory—[Rudolf] Streller, [Luigi] Amoroso, [Paul] Rosenstein-Rodan, [Umberto] Ricci, [Oskar] Morgenstern, [Karl] Bode, and others—turns, in principle, against the central line of thought of equilibrium theories, with their fictitious assumption of the simultaneous rhythm of economic events. The group's criticism is meant to prepare the ground for a dynamic theory. It maintains that "with the realistic assumption of diverse rhythms of [economic] movements, it would . . . be a matter of coincidence if equilibrium came about."[222] For the tendency toward equilibrium is *one* possibility; the alternative is that due to nonsimultaneous rhythms of movements, one change "always brings about other changes, a *perpetuum mobile* of changes, the time coefficients do not equalize and no state of equilibrium emerges at all."[223] Theories of equilibrium would have to prove that this second constellation of

220. Mayer, "Der Erkenntniswert der funktionellen Preis-theorien," 148.
221. Compare Schams, "Komparative Statik," 30.
222. Rosenstein-Rodan, "Das Zeitmoment in der mathematischen Theorie," 131, 134. [Grossman did not signal the ellipsis or interpolation and indicated that the quotation started with "it." Rosenstein-Rodan emphasized "diverse."]
223. [Ibid., 131. *Perpetuum mobile* means "perpetual motion."]

time coefficients cannot occur. They have not provided such a proof, and because of the assumption of the simultaneous rhythm of all economic processes, they have blocked the path to understanding the problem of dynamics.

The "equilibrium system" of the mathematical school only exists thanks to the circumstance that it is "economics without time": "The equilibrium system of the mathematical school, which includes neither time indices nor coefficients, can therefore in no way grasp the real state of equilibrium."[224] And the critique of the mathematical school does not single out one particular aspect of the theory or a particular theorem but rather the theory itself, "because it offers the most precise formulation of a line of thought common to all economic schools, so that its proven defect affects all other formulations even more acutely."[225]

The fundamental error of equilibrium theories is not, therefore, only that "they have regarded moving, changing variables as fixed, as invariant." For if these movements were of the same duration, if they were equitemporal, the real course of the economic process could indeed be grasped as a series of "successive equilibria," each of which could be defined by the equilibrium system.[226] The moment the theory proceeds to grasp nonequitemporal movements, that is, to explicitly express the time factor t, however, as Shams states, "the static system is struck at its weakest point: the assumption of the pseudoconstancy of economic periods."[227] For the incorporation of the time element, that is, divergent periods of movement, shatters the equivalence of the relations that constitute the basis of the mathematical system of the equations and therefore cannot be managed mathematically.[228] So talk about the failure of economic theory is understandable, because it progressively lost all relation to reality. A theory that regards capitalism as a mechanism tending, through self-regulation, toward equilibrium is incapable of comprehending the economic developments of the last few decades, namely, the attempts to establish such an equilibrium through conscious interventions of monopolistic regulation that characterized this period.

So the dominant theory faces a dilemma. Mathematical economics could celebrate its triumph as long as it was dominated by ideas of equilibrium. These, however, failed to explain the economy's dynamic movements. They regarded these movements as

---

224. Ibid., 129.

225. Ibid., 135.

226. Consequently the concept of "moving equilibrium" is a contradiction, as the real movements of the elements of the economy are in constant disequilibrium. Nevertheless Moore did try, in "Moving Equilibria," chapter 5 of his book, to prove that exchange, production, distribution, and accumulation move in lockstep, "as a moving general equilibrium," using empirical material from American potato production over a long period. Moore, *Synthetic Economics*, 93–145. He did not, however, succeed. As Umberto Ricci showed in his critique, Moore did not describe a moving equilibrium, but rather a moving disequilibrium. Ricci, "Die 'synthetische Ökonomie' von Henry Ludwell Moore," 654.

227. Schams, "Komparative Statik," 42.

228. Ibid., 55, or, as Streller formulated this idea: the equilibrium equations would only have been possible at a level of higher abstraction from reality. It is apparent, however, that "an introduction of the time factor 't' into the equation immediately and clearly makes them insoluble." Streller, *Die Dynamik der theoretischen Nationalökonomie*, 12.

mere oscillations around a state of equilibrium or as temporary disturbances prior to the achievement of a new equilibrium,[229] while reality demonstrates long-term disequilibrating movements, exhibiting increasing disequilibrium instead of a tendency toward equilibrium. The reason why all tendencies within the dominant theory emphasized the static character of the economy, its capacity to adjust to the changing needs of society, for over a century—from Ricardo to the present—has clearly been the need to justify the existing economic order as a reasonable, self-regulating mechanism. The concept of self-regulation serves to divert attention away from the actually prevailing chaos of the destruction of capital, the bankruptcy of entrepreneurs and factories, mass unemployment, insufficient capital investment, currency disturbances, and arbitrary redistributions of property.[230] Only in this way is the introduction into economic theory of concepts of statics and dynamics, which originated in theoretical physics, without any justification of such a twofold division of theory, understandable.[231]

The untenability of such a division becomes clear when the fact that there are no immobile economic processes is considered; that the so-called "stationary" economy "moves," is, namely, a circular process. Hence the characteristic distinction between statics and dynamics cannot be that one investigates immobile, the other mobile changing phenomena. Instead, we characterize as static a kinetic economic process that has reached complete equilibrium in its movements and, because all subjective and objective conditions persist, repeats itself forever in unchanging form, from one period to the next (a cyclical process).[232] Consequently, a dynamic economy is not to be understood just as an economy "in motion" (a static economy also moves) but rather as an economic process that has not reached equilibrium in its movement and thus moves in disequilibrium over the course of time. This can only mean, however, that the conditions of this economic process change from period to period, hence the result of the economic process—the economic structure—also experiences continual changes.

Since John Stuart Mill, theory has been forced into this twofold division, but only statics, the tendency toward equilibrium, has been worked on. There has been dis-

---

229. Thus [Thomas Nixon] Carver also recently wrote: "In fact every dynamic movement is either a disturbance of a static condition, or a series of movements by which the static condition is reasserting itself, or rather by which a new static condition is being established after the disturbance." Carver, "The Static State," 29.

230. Ricardo stresses that despite changing economic conditions, the mechanism of self-regulation will distribute capital among individual branches of industry exactly according to their respective needs, "without often producing either the effects of a glut from a too abundant supply, or an enormously high price from the supply being unequal to the demand." Ricardo, *Principles of Political Economy*, 49. Conrad similarly assures us that only the tendency to equilibrium is "to be thanked if" an economy, "lacking centralized management, does not fall into chaos." Conrad, "Die Grundannahme der Gleichgewichtstheorie," 236. Hayek's language is characteristic: he sees merely the economy's "adjustments" but regards the intervals of disturbances and catastrophes between two "adjustments" as "unproblematic." Hayek, *Preise und Produktion*, 23.

231. So the concept of "dynamics" is only vaguely indicated. Within the static line of thought, only statics had to be defined. Dynamics was then the other, the "counterpart" that does not have to be defined and that is somehow supposed to "complement" statics. Streller, *Die Dynamik der theoretischen Nationalökonomie*, 5.

232. Bilimovic, "Zins and Unternehmerginn," 298.

cussion of dynamics and the necessity of "dynamizing" theory, without anyone being able to construct a complete theory of dynamics. Success in breaking away from the dictatorship of these traditional concepts has come late and very slowly. Finally, as Bode states, it has been recognized that there is no point in clinging to the concept of an equilibrium state if, in reality, "equilibrium is nowhere departed from, tended towards or passed through."

Understanding that the equilibrium line of thought is untenable has not, however, made the position of the dominant theory any easier. On one hand, it states that a dynamic theory is needed to explain reality; on the other hand, however, it is forced to admit that the construction of such a theory generates fundamental difficulties.[233]

6.

The discovery, only made by the most advanced, minority wing of the currently dominant theory—and then only after the violent disturbances of the [First] World War—namely, that a dynamic reality cannot be explained by arguments based on ideas of equilibrium, had already been enunciated by Marx in 1867 in the theory of the dual character of labor. This theory was completed in the second volume of *Capital*, in the theory of the various circuits of capital and also of the turnover time of capital. Marx was obliged to set foot here, too, on terrain that had never been entered before. First, he had to create all the categories and concepts that were connected with the time element (circuit, turnover, turnover time, turnover cycles). He correctly raises the objection that classical theory has neglected the investigation of the time element, the form of the circuits and of turnover.[234] Such a disregard was understandable given their merely value-oriented approach. In contrast, Marx's conception of the dual character of all economic phenomena compelled him to look at the economy in its specific movement, not statically. For capital advanced in the form of money can only maintain and multiply itself by changing its natural form in the circuit, transforming itself from the money form into the shape of the elements of production and from these again into the shape of finished products, commodities. Capital must spend a given minimum period of time, objectively determined by the technologies of the processes of production and circulation, in each of these three stages before passing on to the next phase. Capital "is a movement, a circulatory process through different stages. . . . Hence it can only be grasped as a movement, and not as

---

233. "Only static theory can be regarded as being established; dynamic theory is almost totally uninvestigated and unformulated. To this point, apparently, only the necessity for such a theory could be demonstrated." Streller, *Die Dynamik der theoretischen Nationalökonomie*, 26. John Maurice Clark assures us that "We possess a substantially complete static economics, while dynamics is in its infancy . . . and very possibly is destined always to remain in that stage." Clark, "Relation between Statics and Dynamics," 46, 48. Similarly, Hicks mentions "a dynamic theory—the theory which many writers had demanded, but which none, at that time, had produced." Hicks, *Value and Capital*, 4. Compare Harrod, "Studies in the Theory of Economic Expansion," 498; and many others.

234. Compare Marx, *Capital*, vol. 2, 234.

a static thing."[235] The "production time" presented in the first volume of *Capital* is now supplemented in the second volume by an analysis of "circulation time."[236] This not only has consequences for the specific problem of the size of profit but also gives Marx the opportunity to deal with the naked form of motion as such—the question of the duration of the circuits, whether they coincide or are sequential, that is, the conditions for the undisturbed transition from one stage to the next.[237] The circuit of capital proceeds normally only so long as its various phases pass into each other without delay.[238] Marx demonstrates the theoretically postulated conditions for such a normal circuit, which in reality are only present by way of exception: the undisturbed course requires the coexistence of capital in all of its three natural forms. The normal "succession" of each part is conditioned by the "coexistence" of capital, that is, by its constant availability in all three forms—as money capital, productive capital and commodity capital—and by its proportional division into each of these forms.[239] This simple formulation conceals the problem of dynamics. The coexistence of the three forms of capital is identical with their synchronization and thus presupposes given values that are unchanged, because they all fall into the same unit of time. It is precisely only in this case that the "unity of the three circuits" can really be spoken of.[240] In contrast, succession is a process in time and consequently includes the possibility of revolutions in the value of the individual parts of capital, which must impede the smooth transition of capital from one phase to another.[241] Thus, according to Marx, equilibrium would only be possible under the unrealistic assumption that values and technology are constant.[242] Since in reality this condition cannot be realized, the circuit of capital must move "abnormally," that is, in disequilibrium.

The entire presentation is crowned by the analysis of the "turnover of capital," where the circuit of capital through all three stages is understood "not as an isolated act but as a periodic process." The duration of this turnover, given by the sum of production time and circulation time, is called "turnover time" and measures "the periodicity in the capital's life-process, or, if you like, the time required for the renewal and repetition of the valo-

235. Ibid., 185.
236. Ibid., 200.
237. Ibid., 185.
238. Ibid., 133; compare 183.
239. Ibid., 183.
240. Ibid., 184.
241. "Further: since the circulation process of capital is not completed in one day but extends over a fairly long period until the capital returns to its original form, since . . . great upheavals and changes take place in the market in the course of this period, since great changes take place in the productivity of labor and therefore also in the real value of commodities, it is quite clear that between the starting point, the prerequisite capital, and the time of its return at the end of one of these periods, great catastrophes must occur and elements of crisis must have gathered and developed." Marx, "Economic Manuscript of 1861–63 [Notebooks XII to XV]," 126. [Marx emphasized "market" and "value."]
242. "In order for the circuit to run its normal course . . . C-M-C [must] not just include the replacement of one commodity by another, but its replacement in the same value relations." "Thus it is . . . assumed that the commodities . . . do not suffer any change of value during the circuit; if this is not the case, then the process cannot run its normal course." Marx, *Capital*, vol. 2, 153. [Editor's interpolation.]

risation and production process of the same capital value."[243] Finally, following the presentation of the turnover of individual capitals, Marx arrives at the presentation of "The Overall Turnover of Capital Advanced: Turnover Cycles," in order, within this train of thought, to emphasize those elements that operate in the direction of disequilibrium.[244]

In his reproduction schemas, Marx proceeds on the assumption of an identical turnover time of one year for all capitals in all branches of production. While for the dominant theory the synchronization of all movements is a definitive approach, for Marx it is merely a preliminary, simplifying assumption, a first step in the process of successive approximation of reality. He later considers the circumstance that, in reality, "the turnover times of the capitals vary according to their various spheres of investment." This variation in turnover time depends on the natural and technical conditions of production of each kind of commodity (food crops, leather, and so on).[245] In addition to these circumstances, resulting from the process of production and "which distinguish the turnover of different capitals invested in different branches of industry," there are others given by conditions in the sphere of circulation (for example, improved means of transport and communication, which reduce the period during which commodities are moved about).[246] It is self-evident that all these differences in total turnover times must necessarily result in disequilibrium of the system, considering that the original equilibrium in the equations for the reproduction schemas only resulted from the assumption of an equal turnover time for all capitals.

In addition to these sources of disequilibrium due to variations in the total turnover time of the capitals in the various branches of production, there are further differentiating factors within each branch of production, because the turnover times of the fixed and circulating parts of capital are different. With regard to circulating capital, Marx investigates the temporal relation between working period and turnover period, since the size of the circulating capital which functions during both of these periods is conditioned by their durations. Of the three possible cases—that the working period is the same as, longer than, or shorter than the period of circulation[247]—only the first, "in which the working period and the circulation time form two equal halves of the turnover period," allows the undisturbed transition of the capital functioning in the working period into the circulation phase.[248] The same applies in the case in which both periods are indeed unequal but the turnover period "is . . . an exact multiple" of the working period, for example, if the working period is three weeks and the circulation period six, nine, or twelve weeks, and so on.[249] The turnover process only proceeds

243. Marx, *Capital*, vol. 2, 235–36.
244. Ibid., 262–67.
245. Ibid., 236. Compare the analysis of various turnover times for agriculture, p. 317; forestry, p. 321; and cattle raising, p. 322.
246. Ibid., 327.
247. Ibid., 343–55.
248. Ibid., 339.
249. Ibid., 353, 356–57.

"normally," undisturbed, under this "exceptional . . . assumption," which in reality only occurs by chance.[250]

In all the other cases, that is, for the majority of social circulating capital, the necessary modification of the "normal course" occurs during the annual or multiyear turnover cycle. As a result, the circulating capital advanced is "set free" or "tied up."[251] This generates the objective basis as well as the subjective impulses for credit expansion or contraction and also the impulses to expand or contract the given scale of production itself, instead of the originally assumed "normal" transition, on an unchanged scale, from the working period to the circulation period. These impulses do not come from outside but arise endogenously, "simply by the mechanism of the turnover movement," that is, from the temporal difference between the working period and the circulation period.[252] Far from being a primary cause of changes in the scale of production (as monetary theorists of crisis assume), credit expansion and contraction is a dependent variable, conditioned by the turnover mechanism.[253]

And similarly, the time factor (the durability of the means of production) constitutes the basis for the distinction between fixed and circulating capital. The means of labor employed in the production process "only form fixed capital to the extent that the time during which they are in use extends longer than the turnover period of the fluid capital,"[254] that is, to the extent that the "turnover of the fixed component of capital, and thus also the turnover time needed by it, encompasses several turnovers of the fluid components of capital."[255]

This difference in the length of the life of both types of capital results in the variation in the replacement of both kinds of the means of labor, to the extent that we do not consider the value side (as replacement of money) alone but, at the same time, replacement in kind. While labor power and those means of production that represent fluid capital (raw materials) are used up in a shorter period of time and must therefore be continuously renewed, the replacement of fixed capital in kind does not occur continuously but rather periodically.[256] Marx uses this divergence in the time periods necessary for the replacement of both types of capital, in the form of money and in kind, as one of the elements ("the material basis") of his explanation for the periodicity of crises.[257]

---

250. [Ibid., 339.]
251. Ibid., 189.
252. Ibid., 357.
253. Curiously, a misjudgment of the importance of Marx's analysis for the understanding of the dynamic course of the capitalist economy can even be found in Engels, who held the view that Marx had ascribed "an undeserved significance to . . . a matter of little importance," namely, what Marx called the "setting free" of money capital, and that this is the "uncertain [result] of [his] tiresome calculation business." See Engels's note in Marx, *Capital*, vol. 2, 359. [Editor's interpolations.]
254. Ibid., 254.
255. Ibid., 247.
256. Ibid., 533 and following.
257. Ibid., 264.

So long as the process of reproduction and the problem of equilibrium are regarded exclusively from the value side, the problem under consideration here won't be encountered at all, because the distinction between the lifetimes of fixed and fluid capital applies to their natural form, not their value. If Marx's scheme for simple reproduction is regarded merely in terms of value and assumes an annual renewal of all the components of capital, the resultant synchronization of all the movements in the schema would obliterate the specific difference between fixed and circulating capital and hence the whole problem connected with their various replacement times.[258] For both fixed and also circulating capital are renewed annually as values in the schema. The problem first arises when the schema is considered in terms of use value: only now does the difference in the life of each type of capital become apparent and hence also the problem of the different dates of their replacement. (The originally assumed synchronization of replacement dates was only a preliminary approximation, which does not correspond to reality.) While raw materials have to be renewed annually, fixed capital (for example, the 2,000 units in department II of the schema, the consumer goods industry) "is not renewed for the whole of the period during which it functions," because it lasts for several years.[259] Consequently, there can be no sales from department I, which manufactures this fixed capital, to department II for several years. Since, however, the annual productive capacity of department I remains 2,000 units, overproduction must necessarily take place in department I. "There would be a crisis—a crisis of production—despite reproduction on a constant scale."[260] "Normal" production could then only occur in department I if (despite the assumption of simple reproduction in department I) department II was to be expanded over several years,[261] creating a new, additional market for department I each year (the accelerator principle).[262] This is, however, impossible. For the faster expansion of department II, on the basis of the given technology, presupposes an impossible increase in the working population. The second department in the schema would have to double in the second year and triple in the third; the working population employed there would have to grow by 100 percent in the second year of reproduction, 50 percent in the third, and 33 percent in the fourth!

In addition to the reasons for the absence of an equilibrium previously mentioned, there is a much more fundamental and general one, resulting from the structure of the capitalist mode of production, from the tensions that are grounded in the dual character of this mode of production.

---

258. In the schema of simple reproduction, "total value is 9,000, the fixed capital that continues to function in its natural form being excluded by our assumption." Ibid., 473.

259. Ibid., 570.

260. Ibid., 533.

261. "If things are to proceed normally, accumulation in department II must take place quicker than in department I." Ibid., 588.

262. As we see, Marx's accelerator principle is the direct opposite of that propounded in the literature of the dominant theory. See Ibid., 588.

Theories both before and after Marx confine the conditions for equilibrium to submarkets and merely in terms of value.[263] The relation between quantities and values is only analyzed from the perspective of the effect of variations in quantity on marginal values. Equilibrium can always be achieved under such assumptions.[264] In contrast, Marx shows that the issue is not equilibrium in submarkets (money market, labor market, commodity market for the means of production or consumption), just as little equilibrium in the "production process" or the "circulation process." Instead, because Marx regarded the capitalist process of production as a "circuit" in which capital passes through its various stages, he highlighted the idea that equilibrium has to be grasped as an equilibrium within the overall interaction of all these stages. From this perspective, he was the first to carefully define the state of equilibrium in the "process as a whole" and investigate the conditions under which it arises. At the same time, however, he showed that these conditions cannot be realized within the capitalist mode of production. For Marx this signifies, however, that the "normal course," the "state of equilibrium," does not mean an "average," "typical," or "most frequently occurring" process but instead only an imaginary, undisturbed course of reproduction (under fictitious conditions), which never comes about in reality and merely serves as a methodological tool of analysis. As a total social process, the problem of reproduction has to be dealt with in its dual character, that is, "the process of reproduction has to be considered from the standpoint of the replacement of the individual components of C' both in value and in material."[265] Consequently, equilibrium could only be realized if both sets of conditions, those on the value side and those on the use side, are simultaneously fulfilled.

Marx's specific crisis problematic and its solution arises from this comparison of the two series—"the *value* components of the social product . . . with its *material* components." In the circuit C . . . C', "the preconditions for social reproduction can be immediately recognised from the fact that it is necessary to demonstrate what becomes of each portion of the value of this overall product C'."[266] This means not only that, in terms of value, all the commodities produced must be sold on the market, without a remainder. It is also necessary to investigate what then happens to the material mass of things, the use values that have been purchased, to see whether they can in fact be completely employed in the production process (equilibrium in production), including individual consumption.[267] It is therefore a matter of the "transformation of one portion of the product's

---

263. "By its essence, statics only studies one single market." Streller, *Die Dynamik der theoretischen National-ökonomie*, 39.

264. "Equilibrium must be considered as an equilibrium of prices." "There is always a solution of such a system admitting full employment of every factor of production," given only that the condition "that prices must be high enough to equalise supply and demand" is maintained. Cassel, "Keynes' 'General Theory'" 438, 444.

265. Marx, *Capital*, vol. 2, 469. [C' is the expanded value of commodities, after production, in the circuit of capital.]

266. Ibid., 469, 506. [C is the value of the commodities which go into the production process in the circuit of capital.]

267. Marx consequently speaks of the "social balance of production." *Capital*, vol. 3, 1020. As the immediate employment of all factors of production is assumed, stocks lying unused in warehouses are disregarded.

value back into capital, the entry of another part into . . . individual consumption . . . and this movement is not only a replacement of values, but a replacement of materials, and is therefore conditioned not just by the mutual relations of the value components of the social product but equally by their use values, their material shape."[268]

From the above, it is already apparent that the assertion often made in the literature that according to Marx use values lie "outside the consideration of political economy" is based on a misunderstanding. According to Marx, only "use value as such," that is, use value in the sense of subjective utility, lies outside political economy.[269] He counterposes to this use value as "material shape," which is not a subjective utility but an objective thing with a definite, economically important form, a natural form that is exchanged on the market or functions as a means of production in the labor process.[270] Consequently, Marx speaks of "use value or object of utility," of use value or "material shape," of "use value or its physical shape as a commodity," of the "sensuous objectivity of commodities as physical objects," and of the "mass of the means of production" as distinct from their values.[271] Use values, defined in this way, take on crucial importance in Marx's system.[272]

Under the influence of dominant theories, Marxist literature has regarded the problem of equilibrium—insofar as its conditions are specified in Marx's "*tableau économique*"—exclusively from the value side ([Karl] Kautsky, Rudolf Hilferding, Otto Bauer, Rosa Luxemburg, and [Nikolai] Bukharin).[273] There have to be certain quantitative value proportions in both of the departments in Marx's reproduction schemas if all the quantities of value supplied and demanded are to be exchanged without a remainder. The analysis of the material side of the labor process was reduced to the single proposition that in the process of reproduction, department I must produce means of production and department II means of consumption.

Marx's conception of equilibrium, however, is fundamentally different from the above. He shows that, in addition to value proportions, quite definite technical proportions must exist between the mass of labor and the mass of the means of production (machines, raw materials, buildings), in all the departments and subdepartments of the reproduction schemas. These depend on the particular character of the sphere of production under consideration. For the technical labor process, the amount of value these

---

268. Marx, *Capital*, vol. 2, 470.

269. Marx, *Contribution to the Critique*, 270.

270. Marx, "Economic Manuscript of 1861–63 [Notebooks XII to XV]," 120.

271. Marx, *Capital*, vol. 1, 152, 168, 158, 138, 754; also vol. 2, 471, and vol. 3, 137.

272. *Use value* can only be abstracted from to the extent that the matter at hand is the *process of valorization*, the formation of surplus value: "In considering surplus value as such, the original form of the product . . . is of no consequence. It becomes important when considering the actual process of reproduction. . . . Here is another example of how use value as such acquires economic significance." Marx, "Economic Manuscript of 1861–63 [Notebooks XII to XV]," 386 [Marx emphasized "use value"]; similarly, see p. 120.

273. [See Kautsky, "Finance-Capital and Crises"; Hilferding, *Böhm-Bawerk's Criticism of Marx*, 130; Bauer, "The Accumulation of Capital"; Luxemburg, *The Accumulation of Capital*; Bukharin, *Imperialism and the Accumulation of Capital*, 63.]

use values represent is quite immaterial.[274] In factories, such a technical proportionality among factors of production is arranged directly by the technical management. In view of the reciprocal relations of the various branches of production within society, however, it is also the basic condition for the undisturbed course of the production process, because the social division of labor makes the various preceding and subsequent stages of the labor process dependent on one another, as "element[s] of the total labour of society." Despite all their apparent personal independence, producers soon discover that "the independence of the individuals from each other has as its counterpart and supplement a system of all-round material dependence."[275] Only insofar as there is such technical articulation and reciprocal, quantitative accord among individual branches of production is "full employment"[276] of all productive factors in the technical labor process possible, without either unused capacity or shortages of raw materials, machines, or labor power.

In short, the condition for equilibrium in the system of capitalist production as a whole is a dual proportionality of its basic elements. While sale on the market, without a remainder, requires value proportionality within the scope of individual branches of production, for the technical labor process quantitative proportionality of all productive factors, among all branches of production and within each branch as conditioned by the state of technology, is necessary. This technical proportionality is no more present from the outset under the capitalist mode of production than value proportionality, as "the quantitative articulation of society's productive organism . . . is . . . haphazard and spontaneous."[277] Is there any possibility that this dual proportionality is realized at all? This question takes us to the heart of Marx's conception of the problem of equilibrium in the "process as a whole," which is the unity of the technical labor process and the process of value circulation. The difference from the dominant conception is most clearly intelligible in the example of simple reproduction.

"The supposition is that a social capital . . . supplies the same mass of commodity values and satisfies the same quantity of needs in both the current year and the previous year" (that is, it supplies the same mass of use values). Does an equilibrium in reproduction now exist in the case, for example, of a bad harvest reducing the amount of cotton by a half, although it represents the same value as twice as much cotton did previous-

274. "All these things serve in the real labor process because of the relationship which exists between them as use values — not as exchange values, and still less as capital." Marx, "Economic Manuscript of 1861–63 [Notebooks XII to XV]," 398. [Marx emphasized "use values."]

275. Marx, *Capital*, vol. 1, 168, 202–3. Marx therefore speaks of the "interdependent branches of the collective production of a whole society" and of the "bond" that holds it together. Not only are the branches of cattle breeding, which produces hides; tanning, which produces leather; and shoemaking, which works leather up, quantitatively dependent on one another, but those branches that supply them with means of production are too. Marx, *Capital*, vol. 1, 472, 274–75. What results from this and what is important for understanding the dynamics of capitalism is that revolutions in the mode of production in one individual sphere, for example, machine spinning, will necessitate similar revolutions in other spheres, such as weaving and dyeing—otherwise incongruities arise in the technical proportionality between these branches of industry. Marx, *Capital*, vol. 1, 505.

276. [English in the original.]

277. Marx, *Capital*, vol. 1, 202.

ly? In short, does "value . . . remain the same, even though the volume of use values declines"?[278] Seen in terms of value, there would still be "a market equilibrium" in the schema of simple reproduction. In contrast, the schema would necessarily exhibit large disturbances when looked at from the standpoint of the technical labor process: half the spindles and looms would have to be shut down due to the shortage of cotton, that is, the technical scale would be halved. "Reproduction cannot be *repeated* on the same scale."[279] This example shows the inadequacy of the dominant theory's purely value perspective. It assumes that the conditions for equilibrium that are expressed in value equations can always be realized. It does know that capitals that are immobilized in one branch of industry can only be shifted to another branch with difficulty. It treats such instances, however, as "frictions" that only impede the realization of value equilibrium for short periods. In contrast, it regards "adjustment" over longer periods as eminently possible, because the issue here is not so much the transfer of already immobilized old capitals as of the investment of new capitals, thus of "processes of adjustment" within production. These allow the subsequent reestablishment of the correct value proportions on both sides of the exchange equation. In contrast, Marx shows that the value equilibrium asserted by all static theories, to which the economy is supposed to tend, can be established only exceptionally and by chance. This is because the technical labor process gives rise to objective and enduring resistances and blockages that in principle exclude the establishment of such an equilibrium. Even if, when seen from a purely physical point of view, complete freedom and mobility of capital existed, and the transfers in the sense required by the value equations for the establishment of equilibrium took place, equilibrium in the system as a whole would not be achievable, due to the incongruence, in principle, between value proportions and technical, quantitative proportions. It may well be possible for a partial equilibrium to occur temporarily, for example a value equilibrium on the market. But then it becomes apparent that there is no equilibrium in production and various elements of production cannot find employment, or, conversely, that although there is quantitative equilibrium in production, there is no value equilibrium on the market. It follows that with a definite quantitative, technical proportion, which is necessarily given by the scale of production and depends on the size of fixed capital,[280] a value proportion resulting from this technical proportion is also already given. It cannot be changed according to the free will of the entrepreneur so that the theoretically postulated conditions for value equilibrium are satisfied. In short, value proportionality is not very elastic because it is bound up with technical proportionality. Under these circumstances, the incongruence of the two series of proportions and hence the tendency toward the disequilibrium of the system as a whole is unavoidable. On the basis of capitalist production, equilibrium—the "nor-

---

278. Marx, *Capital*, vol. 2, 471. Compare Marx, "Economic Manuscript of 1861–63 [Notebooks XII to XV]," 145.

279. Marx, "Economic Manuscript of 1861–63 [Notebooks XII to XV]," 146.

280. Marx, *Capital*, vol. 2, 245. [This reference is not relevant, unlike 280–87.]

mal course"—is merely our abstraction, a conceptual fiction derived from the "real movement," which is the opposite of this abstraction, namely, constant disequilibrium. "In political economy law is determined by its opposite, absence of law. The true law of political economy is chance."[281]

Not only does Marx deny the regulatory function of the price mechanism, its supposed tendency to balance supply and demand, but he also shows that once this mechanism has fallen into a state of disequilibrium, it continually generates impulses that increase this disequilibrium.[282] Because too much has been produced, there is an impulse to produce still more! From Adam Smith to the present, the dominant schools could only propound the theory of the tendency for the volume of production to adjust to demand with the aid of competition, because they presupposed competition as given, as a kind of occult quality, without ever investigating its origins. "Competition . . . is burdened with explaining all the economists' irrationalities, whereas it is supposed to be the economists who explain competition."[283]

In contrast to the dominant conception, Marx shows that there is no balancing mechanism in the sense of the adjustment of production to demand. According to Marx, an orientation to consumption, that is, adjustment of production to demand, was a characteristic of capitalism's youth, the period before the advent of modern large-scale industry, when there was as yet no large fixed capital.[284] There can be no talk of such an adjustment of production to demand at present, when fixed capital constitutes a predominant and continuously growing share of total capital. The entrepreneur ignores the "market's command" to curtail production, supposedly expressed in falling prices. An orientation toward production instead of consumption is precisely characteristic of the highly developed capitalist economy: that is, production precedes demand. Hence, for the reasons previously provided, there is an inherent tendency to periodically overproduce durable "fixed" capital, for which no profitable employment can be found.[285] But because there is a persistent tendency to overproduce in the sphere producing fixed capital, a compulsion to compete necessarily arises, which does not operate to balance supply and demand. Where, as a consequence of overproduction, there is insufficient living space (market outlow) for all entrepreneurs, individuals are

---

281. Marx, "Comments on James Mill," 211. [Marx emphasized "chance."]

282. "In actual fact, demand and supply never coincide, or, if they do so, it is only by chance and not to be taken into account for scientific purposes; it should be considered as not having happened." Marx, *Capital*, vol. 3, 291.

283. Ibid., 1005.

284. Compare Marx, *The Poverty of Philosophy*, 137. Compare, on the absence of expansionary economic cycles, cyclical booms with subsequent breakdowns under early capitalism "into the eighteenth century." Sombart, *Der moderne Kapitalismus*, 214 and following. [The quotation is on p. 215.]

285. Marx, *The Poverty of Philosophy*, 137. "What Ricardo cannot answer, and neither Mr Say for that matter, is where competition, and the resultant bankruptcies, trade crises etc. come from, if every capital finds its proper employ?" "*If capitals . . . were not so numerous in relation to the uses of capital—competition* would be completely inexplicable." Marx, "Aus David Ricardo," 416. [Marx emphasized only "competition."] The only one of the recent writers to have seen this problem is Willard L. Thorp: "Under competition," he writes, "it is certain that some degree of overcapacity will exist." Thorp, "The Problem of Overcapacity," 491.

compelled to save themselves from collapse at the expense of the others. Far from curtailing output when prices and profits are falling, every entrepreneur with access to the necessary means seeks to produce more cheaply and, indeed, profitably than competitors, by introducing better and cheaper technologies and by expanding the scale of production. So the continual overproduction of fixed capital constitutes a permanent impulse to continually revolutionize technology and hence to continuous revolutions in value, which are characteristic of the capitalist mode of production.[286] Continuous improvements in technology and expansion of the scale of production make general overproduction even worse. The individual entrepreneur has, however, secured the profitability of and markets for his own progressive plant.[287]

So, under the pressure of initial overproduction, the transformation of the entire structure of the capitalist mechanism propagates over the whole breadth of society. At one pole, new, higher technology, together with the enlarged scale of the individual plant, is victorious. The extra profits achieved attract new entrepreneurs, the movement becomes more generalized, and an "upswing" occurs. At the other pole of society, simultaneously and as a direct consequence of the spread of improved technologies and associated revolutions in value (reduction in "socially necessary" labor time), this does not prevent all plants with more backward technologies from being even more threatened by falling prices and overproduction and pressured to withdraw from competition altogether. As, however, the scale of those few new, large plants exceeds the productive capacity of the many small, failing plants, the end result of the movement is growth in the overall scale of social production. And this movement is repeated again and again, as the large, new plants with the most modern technologies soon lose their privileged position because of the generalized application of technological innovations, and the game must begin anew.

Under the pressure of periodically occurring overproduction, the impulse to constantly revolutionized technology and hence also to "periodic revolutions in value" is strengthened. The entrepreneurs who yesterday were able to gain extra surplus value by introducing new processes are today threatened by newcomers with still better technologies and have to be content with the average profit. Tomorrow they may not even cover their costs or may indeed register a loss, and will have to pull out of the market.[288] There is an eternal hunt after extra profits for their own individual plants, a continual attempt to secure an at least temporary, privileged island of extra profit by revolutionizing technology. The "real movement," presented above, shows that there can be no talk of an adjustment of production to demand; rather, production constantly outpaces demand, and the regulatory function of the price mechanism does not exist at all. Far from leading to the curtailment of production, periods of falling prices were in the past and still are today periods of the greatest technological progress and expansion of production. In the face of this now self-evident failure in the construc-

---

286. Marx, *Capital*, vol. 2, 185.
287. Compare Marx, *Capital*, vol. 3, 231–32 [these pages do not seem relevant], 279 and following.
288. Compare Marx, *Capital*, vol. 2, 185.

tion of the existing economic mechanism, the dominant theory also begins to discover that instead of the alleged tendency toward equilibrium, there is perpetual motion of change, a tendency toward disequilibrium;[289] that instead of the regulatory function of the price mechanism balancing supply and demand, situations can arise in which "once destroyed, equilibrium is lost forever."[290]

A theory of dynamic movement must not only point out individual dynamic factors but also make the disequilibrating movement of the system as a whole and its causes intelligible. Beyond that, it has to show the consequences of the dynamic movement for the whole system. In a self-contained theory, Marx sought to grasp not only the sequence of the economic cycle but also the structural changes in the whole system that were its result. Only thus could he show the direction of the overall course of the economic system, its "developmental tendencies." This is not contradicted by the fact that, at a particular level of development, the indicated direction of this course encounters a limit and approaches its end. The validity of the theory is not put in question if it is shown that this limit to the capitalist dynamic is conditioned by and derived from the basic conditions of the system, the dual character of labor.[291]

We have seen how, with the development of the capitalist mode of production, a tendency toward growth in the minimum size of plants prevails.[292] Hence also growth in the capitals required to run a business under "normal" conditions.[293] It follows that, at a given moment, the scale of production, the size of plant, does not depend on the free will of the entrepreneur. "The actual degree of development of the productive

---

289. Compare Rosenstein-Rodan, "Das Zeitmoment in der mathematischen Theorie," 131.

290. Ricci, "Die 'synthetische Ökonomie' von Henry Ludwell Moore," 655.

291. Marx not only regarded a definite level of maturity in the development of the objective factor—the economy—as a precondition for the future higher form of society but also the subjective factor, humanity itself. World history, for him, "is nothing but the creation of man through human labor, nothing but the emergence of nature for man." Marx, "Economic and Philosophic Manuscripts of 1844," 305; compare 292, 333. The "conquest" of the world of objects is, at the same time, the first emergence of this world for humanity. For Marx, its domination, "possessing" it [ibid., 299], does not happen because of a theoretical outlook but rather through labor, through human praxis. In this way, Marx distinguishes himself from Feuerbach. Compare, for example, Marcuse, Studies in Critical Philosophy, 22. The labor whose result is the subjection of nature and the evolution of humanity is not, however, "value-creating" labor but "real," that is, "concrete" labor, which creates useful things; in short, it is the development of human productive power. Since concrete labor is always bound together with value-creating labor in the present economic order, however, the degree of the progressive maturation of concrete labor can only be expressed in its value, in the fall of the rate of profit. It was shown above that the fall in the rate of profit is only the capitalist expression of the wealth of society, of the degree of development of labor's productive power, and hence is also a symptom of the approaching supersession of capital's rule itself. "The decrease in the interest rate is therefore a symptom of the annulment of capital only inasmuch as it is a symptom of the growing domination of capital in the process of perfecting itself—of the estrangement which is growing and therefore hastening to its annulment." Marx, "Economic and Philosophic Manuscripts of 1844," 316.

292. Having shown in Das Akkumulations- und Zusammenbruchsgesetz the consequences that arise for the problem of equilibrium by considering the process of accumulation in terms of value, I confine myself here to emphasizing those moments that impede the attainment of a state of equilibrium from the material side of the technical labor process and increase the incongruence, already described, between material and value proportions even more.

293. Marx, Capital, vol. 1, 777.

forces compels him to produce on such and such a scale."[294] This is, therefore, something given by the technology. It is self-evident that this makes accord between the technical proportions and the required value proportions more difficult. In the course of capitalist development, the tendency toward growth in the organic composition of capital prevails. An ever-larger part of a given capital is transformed into means of production (MP) and an ever-smaller part into labor power (LP).[295] Looked at from the value side, the ratio $c:v$ does grow, however, because of the slower pace of technological progress (cheapening, in value terms, of the means of production) than the quantitative growth in the ratio of MP to LP. The difference between capital's rates of growth in terms of the quantity [of commodities] and value makes the congruence of value and physical proportions even more difficult than previously.

Further, the analysis of the technical labor process yields the law of the uneven development of the individual branches of production.[296] It is precisely the example of this disproportionality in development that best illustrates the distinction between Marx's conception and that of the dominant theory. The latter represents uneven development as capital accumulation in different branches as being different in value terms, for example, 20 percent in one, 35 percent in another, and so on; and disturbances as arising from such value disproportions. According to Marx, this can happen, but does not have to; and does not get to the essence of the problem. Even if all spheres were to have accumulated evenly in value terms, for example, by 1 percent, disturbances must nevertheless arise if the expansion in material terms is not proportionally the same in all branches of production. For with the same percentage growth in capital in all branches, the material expansion in the various branches can vary in size and amount, for example, to 5 percent in one sphere and 20 percent in another. This is conditioned by the specific technological character of each sphere, and according to Marx, it is these characteristics that underlie leaps in technological development.[297]

The contradiction, in the abstract, between possible, continuous accumulation of

---

294. Marx, *The Poverty of Philosophy*, 118. The significance of this statement first becomes entirely apparent if we compare it with Böhm-Bawerk's view, according to which the scale of production can be determined arbitrarily and is not technically given. According to Böhm-Bawerk, "any given total of present goods, be it large or small, is sufficient to purchase and remunerate the total supply of labor existent in an economic community. All that is required is to bring about a corresponding contraction or extension of the production period." Böhm-Bawerk, *Capital and Interest*, vol. 2, 354. It is simply to be wondered why unemployment continues to exist, when it appears so easily abolished.

295. Marx, *Capital*, vol. 1, 773–75.

296. "The specific degree of development of the social productivity of labour differs from one particular sphere of production to another." Marx, *Capital*, vol. 3, 263.

297. "If all other capitals have accumulated at the same rate, it does not follow at all that their production has [also] increased at the same rate. . . . The same value is produced in both cases, but the quantity of commodities in which it is represented is very different. It is quite incomprehensible, therefore, why trade A, because the value of its output has increased by 1 percent while the mass of its products has grown by 20 percent, must find a market in trade B, where the value has likewise increased by 1 percent, but the quantity of its output only by 5 percent. Here, the author has failed to take into consideration the difference between use value and exchange value." Marx, "Economic Manuscript of 1861–63 [Notebooks XII to XV]," 306–7.

value and the fact of discontinuous, jerky material expansion is related to, but not identical with, the above law. Vulgar Marxist literature is fond of looking at accumulation in purely value terms and assuming that any arbitrary amount of value can be accumulated (see, for example, Laurat):[298] that 50 percent of the surplus value is consumed by the capitalist and the other 50 percent steadily accumulated each year. It does not ask whether this surplus value destined for accumulation is large enough to acquire the quantities of means of production required for the expansion of production. The assumption that any small increase in profit can correspond to an equally small growth in the technological apparatus of production, that is, the presupposition of the infinite divisibility of goods, underpins this conception. In contrast, Marx emphasizes that such a parallel relation between value accumulation and material accumulation does not exist, because not every dollar earned is accumulated, that is, can be converted into the material elements of production. For the expansion of the scale of production, a certain minimum amount of capital is usually required, to buy a whole set of technically connected machines making up a unit (for example, in the textile industry).[299] Expansion can only take place, therefore, by this unit, or multiples of it.[300] Such material relations—and consequently also the value relations they bear—consequently determine the minimum amount of money capital necessary for expansion and vary from industry to industry.[301] In short, according to Marx, "the proportions in which the productive process can be expanded are not arbitrary, but are prescribed by technical factors."[302] While, for example, the entire surplus value (or even part of it) suffices and is employed for the expansion of production in one branch, in others the surplus value is saved up for several years until it reaches the minimum size necessary for "real accumulation."[303] Consequently, while one branch of production may be expanded every year, expansion in others only occurs at intervals of several years.

The incongruence between the value side and the material side of the process of reproduction, which we have examined from the side of production, is increased still more by impulses that come from the demand side. An even, proportional expansion of all the spheres of production rests on the tacit assumption that demand (consumption) can be expanded just as evenly and proportionally. In contrast, Marx emphasizes that the individual or productive use of certain commodities is constrained, inelastic, which must likewise result in an uneven material expansion of production in various spheres. No one who finds two tractors sufficient for the cultivation of their land will buy four simply because their price has fallen by half. Demand for tractors is, all other things being equal, not dependent on their price alone but is rather determined by the area to be cultivated, that is, quantitatively. "But the use value—consumption—depends not

298 [Laurat, *Un système qui sombre.*]

299. Compare Marx, *Capital*, vol. 2, 162–63.

300. Marx, *Capital*, vol. 1, 465–66.

301. Marx, *Capital*, vol. 2, 162–63, and vol. 1, 422, 424.

302. Marx, *Capital*, vol. 2, 158.

303. Ibid., 565.

on value, but on the quantity. It is quite unintelligible why I should buy 6 knives because I can now get them for the same price that I previously paid for 1."[304]

All these moments exclude symmetry in technical and value movements; consequently, they impede the doubly proportional expansion of the productive apparatus, in both value and quantitative terms, that theory postulates as the condition for equilibrium. The realization of this equilibrium cannot be an enduring rule. With the constant impulse to revolutionize technology and values, the coordination of the value and material sides of the productive apparatus must become more and more difficult and their incongruence constantly grow. The two sides of the productive apparatus move in opposite directions, following technological change and the development of the productive forces: the values of individual commodities have a tendency to fall, while the mass of material goods increases. Under such circumstances equilibrium, the "rule" presupposed by political economy, can only occur, as it were, by chance within the general irregularity, as a momentary point of transition in the midst of constant disequilibrium.[305]

---

304. Marx, "Economic Manuscript of 1861–63 [Notebooks XII to XV]," 307. The fact of inelastic demand, along with the role of money, constitutes the main argument in Marx's critique of the James Mill–Say theory of the identity of demand and supply, by means of which the possibility of generalized crisis is denied. See ibid., 290–92.

305. "A mode of production whose laws can only assert themselves as blindly operating averages between constant irregularities." Marx, *Capital*, vol. 1, 196.

The Evolutionist Revolt
against Classical Economics[1]

1. In France: Condorcet, Saint-Simon, Simonde de Sismondi

Any theoretical analysis of a contemporary economic system must lead to the formulation of a standard with which to evaluate the existing level of development. To have any validity, such a standard must be worked out of the developmental process itself and not merely from the level attained at the moment of analysis. It will therefore be useful to the present-day theorist to look back and see how dynamic or evolutionary thinking actually entered the field of economic theory. The problem has not been adequately or at all accurately presented in our economic literature. Thus, Richard T. Ely writes: "It is probably due to Herbert Spencer more than to any other person that we have come to recognize the applicability of evolution to the various departments of the social life of man."[2] But the essay of Spencer to which he refers did not appear until 1857, decades after others were already using evolutionary notions in the social sciences.[3] John Bagnell Bury, to cite a more recent example, wrote a whole book on the idea of progress without even mentioning [Jean Charles Léonard Simonde de] Sismondi or Richard Jones—the two men who first worked out the idea of the historical succession of ever more advanced economic stages.[4] In German economic literature either the problem is not discussed at all, as in [Karl] Bücher's widely known study of the rise of national economy,[5] which does not once mention feudalism or capitalism; or

---

1. Originally published under this same title in two parts, in the *Journal of Political Economy* in 1943.
2. Ely, *Studies in the Evolution of Industrial Society*, 6–7.
3. Spencer, "Progress: Its Law and Causes," 1–60.
4. Bury, *The Idea of Progress*.
5. Bücher, *Die Entstehung der Volkswirtschaft*.

else the sole responsibility for what they call the "sociologizing" of economics is falsely attributed to [Georg Wilhelm Friedrich] Hegel and his school.[6] [Edmund] Whittaker, too, in a recent book, makes the mistake of overestimating the German representatives of historicism—the German historical school and Hegel. At the same time, speaking of the French and English, he mentions the economic views of [Henri] Saint-Simon, Sismondi, James Steuart, and Richard Jones, but not their ideas on evolution. [Marie-Jean-Antoine-Nicolas de] Condorcet is not mentioned at all.[7]

The purpose of the present study is to show the decisive role of French and English economists in laying the basis for modern evolutionary theories of economics, and particularly for the work of Karl Marx. It is fully consistent with the general neglect of our problem that Marx's contribution to the "sociologizing" of economics is also widely misconstrued. According to [Werner] Sombart, for example, the importance of Marx lies not so much in the field of economic theory as in the field of sociology. "Marx," he writes, "applied evolutionary thinking to the social process."[8] He gives us "an insight into the historical character of the economy, into *its constant changeability in the course of history*. He first created the *concept of the economic system* and made it the subject of economic science."[9] Sombart thus arbitrarily gives Marx credit for accomplishments he never claimed and thereby conceals and distorts the picture of Marx's real work.[10] Unfortunately, Sombart's view has been widely echoed, even in socialist circles. Eduard Heimann, for example, repeats that Marx's decisive contribution to the growth of economics, his truly "Copernican significance," does not lie in specific theories, such as the theory of surplus value, the theory of concentration, or the theory of crisis, but in his having for the first time "historicized" or "sociologized" economics. It was Marx, he writes, who "first conceived [capitalism] to be historical, and therefore time bound, transformable and transitory." Marx was able to discover this insight because he was the "heir and executor of Hegel's thinking" and because he possessed the "political will" to attack static capitalism.[11]

We can easily dispose of the allegedly Hegelian basis for the "historicizing" of economics. All the great theorists of the French Enlightenment, with the exception of

---

6. Thus [Rudolf] Kötschke (*Grundzüge der deutschen Wirtschaftsgeschichte*, 12–15) has a section on the history of the idea of stages in economic development in which the names of Saint-Simon, Sismondi, James Steuart, and Richard Jones never appear. Kötschke, furthermore, follows Bücher's precedent in discussing the sequence not of complete economic structures, such as feudalism or capitalism, but only of partial units: village economy, town economy, territorial economy. Similarly, [Werner] Sombart speaks of individual economy, transition economy, social economy. And, according to Richard T. Ely, the various stages are not characterized by the different types of social organization; rather, various occupational activities, such as hunting or fishing, agriculture or cattle raising, are just different historical "stages" (hunting stage, fishing stage, etc.). Ely, *Studies in the Evolution of Industrial Society*, 26, 39.

7. See Whittaker, *History of Economic Ideas*.

8. Sombart, *Das Lebenswerk von Karl Marx*, 16.

9. Ibid., 53–54. Italics are mine.

10. It has frequently been pointed out that Sombart's historical statements simply do not stand up under close scrutiny. See, for example, Adolf Schaube's criticism of Sombart's account of certain early English developments in "Die Wollausfuhr Englands."

11. Heimann, "Karl Marx' Bedeutung," 165, 168.

Rousseau, held the philosophic view that history was an endless progress marking man's path to reason.[12] Endless progress necessarily implies that the existing reality, the given state of affairs, will be negated and will not continue to exist indefinitely. Hegel, on the other hand, thought that history had reached its goal in his own day, that the idea and reality had found their common ground.[13] On this point, Marx was closer to the French tradition than to Hegel.

In the *Philosophy of Right*, Hegel patterns the notion of freedom after the free ownership of property.[14] The historical process thus becomes a glorification of the history of the middle class, and Hegel's *Philosophy of History* ends with the consolidation of middle-class society.[15] Here was a social system no longer to be transcended. We shall see that the French tradition, from Condorcet through Saint-Simon and his disciples to Sismondi and [Constantin] Pecqueur, was very different. For them the idea of historical progress ruled by reason tended to turn away from the possessing classes in favor of "the great mass of those who live by their work" (Condorcet). They stood opposed to the existing oppressive social system. Progress does not end with middle-class society. Quite the contrary, it will continue to unfold in the future in new social structures. Whereas one trend in eighteenth-century thought, influenced by the religious tradition of the Garden of Eden, placed the golden age in the past, at the beginning of man's history, Saint-Simon turned the sequence around. "The golden age," he wrote, following an idea of Condorcet's, "which a blind tradition had always placed in the past, lies ahead of us." Here, too, Marx is linked to French thought, not to Hegel.

We must remember that Hegel's *Philosophy of History* was a relatively late work, published posthumously in 1837, four years after Richard Jones had already appeared with his historical study of economics.[16] Hegel, furthermore, as we shall see later, expressly rejected the concept that must lie at the base of any genetic theory of development, namely, that a higher, more developed phase proceeds from the preceding, lower phase.

On the other hand, a genuinely powerful influence on evolutionary thinking must be assigned to the revolution in astrophysics brought about by the publication of [Pierre-Simon] Laplace's *The System of the World* in 1796. Laplace denied the unchanging character of "eternal" nature and offered his famous theory of the evolution of the planetary system through purely mechanical phenomena of the attraction and repulsion of atoms, from a rotating ball of gas that by cooling and contraction threw off segments of its surface. These segments in turn united to become the planets. Both the earth and the

---

12. Turgot, for example, in his second Sorbonne discourse, "Sur les progrès successifs de l'esprit humain," spoke of the "total mass of the human species, who, by alternations . . . of goods and of evils, marches steadily, though with slow steps, to an ever greater perfection" (53–54).

13. Marcuse, *Reason and Revolution*, 226.

14. [Hegel, *Outlines of the Philosophy of Right*, 50–51, 57 and following.]

15. [Hegel, *Lectures on the Philosophy of History*, 472–77.]

16. [Ibid.] Fifty years before Hegel, Gotthold Ephraim Lessing, the most prominent figure of the German Enlightenment, advanced certain evolutionist ideas in his essay *The Education of the Human Species* (1780); these ideas were strongly influenced by Adam Ferguson's *Essay on the History of Civil Society* (1767). Later on Lessing's essay, translated into French (1829), belonged to the Saint-Simonian propagandist literature.

entire solar system were formerly nonexistent, and the time will come when the sun will be extinguished and the universe will break apart.[17] At one time the earth was an uninhabited and unformed mass of gas. It required millions of years for the cooling of the earth's crust to create the conditions that brought into existence the lower organic forms and eventually man himself.

This evolutionary theory of astrophysics had already appeared in 1755 in an anonymous publication by Immanuel Kant. It had failed to make headway against the biblical tradition of Genesis, however, and had passed unnoticed. Kant himself knew that he had "traveled on a dangerous journey" and went to great pains in his preface to ward off the charge of atheism.[18] It required the intellectual atmosphere of the French Revolution to obtain recognition for such a work as Laplace's *System*.

Finally, it must be noted that the sociologizing of economics is not and cannot be regarded as a purely intellectual development flowing from Hegel's dialectics or any other book. While the thinkers of the Enlightenment strove to deduce the eternal laws of a rational "natural order" from nature and from the properties of the human individual, the advocates of the evolutionary idea whom we are dealing with here based their universal laws and predictions on *history*, on actually observed *evolutionary tendencies*. Their ideas are the theoretical reflection of such great historical phenomena as the French and American revolutions and the industrial revolution in England.[19] Above all, it was the outbreak of the French Revolution that, like the eruption of a volcano, exposed the weaknesses of eighteenth-century rationalism. What caused such an eruption? To answer that question, man turned to history.[20]

CR

The classical economists had also made some investigations of the past. Adam Smith, for example, revealed considerable historical knowledge, as in chapter 4 of book 1, "Of

---

17. The influence of these views on Saint-Simon is clearly seen in his *Mémoires sur la science de l'homme* (1813), 194.

18. Kant, *Universal Natural History*, 7.

19. Contemporaries were astounded at the rapid postrevolutionary progress of the United States, both in size of population and in development of agriculture, as contrasted with its "stagnation" under British rule. As one analyst phrased the problem, the United States was a country "where from a few adventurers, a power is now rising." And he continued: "The history of the world has furnished few instances of so great a tract of country undergoing a change, from an uncultivated and barbarous, to a civilised state; and it will well merit the attention of mankind to observe the different steps and the progress upon so large a scale." Playfair, *Commercial and Political Atlas*, 29–30. [See also Grossman's essay on Playfair, chapter 5 of the present volume, 231–51.]

20. The so-called German historical school of law, which received its programmatic statement in [Friedrich Carl] Savigny's *Vom Beruf unserer Zeit zur Gesetzgebung und Rechtswissenschaft* in 1814, was itself only a by-product of the French Revolution. It was the answer of the conservative elements in Germany to the revolutionary method of lawgiving. Against the latter they insisted upon the slow method of historical, organic evolution. They thus condemned progress in the name of continuity. Marx's "Philosophical Manifesto of the Historical School" (against [Gustav] Hugo) is a most penetrating criticism of the methodological presuppositions of the historical school of law (see Hook, *From Hegel to Marx*, 141–44).

the Origin and Use of Money" or chapter 11, "Digression concerning the Variation in the Value of Silver during the Course of the Four Last Centuries" and, above all, in book 3, on the "Progress of Opulence in Different Nations."[21]

The classical economists never reached the point, however, of permitting the idea of development to bring order out of the chaos of economic facts. Adam Smith distinguished between advancing, stationary, or declining conditions of society,[22] and [David] Ricardo talked about the "progress" or "natural advance of society," of "an improving society" advancing from poverty to a flourishing condition.[23] But neither one knew of phases of development, only of datable conditions of one and the same capitalist society—conditions that varied in size of population, extent of capital accumulation, or knowledge of agricultural techniques[24] and not in their fundamental structure.[25] In his chapter entitled "On the Accumulation of Capital," Adam Smith's account of the historical development of England from the invasion of Julius Caesar is characteristic. He writes: "When we compare the state of a nation at two different periods and find that the annual produce of its land and labour is evidently greater at the latter than at the former, that its lands are better cultivated, its manufactures more numerous and more flourishing, we may be assured that its capital must have increased during the interval between the two periods."[26]

"In different stages of society," wrote Ricardo in a similar vein, "the accumulation of capital . . . is more or less rapid," so that in new settlements with little capital, for example, it is very slow.[27] The "different stages" are thus nothing but levels of the same capitalist system of economy. Marx commented sarcastically that "the bourgeois form of labor is regarded by Ricardo as the eternal natural form of social labor. Ricardo's primitive fisherman and primitive hunter are from the outset owners of commodities who exchange their fish and game in proportion to the labor time which is objectified in these exchange values."[28]

The classical economists lacked an understanding of the real developmental sequence and changes of economic systems. Just as Rousseau in the *Social Contract* ex-

---

21. [Adam Smith, *Wealth of Nations*, vol. 1, 19–25, 161–92, 336–74.]

22. Ibid., book I, chapter vii, 48–56.

23. Ricardo, *Principles of Political Economy*, 52–63.

24. Ibid., 5–32.

25. Richard Schueller did not succeed in clearing the classics of the charge of unhistoricism. All he shows is that Smith and Ricardo emphasize the temporal, local, or cultural differentiations, which result in modifications of the general laws of prices, average profits, rents, and wages. Schueller, *Die klassische Nationalökonomie*, 16. But such differentiations can occur within a given economic system regarded as permanent and have nothing in common with the fundamental idea of the theory of evolution, that is to say, with the theory of successive and different economic structures—an idea that is entirely absent from the classics and that Schueller does not discuss at all.

26. Adam Smith, *Wealth of Nations*, vol. 1, 307.

27. [Grossman's paraphrase is inaccurate. Ricardo wrote: "In new settlements, where the arts and knowledge of countries far advanced in refinement are introduced, it is probable that capital has a tendency to increase faster than mankind." *Principles of Political Economy*, 55–56.]

28. Marx, *Contribution to the Critique*, 300.

plained the origin of social institutions rationalistically, the classicists took a rationalistic rather than a genetic approach to the past.[29] All previous societies were measured with the rational yardstick of free trade. That is why they knew of only two ideal states: the "original state of things," occurring before the fall from grace, as it were, and the bourgeois state in their own days of more or less free trade and competition. All intervening epochs, with their severe limitations upon trade and industry, were condemned as unfit and erroneous. They were never discussed in terms of the limitations and conditions of their own time.[30]

We have become so accustomed to the idea of historical development that it is difficult for us to imagine such a lack of historicism. How did the change in our thinking come about? It must be stressed that we are not concerned with individual, isolated representatives of the evolutionary idea; such representatives appeared as early as the Middle Ages[31] and the Renaissance (Vico).[32] The subject of our analysis is a current of thinking that emerged in the social sciences during the last third of the eighteenth century and became triumphant during the first half of the nineteenth century: the concept of the evolution of human society through a succession of economic stages, each superior to the preceding one. Six men are the main representatives of this current: Condorcet, Saint-Simon, and Sismondi in France; Sir James Steuart and Richard Jones in England; and, finally, Karl Marx, who synthesized and completed the whole development. Thereafter the theory of evolution through the succession of definite economic structures was not further developed and fell into discredit with the dominant school.[33]

The great revolution in thought brought about by the French Revolution was most notable in the handling of social problems. Ever since Descartes, the notion of the unity of all knowledge had been generally prevalent. All phenomena, it was believed, no matter how complicated, can ultimately be understood by the same method—the mathematical method of the natural sciences. With the French Revolution, however, the idea arose that social phenomena constitute a special class, requiring special treatment and a special methodology. Eternally unchanging laws may be valid for the natural sciences, because nature is eternal and unchanging, but human society undergoes constant change (progress) from epoch to epoch. The particular task of the social sciences is therefore not to seek for eternal laws but to find the law of change itself.

---

29. [Rousseau, *Rousseau's Social Contract and Discourses*.]

30. It was this attitude that Marx had in mind when he wrote: "Hence the pre-bourgeois forms of the social organisation of production are treated by political economy in much the same way as the Fathers of the Church treated pre-Christian religions." From such a point of view, feudal institutions are "artificial," bourgeois institutions "natural." Marx, *Capital*, vol. 1, 175.

31. Ibn Khaldun (1332–1406) in his work *Muqaddimah* (*Prolegomena*).

32. [Vico, *New Science of Giambattista Vico*.]

33. Whittaker approvingly quotes the opinion of the English historian Frederic William Maitland directed against "architects of stage-systems," who are "prescribing a normal program for the human race in decreeing that every portion of mankind must move through one fated series of stages." Whittaker, *History of Economic Ideas*, 3.

It is true that the application of eternal natural laws to human society was still given formal recognition; but in actual practice, men like Condorcet, Saint-Simon, and Richard Jones began to make sharp differentiations. Eventually, with the further spread of new sciences such as chemistry and biology, in which mathematical analysis played no role, an open revolt set in against the application of the methods of natural science to the study of society. Auguste Comte waged a bitter struggle against the "metaphysical prejudice that no real certainty can exist outside mathematics" and the "empty scientific overlordship temporarily granted the mathematical spirit." In the last "lesson" of his *Course*, Comte wrote: "Instead of seeking blindly for a sterile scientific unity, as oppressive as it is chimerical, in the reduction of all phenomena to a single order of laws, the human mind will eventually consider the different classes of events as having their special laws." He went on to say that "the laws of organic phenomena or social phenomena are established by the predominance of specific methods: the comparative method in biology, the historical method in sociology."[34]

CR

The pioneer of the new approach is Condorcet (1743–94). According to him, the great revolution of his own time can be understood only through "the picture of revolutions which preceded and prepared the way for it."[35] Historical development "is subject to . . . general laws. . . . The result which every instant presents, depends upon that offered by the preceding instants, and has an influence on the instants which follow. . . . This picture, therefore, is historical; since subjected as it will be to perpetual variations, it is formed by the successive observation of human societies at the different eras through which they have passed." The student's task is to discover "the laws of . . . change" of the steady progress of spiritual and social development "towards knowledge and happiness." Progress, Condorcet continues, "may doubtless be more or less rapid, but it can never be retrograde."[36] The certainty of progress can be derived from the fact of the American and French revolutions. By freeing themselves from their tyrannical rulers, the two countries give us the symbol of progress and free us from antiquated preconceptions. We must construct "an art . . . of foreseeing the future improvement of the human race, and of directing and hastening that improvement," and "history . . . must form the principal basis of this art."[37] "From these observations on what man has heretofore been, and what he is at present, we shall be led to the means of securing and of accelerating the still further progress, of which, from his nature, we may indulge the hope."[38]

---

34. Comte, *Cours de philosophie positive*, vol. 6, 413, 521. [The first quotation and the first part of the final quotation cannot be located, although they do express Comte's position; the words after the colon are at p. 397].

35. Condorcet, *Outlines of an Historical View*, 22.

36. Ibid., 9–11.

37. Ibid., 21.

38. Ibid., 11.

We have already seen that the idea of development, of history as a continuous movement of causally linked processes, was worked out before the French Revolution. There was no place in such a conception for a theory of historical stages, however. The spokesmen of the eighteenth-century Enlightenment were convinced that, as soon as reason had discovered the truth, the existing irrational state of affairs would immediately be replaced by a state of perfection. The prevailing irrational conditions were nothing more than the unnecessary products of "error" or "prejudice." The rationalists therefore believed that, with the progress of reason, there would be an unbroken, straight-line rise to perfection. Then came the French Revolution, with its tremendous political and social upheavals, its frightful party and class conflicts; yet it failed to bring about a state of perfection. Rationalism received a mortal blow. The revolution and its aftermath demonstrated that moral and legal relationships did not depend on reason alone, that economic interests were a more important factor in determining the political position of each group in the population.

Condorcet, himself a member of the Girondist party, promptly incorporated this disillusioning experience into his conception of history.[39] The ultimate aim of a state of perfection was not abandoned, but the idea of progress became more differentiated into a succession of stages and periods. He now saw that historical development was an uneven process, in which desirable progressive aims are constantly, though temporarily, being turned into their opposite, into backward steps, until they are finally realized in a new and higher stage. The French Revolution failed to accomplish what its spokesmen had hoped because both the ideas and the social relationships were incomplete *and not yet ripe* for a state of perfection.[40] The conclusion was therefore inevitable that it is not possible to move directly from any given condition to perfection through the demands of reason. Certain specific preconditions must first be fulfilled. And that means that past history should be looked upon not as merely an error that could have been avoided by proper insight but as historically determined and therefore as necessary and unavoidable. In other words, historical development encompasses not only the elements of rational progress but also those of irrational progress. "The history of general errors: . . .the manner in which general errors are introduced, propagated . . . among nations, forms a part of the picture of the progress of the human mind."[41] Thus Condorcet arrived at his stage theory. The "errors" of the past, and especially of the revolution, were a necessary part of a transitional stage in the road to perfection.

After formulating this general theory, Condorcet proceeded to sketch the social evolution of human progress in nine epochs, each representing a higher stage than its predecessor, concluding with a preview (the tenth epoch) of the "future progress of the human spirit." He found two fundamental tendencies in history.

39. See Mannheim, *Ideology and Utopia*, 200.
40. See Cunow, *Die Marxsche Geschichts-, Gesellschafts- und Staatstheorie*, 158.
41. Condorcet, *Outlines of an Historical View*, 19–20.

1. There is a certain regularity in the development of mankind, so that the backward nations will eventually go through the same process of growth that the most advanced nations have already traversed.[42] Condorcet was therefore convinced that the immense distance that separates these people (the most enlightened) from "the slavery of countries subjected to kings, the barbarity of African tribes, and the ignorance of savages" will "gradually vanish," until historical development has accomplished "the destruction of inequality between different nations. . . . Every nation [will] one day arrive at the state of civilization attained by those people who are most enlightened . . . as the French, for instance, and the Anglo-Americans."[43] This goal is realizable because "the march of these people will be less slow and more sure than ours has been, because they will derive from us that light which we have been obliged to discover, and because for them to acquire the simple truths . . . we have obtained after long wandering in the mazes of error, it will be sufficient to seize upon . . . proofs in our . . . publications."[44]

2. The development of social progress is uneven as compared with the progress of knowledge. "We perceive," he wrote, "that the exertions of these last ages have done much for the progress of the human mind, but little for the perfection of the human species. . . . We behold vast countries groaning under slavery. . . . In a few directions, our eyes are struck with a dazzling light," while the great mass of mankind is "consigned over to ignorance and prejudice."[45]

What is responsible for this lag? Up until now history was the history of individuals instead of being the history of the masses. "The mind of the philosopher reposes with satisfaction upon a small number of objects" and forgets "the spectacle of the stupidity, the slavery, the extravagance, and the barbarity" that characterizes the great majority of people.[46] "Hitherto, . . . history . . . has been merely the history of a few men. That which forms in truth the human species, the mass of families, which subsist almost entirely upon their labour, has been forgotten . . . the chiefs only have fixed the attention of historians." This is all wrong. Whether we are concerned with a discovery or an important theory, a legal system or a political revolution, we must always examine its effects on the largest section of each society, "the true object of philosophy." Until now, that is precisely the part of "the history of the human species" that is "the most obscure, the most neglected."[47] Condorcet proceeded to explain this neglect in a purely intellectual way, as the failure of science and knowledge to pay sufficient attention to the social condition of the great mass of working people, who, during the two revolutions, had taken their first active role on the stage of history and thereby demonstrated their importance. Behind the intellectual explanation, however, there was an important in-

---

42. Bury's statement that "Condorcet cannot be said to have deduced any law of social development" is completely false. Bury, *The Idea of Progress*, 212.
43. Condorcet, *Outlines of an Historical View*, 251. [Editor's interpolation.]
44. Ibid., 257–58.
45. [Ibid., 245.]
46. Ibid.
47. Ibid., 246, 248.

sight into historical development, which necessarily brought the economic factor into the foreground. With Condorcet the idea of natural laws of historical development and the collectivist view of history as a history of the masses were born.[48]

༙

Leaning heavily on Condorcet,[49] Saint-Simon (1760–1825) sought to give history the strictly scientific character and certainty that marked astronomy and chemistry.[50] As his starting point Saint-Simon takes the fact of the French Revolution, which he seeks to fit into the whole sequence of historical changes. By this method he hopes to discover the basic forces of history. His ultimate purpose is to found a *politique scientifique*, based on systematized historical observations and destined to replace the hitherto current *politique métaphysique* based on abstract hypotheses, which in reality is only a kind of theology.[51] History, Saint-Simon thinks, can be made into a science only if the student learns from historical experience and "laws" how to predict the future on the basis of the past. "The wise [or knowing] man . . . is the man who foresees."[52]

Saint-Simon's philosophy of history has a history of its own. Originally he too accepted a purely intellectual theory and considered the growth of knowledge to be the determining factor in the historical transformations of society. After 1814, however, he turned to an economic conception. Retaining the formal framework of his earlier view, that is, the idea of the progressive development of historical phenomena causally determined by some basic force, Saint-Simon substituted the economic factor for intellectual enlightenment as the driving force. Material production and the law of property, he now stated, were the base of society. In all social changes the strongest determining

---

48. See Hayek, "The Counter-revolution of Science."

49. In *L'organisateur* (1819) Saint-Simon praises Condorcet's *Outlines*: "It is the first attempt to constitute history . . . by treating it as a real science," he says, "but this attempt, sufficient to indicate the goal of history, will not suffice to achieve it." Saint-Simon, *L'organisateur*, 72–73.

50. Saint-Simon, *Mémoires sur la science de l'homme*. For the following discussion see Bazard, *The Doctrine of Saint-Simon*, Muckle, *Die grossen Sozialisten*, Weill, *L'école saint-simonienne*, Spühler, *Der Saint-Simonismus*, Volgin, "Über die historische Stellung Saint-Simons," and Hayek, "The Counter-revolution of Science."

51. Saint-Simon, *Du système industriel*, first part, 20. ["Scientific politics," "metaphysical politics"].

52. Saint-Simon, *Lettres d'un habitant de Genève*, 36. In *Memoire sur la science de l'homme* Saint-Simon criticized previous historical writing: "It is a collection of facts. . . . These facts are not bound together by any theory . . . they do not provide the means for determining what will happen from what has happened" (246). "The future is made up of the last terms of a series of which the past constitutes the first term" (172).

Enfantin insisted later that the theory of history was the most complete and elaborate part of Saint-Simonism and that it "justified our claim that it was *science*. . . . We demonstrated . . . a LAW, . . . a REGULAR ORDER where only *chaos* and *confusion* had been seen . . . we showed the steady march of humanity toward UNIVERSAL ASSOCIATION." Enfantin, "Deuxième enseignement," 55, 60 [Emphases in Enfantin's original text, but not Grossman's translation.] The Saint-Simonians were also the first (in 1832) to raise the important problem of the uneven development of the West and the Orient. How was it possible, they asked, to reconcile the stationary or retrogressive conditions in Asia and Turkey with the law of continuous progress? Enfantin, "Dix-huitième enseignement, " 135–40, and *Les mémoires d'un industriel*, 167–68. [The pages Grossman refers to are not relevant.

factor is not the spiritual element but the organization of property: "The national character is powerless against objective developments. . . . There is no change in the social order without a change in property."[53] In his *Views on Property and Legislation* (1818),[54] Saint-Simon develops his idea of the dependence of the legal superstructure upon the economic base: he emphasizes that while parliamentary government is merely a *form*, it is the structure of property relations that is the fundamental thing and therefore "this structure is the *real foundation* of the social edifice," implying that with the revision of property relations the whole social order can be changed.[55] "Thus putting it briefly, politics is the *science of production*, whose object is to discover the order of things most favorable to all sorts of production."[56]

The exposition of Saint-Simon's ideas on the historical sequence of various economic structures must be preceded by a short summary of his philosophy of history. "The universe," says Saint-Simon, "is ruled by a single immutable law," and the science of man is part of physical science.[57] The study of history enables us to demonstrate the sequence of organic and critical epochs in the life of nations.[58] In the organic epochs mankind "moved with regularity under the sway of common beliefs," as well as common institutions, whereas during the critical epochs "all forces were engaged in destroying the principles and institutions which had guided the preceding society,"[59] because new facts have emerged and society has new needs that cannot be satisfied within the narrow frame of old institutions and beliefs.[60] In such epochs, dominant religious and political institutions and ideas binding together the culture of a given epoch lose their harmonious unity and organic character; they are undermined by new critical elements, and the society enters a revolutionary crisis: the old creeds and institutions become the targets of attack. At first weak, the new elements, by repeated assault, shake the old order to its foundations and in the end overthrow it. Thus a fundamental change in the basic factor of a given period destroys the superstructure, and society is driven

---

53. Saint-Simon, *De la réorganisation de la sociéte*, 241–42.

54. [Saint-Simon, *Vues sur la propriété*.]

55. Saint-Simon, *L'industrie ou discussion politiques*, 43, 82–83.

56. Thierry, *L'industrie ou discussion politiques*, 188. [Grossman implies that this was a work by Saint-Simon. It was written, under Saint-Simon's influence, by his student and adopted son Augustin Thierry]. This new conclusion was forced upon Saint-Simon by the course of the French Revolution, which preserved the economic-legal structure of the bourgeoisie, and thus of the society, throughout the rapid series of changes in the political constitution when, between 1789 and 1814, France changed its political constitutions ten times. (See Saint-Simon, *De la réorganisation de la sociéte*, 228).

57. Saint-Simon, *Mémoires sur la science de l'homme*, 173, 309; also, Saint-Simon, *Lettres d'un habitant de Genève*, 55.

58. Only the technical terms "organic" and "critical" epochs were introduced by the school ([Philippe] Buchez, [Saint-Amand] Bazard); the distinction between these epochs was introduced by Saint-Simon himself. More generally it must be stated against the views of Hayek, who gives too much credit to the Saint-Simonian school, that almost all the important doctrines of the school can be found in Saint-Simon himself; the school only developed and systematized them. [Hayek, "The Counter-revolution of Science," 135 and following.]

59. Bazard, *The Doctrine of Saint-Simon*, 206–7.

60. Ibid., 207–8.

into anarchy. The crisis is overcome only after a reconstruction of the foundations has created the conditions for the development of new cultural elements, common institutions, and beliefs; then a new organic period begins. Thus the historical process does not follow a straight and continuous line but is interrupted by periodic setbacks. Nevertheless, Saint-Simon regards this succession of progressive and regressive periods as useful and necessary. For each setback is only the expression of new forces facilitating the transition from the existing to a more advanced social system.[61]

Particularly interesting are the concrete illustrations of this theory given by Saint-Simon and further developed by [Saint-Amand] Bazard. Pre-Socratic Greece, dominated by polytheism, constituted an "organic" period. This was followed by a long "critical" period, from Socrates to the barbarian invasions, during which ancient religion suffered a slow process of disintegration. The Middle Ages, says Saint-Simon, are generally regarded as a period of barbarism and ignorance; what is overlooked is that with the Middle Ages mankind entered a new organic period, after Charlemagne had created the social organization and Pope Gregory VII the spiritual organization that gave European society a homogenous character for centuries to come.[62] These institutions proved advantageous as a whole; this was the "period of splendor of the feudal system," during which Europe waged few wars, and these unimportant.[63] The modern critical period began with Copernicus, who destroyed the scientific armor of the Christian religion, and with Luther, who undermined the political power of the papacy, thus breaking the bond that united all the European countries. Carried further by [Francis] Bacon, [René] Descartes, Galileo [Galilei], [Isaac] Newton, and [John] Locke, this spiritual revolution led finally to the French Revolution—the peak of critical dissolution, the collapse of the power of Catholicism.[64] Simultaneously with that dissolution of European unity there began the struggle of the European powers for the domination of the world, from Charles V through Philip II and Louis XIV until Napoleon.[65]

It is against the background of this succession of organic and critical epochs that Saint-Simon shows us the sequence of the various socioeconomic systems—his most brilliant contribution. In contrast to the theoretical individualism of the classical economists and the eighteenth-century Enlightenment, Saint-Simon regards history as an objective process, as the slow, century-long maturation of successive, ever more advanced social systems. The whole population contributes to this process, but not as separate individuals; Saint-Simon stresses *the primacy of the class* over the individual and the nation; he regards historical development, "the march of civilization," as the result of class relations. The so-called "creators," or great men of history, such as Luther, Wy-

---

61. Saint-Simon, *De la réorganisation de la sociéte*, 166.

62. Saint-Simon gives a particularly interesting analysis of the organic period of the Middle Ages in *Du système industriel*, second part, 90 [this page does not seem relevant], *Mémoires sur la science de l'homme*, 170, 243, *De la réorganisation de la société*, 173, *L'organisateur*, 89, and *Catéchisme des industriels*, 174.

63. Saint-Simon, *L'organisateur*, 88.

64. Saint-Simon, *Mémoires sur la science de l'homme*, 191–94, and *L'organisateur*, 99 and following.

65. Saint-Simon, *De la réorganisation de la sociéte*, 174.

cliffe, Huss, merely express the new that had slowly come into being. "Nobody creates a system of social organization; the concatenation of interests and ideas which had been formed is noticed and pointed out, that is all."[66] The "real constitution" cannot be *invented* but only *described*. The "veritable constituent power" belongs neither to the king nor to the constituent assembly but to the "march of civilization," observed and formulated into a "general law" by the philosopher.[67] The seemingly unlimited power of kings is in reality limited by the existing social structure; when general conditions are not ripe, even absolute kings cannot accomplish much, as is shown by the failure of Emperor Joseph II's (1780–90) attempt to restrict the privileges of the nobility and the church in Austria.[68] Every social organization of the past, however deficient it may seem to us, was justified at the time of its birth because it corresponded to the degree of scientific enlightenment and to the productivity of social labor conditioned by it.[69] That for Saint-Simon the economic factor is predominant can also be seen from the fact that, according to him, the leading class in *production* must also be the *politically* ruling class. In the Middle Ages, because the nobility played a leading part in agriculture, it also wielded political power beginning with the eleventh century (in alliance with the clergy as representatives of spiritual power), and these classes "subjugated the rest of the population to exploit it for their own profit."[70] But after Louis XI (died 1483) the kings, alarmed by the power of their big feudal vassals and desirous of strengthening their own power, allied themselves with the new class of *industriels* that had arisen in the womb of feudal society, against the nobility.[71] In their class strategy directed against the nobility, the kings encouraged the nobles to live in luxury, to settle at the royal court, and so on; this led to the farming out of the noblemen's estates and deprived them of any active function in the productive process. Thus it alienated them from the nation. "From that time on they ceased to have any *political* importance in the country, because they were no longer the leaders of the people in their everyday *labors*."[72]

After the kings had thus succeeded in destroying the power of the nobility, they turned against the growing power of the industrial class. Under Louis XIV, with the establishment of banking in France, the power of the industrial class grew tremendously and surpassed that of all other classes. Louis XIV, changing the previous class strategy of the French kings, went over to the side of the nobility and pursued a policy directed *against* the *industriels*. As a result, the monarchy came into contradiction with historical development; it allied itself with a class doomed to perish in its struggle with the new class, which to an ever-increasing extent concentrated in itself all the economic and

66. Saint-Simon, *L'organisateur*, 178–80.

67. Saint-Simon, *Du système industriel*, second part, 188.

68. Saint-Simon, *Catéchisme des industriels*, 54.

69. Saint-Simon, *Du système industriel*, first part, 72, and *L'organisateur*, 38; also *Catéchisme des industriels*, 170 [this page does not seem relevant].

70. Saint-Simon, *L'organisateur*, 41. [The words "subjugated the rest of the population" are not from Saint-Simon's text.]

71. Saint-Simon, *Catéchisme des industriels*, 21.

72. Ibid., 24. Italics are mine.

spiritual forces of the nation.[73] When the French Revolution broke the power of feudalism and the nobility, the end of the monarchy allied with the nobility was inevitable.

The revolution was a gigantic, destructive force; room was now made for the unfettered development of industry. But the revolution, says Saint-Simon, is not yet completed, for the task of every social movement is the creation of a superior social and political organization, and up until now no unified social and cultural organization of society has been created.[74] Production through competition has prevailed and created a wavering chaos, which lacks any principle of integration; self-interest is triumphant everywhere. However, "no system can be replaced by the *critique* that overthrows it; only a *new system* can replace an old one." Saint-Simon tried to develop this positive system of the future in *The Organizer*, whose very name was a program.[75]

He does not, however, condemn capitalism, with its base in individual freedom and its dispersal of forces. He regards capitalism as a necessary stage of evolution that won its right to existence through its victory over the restrictive feudal economy. But capitalism cannot last long. The restoration period will not bring stabilization, and the danger of new disorder will be present as long as the leading class in production—the industrial class—is not also the leading political class. The term "industrial class" is taken here not in its modern meaning but as denoting all those who do productive work, including the entrepreneurs, not in their character as capitalists but as the technical and commercial directors and organizers of industry, in opposition to the *oisifs*, or the idle (the unproductive wing of the bourgeoisie: rentiers, the military, bureaucrats). The majority of the industrial class, however, consists of the "least educated and poorest men." This class is "the only useful one."[76] Economic evolution shows that "this class is increasing steadily at the expense of the others; it must end by becoming the only class."[77]

According to Saint-Simon the restoration period is a *period of transition*. A parasitical group consisting of the unproductive portions of the bourgeoisie mentioned above (rentiers and so on), the *classe intermediaire*, has wedged itself between the old, defeated nobility and the industrial class; this intermediate class seized power during the revolution and concluded a compromise with the old nobility during the restoration; at present it forms the royal bureaucracy and exploits the industrial class.[78] Such a situation is untenable for any length of time, because it is based on "*two antagonistic principles*": economic and social power is held by one class, while political power is held by another. "The nation is essentially industrial and its government is essentially feudal."[79] The time is now nearer for a new organic period that will overcome the present disorganization.

73. Ibid., 25, 30, 32, and *L'organisateur*, 103–4.

74. Saint-Simon, *Du système industriel*, first part, 28, 39–40.

75. Saint-Simon, *l'organisateur*, 6.

76. Saint-Simon, *L'industrie ou discussion politiques*, 74.

77. Ibid. Elsewhere Saint-Simon says that the industrial class comprises 29.5 million of the 30 million Frenchmen. Saint-Simon, *Du système industriel*, second part, 187.

78. Saint-Simon, *Catéchisme des industriels*, 8, 34–9, 41, 67.

79. Ibid., 33–34 [emphasised in Saint-Simon's text]. This passage contains the germ of the important (Lenin's) theory that transitional periods are characterized by dual rule.

The economy of the future, he explains, will be a system of association completely different from all previous systems. Its main task will be to improve the lot of the class whose sole means of subsistence is the work of its hands, which constitutes the majority of the population. For the time being, no one is concerned about this class kept in silent subjection by the ruling classes.[80] But the increasing significance of the new organization "will make them pass from the governed to the governing."[81] The people will no longer be subjects; men will cease to command one another and will be partners, and there will no longer be any need for "government" but only for "administration." The repressive functions of the state are needed only when the majority of the population is exploited by the ruling class. With the abolition of exploitation the repressive functions of the state will disappear.[82] The social organization will have only one purpose: the fullest possible satisfaction of human needs and the increase of social wealth.

The rise of this system is not a utopian dream of an individual but the necessary outcome of the development of civilization during the last seven hundred years. Mankind has always moved in the direction of the industrial system, and, once constituted, "this system will be the *final system*."[83]

Saint-Simon's philosophy of history unquestionably exerted a great influence on the further development of evolutionary thinking in France, England, and Germany. There is a widespread belief that evolutionary ideas in France and in England were developed under German influence; it is important to stress that the exact opposite is true and that particularly after the July revolution (1831) Paris became the mecca of the liberals of all Europe and that many young Hegelians and members of the Young Germany movement were strongly influenced by the Saint-Simonians.[84]

With regard to the further development of the historical approach to political economy, it is particularly interesting to note that Friedrich List's "natural law of historical development," according to which social evolution must necessarily pass through definite stages—an idea readily accepted by the historical school of German economists—is of Saint-Simonian origin.[85] That Bruno Hildebrand, another German economist of the historical school, who propounded the theory of definite stages of economic development, derived his ideas from the Saint-Simonians has been pointed out by Johann Plenge.[86]

80 Saint-Simon, *Du système industriel*, first part, 81.

81. Saint-Simon, *Catéchisme politique des industriels*, 14.

82. Saint-Simon, *Catéchisme des industriels*, 44, 106. This passage foreshadows the Marxist theory of the 'withering away' of the state in the classless society. [The phrase, now widely used in English, has been rendered as 'dies out' in more recent translations of Engels, *Anti-Dühring*, 268 and its condensation into Engels, *Preface*, 321, which was for a long time the main introductory Marxist text in the German-speaking world. Grossman exaggerates: Saint-Simon argued that, instead of being dominant in government, in the future society the military and legal officials would be subordinate to the most capable administrators.]

83. Saint-Simon, *Catéchisme des industriels*, 166; see also 42.

84. See especially Hayek, "The Counter-revolution of Science," 283 and following; also Suhge, *Saint-Simonismus und Junges Deutschland*, 47, 87, and Shine, *Carlyle and the Saint-Simonians*, chapter 4.

85. Hayek, "The Counter-revolution of Science," 291.

86. Plenge, *Stammformen der vergleichenden Wirtschaftstheorie*, xv.

ରେ

A real pioneer was Simonde de Sismondi (1773–1842), who was not only a historian but also a remarkable theorist.[87] He made important contributions in various fields of economic theory and especially in his critique of the static, harmonistic conceptions of Ricardo, Jean-Baptiste Say, and [Thomas] Malthus. Against their abstract, deductive method, he insists upon experience, history, and observation.[88] Rejecting the prevailing glorification of free competition, Sismondi points to the crises of 1814 and 1818, the transformations in England during the first two decades of the nineteenth century, the poverty of the working class that grew out of free competition, the concentration of masses of workers in the new industrial centers, the flight from the soil, the growth of the slums, and the creation of the modern proletariat. This dark picture is very different from the rosy pictures painted by his contemporaries. More than that, Sismondi draws an equally dark view of the future in his first theory of crises. Crises, he argues, are not something accidental, the product of noneconomic factors such as drought or war, as Ricardo taught, but are storms necessarily resulting from the very nature of capitalism. They will become increasingly severe with the future development of capitalism. Since the purchasing power of the working class is never large enough to take all of one year's production, and since the productive power of industry grows more rapidly than the limited purchasing power of the workers, this gap must grow wider as capitalism develops.[89]

This is the point at which Sismondi's theory merges with his sociologizing of economics. Just as he gave a preview of future developments, so he also examined the past systematically; and in 1819 he offered the first general explanation of the development of the existing economic system of the most advanced countries (England and France) out of the conditions of the past—conditions that had by no means disappeared from the world. Modern capitalism is thus conceived as a sort of island in a sea of other, older forms of economy.

Sismondi traced the history of agriculture, for example, from patriarchal exploitation at the dawn of cultural history through slave exploitation in antiquity, serfdom in

---

87. See Grossman, "Simonde de Sismondi and His Economic Theories," in the present volume.

88. See the standard biography, Salis, *Sismondi, 1773–1842*, 407. While Saint-Simon had developed the historical, evolutionary theory, showing the transitory character of the existing social order, his economic critique of existing society remained unelaborated and lacking in precision. (See Henri See, *La notion de classes*, 6.) It was only Sismondi who completed the historical criticism by adding the elements of an economic critique of society, namely, the theories of concentration of capital, periodic crises, unemployment, economic exploitation, pauperism, and insecurity of the working masses—all necessarily resulting from the existing social organization. (See Grossman, "Simonde de Sismondi and His Economic Theories," 65.)

89. There are, of course, other important distinctions between Sismondi and his contemporaries. Thus, against Ricardo's differential land-rent theory, according to which rent arises from better soil but not from the less fruitful, Sismondi shows that even the worst land gives rise to rent. "All land," he said, "yields rent." Sismondi, *New Principles of Political Economy*, 229. [Sismondi expressed this idea but did not use the words Grossman attributes to him on the page he cites.] It is no wonder that Ricardo's disciple, McCulloch, bitterly attacked this work in the *Edinburgh Review*. [In fact, the anonymous review of books by Robert Owen, which included a critique of Sismondi, was written by Robert Torrens in 1819.]

the Middle Ages, *métayer* system (share farming) and corvée labor in the early modern period to modern capitalism, in which large-scale exploitation (*bail à ferme*) reveals its tremendous superiority over small-scale exploitation because the former can "substitute capital for human forces."[90] This superiority means that small-scale production will ultimately disappear. Sismondi then traces industrial production from the guild organization in the towns of the Middle Ages to the development of capitalism. He shows how the capitalist system follows from the separation of the independent handworker from the means of production. In its pure form this system would involve the coexistence of but two classes—the wage earners and the owners of the means of production. In actual fact, however, there still remains a third group held over from the earlier stage—the peasants and craftsmen.[91]

Underlying Sismondi's account of the historical development of agricultural and industrial production is his notion of the difference between dominant and subordinate economic forms. When specific institutions are carried over into a new system, their relation to the whole is altered, and a decisive change occurs in their function. Thus the once-dominant role of the peasant and craftsman has disappeared. What remains is merely a fragment of the past, occupying a subordinate role in the new capitalist economy.

Sismondi was also a pioneer historian. Before his work appeared, the history of medieval Italy was virtually unknown. To the eighteenth-century rationalists the Middle Ages appeared as an era of barbarism and darkness, of interest to none but antiquarians. Sismondi was one of the first to understand that the liberation of the medieval Italian towns prepared the foundation of bourgeois society in Italy earlier than anywhere else.[92] Sweeping aside the classical evaluation of these earlier economies as "irrational," he showed the historical justification for their existence. Each of these earlier systems grew spontaneously out of contemporary conditions, spread without compulsion, and eventually became a dominant form because, from the standpoint of the development of liberty, it represented an economic and social advance over its immediate predecessor. Only when the dominant system passed the peak of its development and creativity did it degenerate and become a hindrance to further progress. It then sought to maintain itself by force against the rise of new economic forms, only to be compelled to give way in the end to a new and more progressive system.[93] The economic development of man is thus not a mere succession of different economic systems but a development toward even greater progress and freedom.[94]

---

90. Sismondi, *New Principles of Political Economy*, 143–96. [The closest expression, in both the original French and the published English translation, to the text Grossman quotes is "Cultivation on the great scale . . . invents machines, in which the wind, fall of water, the expansion of steam, are substituted for the power of limbs." Ibid., 185.]

91. See Grossman, "Simonde de Sismondi and His Economic Theories," 41.

92. See Grossman, "Sismondi, Jean Charles Leonard Simonde de (1773–1842)," 69.

93. See Grossman, "Simonde de Sismondi and His Economic Theories," 77.

94. In a recent article, Anthony Babel criticizes Sismondi for failing to give a precise definition of progress. As a matter of fact, Babel failed to discover not only the definition but also the very conception itself, as outlined above. He does not see Sismondi's discussion of the historical sequence of progressively freer

Characteristic of Sismondi's insight is that he projected this historical development into the future. In view of the long process of the rise and decline of economic systems, he argues, we cannot assume that the existing bourgeois wage-labor system represents the final form of society.[95] On the contrary, we must assume that "our actual organization . . . the dependency of the worker" will also be transcended and replaced by a better system in the future.[96]

Sismondi is thus a forerunner of the Marxist doctrine of the historical development of different economic systems in the direction of a progressive unfolding of the forces of production. "It is one of the civilizing aspects of capital," Marx wrote, "that it extorts this surplus labor in a manner and in conditions that are more advantageous to social relations and to the creation of elements for a new and higher formation than was the case under the earlier forms of slavery; serfdom, etc."[97] What escaped Sismondi, however, was a realization of precisely which factors constitute the driving force of historical development. His investigations into the history of the free Italian towns from the twelfth to the sixteenth century convinced him that the characters of nations, their energy or weakness, their culture or backwardness, are not the products of climate or racial peculiarities but the results of social organization and political institutions. The real motive power of politics and the interdependence between politics and economics, however, he did not see.

Sismondi's doubts about the permanence of the capitalist system could not be forgiven by the representatives of the official doctrine. Among his contemporaries he was recognized chiefly as a historian and historian of literature. Later on, after 1850, the protagonists of social reform, exaggerating Sismondi's really limited faith in reform measures, hailed him as a precursor. But as a theorist he fell into oblivion for more than a century.

2. In England: James Steuart, Richard Jones, Karl Marx

Alongside the trend of thought linked with the French Revolution, another important movement grew out of the industrial revolution in England. Every year new technical processes were increasing the productivity of industry. The equilibrium of society was overthrown, to the detriment of the country districts and to the advantage of the towns, which were rapidly increasing both in number and in size. The workmen affected by the rapid introduction of machinery were in revolt against the novel conditions.[98] England was steadily moving away from the Continental type of agricultural nations, and this rapid process of differentiation demanded an explanation of its historical roots. "Why

---

economic systems as a whole and loses himself in a mass of details about technical, religious, or political progress. Babel, "La notion de progrès," 298 and following.

95. See Grossman, "Simonde de Sismondi and His Economic Theories," 111.

96. [Sismondi, *New Principles of Political Economy*, 558.]

97. Marx, *Capital*, vol. 3, 958.

98. Halévy, *Economic Life*, 79–80.

have not all civilized societies," wrote Lord Lauderdale, "derived equal benefit from them [that is, from the new technical inventions]—and what are the circumstances that retard the progress of industry in some countries, and that guide its direction in all?"[99]

The tremendous leap in production, on the other hand, particularly during and after the Napoleonic Wars, resulted in a marked increase in trade and extension of the world market. One of the consequences was the establishment of close economic and cultural contact between Western European capitalism and the more backward economies of southern and eastern Europe, South America, and, above all, Asia. A clear understanding by means of historical comparison was thus afforded of the different economic systems still existing in different parts of the world and of the changeability of specific economic institutions, such as property. These new insights, together with the influence of the French Revolution previously discussed,[100] inevitably led to a better understanding of the historical development of all social institutions and to the formulation of the inductive method in the field of history and economics, which in the field of history is associated with the name of Auguste Comte.[101]

⌀

The chief representative of evolutionary ideas in the field of economics in England is the Reverend Richard Jones; but the way was prepared for Jones by the work of Sir James Steuart (1712–80), whose *Inquiry into the Principles of Political Economy* reveals an evolutionary approach to economic problems. He argues that the "speculative person" or theorist must use not only deduction but also the inductive method grounded on observation. On the one hand, he must consider the universal factors—he must "become a citizen of the world."[102] In analyzing individual branches of the economy—population, agriculture, trade, industry, interest, or money—he cannot remain satisfied with mere description, "the nature of the work being a deduction of principles, not a collection of institutions."[103]

On the other hand, Steuart warns against too-easy generalizations that are not properly based on experience, against the "habit of running into what the French call

---

99. Lauderdale, *Inquiry into the Nature*, 304.

100. Ibid., compare with 196 and 200 in the present volume.

101. We need not spend any more time on Comte, because he made no contribution to the particular problem under discussion. In his remarks on the method of historical comparison he assumes the validity of the same law of evolution for all peoples, since he holds that they all go through the same successive stages. His three-stage theory, however, has nothing to do with the succession of constantly higher, objective economic systems but deals only with intellectual advances. Man's interpretation of facts advanced from the attribution of all phenomena to supernatural agencies to the use of metaphysical abstractions and finally to scientific laws of succession and similitude. The "law" of the three stages is thus no historical law at all. It offers no causal, genetic explanation of development but merely a schematic description of historical sequences. See lesson 48 in Comte, *Cours de philosophie positive*, vol. 4, 151–247; see also Maudit, *Auguste Comte et la science économique*, 89, and Krynska, *Entwicklung und Fortschritt*, 78.

102. Steuart, *Inquiry into the Principles*, 3.

103. Ibid., viii.

systèmes. These are no more than a chain of contingent consequences, drawn from a few fundamental maxims, adopted, perhaps, rashly."[104] "If one considers the variety . . . in different countries, in the distribution of property . . . of classes, [and so on] . . . one may conclude, that . . . principles, however universally true, may become quite ineffectual in practice."[105]

Political economy must be adjusted to these differences. That is why, in approaching political economy, Steuart conducts "himself through the great avenues of this extensive labyrinth" of facts "by this kind of historical clue,"[106] and he promises to treat the subject "in that order which the revolutions of the last centuries have pointed out as the most natural."[107]

In the second chapter of book I, entitled "Of the Spirit of a People," Steuart offers a sketch of the historical development of Europe "from the experience of what has happened."[108] The "great alteration in the affairs of Europe within these . . . centuries, by the discovery of America and the Indies," namely, the rise of industry and learning and the introduction of trade, led to the "dissolution of the feudal form of government" and the introduction of "civil and domestic liberty."[109] These, in turn, "produced wealth and credit; these again debts and taxes; and all together established a perfectly new system of political economy."[110] All these factors "have entirely altered the plan of government everywhere. . . . From feudal and military, it is become free and commercial."[111]

The social transformation has led, in turn, to corresponding changes in "the manners of Europe,"[112] and the two together are changing the spirit of the people, slowly, to be sure, but nonetheless unmistakably, when we compare any two succeeding generations.[113]

❧

The "sociologizing" of economic categories and institutions was carried through still more penetratingly and systematically by the Reverend Richard Jones (1790–1855), a man who has not been properly appreciated except by Marx.[114] Jones was the first

---

104. Ibid., ix
105. Ibid., 3.
106. Ibid., 16
107. Ibid., 150.
108. Ibid., 16.
109. Ibid., 150.
110. Ibid
111. Ibid., 10.
112. Ibid., 11.
113. Ibid.
114. Marx's evaluation is restated by Hilferding in "Aus der Vorgeschichte" and by Eric Roll in *History of Economic Thought*, 309–16. We have already noted that Marx never claimed credit for having first introduced the historical factor into political economy. He pointed, besides Sismondi, to two men: James Steuart (1767) and, even more important, Richard Jones (1831), who though ignorant of the Hegelian dialectic was thoroughly familiar with the historical conditions of earlier epochs and with the economic conditions of the backward spheres of eastern Europe and Asia. Jones, a friend of Malthus and his successor as a professor

Englishman to criticize the classical economists from the standpoint of the historical school. He sharply attacked their attempts to deduce economic laws valid for all times and all countries. He wrote:

> We must get comprehensive views of facts, that we may arrive at principles which are truly comprehensive. . . . [If] we determine to know as much as we can of the world as it has been, and of the world as it is, before we lay down general laws as to the economical habits and fortunes of mankind or of classes of men: there are open to us two sources of knowledge—history and statistics, the story of the past, and a detail of the present condition of the nations of the earth. [On the other hand, i]f we take a different method, if we snatch at general principles, and content ourselves with confined observations, two things will happen to us. First: what we call general principles will often be found to have no generality. . . . At every step of our further progress, we shall be obliged to confess [that they] are frequently false; and secondly . . .[115]

Jones was especially sharp in his criticism of the supposed universality of Ricardo's laws. He held that they have but limited historical validity, specifically only where Ricardo's presuppositions agree with the actual conditions. They are valid neither for the past nor for the future, because in different epochs the conditions change and no longer coincide with Ricardo's premises.[116]

This approach is genuinely epoch making when contrasted with the "eternal" laws of the classicists. Just before the publication of Jones's major work,[117] his friend William Whewell hailed him as the founder of the inductive system of political economy, in contrast to Ricardo, the master of the deductive method, and expected that Jones's book would *faire époque*.[118] Actually, the work received scant notice. Among the classical economists, only [John Ramsay] McCulloch gave it some attention, and he dismissed it as "superficial" and unimportant. John Stuart Mill describes Jones's "essay on distribution"[119] as a "copious repertory of valuable facts on the landed tenures of different countries"; Jones's evolutionary ideas are not mentioned.[120] Much more recently Böhm-Bawerk, in his history of economic theory, the third German edition of which appeared in 1914, that is, after the publication of Marx's study of Jones in his *Theories*

---

of economics at East India College, Haileybury, was an expert on Asiatic conditions, particularly in India, Persia and Turkey. In his *Essay on the Distribution of Wealth* (1831), book 1, "Rent," Jones lists as [the] source of his historical analysis in an appendix a copious literature about Asiatic and South American countries. Particularly amazing is the knowledge of Asiatic economic conditions that Jones revealed in a work published twenty years later, *Textbook of Lectures on the Political Economy of Nations*.

115. Jones, *Introductory Lecture on Political Economy*, 31–32. The extracts given above have been rearranged somewhat.

116. A theory of rent, for instance, based on the English type of land system, which assumes individual ownership and free competition, cannot be applied to oriental societies, in which joint ownership and absence of competition are the rule.

117. Jones, *Essay on the Distribution of Wealth*.

118. "*Faire époque*" means "make history."

119. [That is, *Essay on the Distribution of Wealth*.]

120. John Stuart Mill, *Principles of Political Economy*, 176.

of Surplus Value, could not say more than that Jones "contribute[s] nothing of great consequence to our subject."[121] Marian Bowley disposes of him briefly by saying that he "looked upon sociology as a branch of economics, thus revising Comte's treatment of economics as a branch of sociology," and that he "criticised the classics for ignoring the relativity of economic laws."[122]

Though Jones's influence on his immediate contemporaries was thus slight, he exercised a powerful indirect influence through Marx. He is one of the few economists of whom Marx speaks with deep acknowledgment, despite the fact that Jones, a friend of Malthus, was very conservative in his political thinking and rejected Ricardo's doctrine of the opposition of class interests in favor of a faith in class harmony.[123] Marx recognized the limited, bourgeois character of Jones's horizon but called him the last representative of the "true science of political economy"[124] and made a special analysis of each of his major works; we find in this analysis frequent references to Jones's superiority over the classical economists.[125]

Jones was not a theorist in the classical sense of developing categorical concepts by sharp, logical deduction from a given set of presuppositions. He was a historian. But unlike the discredited school of [Wilhelm] Roscher, who substituted for theoretical laws an unthinking, chronological accumulation of unanalyzed descriptive material, Jones considered it his function to test and correct the prevalent theories against actual historical developments and to formulate concrete experience into new theoretical viewpoints and categories. With Thomas Hodgskin, for example, he was one of the earliest opponents of McCulloch's wage-fund theory, which held that there is a special fund of fixed magnitude for the employment of workers. Unlike Hodgskin, however, whose critique (1825) of this theory was a beautiful exercise in logic, Jones went to history to show that such a wage fund never really existed in fact. Quite the contrary, given a fixed amount of capital, there is continual fluctuation between its constant (for machines and raw material) and its variable (for wages) elements.[126] To this important

---

121. Böhm-Bawerk, *Capital and Interest*, vol. 1, 69; see also the recent monograph of Hans Weber, *Richard Jones, and Marx*, "Economic Manuscript of 1861–63 [Notebooks XV to XX]."

122. Bowley, *Nassau Senior*, 40. We have already called attention to Eric Roll's discussion of Jones, which does benefit from Marx's analysis but does not discuss Jones's position with respect to our particular problem. Nai-Tuan Chao's thoroughgoing thesis deals only with Jones's system of political economy: his theory of production and distribution, rent, wages, and profit. Chao, "Richard Jones," 15 and following. Jones's evolutionary theories, particularly his theory of the succession of economic stages, are not mentioned.

123. Jones, *Essay on the Distribution of Wealth*, 328.

124. Marx, "Economic Manuscript of 1861–63 [Notebooks XV to XX]," 345.

125. For example: "Jones marks a substantial advance on Ricardo"; "It is here that Jones' superiority is most striking." Marx, "Economic Manuscript of 1861–63 [Notebooks XV to XX]," 322. "One can see what a great leap forward there was from Ramsay to Jones." Ibid., 344. Altogether, Marx devoted seventy pages to the discussion of Jones [in the third volume of the edition of *Theorien über den Mehrwert* edited by Karl Kautsky, which is now superseded by the *Collected Works* edition of Marx's economic manuscripts of 1861–1863; for the extensive discussion of Jones, see Marx, "Economic Manuscript of 1861–63 [Notebooks XV to XX]," 320–71].

126. "The amount of capital devoted to the maintenance of labour may vary, independently of any changes in the whole amount of capital." Jones, "Introductory Lecture on Political Economy," 52.

theoretical conclusion Marx appended the gloss: "This is an important point";[127] and he developed it still further in critical opposition to the classical school in the chapter on "The So-Called Labour Fund."[128]

Jones went still further. Whereas the wage-fund theory held that there is a rigid law of wages, that is, that wages can rise only if the number of workers decreases or if the amount of capital increases,[129] Jones showed by historical evidence that it is possible—and at given historical moments it actually occurs—that "great fluctuations in the amount of employment, and great consequent suffering, may sometimes be observed to become more frequent as capital becomes more plentiful."[130] This happens in the "periods of transitions of the labourers from dependence on one fund to dependence on another," that is to say, in the period of the transition from an economy of independent peasants and handicraftsmen to a system in which those groups become a propertyless proletariat.[131] Such a "transfer"—the loss of economic independence through the loss of ownership of the means of production—obviously cannot be accomplished without serious disturbances.[132] Marx commented that Jones had here hit upon the germ of the idea of "primitive accumulation," that is, the antecedent of capital formation, and had thus begun the necessary process of replacing the "absurd" and rationalistic notion of capital formation through "savings" by a more realistic and historically correct view.[133]

Even more important insights into the historical roots of the capitalist system are to be found in Jones's discussion of various systems of production. He was well aware of the fact that different systems have succeeded one another in the past and sought to work out their essential characteristics. The decisive factor in differentiating these various systems is *the way in which human labor is organized*. As this factor changes, the whole economic system changes. That is why Jones does not follow a chronological arrangement in describing the succession of economies but begins with the capitalist system as a yardstick with which to measure and differentiate earlier systems.

---

127. Marx, *Theorien über den Mehrwert*, vol. 3, 476. [Although it was not apparent to Grossman, this phrase is Kautsky's rather than Marx's. Marx prefaces the quotation from Jones with "Richard Jones sums up correctly in the following passage." See Marx, "Economic Manuscript of 1861–63 [Notebooks XV to XX]," 371.]

128. "It has been shown in the course of this inquiry that the capital is not a fixed magnitude." Marx, *Capital*, vol. 1, 758.

129. McCulloch, *Discourse on Political Economy*, 61–62.

130. Jones, "Introductory Lecture on Political Economy," 52.

131. "Transfer of the labouring cultivators to the pay of capitalists . . . Transfer of non-agricultural classes to the employ of capitalists." Ibid., 52–53. [Jones emphasizes "labouring cultivators."]

132. Ibid., 52–53. The uprising of propertyless peasants in Norfolk in the middle of the sixteenth century, when enclosures were made on a tremendous scale, is well known. This uprising was crushed, and "multitudes of dispossessed and impoverished villagers flocked to the towns." Gibbins, *Industrial History of England*, 88–89. It is not hard to see why it is just in this period there occurs for the first time in history the application of the word *proletarii* in the modern sense, to denote propertyless day laborers, wage workers, and "poore husbandmen" as a "fourth sort or classe" of society. See Thomas Smith, *De republica Anglorum*, book 1, chapter 24, 12–13.

133. "What Jones calls 'TRANSFER' here, is what I call 'primitive accumulation.'" Marx, "Economic Manuscript of 1861–63 [Notebooks XV to XX]," 336.

Like Sismondi, he considered the "transfer," that is, the separation of the once-independent producers (peasants and craftsmen) from their means of production, to be the necessary historical precondition for capitalism. Through the "transfer" process they became wage workers dependent on the capitalist. "The first capitalist employers," he wrote, "those who first advance the wages of labour from accumulated stock, and seek . . . profits . . . have been ordinarily a class distinct from the labourers themselves."[134] This development had so far been limited pretty much to England,[135] and even there it was historically a late phenomenon.[136] In previous centuries the handworkers were supported not by advances from capital but by land revenue, "the surplus produce" of the land.[137] This surplus produce "may be handed over to individual landowners" or it "may be paid to the state."[138] In the latter case "the wages of such workmen were obviously derived directly from the revenue of their great customer, and not from an intermediate class of capitalists," and it "is in Asia that we observe this particular fund . . . in full and continued . . . predominance."[139] In Europe the number of workers paid out of land revenues is still large but no longer predominant, and "in England itself, . . . the body is comparatively small."[140]

Jones shows the superiority of the capitalist system over preceding forms. In China and throughout the East, for example, tailors and other artisans wander all over the city, day in and day out, seeking work in their customers' homes, and thus waste a great deal of time, while under capitalism the workers became sedentary and "can now labour continuously." Finally, on this basis, where one capitalist employs many workers, an organized division of labor becomes possible.[141]

It is on the basis of such concrete historical material that Jones developed his idea of the *sequence of economies through which every nation must pass, though at different tempos* according to their varying conditions. After a given economy becomes dominant, it begins to lose that position while still remaining very widespread, and it slowly becomes more and more subordinate to a new form. When Jones says that "England is much in advance of other nations," he does not mean that English conditions are better but merely that "in arriving at our present position, we have passed through and gone beyond those, at which we see other nations. . . . *The future of all other people will, however, at some time, be like our present.*" This succession theory has exceedingly broad implications, as he himself recognized: "the prophecy is bold."[142] Following Condorcet, he sees an easier road ahead for the younger nations. They have "better hopes for the future" because "if they assume our economic organisation and power,

134. Jones, *Textbook of Lectures on the Political Economy of Nations*, 444–45.
135. Jones, "Introductory Lecture on Political Economy," 52.
136. Jones, *Textbook of Lectures on the Political Economy of Nations*, 454.
137. Ibid., 440.
138. Ibid.
139. Ibid., 442, 444.
140. Ibid., 443.
141. Ibid., 395, 396, 397, 455. [Jones emphasized "can."]
142. Jones, "Introductory Lecture on Political Economy," 19, 21. Italics are mine.

[they] may escape many of the evils that have afflicted our progress, or from which we suffer now."[143]

Jones goes still further. Not only does he predict that every nation must ultimately attain the highest economic form so far developed—capitalism—but he sees the possibility of still further development in the future to a socialized form of production in which the separation of the wage worker from the means of production will be ended. Capitalism is thus a historical and transitory, though necessary, stage on the road to a more advanced economy of the future.

> A state of things may hereafter exist, and parts of the world may be approaching to it, under which the labourers and the owners of accumulated stock, may be identical; but in the progress of nations, which we are now observing, this has never yet been the case. . . . [The present system in which] a body of employers pay the workers by advances of capital . . . may not be as desirable a state of things as that in which labourers and capitalists are identified; but we must still accept it as constituting a stage in the march of industry, which has hitherto marked the progress of advancing nations.[144]

Having shown the way in which historical economies succeed one another, Jones then tried to differentiate those elements in the economy that are particularly active and decisive in the process of transformation from the more passive and secondary ones. He was not interested in the traditional categories of political economy—profit, rent, wages, and so on—but in the changes in production insofar as they influence the growth of productive power and the character of the economy itself. His study of history led him to the conclusion that "changes in the economical structure of nations" teach us to understand the secrets of ancient and of modern history;[145] on the other hand, that changes in the structure of the economy are closely linked with changes in the institution of property, and that the differing property relations correspond to different stages in the development of productive power.[146] For Jones, therefore, the

> economical structure of nations [is made up of] relations between the different classes which are established in the first instance by the institution of property in the soil, and by the distribution of its surplus produce; afterwards modified and changed (to a greater or lesser extent) by the introduction of capitalists, as agents in . . . feeding and employing the labouring population. . . . An accurate knowledge of that structure can alone give us the key to the past fortunes of the different people of the earth, by displaying their economical anatomy, and showing thus, the most deeply-seated sources of their strength, the elements of their institutions, and causes of their habits and character. It is thus we must learn the circumstances which divide them into classes.[147]

---

143. Jones, *Textbook of Lectures on the Political Economy of Nations*, 412.
144. Ibid., 445. [Grossman's interpolation, reduced by words from Jones's text that are part of the quotation.]
145. Jones, "Introductory Lecture on Political Economy," 34.
146. Marx, "Economic Manuscript of 1861–63 [Notebooks XV to XX]," 321.
147. Jones, "Introductory Lecture on Political Economy," 21–22. With the expression "economical anatomy" Jones foreshadows the famous phrase of Marx in the preface to the *Critique of Political Economy* that legal relations and forms of state cannot be understood by themselves and that they are rooted in material

In other words, the economic structure, as thus defined, is the key to social relationships:

> There is a close connection between the economical and social organisation of nations. . . . Great political, social, moral, and intellectual changes, accompany changes in the economical organisation of communities. . . . These changes necessarily exercise a commanding influence over the different political and social elements to be found in the populations where they take place: that influence extends to the intellectual character, to the habits, manners, morals, and happiness of nations.[148]
>
> As communities change their powers of production, they necessarily change their habits too. During their progress in advance, all the different classes of the community find that they are connected with other classes by new relations, are assuming new positions, and are surrounded by new moral and social dangers, and new conditions of social and political excellence.[149]

This superstructure, in turn, "react[s] on the productive capacities of the body."[150]

Only after he has shown the historical relationship of capitalism to earlier systems does Jones turn to the problem of modern land rent. Here, too, he resorts to historical study and shows how modern ground rent developed out of earlier forms. Rent takes on a completely different character within each economy. In one case it is the dominant institution; in another it becomes subordinate to capital, and the landowning class no longer participates directly in production. Jones differentiates five historical types of rent: (1) labor rent, that is, slave and serf rent; (2) an intermediate form of rent, which is the transition from type 1 to type 3; (3) rent in kind; (4) money rent of the precapitalist period; and, finally (5) in the capitalist period, farmer's rent (in the Ricardian sense). The latter differs from all others and can exist only in a society based on the capitalist mode of production, because rent, as a surplus above the average profit, requires as its precondition the development of the industrial average profit rate. In sum, every specific form of property has its corresponding form of labor and of rent.[151]

Jones rejected Ricardo's theory of a "continuous diminution in the returns to agriculture, of its assumed effects on the progress of accumulation."[152] By historical illustrations he showed that rents were actually highest in countries where agriculture was very productive, and he thus destroyed the *historical basis* of Ricardo's theory of rent. As the classical theory of profits and wages was closely connected with the theory of

---

conditions of life—that "the anatomy of this civil society . . . has to be sought in political economy." Marx, *Contribution to the Critique*, 262. It was Sir William Petty who first (1672) introduced the expression "political anatomy" to denote the knowledge of the economic structure of a country, its "symmetry, Fabrick and Proportion," as the basis for understanding the "Body Politick." Petty, *The Political Anatomy of Ireland*, 129.

148. Jones, *Textbook of Lectures on the Political Economy of Nations*, 405–6. Rearranged.

149. Ibid., 410–11.

150. Ibid., 406. [Editor's interpolation.]

151. Ibid., 185, 188. Marx points out that in Jones's work *On Rent* (1831 [that is, *On the Distribution of Wealth*]) he starts with the different forms of real property, whereas two years later in his "Syllabus" he analyzes the different forms of labor that correspond to those types of property. Jones "A Syllabus of a Course"; Marx, "Economic Manuscript of 1861–63 [Notebooks XV to XX]," 321.

152. Jones, *Textbook of Lectures on the Political Economy of Nations*, xiii.

rent, the collapse of the latter endangered the classical theory as a whole.

It is not hard to see why Jones earned the enmity of the classical school and, on the other hand, the strong approbation of Marx. Jones, the latter wrote, is characterized "by what has been lacking in all English economists since Sir James Steuart, namely, a sense of the historical differences in modes of production."[153] "What distinguishes Jones from the other economists (except perhaps Sismondi) is that he emphasizes that the essential feature of capital is its socially determined form [*Formbestimmtheit*]."[154] Probably the highest praise Marx could give Jones was to contrast his presentation of genetic developments with Ricardo, who "developed nothing."[155]

It is worth noting here the emphasis placed by John Stuart Mill on the intellectual backwardness of England—the country that in his judgment was "usually the last to enter the general movement of the European mind."[156] Mill underscored the charge that, whereas "the doctrine that . . . the course of history is subject to general laws . . . has been familiar for generations to the scientific thinkers of the Continent" (France), it was opposed in England well into the second half of the nineteenth century because it conflicted with "the doctrine of Free Will."[157] The fate of the new science of geology is particularly revealing in this context. The foundation for a rational evolutionary system of geology was laid in Italy by [Cirillo] Generelli, a Carmelite friar, in 1749; in France by [Nicolas] Desmarest (1777) and [Jean-Baptiste] Lamarck (1802); in England by [James] Hutton (1785). Hutton, however, was accused of heresy; evolutionary ideas were condemned as incompatible with the biblical account of Genesis.

It was in such an antievolutionary atmosphere that Jones, like Sismondi before him, had the courage to attack the whole structure of the classical economists, not merely specific doctrines, and to cast doubts upon the permanence of the capitalist system. Their critique of the existing economic order, their emphasis upon its historical, transitory character, was considered a heresy, which could not be forgiven. *As theorists*, both men were ignored by the representatives of the dominant school and left in oblivion for nearly a century.

સ્ર

It is apparent that by the time Karl Marx (1818–83) began his work in the forties of the last century, the application of evolutionary concepts to economic institutions and the formulation of the doctrine that economic systems are historical in character had been

---

153. Marx, "Economic Manuscript of 1861–63 [Notebooks XV to XX]," 320. [Marx emphasized "historical."]

154. Ibid., 341. [In the original published version the word *Formgestimmtheit* was used, a typographical error not apparent in a late draft of the translation of the article.]

155. Marx, *Theorien über den Mehrwert*, vol. 3, 451, and following. [The phrase quoted is not present at the points indicated by Grossman in either Kautsky's edition or the 1991 *Collected Works* edition, although Marx writes there that "Jones' analysis . . . distinguishes him from, and shows his superiority over, all his predecessors." Marx, "Economic Manuscript of 1861–63 [Notebooks XV to XX]," 321.]

156. John Stuart Mill, *A System of Logic*, 643.

157. Ibid., 644.

basically accomplished. Marx himself pointed that out repeatedly, though it was left to him to complete and sharpen the analysis. He took over the heritage of Saint-Simon and Sismondi in France, of James Steuart and Richard Jones in England, and of certain elements in Hegel's philosophy of history, and introducing certain new ideas of his own created an integrated, original theory.

We need not underline the point and we assume it as well known that for Marx the Hegelian "development" meant something quite different from what the eighteenth-century Enlightenment, the Saint-Simonians, or even Sismondi, Jones, and positivists like Auguste Comte understood by this term. To men oriented to the natural sciences of their day, development meant nothing more than the generalization of an empirically and inductively constructed series of particular observations,[158] whereas Marx, like Hegel, understood the relationship between the particular and the universal quite differently, viewing the historical "object" as made up not of individual observations but of the "*cultural whole*" of social-collective unities.[159] Using the genetic method of the dialectic, with its constant creation and synthesis of opposites, Marx sought to grasp the evolution of these collective unities in their historical necessity. Every present moment contains both the past, which has led to it logically and historically, and the elements of further development in the future.

At the same time there is a fundamental point at which Marx is joined with Sismondi and Jones against Hegel—one that must not be overlooked in ascribing the "historicizing" of economics to Hegelian influence. For the former, historical development, occurring in the external world in time, is a succession of objective economic stages of different economic structures whereby the higher stage develops out of the lower. In other words, history does not have a relativistic character; it does not depend on the accident of the observer's point of view, ideals, or standards. What Marx did was to remove the study of history from that subjective level to a higher one, where objective, measurable stages of development are perceived. He fulfilled Saint-Simon's hope of making history a science.

Hegel was flatly opposed to such a doctrine. The German word *Entwicklung* has two different meanings, translated into English (and French) by two distinct words—"development" and "evolution." Hegel always used the term in the first sense, meaning the unfolding and dissection of the various component elements (*Gedankenbestimmungen*) contained in the *Begriff* ("notion of the essentials of a thing"). Development is possible only under the rule of the *Begriff* and *hence takes place in the sphere of logic*. "Metamorphosis," Hegel wrote, "pertains only to the Notion as such [that is, to the notion of the essential in contrast to the notion of phenomena], since only its alteration is develop-

---

158. See Troeltsch, *Die Dynamik der Geschichte*, 6–7. From the antipositivists' viewpoint the relationship between the particular and the universal is presented in the excellent book by Cohen, *Reason and Nature*, 161.
159. "Just as generally in the case of any historical, social science, so also in examining the development of economic categories it is always necessary to remember that the subject [is] . . . modern bourgeois society," Marx, "Introduction," 43. [Marx does not seem to have used the phrase "cultural whole" or "cultural totality."]

ment."[160] Hegel therefore attacked the concept of the natural philosophers (and thus also of the sociologists) that evolution as an objective process in history is the "external real production" of a higher stage from a lower one. He insisted, on the contrary, that it is the "the dialectical Notion which leads forward the stages, is the *inner side* of them."[161] That is why in *The Philosophy of History* he saw the various stages in world history not as an objective process in the *sphere of real history* but as a process within the *sphere of logic*.[162] World history is to Hegel the progress within man's *consciousness* of the idea of freedom, and it is this development of consciousness that determines the four principal levels achieved by the various peoples: the oriental world, the Greek, the Roman, and the Germanic world.[163]

Marx, on the contrary, uses the term *Entwicklung* mostly in the second sense, meaning not development within the sphere of *logic* but, like Sismondi and Richard Jones, evolution as an objective process in the sphere of *real history*.[164]

With such a point of view, writes [Georg] Lasson, "Hegel *must* reject the theory of [biological] evolution. Long before Darwin he had discarded all of Darwinism as an unclear confusion of the *notion* and external *existence*."[165] Hegel himself said of the idea of evolution as an objective process in the external world: "A thinking consideration must reject such nebulous . . . ideas as in particular the so-called . . . origination of the more highly developed animal organisms from the lower and so on."[166]

Marx, on the contrary, accepts the idea of the rise of more developed structures from the lower, and for this reason he was one of the first to acknowledge the importance of Darwin's work. In a similar way, as Darwin uses nature's technology, that is, the formation of the organs of plants and animals, as instruments to explain the origin and development of species, Marx wishes to use the history of human technology as an instrument "that *distinguishes different economic epochs*,"[167] as the "productive organs of man in society . . . are the material basis of every particular organisation of society"[168] and the "instruments of labour . . . supply a *standard of the degree of development* which human labour has attained."[169]

---

160. Hegel, *Hegel's Philosophy of Nature*, 20, paragraph 249. [Hegel emphasised '*Metamorphosis*' and '*its*'].

161. Ibid. Italics are mine [Hegel emphasized "stages."]

162. Hegel, *Lectures on the Philosophy of History*, 58–59.

163. Ibid., 109–116, and Fischer, *Hegels Leben, Werke und Lehre*, 748.

164. For that very reason Marx directs his criticism against Proudhon's notion of evolution: Proudhon, he says, has accepted the "Hegelian trash" and is "unable to follow the real course of history. . . . The evolutions of which Mr Proudhon speaks are presumed to be evolutions such as take place in the mystical bosom of the absolute idea." Marx to Pavel Vasilyevich Annenkov, December 28, 1846, 97, and Marx, *The Poverty of Philosophy*, 168, 169.

165. Lasson, foreword to *Enzyklopädie der philosophischen Wissenschaften*, xvii.

166. Hegel, *Hegel's Philosophy of Nature*, 20, paragraph 249. [Hegel emphasized "origination."] See also Renouvier, *Les principes de la nature*, 271.

167. Marx, *Capital*, vol. 1, 286. [Grossman's emphasis.] Long before the publication of Darwin's work, in one of his earliest works—the 1847 critique of Proudhon (1847 [[*The Poverty of Philosophy*])—Marx had already emphasized the fundamental significance of human technology for the characteristics of a given society.

168. Marx, *Capital*, vol. 1, 493.

169. Ibid., 286. [Grossman's emphasis.] Alongside this technological factor, the social factor is equally significant for the distinction of economic epochs from one another, namely, "the particular form and mode in

In sum, Marx refuses to follow Hegel on the basic question of the concept of de-velopment but works rather from the conception of Sismondi and Richard Jones. For Marx, evolution is an objective process of history whereby each historical period or social structure is *marked by specific objective tendencies*[170] that can be discovered from the nature of the technological instruments and from the social organization of labor in the use of those instruments.[171]

From the basic point of view, Marx saw that the history of economic organization is a series of economies, each more advanced than its predecessor because of changes in the method of production: "In broad outline, the Asiatic, ancient, feudal and modern bourgeois modes of production may be designated as epochs marking progress in the economic development of society."[172]

Throughout Marx's writings there are scattered but nonetheless profound charac-terizations of each of these epochs.[173] His main efforts, however, were not directed to the precapitalist forms but to a systematic analysis of the genesis and development of the specific historical phases of capitalism[174] and to the transition from capitalism to socialism.[175] Marx views "the development of the economic formation of society . . . as a process of natural history,"[176] and his aim "lies in the illumination of the special laws that regulate the origin, existence, development and death of a given social organism and its replacement by another, higher one"[177] whereby society "can neither leap over the natural phases of its development nor remove them by decree. But it can shorten and lessen the birth-pangs."[178]

---

which this connection [between laborers and means of production] is effected." Marx, *Capital*, vol. 2, 120.

170. As early as 1847 Marx wrote, against Proudhon: "The hand-mill gives you society with the feudal lord; the steam-mill, society with the industrial capitalist." Marx, *The Poverty of Philosophy*, 166.

171. Elsewhere, in the section "The Capitalistic Character of Manufacture," Marx differentiates the specific tendencies of the manufacturing period from the trends under industrial capitalism and lays the basis for the differences in the fact that "in manufacture the transformation of the mode of production takes *labour power* as its starting point. In large-scale industry, on the other hand, the *instruments* of labour are the starting point." Marx, *Capital*, vol. 1, 492. [Grossman's emphasis. This quotation, and Marx's discussion of the difference between manufacture and large-scale industry, actually comes from the following section, the first in the next chapter of *Capital*.]

172. Marx, *Contribution to the Critique*, 263.

173. Thus he contrasted the unceasing technical revolutionizing of our economy with the *static economic structure of Asiatic societies*, notably India, and saw the explanation in the fact that production was there orga-nized in self-sufficing communities "based on possession of land in common, on the blending of agriculture and handicrafts and on an unalterable division of labour." Marx, *Capital*, vol. 1, 477–78. In this connection the form of taxes, namely, taxes in kind, played an important role. Ibid., 239. In countries where central governments, by the use of artificial irrigation, made it possible to transform deserts into fertile fields, "a single war of devastation has been able to depopulate a country for centuries, and to strip it of all its civili-zation." Marx, "The British Rule in India," 127.

174. For a good historical application of Marx's theory of the earlier stages of capitalism, see Pirenne, "Stages in the Social History."

175. Marx, *Critique of the Gotha Program*.

176. Marx, *Capital*, vol. 1, 92.

177. Ibid., 102.

178. Ibid., 92.

Marx showed, for instance, that industrial capitalism did not develop out of hand-icraft or out of accumulated rent from landed property (as Max Weber and Sombart later taught) but from the merchant. The latter, by progressively subordinating the production of the craftsman and transforming him into a proletarian, brought about the transition from mercantile to industrial capitalism. Starting with the decentralized workshop under the command of the merchant capitalist (domestic system), produc-tion moved into the various phases of the period of manufacture (cooperative, hetero-geneous, and organic manufactures) and finally into modern large-scale industry based on the machine. Marx did not stop with the delineation of the broad lines of historical development, however. He continued the application of the genetic method to the in-dividual organs, institutions, and functions of the capitalist mechanism.

We cannot go into the details of Marx's historical analysis. The important point to emphasize is that Marx never remained within the narrow framework of historical description but always made use of historical insights to deepen his theoretical under-standing of the laws of development. *This close link between history and theory* is one of the factors that differentiates Marx from all his predecessors. An example will serve to illustrate this point. A study of the demography of antiquity, the Middle Ages, and the modern world led Marx to the insight that there is no universally valid law of population, as Malthus had taught, but that the modern trend toward the creation of a relatively surplus population "is a law of population peculiar to the capitalist mode of production; and in fact every particular historical mode of production has its own special laws of population, which are historically valid within that particular sphere."[179]

This type of historical analysis also led to important conclusions in economic the-ory. When Sombart raises the accusation that Marx "hardly ever *defines* . . . his con-cepts . . . such as capital, factory, plant, accumulation," he shows that he misses the true sense of Marx's historicism and even of Marxist terminology: he uses the word *Begriff* in the sense of "definition"; the word "concept" or "notion," however, is used by Marx in the specifically Hegelian sense as the notion of the essence of a thing, as contrasted with the definition as merely the notion of the phenomena.[180]

Marx rejects the view that knowledge consists in classifying and defining and that the task of science is simply to discover a rational criterion for classification. This is the static approach of the classicists, looking upon social phenomena as unchangeable structures. Marx, on the other hand, is a spokesman of the new, dynamic approach. That is why social phenomena, in his judgment, are actually indefinable. They have no "fixed" or "eternal" elements or character but are subject to constant change. A definition fixes the superficial attributes of a thing at any given moment or period and thus transforms these attributes into something permanent and unchanging.[181] To understand things it

---

179. Ibid., 783–84.
180. Sombart, *Das Lebenswerk von Karl Marx*, 52.
181. Marx made his point of view quite clear in his polemic against Cherbuliez: "Previously profit ought to have been explained. But nothing emerged except a DEFINITION of it which merely states the form in which it appears . . . a statement that profit and rate of profit exist, without, however, anything being said

is necessary to grasp them genetically, in their successive transformations, and thus to discover their essence, their "notion" (*Begriff*). It is only a pseudoscience that is satisfied with definitions and the phenomenal aspects of things.[182] Without devoting more space to a characterization of Marx's analysis, we turn to an examination of the fruits of his analysis. By attributing to Marx the first application of evolutionary thinking to economics, critics have obliterated the original contribution that Marx really did make to our understanding of history and the specific differences between Marx and his predecessors. They have reduced his historical conceptions to a level that does not go beyond the horizon of bourgeois liberalism, that is, beyond the idea of evolution in the direction of constant progress "from the incomplete to the complete"—to quote Hegel.

∝

The fundamental characteristic of Marx's historicism and the mark that distinguishes it from his predecessors is not the doctrine of the historical succession of economic systems but a special theory that, in addition to evolutionary changes *within* a given system, explains the objective and subjective conditions necessary for the *transition from one system to another*. Briefly stated, it is that within the existing economy a new economic form arises and grows, that the two enter into ever-sharper conflict with each other and that through the violent resolution of the conflict the new economy finally takes over.

Within this general theory there are three special theories: (1) a doctrine of a "universal social dynamic" of structural changes in society, valid for all "antagonistic" societies; (2) the theory of the *objective developmental tendencies of capitalism;* and (3) the theory of the subjective bearer of change, that is, the class-struggle theory. Obviously, the second, unlike the two others, deals only with the special historical phenomenon of the transformation from capitalism to socialism. Like Condorcet and Saint-Simon, Marx teaches that the idea of evolution must be applied to the future as well as to the past, for one must seek in the perceptible structural changes of the present the lines of future development.[183]

---

about their nature." Marx, "Economic Manuscript of 1861–63 [Notebooks XV to XXI," 296–97. Elsewhere, in speaking of the economists, Marx says that their "definitions . . . are expanded into trivial tautologies," whereas the task of science is not the construction of abstract definitions but "by way of thinking . . . the *reproduction of the concrete*." Marx, 'Introduction,' 24, 38. [Grossman's emphasis.] There are, therefore, no "eternal" economic categories; every category is only "the theoretical expression of historical relations of production, corresponding to a particular stage of development in material production." Marx, "On Proudhon," 29. [Marx emphasized the entire text.]

182. "The vulgar economists confine themselves to systematising [the phenomena] in a pedantic way, and proclaiming [them] for everlasting truths." Marx, *Capital*, vol. 1, 175. [The second interpolation is Grossman's; the first is made necessary by the difference between this and the translation of *Capital* Grossman used.]

183. As early as 1843, Marx wrote to Arnold Ruge that we must not be concerned with "constructing the future" or "dogmatically anticipat[ing] the world, but only want to find the new world through criticism of the old one." Marx, "Economic and Philosophic Manuscripts of 1844," 142. [Editor's interpolation.] Twenty years later Marx wrote to Schweitzer that Proudhon and the utopians were hunting for a "science" by which

We have already seen that Saint-Simon and his school knew that the industrial system grew up within, and as a bitter enemy of, the feudal system of the later Middle Ages. For the Saint-Simonians, however, this insight was no more than a singular historical observation. Marx developed this observation into what we might call a universal birth story of a social system. Every new economic system, he taught, is born directly within the old and goes through a long process of maturation before it can displace its predecessor and become dominant. "New superior relations of production never replace older ones before the material conditions for their existence have matured within the framework of the old society."[184] The displacement of the old system by the new is not an arbitrary process to be accomplished at any chance moment. It requires the existence and slow maturation of certain necessary subjective and objective factors.[185]

For the first time in the history of ideas we encounter a theory that combines the evolutionary and revolutionary elements in an original manner to form a meaningful unit. Gradual changes in the productive forces lead at some point in the process to sudden changes in the social relations of production, that is to say, to political revolution. By underlining the evolutionary aspects, Marxism sharply distinguishes itself from the voluntarism of the utopian socialists as well as from the pseudorevolutionarism of putschists or partisans of the coup d'état. At the same time, Marxism does not give up the idea of revolution but regards it as the necessary conclusion of the evolutionary process and as the instrument for achieving the transition to a new economic structure. This theory rests primarily on the fact that productive forces, legal property relations, and political power are subject to the law of uneven development.

Changes in the productive forces release a relatively rapid and dynamic element, out of which grows the assault against the structure of the old society as a whole. Legal property relations, on the other hand, and political power, which rests upon them, constitute the passive, conservative, static element, guarding the existing society against change. The latter element changes slowly, long after the changes in the productive forces and as the result of those changes. The new economic forces thus clash with the antiquated political and property relations, which no longer correspond to the new needs and fetter further progress. "Then begins an era of social revolution," in which the antiquated legal and political relations are broken and replaced by new ones that are appropriate to the new economic forces.[186] Since the antiquated laws express only the vested interests of their creators, and since these will never voluntarily renounce their

---

the social question was to be solved a priori "instead of deriving their science from *a critical knowledge of the historical movement*, a movement which itself produces the material conditions of emancipation." Marx, "On Proudhon," 29. [Grossman's emphasis; Marx emphasized "material conditions of emancipation."]

184. Marx, *Contribution to the Critique*, 263. Elsewhere Marx emphasized, (May 1871) that the working class can expect no "ready-made utopias. . . . They have no ideals to realize, but to set free elements of the new society with which the old collapsing bourgeois society itself is pregnant." Marx, *The Civil War in France*, 335.

185. "They [the working class] know that in order to work out their own emancipation . . . they will have to pass through long struggles, through a series of historic processes, transforming completely circumstances and men." Marx, *The Civil War in France*, 335.

186. Marx, *Contribution to the Critique*, 263.

privileges, the disappearance of the old laws entails the disappearance of their creators, the former ruling classes.

In his second special theory, dealing with *the objective developmental trends within capitalism*, "the natural laws of its movement," Marx tries to show that there is a limit to the development of capitalism: that it must reach a peak after which a *declining phase* will set in, and that at a certain point the further functioning of the system will become impossible and its collapse inevitable.[187] The system must be transformed not only because the working people reject it but also because the ruling classes cannot find any way out. During this critical period, despite progress in restricted sectors (technology, chemistry), the system as a whole loses its progressive character, and the symptoms of its disintegration grow more and more numerous; the system becomes a fetter on further development and can preserve itself only by violence and increasingly severe repression of the newly emerging social forces. In the end, however, it must be defeated in the conflict with these forces and yield to them. Thus progress is achieved only at the price of the misery and humiliation of individuals and entire peoples.

No predecessor of Marx had a similar theory. It is true that the Saint-Simonians wanted to make history an exact science and conceived the future to be a necessary product of the past, but they never got beyond the mere postulate and never attempted to work out a theory of the future tendencies of capitalism. Nor did Sismondi or Richard Jones. Their prediction that capitalism would be replaced by a higher form of economy did not rest upon theoretical arguments but merely on historical analogy: since all previous economic systems were transitory, they argued, we must assume the same to be true of capitalism.

Marx undertook to demonstrate the historical necessity of the decline and final disintegration of capitalism. When the process of accumulation reaches a certain point, he shows, there will be a transformation of quantity into quality. A condition of over-saturation with capital will arise, and no adequate new possibility for capital investment will be available. All further accumulation of capital will become impossible, and society will enter a permanent period of growing accumulation of idle capital, on the one hand, and of large-scale permanent unemployment on the other. Thus the process of disintegration will begin. The property owners' fear of losing their privileges gives the spiritual and political life of this period a reactionary character. In short, the whole structure of capitalism will be shaken to its roots, and the basis will have been laid for great political and economic transformations.[188] It is true, of course, that Bazard and

---

187. Marx, *Capital*, vol. 1, 92. It must be stressed that Marx does not use the word "trend" or "tendencies" in the usual sense of the term; by "trend" he means "tendencies winning their way through and working themselves out *with iron necessity*." Ibid., 91. [Grossman's emphasis.] The other factors and countertrends can weaken or slow up the dominant trend but not prevent it from asserting itself. Elsewhere Marx speaks about "that higher form to which present society is *irresistibly tending* by its own economical agencies." Marx, *The Civil War in France*, 335. [Grossman's emphasis.]

188. For a detailed study of this theoretical analysis, see Grossmann, *Das Akkumulations- und Zusammenbruchsgesetz*.

later Pecqueur, following Sismondi, foresaw the crises, the misery, and the uncertainty of the working class. These insights remained mere particular observations with them, however, and not, as with Marx, elements of a steadily worsening disease of the system from epoch to epoch that would lead to ultimate paralysis.

The third element in Marx's general theory is that no economic system, no matter how weakened, collapses by itself in automatic fashion. It must be overthrown. The theoretical analysis of the objective trends leading to a paralysis of the system serves to discover the "weak links" and to fix them in time as a sort of barometer indicating when the system becomes ripe for change. Even when that point is reached, change will come about only through active operation of the subjective factors. This part of the theory Marx developed in his study of the class struggle. Marx has frequently been charged with a "fatalistic" theory of the "historical necessity" of social development in some given direction. Such a charge rests on a serious misunderstanding of the theory of the class struggle. In all his writings Marx characteristically emphasizes the unity of theory and practice. This so-called "historical necessity" does not operate automatically but requires the active participation of the working class in the historical process. This participation, however, is itself not something arbitrary but follows from the pressure of the objective factors. The student of history and the forward-looking practical politician must therefore consider this subjective factor as in fact another objective condition of the historical process.[189]

While, for instance, Saint-Simon and his school do not give the working class any political role in the transformation of society, the main result of Marx's doctrine is the clarification of the historical role of the proletariat as the carrier of the transformative principle and the creator of the socialist society. To Marx, activity is an integral part of thinking, and truth cannot be discovered by a merely contemplative attitude but only by action. This is the meaning of Marx's eleventh thesis on Feuerbach: "The philosophers have only interpreted the world in various ways; the point is to change it."[190] If philosophers from Montesquieu to Feuerbach taught that man is a product of his natural and social environment, Marx observes that to an even greater extent man is influenced by his action on his environment. In changing the historical *object*, the *subject* changes himself.[191] Thus the education of the working class to its historical mission must be achieved not through theories brought in from outside but by the everyday practice of the class struggle. This is not a doctrine but a practical process of existing conflicts of interests in which doctrines are tested and accepted or discarded. Only through these struggles does the working class change and reeducate itself and become conscious of

---

189. Of course, class struggle is not to be understood in the primitive sense that the workers must blindly attack the entrepreneur class wherever the two come into contact. Both the content and the form of the class conflicts are themselves determined by the attained level of historical development and by the concrete historical situation.

190. [Marx, "Theses on Feuerbach," 5. Marx emphasized "interpreted" and "change."]

191. Marx, *Capital*, vol. 1, 283.

itself. Marx's attack on the "*fatalist* economists"[192] is only an illustration of the fact that his dialectical concept of history has a twofold significance. In this he follows Hegel, for whom history has both an objective and a subjective meaning, the history of human activity (*historia rerum gestarum*) and human activity itself (*res gestas*).[193] The dialectical concept of history is not merely an instrument with which to explain history but also an instrument with which to make history. "Men make their own history, but they do not make it . . . under circumstances chosen by themselves, but under circumstances directly encountered, given and transmitted from the past."[194]

It is in this double sense that the Marxist theory of the class struggle is to be understood. On the one hand, it is an expression of the existing conflict of interests between classes. At the same time, it transcends the mere statement of an existing factual condition, not as a fatalistic expectation of evolution but as a guide to the active participation of the working class in the historical process. By this activity the objective tendencies can be realized and the forces of a reactionary but powerful minority that stand in the way of further development and progress overcome. In this latter sense the class struggle has always been a decisive subjective factor in history.[195]

It is worth repeating that no one before Marx understood history in this way. It is true that in the first third of the nineteenth century the ideologists of the victorious revolutionary French bourgeoisie—the historians Augustin Thierry, [François] Mignet, and above all François Guizot clearly recognized that the past centuries were dominated by class interests and class struggles. But they never went beyond the description of actual conditions, that is, the struggles of the rising bourgeoisie against the landowning feudal class. They recognized class struggles only in the past and failed to see their continuation in their own time, in the existing relations between the working class and the bourgeoisie. In Marx the class struggle is not merely a description of actual facts but a part of an elaborated historical theory: he explains genetically the necessary emergence of class conflicts in various historical epochs and explains their origin, form, and intensity by the development of the productive forces in each period and by the position individuals and classes occupy in the productive process. This endows the doctrine of the class struggle with a concrete and profound meaning.[196]

On the other hand, Saint-Simon and his school, as we have seen above, had also recognized past class struggles only in a factual sense and did not admit them for their own time. The Saint-Simonians feared to arouse the hopes of the proletariat; and, convinced that progress must come through the elite of the upper classes, they wanted above all

---

192. Marx, *The Poverty of Philosophy*, 176.

193. Hegel, *Lectures on the Philosophy of History*, 63, and Fischer, *Hegels Leben, Werke und Lehre*, 739.

194. Marx, *Eighteenth Brumaire of Louis Bonaparte*, 103.

195. Sismondi, for instance, says that "the freedom of the Occident results from the rebellion of the non-owners" (against a small minority of landowners). "Between the tenth and the twelfth centuries, people without land reconquered freedom for the future generations." Sismondi, *Histoire des républiques italiennes*, 499, 107.

196. See Plekhanov, "Initial Phases of the Theory," 466–67, *Die neue Zeit* 31 (1903): 298, 304, and Tiumeniev, "Marxism and Bourgeois Historical Science," 235–319.

to win these upper classes over to their views.[197] Though the writings of Bazard, [Barthélemy Prosper] Enfantin, and later Pecqueur contain references to the struggle of the working class against the dehumanizing effects of capitalism, these remain isolated statements of fact.[198] In principle, the Saint-Simonians accepted the idea that progress was a continuous transition from antagonism to peaceful association. Thus Pecqueur regards class struggle as an evil, like every other form of struggle, and compares it to war. He expects that in the future all forms of struggle will be less violent and that peaceful methods of production and distribution will develop. There is a wide gap between this view and the overpowering generalization of the *Communist Manifesto*: "The history of all hitherto existing society is the history of class struggles." Here, class struggle is not regarded as an evil but as a dynamic force, the lever of history. By fighting for its rights against the ruling class, the exploited and oppressed class creates a new historical situation. New rights are wrested from the ruling class, and the whole of society is thereby raised to a new and higher level. In this conception, class struggle does not end with the abolition of feudalism by the bourgeoisie; it is also typical of the relations between the bourgeoisie and the working class. According to Marx, the process of history on the road of progress, far from becoming increasingly peaceful, increases in violence with the development of capitalism, and class conflicts become the decisive instrument in the transition from capitalism to collectivism.

---

197. Weill, *L'école saint-simonienne*, 56, 293.

198. "One fact is certain, general . . . it is the silent but very decisive struggle of the workers against their masters . . . with a view to forcing the captains of industry to raise their wages." Pecqueur, *Économie sociale des interets*, vol. 2, 126. "How can one not see that to leave [the wage earners] dependent on the insufficiency of a fluctuating wage is to wish to find oneself surrounded in times of crisis and general unemployment by a famished multitude, to create riot and civil war, and perhaps to arm new Spartacuses." Ibid., 108. [Grossman's translation mistakenly has "Spartans" instead of "Spartacuses."]

W. Playfair,
the Earliest Theorist
of Capitalist Development[1]

Simonde de Sismondi is regarded as the earliest representative of the doctrine of the objective tendencies of capitalist development. But Sismondi reflects not so much the French as the English industrial experience, and we know that in 1817 he went to England, the home country of the industrial revolution, to collect material for his *New Principles*. This is not surprising: British capitalism was the most developed at that time. It would be surprising, however, if the basic trends of capitalism, which manifested themselves in early nineteenth-century England more clearly than anywhere else, had not left any trace in English economic literature. In Playfair we rediscover a missing link; it shows that the English industrial experience found its expression not only indirectly, via Sismondi in France, but also directly in England.

"Trend spotting," or discovery of the objective developmental trends of capitalism, is the primary aim of modern economic science. It is also one of the essential elements of Marxian economics. Nevertheless, there prevails great confusion about the genesis of this important doctrine. Some writers attribute the first formulation of the fundamental tendencies of capitalism to Karl Marx; others maintain that Marx borrowed them from his forerunners, particularly Sismondi.

Can one agree with Professor Charles Rist, who declares that of all the ideas that Marx took over from Sismondi, "the most fertile idea borrowed by Marx was that which deals with the concentration of wealth in the hands of a few powerful capitalists,

---

1. Originally published in the journal *Economic History Review* in 1948.

which results in the increasing dependence of the working classes. This conception . . . forms a part of the very foundation of Marxian collectivism"?[2]

Nothing is more contrary to truth than this assertion. The concentration of wealth, the trend toward large-scale production, and the growing proletarianization of the working classes in the first half of the nineteenth century were not theoretical conceptions but statements of empirically observable facts. Marx did not have to "borrow" from Sismondi facts that could be easily ascertained from contemporary English industrial statistics and that served as the common starting point for all critiques of capitalism by the leaders of the working-class movement in France in the middle of the nineteenth century.

Who was the first to discover and to establish these objective tendencies? In the preface to the first volume of *Capital* Marx declares that "it is the ultimate aim of this work to reveal the economic law of motion of modern society," namely, to show "its tendencies," which Marx regards as "the natural laws of capitalist production."[3] He is referring to objectively ascertainable tendencies, which Marx and Engels describe elsewhere as the concentration of capital and land in a few hands, the ruin of the petty bourgeoisie and peasants, the misery of the proletariat, the crying inequalities in the distribution of wealth, and the industrial war of extermination among the nations.[4]

However, Marx and Engels were not the first to establish the existence of such tendencies. As early as 1843, Victor Considerant, the Fourierist leader in France,[5] clearly formulated all these tendencies in his pamphlet *Principles of Socialism, Manifesto of Democracy in the 19th Century*.[6] Particularly important are paragraphs VII, VIII, and XI.

Paragraph VII (the tendency to the destruction of the small and medium industries): the result of free competition "is the direct reduction of the proletarian masses to collective serfdom . . . the progressive crushing . . . of small and medium industry . . . under the weight of big property, under the colossal wheels of big industry and big trade."[7]

Paragraph VIII (concerning the tendency to the concentration of capital and the impoverishment of the working masses): "Society tends more and more distinctly to be divided into two great classes: a small number possessing everything or almost everything . . . and the great number possessing nothing, living in absolute collective dependence upon the owners of capital and the instruments of production, compelled

---

2. Rist, "Sismondi and the Origins," 198.

3. Marx, *Capital*, vol. 1, 92, 91.

4. Marx and Engels, *Manifesto of the Communist Party*, 489–91.

5. [Considerant led the followers of the utopian socialist Charles Fourier.]

6. First published as a programmatic statement in the first issue of *Democratie pacifique*, the daily organ of L'École Sociétaire (August 1, 1843). The quotations refer to the second (1847) edition, Considerant, *Principes du socialisme*. A few months after the appearance of Considerant's manifesto of 1843, Parke Godwin, an American Fourierist, published a pamphlet, *Democracy Constructive and Pacific*, that follows Considerant closely and in which the developmental trends of capitalism are defined. I am indebted to Mr Maurice Buchs, who is preparing a new study in French entitled "Le fouriérisme aux Etats Unis," for having drawn my attention to Godwin.

7. Considerant, *Principes du socialisme*, 9.

to hire for precarious and ever-decreasing wages their hands, talents, and energies to the feudal lords of modern society."[8]

Finally, Considerant emphasizes the fact in paragraph XI, that as an inevitable result of free competition there arises the tendency to the formation of big monopolies in every branch of business.[9]

Nor was Considerant the first to discover these tendencies. Several years before him, all the tendencies described above had been formulated, with masterful conciseness and precision, by Constantin Pecqueur. In his *Social Economics* this writer predicts that as a result of the introduction of machines, "the various small industries, agricultural, manufacturing and commercial, will disappear quite generally. . . . As small industry will disappear, the small industrialists . . . will degenerate into wage laborers, a mass of serfs working day by day in the manufactures, into proletarians without a future; and all the big industries will be monopolized exclusively by an industrial feudalism."[10]

A few other authors propounding similar ideas could be quoted. Their primary source in France was Sismondi's book, *New Principles*, in which the fundamental developmental tendencies of capitalism were clearly stated as early as 1819. As regards the tendency to concentration, Sismondi shows that as capitalism progressively accumulates, it concentrates in large-scale manufactures.[11] He formulates the tendency to the destruction of small and medium enterprises in industry and trade.[12] As for the tendency to the impoverishment of the laboring masses, he observes that, as a result of the technological advances that extend to a growing number of branches of industry, new masses of workers constantly become unemployed; to find employment they are ready to work for starvation wages and as a result become physically and morally degraded, sinking below the level of beasts. Every technological revolution is followed by a new deterioration of the status of laborers.

However, Sismondi, too, had a predecessor. This article attempts to show that the true originator of the doctrine of the objective developmental trends of capitalism was William Playfair (1759–1823), a British economist, who until now has remained completely unnoticed.

Such revaluation of a forgotten economist has more than a merely personal significance. If it can be established that the conception of the objective fundamental tendencies of capitalism—the ideas of the growing accumulation of capital in a few hands, of

---

8. Ibid., 11.

9. Ibid., 13.

10. Pecqueur, *Économie sociale des interets*, vol. 2, 101. See also vol. 1, 269. [Here "manufactures" means "factories."]

11. "It is worthy of mention that . . . the effect of increasing capital is generally to concentrate labor in very large manufactories." Sismondi, *New Principles of Political Economy*, 275. "Discoveries in mechanical arts have always the remote result of concentrating industry within the hands of a smaller number of merchants." Ibid., 561. [Here "manufactures" means "factories."]

12. "They discover the economy which exists in management on a greater scale . . . the employment common to a greater number of men at once, of light, fuel, and all the powers of nature. Thus small merchants, small manufacturers disappear." Sismondi, *New Principles of Political Economy*, 562.

the disappearance of the middle classes, of the necessity of capital export, et cetera, can be found for the first time not in Sismondi, 1819, but in Playfair, as early as 1805, this means that all these tendencies had become sufficiently perceptible in England and objectively ascertainable fourteen years before the publication of Sismondi's book, and for that very reason could be formulated at that early date.[13]

Furthermore, it is noteworthy that while the previously known French theorists of the objective trends of capitalism were utopian or petty-bourgeois socialists, or semisocialists, who sharply criticized capitalism and proposed to replace it by another more or less socialist form of society, Playfair was a spokesman for the petty bourgeoisie. He too criticizes the failings of capitalism, but his critique is purely sentimental. He does not conceive of any way out of the situation; despite all the failings of capitalism that he points out, he wants to preserve it and does not propose to replace it by another system.

Playfair is not a theoretician comparable to the classical economists, that is to say, he is not an analyst. He does not precede his exposition by any general principles, such as a theory of value, from which he might draw inferences by way of logical deduction. He applies the reverse procedure—the method of the historical school. He describes the real processes and the observed developmental tendencies, and theorizes rarely. In this "inquiry . . . there has been an invariable rule, never to oppose theory and reasoning to facts but to take experience as the surest guide."[14] The result is a surface treatment and a lack of depth and analysis. But he is an excellent observer. Playfair is interested above all in the fate of the British Empire and its future economic development as a basis for its political power. In order to foresee that future fate, Playfair first strives to discover a general law of historical development, a law valid for all nations and all times from antiquity to the modern era, so that Britain would represent only a special case in the application of the general law, only its modification under the particular circumstances of modern capitalism, which can be understood only as such. For that reason Playfair's exposition of Britain's developmental trends would be difficult to understand without a discussion of his general historical law of the rise and decline of nations.

---

13. William Playfair, known as an anti-Jacobin pamphleteer and statistician, has remained entirely unnoticed in the history of economic ideas, although his book, *Inquiry into Permanent Causes of the Decline and Fall of Powerful and Wealthy Nations*, 1805, had some success in his time and was published in a second edition in 1807—Playfair is not even mentioned in any early or recent history of economic theories. Furthermore, Playfair's name is not mentioned in the 1941 edition of the *Encyclopaedia Britannica*, nor in the American *Encyclopaedia of the Social Sciences* edited by Edwin Seligman (1930–35), nor in James Bonar's monograph *Malthus and His Work*, 1924, although it deals with a period in which both Malthus and Playfair were active. Only two English dictionaries contain short biographical and bibliographical notices on Playfair: Robert Palgrave's 1913 *Dictionary of Political Economy*, vol. 3, 116, and Stephen and Lee's 1921–22 *The Dictionary of National Biography*, vol. 15, 1300. But even these notices are confined to enumerating the titles of Playfair's writings; his economic theories are not mentioned. *Economic Journal* (*Economic History* supplement), 1935, contains an article [Funkhouser and Walker, "Playfair and His Charts."]

14. Playfair, *Inquiry into Permanent Causes*, 276.

1. The Dominant Tendencies of Capitalism

While contemporary French evolutionists such as [Anne-Robert-Jacques] Turgot (1750), [Marie-Jean-Antoine-Nicolas de] Condorcet (1795), and Count [Henri] Saint-Simon (first publication in 1802) assumed the existence of a law of continuous cultural and economic progress, Playfair rejects such an idea.[15] His law of the rise and decline of nations is based on the idea that mankind marks time without moving forward; that states, just like individuals, go necessarily through periods of infancy, manhood, and decrepitude, and then die; that all of them begin with "their original state of poverty,"[16] that they subsequently gradually develop into centers of wealth and power, and that in the end, after reaching the climax of their wealth, through the operation of the same general law, inevitably relapse into barbarism and poverty; their place is then taken by other, culturally and economically backward nations, so "that the greatness of nations is but of short duration."[17]

To prove the existence of such a historical law, Playfair briefly outlines the rise and fall of all the civilizations he knows for a period of more than three thousand years, covering antiquity, the Middle Ages, and modern times. Under "the pressure of necessity"[18] the poor countries with "superior energy" attack the wealthy nations either by peaceful methods or by war, producing always the same effect: "the triumph of poverty over wealth."[19] "The effeminacy and luxury of the rich,"[20] operating persistently "from generation to generation,"[21] undermines the energy and activity of the wealthy.

This general law of historical development works in "modern" (that is, capitalist) industrial countries only with some modifications, because of the presence of "some particular causes that operate in some modern nations."[22] One of these "particular causes" is the tremendous development of modern military technique and mechanical warfare. In the past, the triumph of poverty over wealth was possible because the backward nations under the pressure of necessity were energetic, martial, and brave. In modern times, however, wars no longer favor poor nations, [as] "bodily strength has but little effect, while the engines of war can only be procured by those resources which wealth affords." To constitute and equip an army with modern engines, "a very considerable degree of wealth is necessary."[23] Courage and bravery, the fighting qualities of the poor nations, no longer prevail against modern weapons. While in the past wealth and luxury led to the decline of the wealthy nations, in modern times the situation is reversed:

---

15. [Turgot, "Sur les progrès successifs de l'esprit humain"; Condorcet, *Outlines of an Historical View*; Saint-Simon, *Lettres d'un habitant de Genève*. See also chapter 4 in the present volume.]
16. Playfair, *Inquiry into Permanent Causes*, iv.
17. Ibid.
18. Ibid., 167.
19. Ibid., 19.
20. Ibid., 177.
21. Ibid., 81.
22. Ibid., 164.
23. Ibid., 18.

victory is decided not by martial virtues but by wealth; therefore, the main task of the government is now to preserve wealth and prosperity.

Having formulated the general law in book 1, Playfair confines his analyses in books 2 and 3 to the "modern," i.e., capitalist nations, inquiring into the specific causes that determine the rise and fall of such nations. He eliminates "a variety" of local or accidental causes (for example, wars) and attempts to deal only with fundamental causes "operating in all of them," namely, "the interior causes of the decline of wealthy nations, arising from the wealth itself," that is, from the degree of accumulation of capital achieved in a given period.[24] Playfair distinguishes three phases of such accumulation: in the first, less capital is available than can be invested; in the second, there is sufficient capital; in the third—on which he concentrates almost exclusively—there is more available capital than can be profitably invested. Therefore, capital reaches insuperable limits—"its bounds"—to further accumulation.[25] All nations begin their development as agrarian countries, then become manufacturing countries, and finally change into creditor nations that must export the available surplus capital.[26]

According to Playfair, Britain has entered, or is about to enter, this third phase, and he analyzes it in the light both of arguments drawn from observation of contemporary conditions in Britain and of arguments drawn from the experience of previous centuries, particularly from the history of Holland, Genoa, and Venice. In the course of this analysis he attempts—and he is the first economist to do so—to formulate the developmental trends of capitalist accumulation.

During the whole period embracing the first two phases of capital accumulation, which is identical with the period of progressive industrialization, Playfair observes three fundamental tendencies of development:

1. The tendency of capital to concentrate in a few hands.
2. The tendency of the productive classes to become poorer.
3. The tendency of the middle classes to disappear.

When the third phase, that of superabundance of capital, is reached, a fourth fundamental tendency begins to operate—the tendency of every industrial nation to become a creditor or investor nation.

But this means the end of progressive industrialization and expansion, that is, a tendency to a stationary state and the beginning of disintegration and decline. Thus the general law of rise and decline remains valid also for modern, capitalist states, although its outward form is modified.

---

24. Ibid., 90.
25. Ibid., 200.
26. Ibid., 161, 200, 270.

The Natural Tendency of Wealth to Accumulate in the Hands of a Few

The tendency of wealth to accumulate in the hands of a few was often asserted as a fact. Thus [Paul Henri Thiry] d'Holbach wrote in 1773: "Wealth . . . gradually accumulates in a small number of hands; to favor a few shrewd citizens, all others are reduced to indigence."[27] Playfair—and this is his contribution—does not confine himself to a vague, general statement that seems to apply to all epochs, and he does not explain the concentration of capital by the personal shrewdness of a few but regards it as the natural and inevitable result of the accumulation process in modern industrial states. In contrast to the belief of eighteenth-century economists that fundamental economic structures are the result of legislation, he shows that, parallel to this accumulation, the differentiation and inequality of possessions increase as a natural result of the economic process, quite independently of existing legislation or the political form of the state (that is, both in despotic and free states). Moreover, he shows the effects of the concentration of capital on all social classes—the enrichment of a few big entrepreneurs, the ruin of numerous small entrepreneurs who lose their economic independence, the decline of wealth based on rentier income, the automatic enrichment of the landowning class, the specific role of credit in the centralization of big fortunes, and, as a consequence of the concentration process as a whole, the widening of the gap between the impoverished and degraded classes and the wealthy upper classes. "In the career of wealth, in its early state, when individual industry is almost without any aid from capital, men are as nearly on an equality as the nature of things can admit. But in proportion as capital comes into the aid of industry, that equality dies away, and men, who have nothing but industry, lose their means of exerting it with advantage; some become then incapable of maintaining their rank in society altogether."[28] "In every country, the wealth . . . has a natural tendency to accumulate in the hands of certain individuals, whether the laws of the society do or do not favour this accumulation," as a result of which the "unequal division of property" is accentuated.[29]

This tendency of productive, industrially employed capital to concentrate is intensified by the specific function of credit. Profits are primarily created by productive activity. But this mode of enrichment is relatively slow. Big fortunes can be accumulated with the help of long-term credits: "In countries where the common practice is to sell, chiefly, for ready money, great fortunes are seldom gained. . . . But in a country that gives long credits, or in a branch of trade on which long credits are given, we always see some individuals gaining immense fortunes."[30]

---

27. Holbach, *Système social*, vol. 3, 74.
28. Playfair, *Inquiry into Permanent Causes*, 156.
29. "Of the internal causes of decline, arising from the unequal division of property, and its accumulation in the hands of particular persons." Playfair, *Inquiry into Permanent Causes*, 125.
30. Ibid., 181–82. Compare Marx: "The credit system . . . is . . . an enormous social mechanism for the centralisation of capitals." *Capital*, vol. 1, 777–78.

On the basis of the observation that as capital accumulates, the rate of interest sinks (Turgot, Adam Smith),[31] Playfair concludes that in the course of the accumulation process the relative position of an owner of a definite amount of money capital deteriorates. If the rate of interest drops from 4 percent to 2 percent, a capital of £1,000 brings in the same income as previously a capital of £500. Capital accumulation is thus accompanied by depreciation of money capital, and as a result of this tendency to depreciation, large money fortunes are not permanent; they shrink after two or three generations. To counteract this tendency and maintain the former relative position of money capital, much energy, work, shrewdness, and willingness to take risks are required.[32]

In contrast to this constantly threatened position of the moneylender, the relative position of the landowning class grows progressively stronger. As capital accumulation in industry increases and the rate of interest falls, the value of land automatically rises, without the intervention or work of the landowner. Therefore, this form of property and its concentration in a few hands is the most dangerous.[33]

The Tendency of the Number of Poor to Increase in Countries Advancing in Wealth

In the seventeenth century, England was faced with a chronic problem of pauperism— pauperism in an agricultural country. The new pauperism was very different; it was a consequence of industrialization. What distinguishes Playfair from his predecessors in calling attention to this fact is that in contrast to the countless remedies proposed by older economists for curing idleness by corrective or punitive legislation, he regards the increase in the number of the poor as a natural consequence of concentration of capital and wealth: "the alarming and lamentable increases of the poor in proportion, as a nation becomes rich."[34]

Playfair calculates that the number of the poor has grown faster than the total population.[35] These victims of poverty, he says sarcastically, are "filling prisons, poor houses

---

31. Adam Smith, *Wealth of Nations*, vol. 1, 313–20.

32. "A fortune lent at interest, diminishes as the value of money sinks." "The depreciation of money that takes place in every country that grows rich, falls nearly all on the lender at interest." Playfair, *Inquiry into Permanent Causes*, 129, 162–63. "A fortune engaged in trade is liable to risks, and requires industry to preserve it: but industry . . . never is to be found for any great length of time in any single line of men." Ibid., 129. "We find that wealth seldom goes amongst people of business past the second, and almost never past the third generation." Ibid., 89.

33. The thousand pounds laid at interest, after thirty years, is always worth 1,000 pounds. But land bought for 1,000 pounds would be worth 2,000 pounds. Playfair, *Inquiry into Permanent Causes*, 163. [Although Grossman originally put this sentence inside quotation marks, it is not a direct quote. It is, however, a fair summary of Playfair's point.] "An estate in land augments in value, without augmenting in extent, when a country becomes richer." "Of all the ways in which property accumulates, in particular hands, the most dangerous is landed property." Playfair, *Inquiry into Permanent Causes*, 129.

34. Ibid., 87–88.

35. Ibid., 88. Playfair's contemporary, James Mill, states "that the paupers are equal to nearly one third of the whole male population, including old men, young men, or children." *Commerce Defended*, 101.

and hospitals," "illustrating the effect of wealth," and he devotes a whole chapter to the problem "Of the Increase of the Poor, as General Affluence Becomes Greater."[36]

Playfair distinguishes between two types of poverty. The first, which exists "in every nation," comprises people who are poor for general, demographic, natural reasons, such as "the lame, the sick, the infirm, the aged, or children unprovided for." The number of those "in proportion to the total number of inhabitants, will be pretty nearly the same at all times; for it is nature that produces this species of helpless poverty." "There is another species of poverty, not of nature's creation. . . . That new species of poverty is occasioned by the general wealth, since it increases in proportion to it." "As this tendency is uniformly felt . . . over the whole country when it advances in wealth . . . it must operate, in length of time, in producing the decline of the whole nation."[37]

For even though the enrichment of some and the impoverishment of others takes place in such a way that they "change places gradually and without noise," the final result is nevertheless that "such changes are attended with . . . violent commotion." "The lower classes become degraded and discouraged, as is universally found to be the case in nations that have passed their meridian." While some men remain idle because of their wealth, "others, who are depressed below the natural situation of men, are bringing them [their children] up to feel the extreme pressure of want. . . . Neither the powers of their body, nor of their mind, arrive at maturity." "Whilst the foundation of idleness and poverty is laid in, for one part of a nation, from the affluence of their parents, another portion seems as if it were chained down to misery from the indigence in which they were born and brought up."[38]

This social sickness is not the result of accidental external causes but of "the interior cause"—the accumulation of capital. That is why this sickness is inherent in the nature of the economic organism, and it becomes accentuated with the growth of this organism—a process that Playfair illustrates by quoting from [Alexander] Pope:

> "The great disease that must destroy at length,
> Grows with our growth, and strengthens with our strength."[39]

> In all new and rising states the higher orders . . . as they increase in wealth and have lost sight of its origin, which is industry, they change their mode of thinking; and by degrees, the lower classes are considered as only made for the convenience of the rich. The degradation into which the lower orders themselves fall, by vice and indolence, widens the difference and increases the contempt in which they are held. This is one of the invariable marks of the decline of nations.[40]

But the rich consider only their own advantage; the richer they become, the more

---

36. Playfair, *Inquiry into Permanent Causes*, 88, 156–60.
37. Ibid., 88–89.
38. Ibid., 89, 132, 156.
39. Ibid. [Playfair paraphrased Pope's couplet, "The young disease, which must subdue at length/Grows with his growth, and strengthens with his strength." Pope, "Essay on Man," 204.], 90.
40. Ibid., 263.

selfish they are; they hold the poor responsible for their poverty and treat them worse than beasts: "It has been noticed that in every society, as wealth increases, hospitality [which existed in a less advanced state of society] dies away. . . . The social feelings become less active, and men turn selfish and interested, thinking for themselves and careless for the community; while, on the one hand, the causes for poverty increase, on the other, the means of relief are misapplied, neglected."[41]

The Tendency of the "Middling Classes" to Disappear

Concentration of wealth, on the one hand, and the growing number of impoverished masses, on the other, take place at the expense of the middle classes, that is, "those immediately above" "the inferior classes."[42] These middle classes gradually disappear. "The consequence of great fortunes, and the unequal division of property, are that the lower ranks . . . become degraded, disorderly and uncomfortable, while the middling classes disappear by degrees." Such an exasperation of economic antagonisms as a result of the unequal division of property is dangerous and leads the nation to inevitable ruin.[43]

Playfair is not a radical. He praises the middle class and believes in their great task of assuring economic and political progress, the material and spiritual elements of which are concentrated in that class. The rich have always managed to shift burdens to the others; as for the large masses of the productive workers, they have neither the leisure nor the resources to steer the ship of state. Nor has Playfair a high opinion of the landowners, rentiers, and all those who receive a fixed, unearned income. He contrasts "the most useful class," that is, "those whose income is regulated by their efforts . . . that is to say, the productive labourers of the country" with "those whose incomes are fixed, that is principally the unproductive labourers . . . the drones of society."[44] "Where there is no regular gradation of rank and division of property, emulation, which is the spur to action . . . is . . . destroyed."[45] "The higher classes can never be made to contribute their share towards the prosperity of a state. . . . The higher class . . . can never be very numerous; and being above the feeling of want . . . there is nothing to be expected of them towards the general good." "From the working and labourious classes, again, little is to be expected . . . they have neither leisure, nor other means of contributing to general prosperity as public men; they, indeed, pay more than their share of taxes in almost every country; but they cannot directly, even by election, participate in the government of the country." "It is in the middling classes that the freedom, the intelligence, and the industry of a country reside. . . . Where there are no middling classes to

---

41. Ibid., 159. [In the original the "one" was "other"; Grossman corrected this.]
42. Ibid., 133.
43. Ibid., 126, 128.
44. Ibid., 167–68.
45. Ibid., 132.

connect the higher and lower orders . . . a state must gradually decline."[46]

The rapid disappearance of the middle class is particularly dangerous because this increases the distance between the mass of the poor and the class of the wealthy, and the contrasts between want and riches are brought into sharp focus: "The strongest bond of society is thereby broken; the bond that consists in the attachment of the inferior classes to those immediately above them. Where the distance is great there is but little connection. . . . The whole society becomes, as it were, disjointed."[47]

Despite Playfair's sympathy for the middle classes, he has no illusions about the actual development of capitalism. He knows that the wheel of history cannot be stopped. The middle classes are disappearing and social inequality operates permanently, even in the opening stages of capital accumulation when the nation is still poor in capital; but it operates with particular intensity at the higher stages of accumulation and capital saturation: "[The] tendency to [inequality] increases very rapidly of late years." "But if this progress goes on, while a nation is acquiring wealth, how much faster does it not proceed when it approaches its decline? It is then, indeed, that the extremes of poverty and riches are to be seen in the most striking degree."[48]

The tendency of agricultural nations to change into industrial nations and later into creditor (investor) nations. Superabundance of capital and lack of investment opportunities in old industrial countries as factors of disintegration and decay.

We have shown that according to Playfair capitalism, from its very beginning, has been accompanied by the three developmental trends described above. We shall pass now to the most important section of Playfair's theory of accumulation—his view that at a specific stage capital accumulation reaches a maximum limit. This results in a profound structural change of the whole economy. It is at this late stage of accumulation that a fourth trend appears—the tendency of industrial nations to change into creditor (investor) nations, which ultimately leads to the disintegration of the whole economic system. For if capital accumulation reaches the third phase (characterized by superabundance of capital), the profits earned in the existing enterprises cannot be profitably absorbed at home; they become "surplus" capital and must therefore be exported: "When capital becomes over abundant,"[49] "if there is not sufficient means of employing capital within a nation or country . . . there are plenty of opportunities furnished by poorer nations."[50]

In other words, the "surplus" capital that cannot be invested at home must be exported to other, economically undeveloped countries. If the "surplus" capital is never-

46. Ibid., 131–32.
47. Ibid., 132–33.
48. Ibid., 129, 131.
49. Ibid., 161.
50. Ibid., 135.

theless invested in the home country and the manufactures are expanded, an unsalable surplus of commodities is inevitably produced, which again can be marketed only in undeveloped countries. Such countries "afford us much reason for hope, and do away [with] one of the causes for fearing a decline that has been stated, namely . . . by not having a market for our increasing manufactures."[51] "The United States promise to support the industry of England now . . . far more than both the Indies. . . . A market for British manufactures [will be] insured for ages to come."[52]

Here we have in germ a formulation of a specific underconsumption theory deriving from surplus capital, a theory that was later developed by Sismondi (1819) and Hegel (1820) and that was popularized in the twentieth century by J. A. Hobson (1911) and Rosa Luxemburg (1913).[53]

[David] Ricardo, in 1817, criticized such a "surplus" theory. According to him, there can be no surplus capital in a country, because any amount of capital can always find profitable investment.[54] Unlike Ricardo, Adam Smith explicitly defended the theory of overabundance of capital inherited from his predecessors John Locke and David Hume.[55]

This theory of Adam Smith of a possible saturation of capital, that is, of a "mature economy" that has acquired "its full complement of riches," was quite current in Playfair's lifetime. Locke (1692) and Hume (1752) had advanced it before Smith in England; in France, it was held by Turgot (1766) and Condorcet (1794).[56] But Playfair goes beyond his predecessors in one very important respect. Smith, for instance, confines himself to stating that in Holland many moneylenders or rentiers lived on the interest of capital lent to foreign nations. Playfair, however, not only refers to investors or rentiers but also is the first to define all the characteristic features of a parasitic creditor (investor) nation living not on productive work but "without labour," on the interests of capital lent abroad.[57] At the same time Playfair conceives of the investor state as the necessary and ultimate phase of industrial development of any country, a phase that inaugurates decline and decay.

According to Playfair, there is a fundamental difference between an individual creditor and a creditor nation. Individuals can withdraw from productive activity at any time. They can sell their real estate and lend their capital abroad against interest. On

---

51. Ibid., 269.

52. Ibid., 268.

53. [Hobson, *An Economic Interpretation of Investment*, 85–86. Hobson had, however, been propounding underconsumptionist arguments since 1894 at the latest: *Evolution of Modern Capitalism*, 167–219. Luxemburg, *The Accumulation of Capital*.] Sismondi, *New Principles of Political Economy*, 264, 276, 561; Hegel, *Outlines of the Philosophy of Right*, 221–24 (paragraphs 245 and 246, and additions to paragraphs 244 and 248).

54. [Ricardo, *Principles of Political Economy*, 193.]

55. Adam Smith cites the example of the Dutch, who lent large amounts of capital to the English, French, and other nations, in *Wealth of Nations*, vol. 1, 82.

56. [Ibid., 86; Locke, *Some Considerations on the Lowering of Interest*; Hume, *Hume's Political Discourses*; Turgot, *Reflections on the Formation*; Condorcet, *Outlines of an Historical View*.]

57. Playfair, *Inquiry into Permanent Causes*, 82.

the contrary, a nation cannot completely cease productive activities and must always put to use its real estate, factories, mines, cultivated land, and so on; only movable goods and money capital can be exported abroad. Therefore only part of a nation can function as a creditor: "The whole nation could not become idle. Such a case never can exist, as that of all individuals in a country becoming sufficiently rich to live without labour." "A nation can never retire; it must always be industrious."[58]

However, although not all individuals in a creditor nation can live comfortably, "without labour," the number of such idle individuals who live on interest coming from abroad is steadily increasing.

Once the state of overabundance of capital is attained, there begins a slow disintegrating process, a retrogression of the industrial state, which in the end must lead to its decline. Two types of change take place: a structural change in the economic basis and, parallel to it, a far-reaching change in the spiritual superstructure.[59]

Playfair is a realist; his analysis of the economic disintegration and ultimate decay of a creditor state are not wishful speculations or conclusions reached by deduction from abstract presuppositions; they have a realistic character, for he takes as a basis of his analyses the historical example of the decline of Holland, a creditor state, and he thinks that if in the future other, for the time being backward nations ever reach the stage of capital superabundance, they will produce analogous symptoms of material and moral disintegration.

According to Playfair, the economic disintegration and decline of Holland was not accidental. Accidents play a great part in the lives of individuals or small human groups, but not in the life of a whole nation. Playfair obviously has in view the statistical law of big numbers, which he was the first to apply to history. The accidental forces inclining in different directions cancel one another, and only the fundamental forces common to the total mass of the nation assert themselves and can be considered the dominant trends. A whole nation can perish only if "interior causes" have prepared it for decay[60]:

> An inquiry into the causes of the revolutions of nations is more perfect . . . than when directed to those of individuals. . . . Nations are exempt from those accidental vicissitudes which derange the wisest of human plans upon a smaller scale. Number and magnitude reduce chances to certainty. The single and unforeseen cause that overwhelms a man in the midst of prosperity, never ruins a nation: unless it be ripe for ruin, a nation never falls. . . . Accident has only the appearance of doing what, in reality, was already nearly accomplished.[61]

---

58. Ibid., 82, 89.
59. In another context Playfair illustrates the parallelism of economic and spiritual development by the following remark, which is reminiscent of Max Weber [*The Protestant Ethic*]: "The reformation in religion, and the establishment of manufactures in England date from nearly the same period. . . . There are, therefore many reasons, from experience, for believing that the Protestant religion is particularly favourable to industry." Playfair, *Inquiry into Permanent Causes*, 265. [Grossman was very familiar with this issue; see his "The Beginnings of Capitalism."]
60. Playfair, *Inquiry into Permanent Causes*, 185.
61. Ibid., xi–xii.

Playfair analyzes the rise and decline of Holland from that standpoint: "As for the Dutch, they continued to increase in wealth til the end of the seventeenth century. . . . In addition to their great industry, the fisheries and art of curing fish, the Dutch excelled in making machines of various sorts, and became the nation that supplied others with materials in a state ready prepared for manufacturing: this was a new branch of business and very lucrative, for, as the machines were kept a secret, the abbreviation of labour was great."[62]

But when Dutch industry became saturated with capital, there were no further profitable investments at home. The additional capital could function only as [a] commercial agent between foreign nations; the Dutch became a nation of intermediaries: "But when they became affluent . . . the manufacturers became merchants, and the merchants became agents and carriers. . . . Dutch capital was employed to purchase goods in one country and sell them in another; the Dutch became carriers of others, instead of manufacturing . . . for themselves." Thus "the solid sources of riches [that is, production] disappeared. . . . The merchants preferred safe agencies for foreigners to trading on their own." "Superiority in manufactures over other countries was continually diminishing; consequently, industry was not so well rewarded, and less active."[63]

According to Playfair, the structural transformation of the country did not stop there. The manufacturer who regressed to the status of a merchant later became a rentier; the industries were neglected, and the nation changed from an industrial into a creditor nation.

> Manufacturers aspire to become merchants, and merchants to become lenders of money or agents.
>
> The Dutch were the greatest example of this. . . . They had long ceased to give that great encouragement to manufactures which had, at first, raised them to wealth and power. . . . They had, in the latter times, become agents for others rather than merchants on their own account; so that the capital, which, at one time, brought in, probably, twenty or twenty-five percent annually, and which had, even at a late period, produced ten or fifteen, was employed in a way that scarcely produced three.[64]

This economic transformation was accompanied by a parallel change of mentality, which reacted on the economic basis and further accentuated its weakness. In an investor nation "it is not merely a neglect of industry . . . that is hurtful; the general way of thinking and acting becomes different."[65]

The mentality of an idle class of rentiers who despise productive work leaves its impress on the whole life of an investor nation. This "degradation of moral character" of an investor nation is again illustrated by Holland. In an industrial country, her manufac-

62. Ibid., 66.
63. Ibid., 66–67. This picture of the decline of Dutch industry is essentially confirmed by a modern historian, C. H. Wilson, in "The Economic Decline of the Netherlands" (1939).
64. Playfair, *Inquiry into Permanent Causes*, 134.
65. Ibid., 90.

turers are a class of robust, active entrepreneurs; in an investor country, wealthy, well-established firms avoid risks, withdraw from productive activity, and live on interest.[66]

> Whatever, therefore, tends to accumulate the capital of a nation in a few hands . . . not only increases luxury, and corrupts morals, but diminishes the activity of the capital and industry of the country.
>
> In all the great places that are now in a state of decay, we find families living on the interest of money, that formerly were engaged in manufactures or commerce. Antwerp, Genoa and Venice, were full of such; but those persons would not have ventured a single shilling in a new enterprise.[67]

In this way, both for objective and subjective, psychological reasons, capital expansion is brought to a standstill, productivity deteriorates, and industry disintegrates. Holland's position deteriorated as a result of an internal development, not of unfavorable external circumstances: "There was no violent revolution, no invasion by an enemy; it was the silent operation of that cause of decline which had been already mentioned."[68]

The foregoing outline of the economic evolution of Holland from an industrial to a parasitic creditor nation is, according to Playfair, not a casual excursion into the history of a specific country. It is on the contrary conceived of as an illustration of a general law of the rise and decline of all modern industrial nations. The economic transformation and the attending processes of material and moral degradation are seen as an inevitable historical stage in the development of every industrial state, which begins the moment its capital accumulation has entered the phase of superabundance and capital export.

Thus Playfair was the first—and for a whole century he remained the only one—to describe this characteristic tendency in the evolution of modern industrial states, the tendency to capital export and to transformation into creditor states. Economic theory neglected this problem during the entire nineteenth century. Only at the beginning of the twentieth century was the problem raised again by John Atkinson Hobson, whose work gave rise to a whole literature; but it is interesting to note that Hobson's economic interpretation of investment, his theory of surplus capital formulated in 1911, does not go an inch beyond Playfair's views expressed as early as 1805.[69]

2. Counteracting Tendencies

What consequences does Playfair draw from his theory of the fundamental developmental trends of capitalism?

The prospect of decay presented Playfair, who assumed it to be a proven truth as regards the whole historical past of more than three thousand years, with considerable

---

66. Ibid., 91, 162.
67. Ibid., 135.
68. Ibid., 67.
69. Hobson, *An Economic Interpretation of Investment*.

theoretical difficulties insofar as he dealt with the future evolution of Britain, then the leading industrial country in the world. The French evolutionists, Condorcet, Sismondi, and particularly Saint-Simon, or utopian socialists like Pecqueur and Considerant were able to point out the contradictions and inadequacies of capitalism because they not only criticized such inadequacies but also rejected the existing social organization and wanted it replaced by a higher form.[70] But Playfair, who criticizes the contradictions of capitalism with equal keenness, is a partisan of capitalism and wants to preserve it despite its evils. The idea of a transition to another, socialist organization is outside his horizon, because in his eyes the existing capitalist form is the highest, and he violently criticizes the French Revolution for its "levelling" tendencies. But if the capitalist basis is retained, then, according to Playfair's own general historical law valid for all epochs, society is threatened with decay, because these tendencies originate in wealth, that is, in the very essence of capital accumulation. The danger is all the more to be feared because history shows that wealth and power "never have been renewed when once destroyed."[71]

Thus the theoretical problem has a practical implication, and Playfair raises the question whether England cannot avert such a tragic end: "It is then worth while to inquire into the causes of so terrible a reverse," [whether] that "degradation which naturally follows, and which has always followed hitherto, may be averted."[72]

He solves this problem by distinguishing between "necessity" and "tendency," and by a new methodological construction in which the dominant tendency is weakened by one or more counteracting tendencies. These do not eliminate the main tendency but check its effectiveness and postpone its ultimate triumph.

If decay were a historical necessity impossible to avert, the "inquiry would be of no utility. It is of no importance to seek for means of preventing what must of necessity come to pass: but if the word necessity is changed for tendency or propensity, then it becomes an inquiry deserving attention." "It merits investigation, whether it is or is not possible to counteract the tendency to decline . . . after having attained the summit of wealth, we may remain there instead of immediately descending."[73]

We know that later Ricardo (1817), John Stuart Mill (1848), and Karl Marx (1867) resorted to the same methodological instrument of a dominant tendency and counteracting tendencies.[74]

Economic theory recorded this as a fact but has never raised the problem of the origin of this idea and has never inquired into the circumstances that led to making such

---

70. See Grossman, "The Evolutionist Revolt," chapter 4 in the present volume.

71. Playfair, *Inquiry into Permanent Causes*, 79.

72. Ibid., iv–v.

73. Ibid., ix, 169.

74. [Ricardo, *Principles of Political Economy*, for example p. 52; John Stuart Mill, *Principles of Political Economy*, 481–91. Grossman refers to the first volume of Marx's *Capital*. Marx's extensive discussion of the tendency for the rate of profit to fall and its countertendencies is, however, in the third volume. Marx, *Capital*, vol. 3, 317–48.]

a distinction between the tendencies. The foregoing passage from Playfair's book shows that he is the originator of the idea and casts light on the circumstances that led him to this important methodological construction. Playfair, the petty-bourgeois theorist, elaborates the counteracting tendencies because he regards them as the theoretical justification of an effort to preserve the existing capitalist society from disintegration and decay, or at least to postpone them for several generations.

This does not mean that Playfair places his subjective wish for the preservation of capitalism above the objective developmental trends; he still thinks that history is governed by necessity. Just as he tries to show the objective inevitability of decline on the basis of the internal structure of the economic organism, "the interior causes," so, remaining true to his methodological principles, he inquires whether objective countertendencies are not active within the economic organism. Only if such objective countertendencies can be discovered is there room for the intervention of the subjective factor—the deliberate effort to strengthen them.

According to Playfair, the task of strengthening and directing these objective countertendencies is incumbent not upon individuals but upon the government: "Government can never be better employed than in counteracting this tendency to decay."[75] This does not eliminate the inevitability of decline, but—and this is all that Playfair expects from his *Inquiry*—it might be possible "to find the means by which prosperity may be lengthened out, and the period of humiliation procrastinated to a distant day."[76]

With the help of such a distinction between "necessity" and "tendency" and between "tendency" and "counteracting tendency," Playfair's general law of rise from barbarism to civilization and subsequent decline can be upheld theoretically with regard not only to the past but also to Britain's future, at the same time the decline of England, even though the existing capitalist basis is maintained, can be averted or at least postponed for long generations.

What are these counteracting tendencies? Playfair enumerates several, of which we shall discuss the most important—export of capital.[77]

Superabundance of capital in an industrial nation entails consequences that Playfair describes in a special chapter entitled "Of the Tendency of Capital and Industry to Leave a Wealthy Country."[78] "If there is not sufficient means of employing capital within a nation or country . . . there are plenty of opportunities furnished by poorer nations." This withdrawal of capital "that operate[s] . . . in some modern nations, is

---

75. Playfair, *Inquiry into Permanent Causes*, 172.
76. Ibid., iv. Playfair emphasizes this idea in the subtitle of his book: *An Inquiry . . . Designed to Show How the Prosperity of the British Empire May Be Prolonged*.
77. The counteracting tendencies listed here—export of commodities and of capital, decentralization of capital, further various forms of unproductive expenditure and waste—are the same as those mentioned forty years later by John Stuart Mill, *Principles of Political Economy*, 487–88. This fact suggests that Mill carefully read Playfair.
78. Playfair, *Inquiry into the Causes*, 161–65.

counteracting this effect, so far as it is occasioned by a superabundance of capital." "As it raises the poor nation nearer the level of the rich one, its effect gradually becomes less powerful."[79]

Nations with superabundant capital indulge in comforts, keep numerous servants, and work less than the poorer nations, just as the sons of a well-to-do father work less than the father worked in his youth.

But the export of capital, though it counteracts the effects occasioned by superabundance of capital, does not eliminate the dominant tendency to decline. These counteracting tendencies relieve the situation of capital-saturated countries only temporarily. In the long run "the intercourse between nations is . . . in favour of the poorer one." "The capital of a rich nation is employed in fostering a rivalship in a poorer nation."[80]

Young nations that appear as rivals of older and wealthier nations enjoy a number of advantages that enable them to rise faster and even to overtake their models. Elaborating on an idea that Condorcet formulated ten years earlier, Playfair observes that the leading nations can develop technology and invent new methods of work only by the hard way of trial and error. The rival young nations need to imitate only the successful inventions, thus saving a great deal of time and expenditure. "The nation that is highest, treads in discovery, invention, etc. a new path. . . . Those who follow have, in general, but to copy, and in doing that, it is generally pretty easy to improve." "So far as method of working and machinery are concerned, the imitating nation has the advantage; it copies the best sort of machine and the best manners of working at once."[81] This, according to Playfair, explains the fact that whereas the old industrial nations that improved their technique step by step are burdened with many obsolete machines, "the nations that have improved in manufactures the latest have always carried them to the greatest perfection."[82]

In this manner the relief experienced by capital-saturated nations through export of capital to backward nations is of short duration. Their economic and technical advantage is only temporary, it disappears by degrees, and England "cannot be expected long to maintain its superiority over others."[83]

It is of little avail to possess a legal or factual monopoly in order to secure superiority: "Holland, Flanders, and France were all originally superior, in the arts of manufacturing most goods, to England."[84]

Nevertheless, these countries lost their superiority to England, because while the rising nation's industrialization is stimulated by high profits, the low profits earned by the advanced nation "which is about being rivalled" produces "a sort of discourage-

---

79. [Ibid., 135, 164, 183. Editor's interpolation.]
80. Ibid., 179, 180.
81. Ibid., 208, 212.
82. Ibid., 211.
83. Ibid., 204.
84. Ibid., 203.

ment and dismay."[85] Such nations with superabundant capital cease accumulating; they tend to a stationary state in which no capital investments take place: "At all events, a day must arrive when the nation that is highest, ceasing to proceed, the others must overtake it."[86] "From this it is very evident, that the nation the farthest advanced in inventions has only to remain stationary a few years, and it will soon be overtaken, and perhaps surpassed."[87]

Thus the export of capital, which brought temporary relief and advantage to the industrial country exporting capital, in time undermines its long-range interests, because the exported capital helps in the industrialization of the rival country: "In this manner it is, that the capital of a rich country supplies the want of it in poorer ones, and that, by degrees, a nation saps the foundation of its own wealth and greatness, and gives encouragement to them in others."[88]

Playfair illustrates this development by the example of Holland: "the Dutch, for the last century, employed their capital in this manner, and, at one time, were the chief carriers . . . giving credit largely. . . . They ruined many of their own manufactures in this manner. . . . There are many manufactures in England that originally rose by means of Dutch capital."[89]

Thus Playfair shows that there is an insoluble antagonism of interest between the industrial and merchant capital of a country. At first the Dutch merchants "ruined many of their own manufactures" by giving large credits to foreigners, earned large profits as merchants and carriers of raw materials and finished commodities; but later "they sunk both as a commercial and manufacturing people."[90]

However, Playfair does not reproach the Dutch merchants with lack of patriotism; he considers their conduct inevitable in a nation that has reached the creditor stage. Every merchant is under pressure of competition and must take the constantly changing circumstances into account. He cannot stop to consider whether he serves or harms his nation; he is guided and driven by the profit incentive, the principle on which the system of private enterprise rests. Should he allow himself to be guided by other motives, he would soon be ruined. The transfer of capital and industry abroad is not the result of the merchant's personal decision but of an objective tendency of industry in a nation that has reached the creditor stage.

The counteracting tendencies, therefore, bring only temporary relief; in the long run, the backward agricultural and colonial countries are industrialized with the help of exported capital and attain the level of the wealthy countries; they, too, enter a stage at which they have accumulated sufficient capital of their own or even have begun to suffer from superabundance of capital. At such a future stage of development, all inter-

---

85. Ibid., 212.
86. Ibid., 208.
87. Ibid., 203.
88. Ibid., 181.
89. Ibid.
90. Ibid.

national credit operations will inevitably stop: "If the time should ever come that capital should be abundant in all nations . . . obtaining credit will not be an object."[91]

For despite the operation of all counteracting trends, the dominant trend, if the changes and rebounds caused by wars are disregarded, asserts itself in the end; all nations will ultimately reach the state of capital saturation, or the stationary state.

The fact that as early as the first half of the nineteenth century, before Karl Marx, a number of authors such as Playfair (1805), Sismondi (1819), Pecqueur (1837), and Victor Considerant (1843) described the objective developmental trends of capitalism raises the question of Marx's relation to his forerunners.[92] If he is not the originator of the idea, what is Marx's contribution to that doctrine?

Marx approached the problem of the developmental tendencies of capitalism not as a historian but as a theoretician. His purpose was not once again to describe these tendencies that had repeatedly been described in contemporary French literature but to explain them. Marx's *Capital* does not contain a single chapter or section in which the above-mentioned developmental trends are described—as is the case with Sismondi, Pecqueur, or Considerant—as empirical facts. In chapter 32, "The Historical Tendency of Capitalist Accumulation," and in chapter 25, "General Law of Capitalist Accumulation," Marx strives to show *why* the trend to concentration (and the associated trends to centralization and to the destruction of the small and medium industries) is the *inevitable* result of capitalist accumulation on the basis of the law of value; his purpose is to show that all these trends are dominated and explainable by the law of accumulation.[93]

At the same time Marx developed an idea that was completely alien to all his forerunners and that is the focal point of Marx's theory of the developmental trends of capitalism: the idea that the trends to concentration and centralization, as well as the disappearance of small industry, follow *one* direction, and that they are only the outward expression of the slow, gradual, long process of socialization of labor—even under capitalism—a process that paves the way for the socialized economy of the future. This process begins with the "scattered private property resting on the personal labour of individuals"; it continues with the "centralisation of the means of production and socialisation of labour"; and it ends with the transformation "of capitalist private property, which in fact already rests on the carrying on of production by society, into social property"—a result that looms only at the end of a long historical transformation of social labor.[94] What Playfair, Sismondi, Pecqueur, and Considerant could not see were the far-reaching implications of this historic process. It is true

91. Ibid.

92. [Sismondi, *New Principles of Political Economy*; Pecqueur, *Économie sociale des interets*; Considerant, *Principes du socialisme.*]

93. [Marx, *Capital*, vol. 1, 762–870, 927–30.] It must be stressed that Marx does not use the word "trend" or "tendencies" in the usual sense of the term; by "trend" he means "tendencies winning their way through and working themselves out with iron necessity," Marx, *Capital*, vol. 1, 91. The other factors and countertrends can weaken or slow up the dominant trend but not prevent it from asserting itself.

94. [Ibid., 929–30.]

that many writers before Marx referred to the regularity of crises and the precarious condition of the working class. However, these insights remained mere observations until Marx showed them to be the inevitable result of another long-term fundamental tendency, which he discovered—the tendency of capital, as technology advances, to increase its so-called "organic composition," that is, the amount of invested fixed capital per worker.

—New York City

References

Adler, Max. *Kant und der Marxismus*. Berlin: Laub'sche Verlagsbuchhandlung, 1925.

————. *Kausalität und Teleologie im Streite um die Wissenschaft*. Vienna: Verlag der Wiener Volksbuchhandlung Brand, 1904.

————. *Marx als Denker: Zum 25; Todesjahre von Karl Marx*. Berlin: Verlag Buchhandlung Vorwärts, 1908.

————. *Marxistische Probleme: Beiträge zur Theorie der materialistischen Geschichtsauffsung und Dialektik*. Stuttgart: Dietz, 1913.

Adorno, Theodor W., and Max Horkheimer. *Towards a New Manifesto*. London: Verso, 2011 [written 1956].

Aftalion, Albert. "Les crises économiques et financières." *Recueil des cours de L'Académie de Droit International de La Haye* 39 (1932): 273–350.

————. *Les crises périodiques de surproduction*. Paris: Rivière, 1913.

————. "L'oeuvre économique de Simonde de Sismondi." Doctoral thesis, University of Paris Law Faculty, 1899.

Amoroso, Luigi. "La meccanica economica." *Giornali degli Economisti* 64 (1924): 45–54.

Andler, Charles. *Introduction historique et commentaire au* Manifeste communiste. Paris: Rieder, 1901.

Anonymous. "Dos 40 yohriger yubileum fun *Kapital*." *Sotsial-demokrat*, July 19, 1907.

————. *Observations on Certain Verbal Disputes in Political Economy*. London: R. Hunter, 1821.

Aristotle. *Aristotle's Politics*. Translated by Benjamin Jowett. Oxford: Clarendon, 1905.

Aucuy, Marc. *Les systèmes socialistes d'échange*. Paris: Alcan, 1908.

Ayres, Leonard P. *Turning Points in Business Cycles*. New York: Macmillan, 1939.

Babel, Anthony. "La notion de progrès chez Sismondi." *Revue international de sociologie* 46 (1938): 296–328.

Bastiat, Frédéric. *Economic Sophisms*. Edinburgh: Oliver and Boyd, 1873 [1845, 1848].

————. *Harmonies of Political Economy*. Translated by Patrick James Stirling. Edinburgh:

Oliver and Boyd, 1880 [1850].

Basu, Deepankar and Panayiotis T. Manolakos. "Is There a Tendency for the Rate of Profit to Fall? Econometric Evidence for the U.S. Economy, 1948–2007." *Review of Radical Political Economics* 45, no. 1 (2012): 76 –95.

Bauer, Otto. "The Accumulation of Capital." Translated by J. E. King. *History of Political Economy* 18, no. 1 (1986): 87–110 [1913].

———. "Die Akkumulation des Kapitals." *Neue Zeit* 31, part 1, nos. 23 and 24 (1913): 831–38, 862–74.

———. *Einführung in die Volkswirtschaftslehre.* Vienna: Verlag der Wiener Volksbuchhandlung, 1956 [written 1927–1928].

———. "Marxismus und Ethik." *Neue Zeit* 24, part 2, no. 41 (1906): 485–99.

Bazard, Saint-Amand. *The Doctrine of Saint-Simon: An Exposition; First Year, 1828–1829.* Boston: Beacon Press, 1958 [1828–1829].

Bernadelli, Harro. "The End of the Marginal Utility Theory?" *Economica*, n.s., 5, no. 18 (1938): 192–212.

Bernstein, Eduard. "Der Kampf der Sozialdemokratie und die Revolution der Gesellschaft." *Neue Zeit* 16, part 1, nos. 16 and 18 (1898): 484–97, 548–57.

———. *The Preconditions of Socialism.* Translated by Henry Tudor. Cambridge: Cambridge University Press, 1993.

———. *Der Revisionismus in der Sozialdemocratie.* Amsterdam: Cohen, 1909.

———. "Sozialistische Oekonomie in England." *Neue Zeit* 15, part 1, no. 2 (1896): 46–54.

———. *Wie ist wissenschaftlicher Socialismus möglich? Ein Vortrag.* Berlin: Verlag der Socialistischen Monatshefte, 1901.

———. *Zur Geschichte und Theorie des Socialismus: Gesammelte Abhandlungen.* Berlin: Edelheim, 1901.

Bilimovic, Alexander. "Irving Fishers statistische Methode für die Bemessung des Grenznutzens." *Zeitschrift für Nationalökonomie* 1, no. 1 (1929): 114–28.

———. "Ein neuer Versuch der Bemessung des Grenznutzens." *Zeitschrift für Nationalökonomie* 4, no. 2 (1934): 161–87.

———. "Zins and Unternehmergewinn im Gleichungssystem der stationären Wirtschaft." *Zeitschrift für Nationalökonomie* 8, no. 3 (1937): 297–32.

———. "Zur Verteidigung der Gleichgewichtsidee." *Zeitschrift für Nationalökonomie* 8, no. 2 (1937): 220–28.

Blanc, Louis. *The Organization of Labour.* London: Clarke, 1848 [1839].

Blanqui, Adolphe. *History of Political Economy.* New York: G. Putnam's Sons, 1885 [1860].

Bode, Karl. "Prosperität und Depression." *Zeitschrift für Nationalökonomie* 8, no. 5 (1937): 597–614.

Böhm-Bawerk, Eugen. *Capital and Interest.* 3 vols. Translated by George D. Huncke and Hans F. Sennholz. South Holland, IL: Libertarian Press, 1959.

———. "On the 'Measurability' of Sensations." In *Capital and Interest,* vol. 3, *Further*

    Essays on Capital and Interest. Translated by Hans F. Sennholz, 124–36 [1888, 1921].

Bonar, James. *Malthus and His Work*. 2nd edition. London: Allen & Unwin, 1924.

Bortkiewicz, Ladislaus. "On the Correction of Marx's Fundamental Theoretical Construction in the Third Volume of *Capital*." Translated by Paul Sweezy. In Eugen von Böhm-Bawerk and Rudolf Hilferding, *Karl Marx and the Close of His System and Böhm-Bawerk's Criticism of Marx*, 199–221. New York: Kelley, 1949 [1907].

————. *Value and Price in the Marxian System*. International Economic Papers, no. 2 (1952).

Boudin, B. Louis. *The Theoretical System of Karl Marx in the Light of Recent Criticism*. Chicago: Kerr, 1907.

————. *Das theoretische System von Karl Marx*. Stuttgart: Dietz, 1909.

Bousquet, Georges-Henri. *Essai sur l'évolution de la pensée économique*. Paris: Giard, 1927.

Bowley, Marian. *Nassau Senior and Classical Economics*. London: Allen & Unwin, 1937.

Bramble, Tom. "Is There a Labour Aristocracy in Australia?" *Marxist Left Review* 4 (Winter, 2012). Available at http://marxistleftreview.org/.

Brauer, Theodor. *Der moderne deutsche Sozialismus*. Freiburg: Herder, 1929.

Bray, John Francis. *Labour's Wrongs and Labour's Remedy*. Leeds: David Green, 1839.

Braunthal, Alfred. *Wirtschaft der Gegenwart und ihre Gesetze: Ein sozialistisches Lehrbuch der Nationalökonomie*. Berlin: Laubsche Verlagsbuchhandlung, 1930.

Brousse, Paul. *Le Marxisme dans l'Internationale*. Paris: Le Proletaire, 1882.

Bucharin, Nikolai. *Imperialismus und Weltwirtschaft*. Vienna: Verlag für Literatur und Politik, 1929.

————. *See also* Bukharin, Nikolai.

Bücher, Karl. *Die Entstehung der Volkswirtschaft*. 5th edition. Tübingen: Laupp, 1906.

Buchs, Maurice. "Le Fouriérisme aux Etats Unis." Doctoral thesis, University of Paris, 1948.

Bukharin, Nikolai. *The Economic Theory of the Leisure Class*. New York: Monthly Review, 1972.

————. *Imperialism and the Accumulation of Capital*, with Rosa Luxemburg, *The Accumulation of Capital an Anti-Critique*. Edited by Kenneth Tarbuck. Translated by Rudolf Wichmann. New York: Monthly Review Press, 1972 [1925–1926].

————. *Imperialism and World Economy*. London: Lawrence, 1929 [1919, written 1914 and 1917].

————. *The Politics and Economics of the Transition Period*. London: Routledge & Kegan Paul, 1979 [1920].

————. "The Programme of the International and the Communist Parties." In *Toward the United Front: Proceedings of the Fourth Congress of the Communist International, 1922*, translated and edited by John Riddell, 479–501. Leiden: Brill, 2012 [1922].

————. *See also* Bucharin, Nikolai.

Burkett, Paul. "Marx's Reproduction Schemes and the Environment." *Ecological Economics* 49, no. 42 (2004): 457–67.

Bury, John Bagnell. *The Idea of Progress*. London: Macmillan, 1920.

Cairnes, John Elliott. *The Character and Logical Method of Political Economy*. New York: Harper, 1875 [1857].

Canard, Nicolas-François. *Principes d'économie politique*. Paris: F. Buisson, 1801.

Carchedi, Guglielmo. *Frontiers of Political Economy*. London: Verso, 1991.

Carchedi, Guglielmo, and Michael Roberts. "The Long Roots of the Present Crisis: Keynesians, Austerians, and Marx's Law." *World Review of Political Economy* 4, no. 1 (2013): 86–115.

Carey, Henry Charles. *The Past, the Present and the Future*. Philadelphia: Carey & Hart, 1848.

Carver, Thomas Nixon. "The Static State and the Technology of Economic Reform." In *Economic Essays Contributed in Honour of John Bates Clark*, edited by Jacob Hollander, 29–45. New York: Macmillan, 1927.

Cassel, Gustav. "Keynes' 'General Theory.'" *International Labour Review* 36, no. 4 (1937): 437–45.

———. *The Theory of Social Economy*. London: Unwin, 1932 [1918].

Chaloupek, Günther. "Marxistische Kritik an der Österreichischen Schule." In *Die Wiener Schule der Nationalökonomie*, edited by Norbert Leser, 195–221. Vienna: Böhlau-Verlag, 1986.

Chao, Nai-Tuan. "Richard Jones: An Early English Institutionalist." Doctoral dissertation, Columbia University, New York, 1930.

Chaptal, Jean-Antoine. *De l'industrie française*. Vol. 2. Paris: Antoine-Augustin Renouard, 1819.

Charasoff, Georg. *Das System des Marxismus: Darstellung und Kritik*. Berlin: Bondy, 1910.

Chayanov, Alexander Vasilyevich. *Die optimalen Betriebsgrössen in der Landwirtschaft*. Berlin: Parey, 1930 [1921].

———. *The Theory of Peasant Co-operatives*. Columbus: Ohio State University Press, 1991 [1919].

———. *The Theory of the Peasant Economy*. Homewood, IL: R. D. Irwin, 1966 [1923].

Clark, John Bates. *The Distribution of Wealth*. New York: Macmillan, 1927.

———. *Essentials of Economic Theory*. New York: Macmillan, 1915 [1899].

Clark, John Maurice. "Business Acceleration and the Law of Demand." *Journal of Political Economy* 25, no. 3 (1917): 217–23.

———. "The Relation between Statics and Dynamics." In *Economic Essays Contributed in Honour of John Bates Clark*, edited by Jacob Hollander, 48–70. New York: Macmillan, 1937.

Cliff, Tony. *State Capitalism in Russia*. London: Pluto, 1974 [1955].

———. "The Economic Roots of Reformism." *Socialist Review* 6, no. 9 (1957). Available at www.marxists.org.

Cohen, Hermann. "Einleitung mit kritischem Nachtrag." In Friedrich Albert Lange, *Geschichte des Materialismus seit Kant*. 5th edition. Leipzig: Baedeker, 1896.

Cohen, Morris Raphael. *Reason and Nature: An Essay on the Meaning of Scientific Method*.

New York: Harcourt, Brace, 1931.

Cole, George Douglas Howard. *Guild Socialism*. London: Fabian Society, 1920.

————. *Selbstverwaltung in der Industrie*. Berlin: Engelmann, 1921.

————. *Self-Government in Industry*. London: Bell and Sons, 1920 [1917].

Cole, George Douglas Howard, and William Mellor. *Gildensozialismus*. Cologne: Rhein-land, 1921.

————. *The Meaning of Industrial Freedom*. London: Allen and Unwin, 1918.

Colquhoun, Patrick. *A Treatise on the Wealth, Power, and Resources of the British Empire*. London: Joseph Mawman, 1814.

Comte, Auguste. *Cours de philosophie positive*. Vol. 4. Paris: Schleicher Frères, 1908 [1838].

————. *Cours de philosophie positive*. Vol. 6. Paris: Schleicher Frères, 1908 [1842].

Condorcet, Marie-Jean-Antoine-Nicolas. *Outlines of an Historical View of the Progress of the Human Mind*. New York: M. Carey, H. & P. Price and Company etc., 1796 .

Conrad, Otto. "Die Grundannahme der Gleichgewichtstheorie." *Zeitschrift für Nation-alökonomie* 7, no. 2 (1936): 234–43.

————. *Der Mechanismus der Verkehrswirtschaft*. Jena: Fischer, 1931.

Considerant, Victor. *Principes du socialisme, manifeste de la democratie au XIXe siecle*. Paris: Librairie Phalanstérienne, 1847 [1843].

Cossa, Luigi. *Histoire des doctrines économiques*. Paris: V. Briard & E. Brière, 1809.

Croce, Benedetto. *Historical Materialism and the Economics of Karl Marx*. London: George Allen and Unwin, 1914 [1899].

————. *Philosophy of the Practical: Economic and Ethic*. London: Macmillan, 1913 [1909].

Cunow, Heinrich. *Die Marxsche Geschichts-, Gesellschafts- und Staatstheorie: Grundzüge der Marxschen Soziologie*. Berlin: Buchhandlung Vorwärts, 1920.

————. "Zur Zusammenbruchstheorie." *Neue Zeit* 17, part 1, nos. 12–14 (1898): 356–64, 396–403, 424–30.

David, Eduard. *Socialismus und Landwirtschaft*. Berlin: Verlag der Socialistischen Mona-tshefte, 1903.

Day, Richard B. "The Theory of the Long Cycle: Kondratiev, Trotsky, Mandel." *New Left Review*, series 1, 99 (1976): 67–82.

Denis, Hector. *Histoire des systèmes économiques et socialistes*. Vol. 2. Paris: V. Giard & E. Brière, 1907.

Dobb, Maurice. *Political Economy and Capitalism: Some Essays in Economic Tradition*. Lon-don: Routledge, 1937.

Douglas, Paul H. "Smith's Theory of Value and Distribution." *University Journal of Busi-ness* 5, no. 1 (1927): 53–87.

Dupuit, Jules. "On the Measurement of the Utility of Public Works." In *Readings in Welfare Economics*, edited by Kenneth J. Arrow and Tibor Scitovsky, 255–83. Home-wood, IL: Richard D. Irwin, 1969 [1844].

Eckstein, Gustav. "Die vierfache Wurzel des Satzes vom unzureichenden Grunde der Grenznutztheorie: Eine Robinsonade." *Neue Zeit* 20, part 2, no. 26 (1902): 810–16.

————. "Zur Methode der politischen Ökonomie." *Neue Zeit* 28, part 1, nos. 10, 11, and 14 (1909 [1904]): 324–32, 367–75, and 489–97.

Eisenhart, Hugo. *Geschichte der Nationalökonomik*. 3rd edition. Jena: Fischer, 1910.

Elster, Ludwig. "J. Ch. L. Simonde de Sismondi: Ein Beitrag zur Geschichte der Volkswirtschaftslehre." *Jahrbücher für Nationalökonomie und Statistik* 48, n.s., 14, nos. 4–5 (1887): 321–82.

————. "Smiths Lehre and die Lehren der sogenannten 'Klassiker der Volkswirtschaftslehre.'" In *Wörterbuch der Volkswirtschaft*, vol. 3, edited by Ludwig Elster. 4th edition. Jena: Fischer, 1933: 211-33.

————, ed. *Wörterbuch der Volkswirtschaft*. 3 vols. 4th edition. Jena: Fischer, 1931–33.

Ely, Richard T. *Studies in the Evolution of Industrial Society*. New York: Macmillan, 1903.

Enfantin, Barthélemy Prosper. "Deuxième enseignement: L'Histoire." In Henri Saint-Simon and Barthélemy Prosper Enfantin. *Oeuvres de Saint-Simon et d'Enfantin*, vol. 14, 45–74 [1831].

————. "Dix-huitième enseignement: L'Histoire." In Henri Saint-Simon and Barthélemy Prosper Enfantin, *Oeuvres de Saint-Simon et d'Enfantin*, vol. 17, 103–40 [1832].

————. *Les mémoires d'un industriel de l'an 2240*. In Henri Saint-Simon and Barthélemy Prosper Enfantin, *Oeuvres de Saint-Simon et d'Enfantin*, vol. 17, 141–214 [1838].

Engels, Frederick. *Anti-Dühring: Herr Eugen Dühring's Revolution in Science*. In *Marx and Engels Collected Works*, vol. 25, 1–309 [1878].

————. "A Critique of the Draft Social-Democratic Programme of 1891." In *Marx and Engels Collected Works*, vol. 27, 217–33 [1891].

————. Friedrich Engels to Joseph Bloch, September 21, 1890. In *Marx and Engels Collected Works*, vol. 49, 33–36.

————. Friedrich Engels to Karl Kautsky, June 26, 1884. In *Marx and Engels Collected Works*, vol. 47, 155–57.

————. Friedrich Engels to Nikolai Danielson, January 5, 1888. In *Marx and Engels Collected Works*, vol. 48, 135–37.

————. Introduction to *The Class Struggles in France*, by Karl Marx. In *Marx and Engels Collected Works*, vol. 27, 506–24 [1895].

————. Preface to *Capital*, vol. 2, by Karl Marx, 83–102 [1884]

————. *Socialism: Utopian and Scientific*. In *Marx and Engels Collected Works*, vol. 24, 281–325 [1878].

Engländer, Oskar. "Böhm-Bawerk und Marx." *Archiv für Sozialwissenschaft and Sozialpolitik* 60 (1928): 368–81.

Espinas, Alfred Victor. *Histoire des doctrines économiques*. Paris: Colin, 1891.

Ferguson, Adam. *Essay on the History of Civil Society*. 7th edition. Boston: Hastings, Etheridge and Bliss, 1809 [1767].

Fichte, Johann Gottlieb. *The Closed Commercial State*. Albany: State University of New York Press, 2012 [1800].

Fischer, Kuno. *Hegels Leben, Werke und Lehre*. Part 2. Heidelberg: Carl Winter's Universitätsbuchhandlung, 1901.

Fisher, Irving. *Mathematical Investigations in the Theory of Value and Prices. Transactions of the Connecticut Academy of Arts and Sciences* 9 (1892): 1–124.

———. *Stabilizing the Dollar*. New York: Macmillan, 1925 [1920].

Ford, Henry. *My Life and Work*. New York: Doubleday, 1922.

Foster, John Bellamy, and Robert W. McChesney. "Listen Keynesians, It's the System! Response to Palley." *Monthly Review* 61, no. 11 (2010): 44–56.

Foxwell, Herbert. Introduction to *The Right to the Whole Produce of Labour*, by Anton Menger. London: Macmillan, 1899.

Freudenthal, Gideon and Peter McLaughlin, eds. *The Social and Economic Roots of the Scientific Revolution: Texts by Boris Hessen and Henryk Grossmann*. Dordrecht: Springer, 2009.

Funkhouser, H. G., and Helen M. Walker. "Playfair and His Charts." In *Economic History*, supplement to *Economic Journal*, 103–9 (1935).

Ganilh, Charles. *La théorie de l'économie politique*. Vol. 1. Paris: Deterville, 1815.

Gibbins, Henry de Beltgens. *The Industrial History of England*. London: Methuen, 1897 [1890].

Gide, Charles, and Charles Rist. *A History of Economic Doctrines*. Boston: Heath, 1915.

Godwin, Parke. *Democracy Constructive and Pacific*. New York: J. Winchester, 1844.

Gonnard, René. *Histoire des doctrines économiques*. Vol. 3. Paris: Nouvelle Librairie Nationale, 1922.

Gorter, Herman. *Der Imperialismus, der Weltkrieg und die Sozial-demokratie*. Amsterdam: Sozial-demokratische Partei Hollands, 1915.

Gossen, Hermann Heinrich. *The Laws of Human Relations and the Rules of Human Action Derived Therefrom*. Cambridge, MA: MIT Press, 1983 [1854].

Gottl, Friedrich. *Die Herrschaft des Wortes*. Jena: Gustav Fischer, 1901.

Gray, John. *The Social System: A Treatise on the Principle of Exchange*. Edinburgh: William Tait, 1831.

Grossman, Henryk (*see also* Grossmann, Henryk). "The Beginnings of Capitalism and the New Mass Morality." *Journal of Classical Sociology* 6, no. 2 (2006 [written 1934]): 201–13.

———. "The Change in the Original Plan for Marx's *Capital* and Its Causes." Translated by Geoffrey McCormack. *Historical Materialism* 21, no. 3 (2013 [1929]): 138–64.

———. "Ekonomiczny system Karola Marksa." *Kultura Robotnicza* 2 (10), no. 32 (1923): 295–99.

———. "The Evolutionist Revolt against Classical Economics." In *Karl Marx's Social and Political Thought: Critical Assessments*, vol. 1, edited by Bob Jessop, 253–74. London: Routledge, 1990.

———. "The Evolutionist Revolt against Classical Economics." In *Thomas Tooke (1774–1858), Mountifort Longfield (1802–1884), Richard Jones (1790–1855)*, edited by Mark Blaug, 1–16. Aldershot, Hants: Elgar, 1991.

———. "The Evolutionist Revolt against Classical Economics: I. In France—Condorcet, Saint-Simon, Simonde de Sismondi." *Journal of Political Economy* 51, no. 5 (1943): 381–96.

———. "The Evolutionist Revolt against Classical Economics: II. In England—James Steuart, Richard Jones, Karl Marx." *Journal of Political Economy* 51, no. 6 (1943): 506–522.

———. *Fifty Years of Struggle over Marxism*. Translated by Rick Kuhn and Einde O'Callaghan. Melbourne: Socialist Alternative, 2014 [1932].

———. Henryk Grossman to Max Horkheimer, June 30, 1937. Na 1 Nachless Max Horkheimer, VI 9.320, Universitätsbibliothek, Goethe Universität, Frankfurt.

———. Henryk Grossman to Max Horkheimer, October 1, 1936. In Horkheimer, *Gesammelte Schiften*. Vol. 15, *Briefwechsel 1913–1936*, 641–42. Frankfurt: Fischer, 1995.

———. *Marx, Classical Political Economy and the Problem of Dynamics*. Translated by Pete Burgess. *Capital and Class* 1, no. 2 (1977 [1941]): 32–55 and 1, no. 3 (1977 [1941]): 67–99.

———. *Marx, Classical Political Economy and the Problem of Dynamics*. Translated by Rick Kuhn. Melbourne: Socialist Alternative, 2015 [1941].

———. *Marx, die Klassische Nationaloekonomie und das Problem der Dynamik*. Mimeograph. New York: Institut für Sozialforschung, 1941.

———. "Polityka przemysłowa i handlowa rządu Terezynansko-Józefińskiego w Galicyi 1772–1790: Referat na V. Zjazd prawnikow i ekonomistow polskich." In *Przeglad prawa i administracyi* (1912): 1–43.

———. "Przycznek do historji socjalizmu w Polsce przed laty czterdziestu." In Karol Marks, Karol Marks: Pisma niewydane, translated by Henryk Grossman, iii–xxvii. Warsaw: Książka, 1923.

———. Review of *Turning Points in Business Cycles*, by L. P. Ayres. *Zeitschrift für Sozialforschung* 8, no. 3 (1939): 490–92.

———. *Simonde de Sismondi et ses théories économiques: Une nouvelle interprétation de sa pensée*. Warsaw: Bibliotheca Universitatis Liberae Polniae, 1924.

———. "Sismondi, Jean Charles Leonard Simonde de (1773–1842)." In *Encyclopaedia of the Social Sciences*, edited by Edwin R. A. Seligman, vol. 14, 69–71. New York: Macmillan, 1934.

———. "The Theory of Economic Crises." In *Value, Capitalist Dynamics and Money*, edited by Paul Zarembka and Susanne Soederberg, 171–80. Research in Political Economy. New York: Elsevier Science, 2000 [19??].

———. "W. Playfair, the Earliest Theorist of Capitalist Development." *Economic History Review* 18, no. 1–2 (1948): 65–83.

Grossmann, Henryk (*see also* Grossman, Henryk). *Das Akkumulations- und Zusammenbruchsgesetz des kapitalistischen Systems (zugleich eine Krisentheorie)*. Hirschfeld: Leipzig, 1929.

———. "Die Anfänge und geschichtliche Entwicklung der amtlichen Statistik in Österreich." *Statistische Monatsschrift*, n.s., 21 (1916): 331–423.

————. "Bolschevismus." In Elster, *Wörterbuch der Volkswirtschaft*, vol. 1, 421–44.

————. "Descartes and the Social Origins of the Mechanistic Concept of the World." In *The Social and Economic Roots of the Scientific Revolution*, edited by Freudenthal and McLaughlin, 157–229 [written 1940s].

————. "Die Fortentwicklung des Marxismus bis zur Gegenwart." In Elster, *Wörterbuch der Volkswirtschaft*, vol. 3, 313–41.

————. *Fünfzig Jahre Kampf um den Marxismus 1883–1932*. Jena: Fischer, 1932.

————. "Die Goldproduktion im Reproduktionsschema von Marx und Rosa Luxemburg." In Max Adler et al., *Festschrift für Carl Grünberg zum 70. Geburtstag*, 152–84. Hirschfeld: Leipzig, 1932.

————. Henryk Grossmann to Paul Mattick, February 19, 1935. In *Marx, die klassische Nationalökonomie und das Problem der Dynamik*, 102.

————. Henryk Grossmann to Paul Mattick, July 18, 1937. In *Marx, die klassische Nationalökonomie und das Problem der Dynamik*, 112.

————. "Internationale: Die dritte Internationale." In Elster, *Wörterbuch der Volkswirtschaft*, vol. 2, 439–49.

————. "Internationale: Die zweite Internationale." In Elster, *Wörterbuch der Volkswirtschaft*, vol. 2, 432–39.

————. "Jaurès, Jean." In Elster, *Wörterbuch der Volkswirtschaft*, vol. 2, 382–83.

————. *The Law of Accumulation and Breakdown of the Capitalist System: Being Also a Theory of Crises*. Abridged English translation by Jairus Banaji. London: Pluto Press, 1992 [1929].

————. *Marx, Classical Economics, and the Problem of Dynamics*. Translated by Paul Mattick Jr. *International Journal of Political Economy* 36, no. 2 (2007 [1941]): 6–83.

————. *Marx, den klassiske nationaløkonomi og dynamikken*. Copenhagen: Rhodos, 1975.

————. *Marx, die klassische Nationalökonomie und das Problem der Dynamik*. Unauthorized edition, ca. 1970 [1941].

————. *Marx, die klassische Nationalökonomie und das Problem der Dynamik*. With appendix "Briefe Henryk Grossmanns an Paul Mattick über Akkumulation." Frankfurt: Europäische Verlagsanstalt, 1969 [1941].

————. *Marx, l'economia politica classica e il problema della dinamica*. Translated by Giorgio Backhaus. Bari: Laterza, 1971 [1941].

————. *Marx, l'économie politique classique et le probleme de la dynamique*. With a preface by Paul Mattick. Paris: Champ Libre, 1975 [1941].

————. "Eine neue Theorie über Imperialismus und die soziale Revolution." *Archiv für die Geschichte des Sozialismus und der Arbeiterbewegung* 13 (1928): 141–92.

————. *Österreichs Handelspolitik mit Bezug auf Galizien in der Reformperiode 1772–1790*. Studien zur Soziale-, Wirtschafts- und Verwaltungsgeschichte, herausgegeben von Carl Grünberg. Vienna: Konegen, 1914.

————. Review of *La loi de Marx sur les capitaux à la lumière des événements contemporains*, by Robert Bordaz. *Zeitschrift für Sozialforschung* 3, no. 2 (1934): 314–15.

————. Review of *Sismondi*, by Elie Halévy. *Zeitschrift für Sozialforschung* 3, no. 2 (1934): 291.

————. "The Social Foundations of the Mechanistic Philosophy and Manufacture." In *The Social and Economic Roots of the Scientific Revolution*, edited by Freudenthal and McLaughlin, 103–56 [1935].

————. "Die Wert-Preis-Transformation bei Marx und das Krisenproblem." *Zeitschrift für Sozialforschung* 1 (1932): 55–84.

Grünberg, Carl. "Sozialistische Ideen und Lehren." In Elster, *Wörterbuch der Volkswirtschaft*, vol. 2, 876–79.

Grünberg, Carl, and Henryk Grossmann. "Sozialdemokratische und kommunistische Parteien." In Elster, *Wörterbuch der Volkswirtschaft*, vol. 3, 238–57.

Gumperz, Julian. *Die Agrarkrise in den Vereinigten Staaten*. Leipzig: Buske, 1931.

Haberler, Gottfried. *Prosperity and Depression*. 3rd edition. New York: United Nations, 1946 [1937].

Halévy, Élie. *Economic Life*. Vol. 2 of *A History of the English People*. Harmondsworth: Penguin, 1937.

Harrod, Roy Forbes. "Studies in the Theory of Economic Expansion." *Zeitschrift für Nationalökonomie* 8, no. 4 (1937): 494–98.

Hasbach, Wilhelm. *Untersuchungen über Adam Smith*. Leipzig: Duncker, 1891.

Hawtrey, Ralph George. *Currency and Credit*. 2nd edition. London: Longmans, Green, 1923.

————. *Trade and Credit*. London: Longmans, Green, 1928.

Hayek, Friedrich August. "The Counter-revolution of Science." *Economica* 8, nos. 30 and 31 (1941): 119–50, 281–320.

————. *Monetary Theory and the Trade Cycle*. New York: Harcourt, Brace, 1933.

————. *Preise und Produktion*. Vienna: Springer, 1931 [1929].

Haynes, Mike. *Russia: Class and Power 1917–2000*. London: Bookmarks, 2002.

Hegel, Georg Wilhelm Friedrich. *The Encyclopaedia Logic: Part 1 of the Encyclopaedia of Philosophical Sciences with the Zusätze*. Translated by T. F. Geraets, W. A. Suchting, and H. S. Harris. Indianapolis, IN: Hackett, 1991 [1817].

————. *Hegel's Philosophy of Nature: Being Part Two of the Encyclopaedia of the Philosophical Sciences*. Translated by Arnold V. Miller. Oxford: Oxford University Press, 2004 [1830].

————. *Lectures on the Philosophy of History*. Translated by J. Sibree. London: Bell, 1914 [1837].

————. *Outlines of the Philosophy of Right*. Translated by T. M. Knox. Oxford: Oxford University Press, 2008 [1821].

————. *Phenomenology of Mind*. Vol. 1. Translated by J. B. Baillie. London: Swan Sonnenschein, 1910.

Heimann, Eduard. "Karl Marx' Bedeutung für die Entwicklung der Nationalökonomie." In *Kapitalismus und Sozialismus*. Potsdam: Protte, 1931.

Henryk Grossman III-155 Collection. Archiwum Polskiej Akademii Nauk. Warsaw.

Herkner, Heinrich. *Die Arbeiterfrage*. 7th edition. Vol. 2. Berlin: W. de Gruyter, 1921 [1894].

Hicks, John Richard. "Equilibrium and the Trade Cycle." *Economic Inquiry* 18, no. 4 (1980 [1933]): 523–34.

———. "A Reconsideration of Value: Part 1." *Economica*, n.s., 1, no. 1 (1934): 52–76.

———. *Value and Capital: An Inquiry into Some Fundamental Principles of Economic Theory*. Oxford: Clarendon, 1939.

Hilferding, Rudolf. *Die Aufgaben der Sozialdemokratie in der Republik*. Berlin: Vorstand der Sozialdemokratischen Partei Deutschlands, 1927. Available at http://library.fes.de.

———. "Aus der Vorgeschichte der Marxschen Ökonomie: 3. Richard Jones." *Neue Zeit* 30, part 1, no. 10 (1912): 343–54.

———. *Böhm-Bawerk's Criticism of Marx*. Translated by Eden Paul and Cedar Paul. In Eugen von Böhm-Bawerk and Rudolf Hilferding, *Karl Marx and the Close of His System and Böhm-Bawerk's Criticism of Marx*, edited by Paul Sweezy, 121–96. New York: Kelley, 1949 [1904].

———. *Finance Capital: A Study of the Latest Phase of Capitalist Development*. London: Routledge & Kegan Paul, 1981 [1910].

———. Review of *Theorie des Geldes und des Umlaufsmittel*, by Ludwig Mises. *Neue Zeit* 30, part 2, no. 52 (1912): 1024–27.

Hillquit, Morris. *Socialism in Theory and Practice*. New York: Macmillan, 1909.

Hobson, John Atkinson. *An Economic Interpretation of Investment*. London: Financial Review of Reviews, 1911.

———. *The Evolution of Modern Capitalism*. London: Walter Scott, 1894.

Hodgskin, Thomas. *Labour Defended against the Claims of Capital*. London: Knight and Lacey, 1825.

———. *Popular Political Economy*. London: Charles Tait, 1827.

Holbach, Paul Henri Thiry d'. *Système social*. Vol. 3. Amsterdam: 1773.

Homan, Paul T. *Contemporary Economic Thought*. New York: Harper, 1928.

Hook, Sidney. *From Hegel to Marx: Studies in the Intellectual Development of Karl Marx*. London: Gollancz, 1936.

Horkheimer, Max. Max Horkheimer to Friedrich Pollock, June 9, 1943. In *Gesammelte Schiften*. Vol. 17, *Briefwechsel 1941–1948*, 453–54. Frankfurt: Fischer, 1996.

———. Max Horkheimer to Henryk Grossman, October 12, 1936. In *Gesammelte Schiften*. Vol. 15, *Briefwechsel 1913–1936*, 660. Frankfurt: Fischer, 1995.

———. "On the Problem of Truth." In *Between Philosophy and Social Science: Selected Early Writings*, 177–218. Cambridge, MA: MIT Press, 1993 [1935].

Horkheimer, Max, and Theodor Adorno. "Diskussion über die Differenz zwischen Positivismus and materialistischer Dialektik." In Horkheimer, *Gesammelte Schiften*. Vol. 12, *Nachgelassene Schriften 1931–1949*, 438. Frankfurt: Fischer, 1985.

Husserl, Edmund. *Logical Investigations*. Vol. 1. Translated by J. N. Findlay. London: Routledge, 2001 [1900/1901].

Hume, David. *Essays, Moral, Political, and Literary*. Vol. 1. London: Longmans, Green, 1889 [1742].

———. *Hume's Political Discourses*. London: Walter Scott, 1906 [1752].

Hyndman, Henry. *The Economics of Socialism*. Boston: Small, Maynard & Company, 1921 [1896 written in 1894].

Ibn Khaldun. *The Muqaddimah: An Introduction to History*. 2nd edition. 3 vols. Translated by Franz Rosenthal. Princeton, NJ: Princeton University Press, 1967 [written 1377].

Ingram, John Kells. *A History of Political Economy*. London: Black, 1915 [1888].

International Institute of Social Research, American Branch. *International Institute of Social Research: A Short Description of Its History and Aims*. New York: Columbia University Archives, 1934.

Jaurès, Jean. *De primis socialismi germanici lineamentis apud Lutherum, Kant, Fichte et Hegel*. Toulouse: Chauvin, 1891.

———. *Histoire socialiste de la révolution française*. Vol. 7. Revised by A. Mathiez. Paris: Librairie de l'Humanité, 1924.

Jessen, Jens. "Sozialistische Ideen und Lehren (II National Sozialismus)." In Elster, *Wörterbuch der Volkswirtschaft*, vol. 3, 341–59.

Jevons, William Stanley. *The Theory of Political Economy*. 5th edition. London: Kelley, 1879 [1871].

Jones, Richard. *Essay on the Distribution of Wealth*. London: John Murray, 1831.

———. "An Introductory Lecture on Political Economy." In *An Introductory Lecture on Political Economy*, 1–42.

———. *An Introductory Lecture on Political Economy, to Which Is Added a Syllabus of a Course of Lectures on the Wages of Labor*. London: John Murray, 1833.

———. "A Syllabus of a Course of Lectures on the Wages of Labor." In *An Introductory Lecture on Political Economy*, 43–59.

———. *Textbook of Lectures on the Political Economy of Nations*. In *Literary Remains Consisting of Lectures and Tracts on Political Economy, of the Late Rev. Richard Jones*, 339–537. London: John Murray, 1859 [1852].

Kant, Immanuel. *Universal Natural History and Theory of the Heavens or an Essay on the Constitution and the Mechanical Origin of the Entire Structure of the Universe Based on Newtonian Principles*. Translated by Ian C Johnston. Arlington, VA: Richer Resources Publications, 2009 [1755].

Kautsky, Karl. *The Agrarian Question*. 2 vols. Translated by Pete Burgess. London: Zwan, 1988 [1899].

———. "Bernstein über die Wertheorie und die Klassen." *Neue Zeit* 17, part 2, no. 29 (1899): 68–81.

———. *Bernstein und das sozialdemokratische Programm: Eine Antikritik*. Dietz: Stuttgart, 1899.

———. *The Economic Doctrines of Karl Marx*. Translated by H. J. Stenning. London: Black, 1925 [1887].

————. "*Das Elend der Philosophie* und *Das Kapital.*" *Neue Zeit* 4, nos. 1, 2, 3, and 4 (1886): 7–19, 49–58, 117–29, 157–65.

————. *Ethics and the Materialist Conception of History.* Translated by John B. Askew. Chicago: Kerr, 1906.

————. "Finance-Capital and Crises." 1911. Available online at Marxists Internet Archive, www.marxists.org.

————. Foreword to *Das Kapital: Kritik der politischen Ökonomie. 2. Der Zirkulationsprozeß des Kapitals*, by Karl Marx. Berlin: Dietz, 1926.

————. *Foundations of Christianity: A Study in Christian Origins.* Translated by Henry F. Mins. New York: International Publishers, 1925 [1889].

————. *Handelspolitik und Sozialdemokratie.* Berlin: Buchhandlung Vorwärts, 1911 [1901].

————. *Die Klassengegensätze im Zeitalter der französischen Revolution.* Stuttgart: Dietz, 1908 [1889].

————. "Krisentheorien." *Neue Zeit* 20, part 2, nos. 2–5 (1902): 37–47, 76–81, 110–18, 133–43.

————. Letter to the editor. *Petite Republique*, September 28, 1899.

————. *The Materialist Conception of History.* Translated by Raymond Meyer and John H. Kautsky. Abridged, annotated, and introduced by John H. Kautsky. New Haven: Yale University Press, 1988 [1927].

————. *The Road to Power.* Translated by A. M. Simons. Chicago: Bloch, 1909.

————. *The Social Revolution.* Translated by A. B. Askew. London: Twentieth Century Press, 1903 [1902].

————. "Der sozialistischen Kongresse und der sozialistische Minister." *Neue Zeit* 19, part 1, no. 2 (1901): 36–4.

————. *Thomas More and His Utopia.* London: A. and C. Black, 1927 [1888].

————. "Verelendung und Zusammenbruch: Die neuste Phase des Revisionismus." *Neue Zeit* 26, part 2, nos. 42 and 43 (1908): 540–51, 607–12.

Kautz, Julius. *Theorie und geschichte der national-oekonomik: Zweite Teil; Literatur-Geschichte der National Oekonomik.* Vienna: Gerold, 1860.

Kelsen, Hans. "Allgemeine Rechtslehre im Lichte materialistischer Geschichtsauffassung." *Archiv für Sozialwissenschaft und Sozialpolitik* 66, no. 3 (1931): 449–521.

Kleinwächter, Friedrich. *Grundlagen der wissenschaftlichen Sozialismus.* Innsbruck: Wagner, 1885.

Kliman, Andrew. *The Failure of Capitalist Production: Underlying Causes of the Great Recession.* London: Pluto, 2012.

————. *Reclaiming Marx's "Capital": A Refutation of the Myth of Inconsistency.* Lanham: Lexington Books, 2007.

Knapp, Georg Friedrich. *The State Theory of Money.* London: Macmillan, 1924 [1895].

Knies, Karl. *Das Geld.* 2nd edition. Berlin: Weidmannsche Buchhandlung, 1885.

Knight, Charles. *The Rights of Industry: 1. Capital and Labour.* Philadelphia: Carey & Hart,

1832 [1831].

Knight, Frank Hyneman. Review of *A History of Economic Thought*, by Erich Roll. *American Journal of Sociology* 46, no. 1 (1940): 104–05.

————. "Statik und Dynamik." *Zeitschrift für Nationalökonomie* 2, no. 1 (1931): 1–26.

Koepp, Carl. *Das Verhältnis der Mehrwerttheorien von Karl Marx and Thomas Hodgskin*. Vienna: Konegen, 1911.

Korsch, Karl. *Kernpunkte der materialistischen Geschichtsauffassung: Eine quellenmäßige Darstellung*. Berlin: VIVA Vereinigung Internationaler Verlags-Anstalten, 1922.

————. "Marxism and Philosophy." In *Marxism and Philosophy*, translated by Fred Halliday, 29–85. New York: Monthly Review Press, 1970 [1923].

———— *Die materialistische Geschichtsauffassung: Eine Auseinandersetzung mit Karl Kautsky*. Leipzig: Hirschfeld, 1929.

Kötschke, Rudolf. *Grundzüge der deutschen Wirtschaftsgeschichte bis zum 17. Jahrhundert*. Leipzig: Teubner, 1923.

Krynska, Salomea. *Entwicklung und Fortschritt nach Condorcet und A. Comte*. Berne: Scheitlin, Spring und Cie, 1908.

Kuhn, Rick. "Henryk Grossman and Critical Theory." *History of the Human Sciences* 29, no. 2 (2016): 42–59.

————. *Henryk Grossman and the Recovery of Marxism*. Chicago: University of Illinois Press, 2007.

————. "Sismondi, Marx and Grossman: Method, Contradictions of the Commodity and Crisis." *Marxism 21* 13, no. 1 (2016): 262–83.

Kuznets, Simon. "Relations between Capital Goods and Finished Products in the Business Cycle." In Asher Achinstein et al., *Economic Essays in Honor of Wesley Clair Mitchell*, 209–67. New York: Columbia University Press, 1935.

Labriola, Antonio. *Karl Marx, l'économiste, le socialiste*. Paris: Rivière, 1910 [1908].

Labriola, Arturo. *La dittatura della borghesia e la decadenza della società capitalistica*. Naples: Morano, 1924.

————. *La speculazione economica*, Naples: Società Editrice Partenopea, 1907.

————. *Studio su Marx*. 2nd edition. Naples: Morano, 1926 [1908].

Lachmann, Ludwig M. "Preiserwartungen und intertemporales Gleichgewicht." *Zeitschrift fur Nationalökonomie* 8, no. 1 (1937): 33–46.

Lafargue, Paul. *Le déterminisme économique de Karl Marx: Recherches sur l'origine et l'évolution des idées de Justice, du Bien, de l'Ame et de Dieu*. Paris: V. Giard et E. Brière, 1909.

Lange, Oskar. "Die allgemeine Interdependenz der Wirtschaftgrössen und die Isoliermethode." *Zeitschrift für Nationalökonomie* 4, no. 1 (1932): 52–78.

Laplace, Pierre Simon. *The System of the World*. 2 vols. Translated by Henry H. Harte. Dublin: Longman, Rees, Orme, Brown and Green, 1830 [1796].

Lasson, Georg. Foreword to *Enzyklopädie der philosophischen Wissenschaften im Grundrisse*, by Georg Wilhelm Friedrich Hegel. 2nd edition. Leipzig: Meiner, 1920 [1905].

Lauderdale, James. *An Inquiry into the Nature and Origin of Public Wealth*. Edinburgh:

Constable, 1804.

Laurat, Lucien. *Un système qui sombre*. Paris: L'Églantine, 1932.

Lederer, Emil. *Grundzügen der ökonomischen Theorie*. Tübingen: J.C.B. Mohr (P. Siebeck), 1922.

———. "Konjunktur und Krisen." In *Grundriß der Sozialökonomie* IV, i, 355–413. Tübingen: J.C.B. Mohr (P. Siebeck), 1925.

Lenin, N., and G. Sinowjew. *Gegen den Strom: Aufsätze aus den Jahren 1914–16*. Hamburg: Verlag der Kommunistischen Internationale, 1921 [1918].

Lenin, Vladimir Ilyich. "The Chain Is No Stronger than Its Weakest Link." In *Collected Works*, vol. 24, 519–21 [1917].

———. *A Characterization of Economic Romanticism (Sismondi and Our Native Sismondists)*. In *Collected Works*, vol. 2, 129–265 [1897].

———. "The Collapse of the Second International." In *Collected Works*, vol. 21, 205–59.

———. *Collected Works*. 45 vols. Moscow: Progress Publishers, 1960–70.

———. *The Development of Capitalism in Russia*. In *Collected Works*, vol. 3 [1899].

———. "The Discussion on Self-Determination Summed Up." In *Collected Works*, vol. 22, 320–60 [1916].

———. *Imperialism, the Highest Stage of Capitalism: A Popular Outline*. In *Collected Works*, vol. 22, 185–304 [1917].

———. "The Junius Pamphlet." In *Collected Works*, vol. 22, 306–19 [1916].

———. *Letters from Afar*. In *Collected Works*, vol. 23, 297–342 [1917].

———. *Materialism and Empiriocriticism*. In *Collected Works*, vol. 22, 17–362 [1909].

———. *The State and Revolution*. In *Collected Works*, vol. 25, 385–498 [1918].

———. *Two Tactics of Social-Democracy in the Democratic Revolution*. In *Collected Works*, vol. 22, 15–140 [1905].

Leroy, Louis-Modeste. *Auguste Walras, sa vie, son oeuvre*. Paris: Pichon et Durand-Auzias, 1923.

Lessing, Gotthold Ephraim. *The Education of the Human Species*. Translated by Frederic W. Robertson. London: Kegan Paul, Trench and Company, 1883 [1780].

Liebknecht, Wilhelm, to Friedrich Engels, January 20, 1868. In *Wilhelm Liebknecht: Briefwechsel mit Karl Marx und Friedrich Engels*, 88. Hague: Mouton, 1963.

Lindemann, Hugo, *Deutsche Städteverwaltung: Ihre Aufgaben auf den Gebieten der Volkshygiene, des Städtebaus und des Wohnungswesens*. Stuttgart: Dietz, 1906 [1901].

———. *Städteverwaltung und Munizipal-Sozialismus in England*. Stuttgart: Dietz, 1906 [1897].

Locke, John. *Some Considerations on the Lowering of Interest and Raising the Value of Money*. In *The Works of John Locke in Nine Volumes*, vol. 4, 1–116. London: Rivington et al., 1924 [1691].

Löwenthal, Leo. Leo Löwenthal to Max Horkheimer, November 26, 1941. In Horkheimer, *Gesammelte Schiften*, vol. 17, *Briefwechsel 1941–1948*, 220–23. Frankfurt: Fischer, 1996.

Lukács, Georg. *History and Class Consciousness: Studies in Marxist Dialectics*. Translated by Rodney Livingstone. London: Merlin, 1971 [1923].

Luxemburg, Rosa. *The Accumulation of Capital*. Translated by Agnes Schwarzschild. London: Routledge and Kegan Paul, 1951 [1913].

————. *Die Akkumulation des Kapitals: Ein Beitrag zur ökonomischen Erklärung des Imperialismus*. In *Gesammelte Werke*, vol. 5. Berlin: Dietz, 1975 [1913].

————. *The Mass Strike*. In *The Essential Rosa Luxemburg: "Reform or Revolution" and "The Mass Strike,"* 111–81. Chicago: Haymarket Books, 2008 [1907].

————. *Social Reform or Revolution*. Translated by Integer. In *The Essential Rosa Luxemburg: "Reform or Revolution" and "The Mass Strike,"* 41–104. Chicago: Haymarket Books, 2008 [1899, 1908].

MacDonald, James Ramsay. *Socialism and Society*. London: Independent Labour Party, 1905.

————. *Sozialismus und Regierung*. With a foreword by Eduard Bernstein. Jena: Diederichs, 1912.

Maito, Esteban Ezequiel. "The Historical Transience of Capital: The Downward Trend in the Rate of Profit since the XIX Century." Unpublished paper, 2015. Available at www.academia.edu.

Makarov, Nikolai Pavlovich. *Krestianskoe khozyaistvo i ego evolyutsiya*. Moscow: Tip. N. Zheludkovoi, 1920.

Malthus, Robert. *Principles of Political Economy, Considered with a View to Their Practical Application*. London: Pickering, 1836 [1820].

Mannheim, Karl. *Ideology and Utopia: An Introduction to the Sociology of Knowledge*. Translated by Louis Wirth and Edward Shils. London: Routledge & Kegan Paul, 1936 [1929].

Marcuse, Herbert. *Reason and Revolution: Hegel and the Rise of Social Theory*. New York: Oxford University Press, 1941.

————. *Studies in Critical Philosophy*. Translated by Joris de Bres. London: NLB, 1972.

Marshall, Alfred, *Principles of Economics*. London: Macmillan, 1890.

Marx, Karl. "Aus David Ricardo: *Des principes de l'économie politique et l'impôt*." In Karl Marx and Friedrich Engels, *Marx-Engels-Gesamtausgabe, Exzerpte und Notizen, 1843 bis Januar 1845*, section 4, vol. 2, 392–427. Berlin: Dietz, 1981.

————. "The British Rule in India." In Karl Marx and Friedrich Engels, *Marx and Engels Collected Works*, vol. 12, 125–33 [1853].

————. *Capital: A Critique of Political Economy*. 3 vols. Translated by Ben Fowkes and David Fernbach. Harmondsworth: Penguin, 1976–81 [1867, 1885, 1895].

————. *The Civil War in France*. In Karl Marx and Friedrich Engels, *Marx and Engels Collected Works*, vol. 22, 307–60 [1871].

————. "Comments on James Mill, *Éléments d'économie politique*." In Karl Marx and Friedrich Engels, *Marx and Engels Collected Works*, vol. 3, 211–34 [written 1944].

————. *A Contribution to the Critique of Political Economy: Part One*. In Karl Marx and

Friedrich Engels, *Marx and Engels Collected Works*, vol. 29, 257–417 [1859].

———. *Critique of the Gotha Program*. In Karl Marx and Friedrich Engels, *Marx and Engels Collected Works*, vol. 24, 75–100 [1875].

———. "Economic and Philosophic Manuscripts of 1844." In Karl Marx and Friedrich Engels, *Marx and Engels Collected Works*, vol. 6, 229–346 [1844].

———. "Economic Manuscript of 1861–63 [Notebooks I to VII]." Karl Marx and Friedrich Engels, *Marx and Engels Collected Works*, vol. 30 [1905–1910].

———. "Economic Manuscript of 1861–63 [Notebooks VII to XII]." Karl Marx and Friedrich Engels, *Marx and Engels Collected Works*, vol. 31 [1905–1910].

———. "Economic Manuscript of 1861–63 [Notebooks XII to XV]." Karl Marx and Friedrich Engels, *Marx and Engels Collected Works*, vol. 32 [1905–1910].

———. "Economic Manuscript of 1861–63 [Notebooks XV to XX]." Karl Marx and Friedrich Engels, *Marx and Engels Collected Works*, vol. 33 [1905–1910].

———. "Economic Manuscript of 1861–63 [Notebooks XX to XXIII]." Karl Marx and Friedrich Engels, *Marx and Engels Collected Works*, vol. 34 [1905–1910].

———. *The Eighteenth Brumaire of Louis Bonaparte*. In Karl Marx and Friedrich Engels, *Marx and Engels CollectedWorks*, vol. 11, 99–197 [1852].

———. "Introduction." In Karl Marx and Friedrich Engels, *Marx and Engels Collected Works*, vol. 28, 17–48 [1903, written 1857].

———. *Das Kapital: Kritik der Politischen Ökonomie*. 4th edition. Vol. 1. In *Marx-Engels-Gesamtausgabe*, section 2, vol. 10. Berlin: Akademie Verlag, 1991 [1890].

———. Karl Marx to Arnold Ruge, March, May, and September, 1843. In Karl Marx and Friedrich Engels, *Marx and Engels Collected Works*, vol. 3, 141–45 [1844, written 1843].

———. Karl Marx to Friedrich Engels, August 27, 1867. In Karl Marx and Friedrich Engels, *Marx and Engels Collected Works*, vol. 42, 407.

———Karl Marx to Friedrich Engels, January 8, 1868. In Karl Marx and Friedrich Engels, *Marx and Engels CollectedWorks*, vol. 42, 514–7.

———. Karl Marx to Ludwig Kugelmann, December 28, 1862. In Karl Marx and Friedrich Engels, *Marx and Engels Collected Works*, vol. 41, 435–37.

———. Karl Marx to Pavel Vasilyevich Annenkov, December 28, 1846. In Karl Marx and Friedrich Engels, *Marx and Engels Collected Works*, vol. 38, 95–106.

———. "On Proudhon" (letter to J. B. Schweitzer, January 24, 1865). In Karl Marx and Friedrich Engels, *Marx and Engels Collected Works*, vol. 20, 26–33.

———. "Outlines of the Critique of Political Economy (Rough Draft of 1857–58) [First Installment]" (also known as *Grundrisse*). In Karl Marx and Friedrich Engels, *Marx and Engels CollectedWorks*, vol. 28, 49–537 [1939, written 1857–1858].

———. "The Philosophical Manifesto of the Historical School of Law." In Karl Marx and Friedrich Engels, *Marx and Engels Collected Works*, vol. 1, 203–10 [1842, 1927].

———. *The Poverty of Philosophy: Answer to the Philosophy of Poverty by M. Proudhon*. In Karl Marx and Friedrich Engels, *Marx and Engels Collected Works*, vol. 6, 105–212 [1847].

————. *Theorien über den Mehrwert: Aus dem nachgelassenen Manuskript "Zur Kritik der politischen Ökonomie" von Karl Marx*. 3 vols. (Vol. 2 printed in two parts.) Edited by Karl Kautsky. Stuttgart: Dietz, 1910 [written 1861–63].

————. "Theses on Feuerbach." In Karl Marx and Friedrich Engels, *Marx and Engels Collected Works*, vol. 5, 3–8 [1888, written 1847].

————. *Zur Kritik der politischen Ökonomie*. In Karl Marx and Friedrich Engels, *Marx-Engels-Gesamtausgabe, Ökonomische Manuskripte und Schriften*, section 2, vol. 2, 95–245. Berlin: Dietz, 1980 [1859].

Marx, Karl, and Friedrich Engels. *Historisch-kritische Gesamtausgabe*. Frankfurt and Berlin: Marx-Engels-Archiv, Verlagsgenossenschaft ausländischer Arbeiter in der UdSSR, and Marx-Engels-Verlag, 1927–41.

————. *Manifesto of the Communist Party*. In *Marx and Engels Collected Works*, vol. 6, 477–519 [1848].

————. *Marx and Engels Collected Works*. Translated by Richard Dixon, et al. 50 vols. New York: International Publishers, 1975–2004.

Masaryk, Tomáš Garrigue. *Masaryk on Marx*. Translated by Erazim V. Kohak. Lewisburg: Bucknell University Press, 1972 [1899].

Maudit, Roger. *Auguste Comte et la science économique*. Paris: Alcan, 1929.

Max-Horkheimer-Archiv. Frankfurt.

Mayer, Hans. "Der Erkenntniswert der funktionellen Preis-theorien." In *Die Wirtschafts-theorie der Gegenwart*. Vol 2: *Wert, Preis, Produktion, Geld und Kredit*, edited by Hans Mayer, 147–239. Vienna: Springer, 1932.

McCulloch, John Ramsay. *Discourse on Political Economy*. Edinburgh: Archibald Constable and Co., 1825.

Mehring, Franz. *Aus dem literarischen Nachlass von Karl Marx and Friedrich Engels*. 3rd edition. Vol. 1. Stuttgart: Dietz, 1920 [1902].

————. *Geschichte der deutschen Sozialdemokratie*. 5th edition. 2 vols. Stuttgart: Dietz, 1913 [1897].

————. "In Sachen Bernstein." *Leipziger Volkszeitung*, March 10, 1898.

————. *The Lessing Legend*. Translated by A. S. Grogan. New York: Critics Group Press, 1938 [1893].

————. "Das sozialistische Endziel." *Leipziger Volkszeitung*, February 10, 1898.

————. "Sozialistische Selbstkritik." *Leipziger Volkszeitung*, February 9, 1898.

Menger, Carl. *Investigations into the Method of the Social Sciences with Special Reference to Economics*. Translated by Francis J. Nock. New York: New York University Press, 1985 [1883].

Mill, James. *Commerce Defended*. London: C. and R. Baldwin, 1808.

Mill, John Stuart. *Principles of Political Economy*. London: Routledge, 1900 [1848].

————. *A System of Logic Ratiocinative and Inductive*. 8th edition. New York: Harper, 1900 [1843].

Mirowski, Philip. *More Heat than Light: Economics as Social Physics, Physics as Nature's Eco-*

nomics. Cambridge: Cambridge University Press, 1989.

Moore, Henry Ludwell. *Synthetic Economics*. New York: Macmillan, 1929.

Moseley, Fred. *Money and Totality: A Macro-Monetary Interpretation of Marx's Logic in Capital and the End of the "Transformation Problem."* Leiden: Brill, 2016.

Muckle, Friedrich. *Die grossen Sozialisten.* Vol. 1, *Owen, Fourier, Proudhon.* Leipzig: Teubner, 1920.

Myrdal, Gunnar. *The Political Element in the Development of Economic Theory*. London: Routledge & Kegan Paul, 1953.

Neurath, Wilhelm. *Die wahren Ursachen der Überproduktion.* Vienna: Klinkhardt, 1892.

Okishio, Nobuo. "Technical Change and the Rate of Profit." *Kobe University Economic Review* 7 (1961): 85–99.

Oppenheimer, Franz. *Kapitalismus, Kommunismus, Wissenschaftlicher Sozialismus.* Berlin: de Gruyter, 1919.

———. *Weder Kapitalismus noch Kommunismus.* Jena: Fischer, 1932.

Owen, Robert. *A New View of Society, or Essay on the Principle of the Formation of the Human Character.* London: Cadell and Davies, 1813.

Palgrave, Robert Harry Inglis. *Dictionary of Political Economy*. Vol. 3. London: Macmillan, 1913.

Pareto, Vilfredo. *Cours d'économie politique.* Lausanne: Rouge, 1896–97.

———. *Manual of Political Economy.* London: Macmillan, 1972.

———. *Les systèmes socialistes.* Vol. 2. Paris: Giard & Brièr, 1902.

Parvus. "Bernsteins Umwälzung des Sozialismus." *Sächsiger Arbeiter-Zeitung*, January 27 and 28, February 8, 9, 12, 18, 22, 24, and 26, and March 9, 11, 24, and 26, 1898.

———. *Der gewerkschaftliche Kampf.* Berlin: Buchhandlung Vorwärts, 1908.

———. *Die Handelskrisis und die Gewerkschaften.* Munich: Ernst, 1901.

———. *Die Kolonialpolitik und der Zusammenbruch.* Leipzig: Leipziger Buchdruckerei Aktiengesellschaft, 1907.

———. *Der Sozialismus und die soziale Revolution.* Berlin: Buchhandlung Vorwärts, 1910.

Paul Mattick Collection. International Institute of Social History, Amsterdam.

Pecqueur, Constantin. *Économie sociale des interets du commerce de l'industrie et de l'agriculture.* 2nd edition. 2 vols. Paris: Dessesart, 1839 [1837].

Périn, Charles. *Les doctrines économiques depuis un siècle.* Paris: Lecoffre, 1880.

Petty, William. *The Political Anatomy of Ireland.* In *The Economic Writings of Sir William Petty*, vol. 1, edited by Charles H. Hull, 121–231. Cambridge: Cambridge University Press, 1899 [1672].

Pietri-Tonelli, Alfonso de. *Traité d'économie rationnelle.* Paris: Giard, 1927.

Pirenne, Henri. "The Stages in the Social History of Capitalism." *American Historical Review* 19 (1914): 494–515.

Playfair, William. *The Commercial and Political Atlas: Representing, by Means of Stained Copper-Plate Charts, the Progress of the Commerce, Revenues, Expenditure, and Debts of England, during the Whole of the Eighteenth Century.* 3rd edition. London: J. Wallis, 1801.

————. *Inquiry into Permanent Causes of the Decline and Fall of Powerful and Wealthy Nations*. London: Greenland and Morris, 1805 [1786].

Plechanow, G. (*see also* Plekhanov, Georgii). *Henrik Ibsen*. Stuttgart: Singer, 1908.

Plekhanov, Georgii (*see also* Plechanow, G.). *Essays on the History of Materialism*. In *Selected Philosophical Works*, vol. 2, 31–182 [1896].

————. *Fundamental Problems of Marxism*. In *Selected Philosophical Works*, vol. 3, 117–83 [1908].

————. "The Initial Phases of the Theory of the Class Struggle." In *Selected Philosophical Works*, vol. 2, 427–73 [1900].

————. *Selected Philosophical Works*. 5 vols. Moscow: Progress Publishers, 1974–81.

Plenge, Johann. *Stammformen der vergleichenden Wirtschaftstheorie*. Essen: Baedeker, 1919.

Pollock, Friedrich. "Sozialismus und Landwirtschaft." In Max Adler et al., *Festschrift für Carl Grünberg*, 397–431. Leipzig: Hirschfeld, 1932.

Pope, Alexander. "Essay on Man." In Alexander Pope, *The Poetical Works of Alexander Pope*. Macmillan: London, 191–226, 1889 [1733].

Post, Charles. "Exploring Working-class Consciousness: A Critique of the Theory of the 'Labour Aristocracy.'" *Historical Materialism* 18 (2010). 3–38.

Rambaud, Joseph. *Histoire des doctrines économiques*. 2nd edition. Paris: Librairie de la Société du Recueil Général des Lois et des Arrêts et du Journal du Palais, 1902 [1899].

Ravenstone, Piercy. *Thoughts on the Funding System and Its Effects*. London: Andrews, 1824.

Renner, Karl. *Marxismus, Krieg und Internationale*. Stuttgart: Dietz, 1918 [1917].

Renouvier, Charles. *Les principes de la nature*. Paris: Colin, 1912 [1864].

Ricardo, David. David Ricardo to Jean-Baptiste Say, January 11, 1820. In *The Works and Correspondence of David Ricardo*, vol. 8, 149–50. Cambridge: Cambridge University Press, 1952.

————. David Ricardo to Thomas Malthus, October 10, 1820. In *Letters of David Ricardo to Thomas Robert Malthus 1810–1823*, edited by James Bonar, 173–77. Oxford: Clarendon, 1887.

————. *The Principles of Political Economy and Taxation*. London: Dent, 1912 [1817].

Ricci, Umberto. "Pareto e l'economia pura." *Giornali degli economisti* 64 (1924): 27–44.

————. "Die 'synthetische Ökonomie' von Henry Ludwell Moore." *Zeitschrift für Nationalokonomie* 1, no. 5 (1930): 649–68.

Rist, Charles. "Sismondi and the Origins of the Critical School." In Charles Gide and Charles Rist, *A History of Economic Doctrines*, translated by R. Richards, 170–98. Boston: Heath, 1915 [1909].

Roberts, Michael. *The Long Depression: Marxism and the Global Crisis of Capitalism*. Chicago: Haymarket Books, 2016.

Roche-Agussol, Maurice. "Die Werttheorie." In Mayer, *Die Wirtschaftstheorie der Gegenwart* Vol 2: *Wert, Preis, Produktion, Geld und Kredit*, 27–38.

Rodbertus, Karl. *Overproduction and Crises*. London: Swan Sonnenschein, 1898 [1850].

Roll, Eric. *A History of Economic Thought*. London: Faber and Faber, 1938.

Rosdolsky, Roman. *The Making of Marx's* Capital. London: Pluto, 1977 [1968].

Rosenstein-Rodan, Paul. "Das Zeitmoment in der mathematischen Theorie des wirtschaftlichen Gleichgewichtes." *Zeitschrift für Nationalökonomie* 1, no. 1 (1929): 129–42.

Rousseau, Jean-Jacques. *Rousseau's Social Contract and Discourses.* Translated by G. D. H. Cole. London: Dent, 1920.

Saint-Simon, Henri. *Catéchisme des industriels.* In Henri Saint-Simon and Barthélemy Prosper Enfantin, *Oeuvres de Saint-Simon et d'Enfantin*, vol. 37, [1823–1824].

———. *Catéchisme politique des industriels.* In *Oeuvres de Saint-Simon*, 1–173 [1823].

———. *De la réorganisation de la société européenne.* In Henri Saint-Simon and Barthélemy Prosper Enfantin, *Oeuvres de Saint-Simon et d'Enfantin*, vol. 15, 155–248 [1814].

———. *Du système industriel,* first part. Henri Saint-Simon and Barthélemy Prosper Enfantin, *Oeuvres de Saint-Simon et d'Enfantin*, vol. 21 [1821].

———. *Du système industriel,* second part. Henri Saint-Simon and Barthélemy Prosper Enfantin, *Oeuvres de Saint-Simon et d'Enfantin*, vol. 22 [1821].

———. *L'industrie ou discussion politiques, morales et philosophiques.* Vol. 2. In Henri Saint-Simon and Barthélemy Prosper Enfantin, *Oeuvres de Saint-Simon et d'Enfantin*, vol. 19, 11–174 [1817].

———. *Lettres d'un habitant de Genève.* In Henri Saint-Simon and Barthélemy Prosper Enfantin, *Oeuvres de Saint-Simon et d'Enfantin*, vol. 15, 7–60 [1802].

———. *Mémoires sur la science de l'homme.* In Henri Saint-Simon and Barthélemy Prosper Enfantin, *Oeuvres de Saint-Simon et d'Enfantin*, vol. 40 [1813].

———. *Oeuvres de Saint-Simon.* Edited by Olinde Rodrigues. Paris: Capelle, 1841.

———. *L'organisateur.* In Henri Saint-Simon and Barthélemy Prosper Enfantin, *Oeuvres de Saint-Simon et d'Enfantin*, vol. 20 [1819, 1820]

———. *Vues sur la propriété et la législation.* In *Oeuvres de Saint-Simon*, 241–364.

Saint-Simon, Henri, and Barthélemy Prosper Enfantin. *Oeuvres de Saint-Simon et d'Enfantin.* Reprint edition. 47 vols. Aalen: Otto Zeller, 1963–64. Available at http://gallica.bnf.fr/.

Salis, Jean Rodolphe de. *Sismondi, 1773–1842: La Vie et l'œuvre d'un cosmopolite philosophe.* 2 vols. Paris: Champion, 1932.

Sartorius, Georg. *Abhandlungen die Elemente des Nationalreichtums betreffend.* Göttingen: Röwer, 1806.

Savigny, Friedrich Carl. *Vom Beruf unserer Zeit zur Gesetzgebung und Rechtswissenschaft.* Heidelberg: Mohr und Zimmer, 1814.

Say, Jean-Baptiste. *A Treatise on Political Economy.* 6th edition. Translated by C. R. Prinsep. Philadelphia: Lippincott, 1867 [1803].

Schams, Ewald. "Komparative Statik." *Zeitschrift für Nationalökonomie* 2, no. 1 (1931): 27–61.

Schaube, Adolf. "Die Wollausfuhr Englands vom Jahre 1273." *Vierteljahrschrift für Sozial- und Wirtschaftsgeschichte* 6, no. 1 (1908): 39–72.

Schmidt, Conrad. *Die Durchschnittsprofitrate auf Grundlage des Marx'schen Werthgesetzes.* Stuttgart: Dietz, 1889.

———. "Nachträgliche Bemerkungen zur Bernstein-Diskussion." *Sozialistische Monatshefte* 3, no. 10 (1899): 493–99.

———. "Positive Kritik des Marxschen Wertgesetzes." *Sozialistische Monatshefte* 16, no. 10 (1910): 604–18.

———. "Die psychologische Richtung in der neueren National-Oekonomie." *Neue Zeit* 10, part 2, nos. 40 and 41 (1892): 421–29, 459–64.

———. "Zur Methode der theoretischen Nationalökonomie." *Sozialistische Monatshefte* 21, no. 10 (1915): 492–502.

———. "Zur Theorie der Handelskrisen und der Ueberproduction." *Socialistische Monatshefte* 5, no. 9 (1901): 669–82.

Schueller, Richard. *Die klassische Nationalökonomie und ihre Gegner.* Berlin: Heymann, 1895.

Schultz, Henry. "The Italian School of Mathematical Economics." *Journal of Political Economy* 39, no. 1 (1931): 76–85.

Schumpeter, Joseph Alois. *Economic Doctrine and Method.* New York: Oxford University Press, 1954 [1934].

———. "Eugen von Böhm-Bawerk." In *Neue oesterreichische Biographie*, vol. 2, edited by Anton Bettelheim, 63–80. Vienna: Amalthea, 1925.

———. *Theorie der wirtschaftlichen Entwicklung.* Leipzig: Duncker & Humblot, 1912 [1911].

———. *Das Wesen und der Hauptinhalt der theoretischen Nationalökonomie.* Leipzig: Duncker & Humblot, 1908.

See, Henri. *La notion de classes chez les Saint-Simoniens.* Paris: Rivière, 1925.

Seligman, Edwin R. A., ed. *Encyclopaedia of the Social Sciences.* 15 vols. New York: Macmillan, 1930–35.

Senior, Nassau. *An Outline of the Science of Political Economy.* New York: Kelley, 1965 [1836].

Shaw, George Bernard. *Report on Fabian Policy and Resolutions Presented by the Fabian Society to the International Socialist Workers and Trade Union Congress, London, 1896.* Fabian Tract 70. London: Fabian Society, 1896.

Shibata, Kei. "Marx's Analysis of Capitalism and the General Equilibrium Theory of the Lausanne School." *Kyoto University Economic Review* 8, no. 1 (1933): 107–136.

———. "The Meaning of the Theory of Value in Theoretical Economics." *Kyoto University Economic Review* 8, no. 2 (1933): 49–68.

Shine, Hill. *Carlyle and the Saint-Simonians.* Baltimore: Johns Hopkins Press, 1940.

Sinowjew, Grigori. *Der Krieg und die Krise des Sozialismus.* Vienna: Verlag für Literatur und Politik, 1924 [1916].

———. *See also* Zinoviev, Grigory.

Sismondi, Jean Charles Léonard Simonde de. "Analysis of a Refutation of *New Principles of Political Economy* published in the *Edinburgh Review* by a follower of Mr. Ricardo."

In *New Principles of Political Economy*, 599–616 [1820].

—. "Clarification Relative to the Equilibrium of Consumption with Production." In *New Principles of Political Economy*, 595–97 [1827].

—. *Études sur l'économie politique*. 2 vols. Paris: Treuttel et Würtz, 1837–38.

—. *Histoire des républiques italiennes du moyen âge*. Vol. 3. Paris: Furne, 1840 [1809].

—. *New Principles of Political Economy*. Translated by Richard Hyse. New Brunswick, NJ: Transaction, 1991 [1821].

—. "Notes on an Article by M. Say, Entitled 'On the Balance of Consumption with Production.'" In *New Principles of Political Economy*, 645–48 [1824].

—. *Nouveau principes d'économie politique*. 2nd edition. Vol. 2. Paris: Delaunay, 1827.

—. "On the Balance of Consumption with Production." In *New Principles of Political Economy*, 617–39 [1824].

Skarbek, Fryderyk. *Théorie des richesses sociales*. Vol. 1. Paris: A. Sautelet, 1829.

Smith, Adam. *Wealth of Nations*. 2 vols. London: Dent, 1910 [1776].

Smith, Thomas. *De republica Anglorum: A Discourse of the Commonwealth of England*. Cambridge: Cambridge University Press, 1906 [1583, written about 1565].

Soden, Julius. *Die National-Oekonomie: Ein philosophischer Versuch*. 2nd edition. Vienna: B. Ph. Bauer, 1815 [1805].

Sombart, Werner. *Das Lebenswerk von Karl Marx*. Jena: Fischer, 1909.

—. *Der moderne Kapitalismus*. Vol. 2, part 1. Leipzig: Duncker & Humblot, 1921.

—. *Socialism and the Social Movement*. London: J. M. Dent, 1909.

—. "Die Störungen im deutschen Wirtschaftsleben während der Jahre 1900 ff." *Verhandlungen der General-versammlung in Hamburg, 14., 15. und 16. September 1903 ... Referate von Werner Sombart, F. Hecht, J. Jastrow*. Schriften des Vereins für Sozialpolitik 113, 121–36. Leipzig: Duncker & Humblot, 1904.

Sozialdemokratische Arbeiterpartei Österreichs. *Protokoll des sozialdemokratischen Parteitages 1926, abgehalten in Linz, vom 30. Oktober bis 3. November*. Vienna: Verlag der Wiener Volksbuchhandlung, 1926.

Spencer, Herbert. "Progress: Its Law and Causes." In *Illustrations of Universal Progress*, 1–60. New York: Appleton, 1878 [1864].

Spiethoff, Athur. "Business Cycles." *International Economic Papers* 3 (1955): 75–171.

—. "Die Krisentheorien von M. Tugan-Baranovsky und L. Pohle." *Schmollers Jahrbuch*, n.s., 27 (1903 [1925]): 679–708.

Spühler, Willy. *Der Saint-Simonismus: Lehre und Leben von Saint-Amand Bazard*. Zurich: Girsberger, 1925.

Stalin, Joseph Vissarionovich. "A Necessary Correction." In *Works*, vol. 12, 143–45. Moscow: Foreign Languages Publishing House, 1954 [1929].

Stammler, Rudolf. *Wirtschaft und Recht nach der materialistischen Geschichtsauffassung: Eine sozialphilosophische Untersuchung*. Leipzig: Veit, 1896.

Staudinger, Franz. *Ethik und Politik*. Berlin: Dümmler, 1899.

—. *Wirtschaftliche Grundlagen der Moral*. Darmstadt: Roether, 1907.

Stead Collection. National Library of Australia, Canberra.

Stephen, Leslie, and Sir Leslie Lee, eds. *The Dictionary of National Biography*. Vol. 15. London: Oxford University Press, 1922.

Steuart, James. *Inquiry into the Principles of Political Oeconomy*. London: A. Millar and T. Cadell, 1767.

Suhge, Werner. *Saint-Simonismus und Junges Deutschland, Germanische Studien*, 164. Berlin: Dr. E. Ebering, 1935.

Streller, Rudolf. *Die Dynamik der theoretischen Nationalökonomie*. Tübingen: Mohr, 1928.

Sweezy, Paul. *The Theory of Capitalist Development*. London: Dobson, 1942.

Süßmilch, Johann Peter. *Die Göttliche Ordnung in den Veränderungen des menschlichen Geschlechts*. Vol. 1. Berlin: Verlag des Buchladens der Realschule, 1761.

Tarnow, Fritz. *Warum arm sein?* Berlin: Allgemeiner Deutscher Gewerkschaftsbund, 1928.

Taylor, George Robert Stirling. *Guild Politics: A Practical Programme for the Labour Party & the Co-operators*. London: Palmer, 1921.

Thierry, Augustin. *L'industrie ou discussion politiques, morales et philosophiques*. Vol. 1. In Saint-Simon and Enfantin, *Œuvres de Saint-Simon et d'Enfantin*, vol. 18, 17–127. [1817].

Thompson, William. *An Inquiry into the Principles of the Distribution of Wealth Most Conducive to Human Happiness*. London: Longman, 1824.

Thorp, Willard L. "The Problem of Overcapacity." In Asher Achinstein et al., *Economic Essays in Honor of Wesley Clair Mitchell*, 477–95. New York: Columbia University Press, 1935.

Tiumeniev, A. I. "Marxism and Bourgeois Historical Science," 235–320. In Nikolai Bukharin et al. *Marxism and Thought*. Translated by Ralph Fox. London: Routledge 1935.

Troeltsch, Ernst. *Die Dynamik der Geschichte nach der Geschichtsphilosophie des Positivismus*. Berlin: Reuther und Reichard, 1919.

Trotsky, Leon. "The Curve of Capitalist Development." *Fourth International* 2, no. 4 (1941): 111–14 [1923].

———. *Results and Prospects*. In *The Permanent Revolution and Results and Prospects*, 125–281. Translated by John G. Wright and Brian Pearce, New York: Pathfinder, 1969.

———. *The War and the International*. Columbo: Young Socialist, 1971 [1914].

Tudor, Henry, and Josephine M. Tudor, eds. *Marxism and Social Democracy: The Revisionist Debate 1896–98*. Cambridge: Cambridge University Press, 1988.

Tugan-Baranowsky, Mikhail. *Modern Socialism in Its Historical Development*. London: Sonnenschein, 1910.

———. *Studien zur Theorie und Geschichte der Handelskrisen in England*. Translation of second Russian edition. Jena: Fischer, 1901 [1894].

———. "Studies in the Theory and the History of Business Crises in England." Translated by Alejandro Ramos-Martínez. In *Value, Capitalist Dynamics and Money*, edited by Paul Zarembka, 53–110. Research in Political Economy. New York: Elsevier, 2000 [1894].

————. *Theoretische Grundlagen des Marxismus*. Leipzig: Duncker & Humblot, 1905.

————. "Der Zusammenbruch der kapitalistischen Wirtschaftsordnung im Lichte der nationalökonomischen Theorie." *Archiv für Sozialwissenschaft und Sozialpolitik* 19 (1904): 273–306.

Turgot, Anne-Robert-Jacques. *Reflections on the Formation and Distribution of Wealth*. London: Macmillan, 1898 [1769–1770, written 1766]

————. "Sur les progrès successifs de l'esprit humain." In *Oeuvres de Mr. Turgot*, vol. 2, 52–92. Paris: Delance, 1808 [1750].

Universität Frankfurt am Main. *Verzeichnis der Vorlesungen Sommer- Halbjahr 1928 und Personalverzeichnis*, 1928.

————. *Verzeichnis der Vorlesungen Sommer- Halbjahr 1930 und Personalverzeichnis*, 1930.

Vandervelde, Émile. *La Belgique ouvrière*. Paris: Cornély, 1906.

————. *Collectivism and Industrial Evolution*. Translated by Charles H. Kerr. Chicago: Kerr, 1901 [1900].

————. *Essais sur la question agraire en Belgique*. Paris: Éditions du Mouvement Socialiste, 1902.

————. *Le Parti Ouvrier Belge, 1885–1925*. Brussels: Maison Nationale d'Édition l'Églantine, 1925.

————. *Le socialisme agraire ou le collectivisme et l'évolution agricole*. Paris: Giard & Brière, 1908.

Varoufakis, Yanis. *Foundations of Economics: A Beginner's Companion*. London: Routledge, 1998.

Vico, Giambattista. *The New Science of Giambattista Vico*. Translated by Thomas Goddard Bergin and Max Harold Fisch. Ithaca, NY: Cornell University Press, 1948.

Volgin, Vjačeslav Petrovič. "Über die historische Stellung Saint-Simons." *Marx-Engels Archiv* 1 (1926): 82–118.

Vollmar, Georg von. *Ueber die nächsten Aufgaben der Deutschen Sozialdemokratie: zwei Reden, gehalten am 1 Juni und 6 Juli 1891 im 'Eldorado' zu München*. München: M. Ernst, 1891.

————. *Ueber Staatssozialismus*. Nürnberg: Wörlein, 1892.

Vorländer, Karl. *Kant und der Sozialismus unter besonderer Berücksichtigung der neuesten theoretischen Bewegung innerhalb des Marxismus*. Berlin: Reuther & Reichard, 1900.

————. *Kant und Marx: Ein Beitrag zur Philosophie des Sozialismus*. 2nd edition. Tübingen: Mohr, 1926 [1911].

————. *Von Machiavelli bis Lenin: Neuzeitliche Staats- und Gesellschaftstheorien*. Leipzig: Quelle & Meyer, 1926.

————. "Zu den philosophischen Grundlagen unseres Parteiprogramms." In Sozialdemokratische Partei Deutschlands, *Das Programm der Sozialdemokratie: Vorschläge für seine Erneuerung*, 10–17. Berlin: Buchhandlung Vorwärts, 1920.

Walras, Léon. *Elements of Pure Economics*. Translated by William Jaffé. London: Allen and Unwin, 1954 [1874].

Webb, Sidney, and Beatrice Webb. *A Constitution for the Socialist Commonwealth of Great*

Britain. London: Longmans, Green and Company, 1920.

———. *The Decay of Capitalist Civilisation*. London: Fabian Society, 1923.

———. *Die Geschichte des Britischen Trade-Unionismus*. Translated by Richard Bernstein. With an afterword by Eduard Bernstein. Stuttgart: Dietz, 1895 [1894].

———. *History of Trade Unionism*. London Longmans, Green and Company, 1894.

———. *Industrial Democracy*. 2 vols. London: Longmans, Green and Company, 1897.

———. *The Prevention of Destitution*. London: Longmans, Green and Company, 1911.

Weber, Hans. *Richard Jones: Ein frueher englischer Abtruenniger der klassischen Schule der Nationaloekonomie*. Zurich: Girsberger, 1939.

Weber, Max. *The Protestant Ethic and the Spirit of Capitalism*. Translated by Talcott Parsons. London: Unwin, 1968 [1904–1905].

Weill, Georges. *L'école saint-simonienne*. Paris: Alcan, 1896.

Weiller, Jean. *La conception classique d'un équilibre économique*. Paris: Rivière, 1934.

Whittaker, Edmund. *A History of Economic Ideas*. New York: Longmans, Green and Company, 1940.

Wicksell, Knut. *Lectures on Political Economy*. Vol. 2. Translated by E. Classen. Fairfield, NJ: Kelley, 1978 [1913].

Wilbrandt, Robert. *Karl Marx: Versuch einer Würdigung*. Leipzig: Teubner, 1920 [1918].

Wilson, C. H. "The Economic Decline of the Netherlands." *Economic History Review* 9, no. 2 (1939): 111–27.

Woltmann, Ludwig. *Der historische Materialismus: Darstellung und Kritik der marxistischen Weltanschauung*. Düsseldorf: Michels, 1900.

Zinoviev, Grigory. "Two Eras of War." *New International* 18, nos. 5 and 6 (1952) and 19, no. 1 (1953 [1916]): 233–44, 323–27, 42–51. Available at www.marxists.org.

———. *See also* Sinowjew, Grigori.

Editor's Acknowledgments

Sandra Bloodworth, Tom Bramble, Günther Chaloupek, Liam Dee, Daniel Gaido, Andrew Gilbert, Ben Hillier, Peter Jones, John King, David Mayer, and Thomas Weiss offered valuable comments on or advice for drafts of essays related to the introduction to the present volume. I am grateful to Daniel Gaido, David Paenson, Geoff McCormack, and the staff of the Archive of the Polish Academy of Sciences for access to materials. The translation of *Marx, Classical Political Economy and the Problem of Dynamics* benefited from reference to previous translations by Pete Burgess and Paul Mattick Jr. The Australian National University's School of Politics and International Relations, when John Ravenhill was its head, provided generous financial support for the project of which this book is one result. My partner Mary Gorman, especially, as well as close friends and Socialist Alternative comrades, continue to provide emotional and intellectual support for my Grossmaniac endeavors.

Index and Glossary

About Haymarket Books

Haymarket Books is a radical, independent, nonprofit book publisher based in Chicago.

Our mission is to publish books that contribute to struggles for social and economic justice. We strive to make our books a vibrant and organic part of social movements and the education and development of a critical, engaged, international left.

We take inspiration and courage from our namesakes, the Haymarket martyrs, who gave their lives fighting for a better world. Their 1886 struggle for the eight-hour day—which gave us May Day, the international workers' holiday—reminds workers around the world that ordinary people can organize and struggle for their own liberation. These struggles continue today across the globe—struggles against oppression, exploitation, poverty, and war.

Since our founding in 2001, Haymarket Books has published more than five hundred titles. Radically independent, we seek to drive a wedge into the risk-averse world of corporate book publishing. Our authors include Noam Chomsky, Arundhati Roy, Rebecca Solnit, Angela Y. Davis, Howard Zinn, Amy Goodman, Wallace Shawn, Mike Davis, Winona LaDuke, Ilan Pappé, Richard Wolff, Dave Zirin, Keeanga-Yamahtta Taylor, Nick Turse, Dahr Jamail, David Barsamian, Elizabeth Laird, Amira Hass, Mark Steel, Avi Lewis, Naomi Klein, and Neil Davidson. We are also the trade publishers of the acclaimed Historical Materialism Book Series and of Dispatch Books.

Also Available from Haymarket Books

Capitalism's Crisis Deepens: Essays on the Global Economic Meltdown
Richard D. Wolff

The Long Depression: How It Happened, Why It Happened, and What Happens Next
Michael Roberts

Zombie Capitalism: Global Crisis and the Relevance of Marx
Chris Harman

About the Editor

Dr. Rick Kuhn is an honorary associate professor in sociology at the Australian National University and long-time socialist activist, who has written extensively on Marxist theory as well as Australian politics and political economy. His *Henryk Grossman and the Recovery of Marxism* won the 2007 Deutscher Prize.